LANCASTRIANS

PAUL SALVESON

Lancastrians

Mills, Mines and Minarets:
A New History

HURST & COMPANY, LONDON

First published in the United Kingdom in 2023 by
C. Hurst & Co. (Publishers) Ltd.,
New Wing, Somerset House, Strand, London, WC2R 1LA
© Paul Salveson, 2023
All rights reserved.

Distributed in the United States, Canada and Latin America by
Oxford University Press, 198 Madison Avenue, New York, NY 10016,
United States of America.

A Cataloguing-in-Publication data record for this book
is available from the British Library.

ISBN: 9781787389335

This book is printed using paper from registered sustainable
and managed sources.

Printed and bound in Great Britain by Bell and Bain Ltd, Glasgow
www.hurstpublishers.com

CONTENTS

LIST OF ILLUSTRATIONS

All photos by author unless provenance otherwise stated.

ACKNOWLEDGEMENTS

I am very grateful for the kind and friendly assistance from many librarians and academic colleagues, mostly across Lancashire. Particular thanks must go to the staff of Bolton History Centre at Bolton Public Library and Museums Service and their colleagues at Farnworth branch; Oldham Local Studies and Archives; Blackburn Library's Local Studies section and their Darwen branch; Rochdale (Touchstones) and their excellent branch library at Heywood; the University of Bolton Library (keepers of the Lancashire Authors' Association Special Collection); and Salford Local Studies Library. Over several years I have benefited from the help of staff in Manchester Central Library, the Portico Library, John Rylands Library, University of Liverpool Library and Lancashire Libraries (particularly Accrington).

I am indebted to the work of those who have gone before. I once had the pleasure of meeting Ms. Jessica Lofthouse—back in 1976 at a public meeting calling for the re-opening of the Blackburn to Clitheroe railway line. Her writing on Lancashire is often insightful and entertaining; she belongs to a different age but her work always repays study. The Lancashire novelist, Walter Greenwood, wrote a fine survey of Lancashire and this book owes much to Greenwood's chatty and engaged approach, as well as that of Allen Clarke's *Moorlands and Memories*.

I was fortunate to have been taught by Professor John Marshall when I was a student at Lancaster in the 1970s. His knowledge of Lancashire was encyclopaedic and I am forever in his debt; I'm equally grateful to Professor John Walton who was at Lancaster in the same period and became a good friend in later years.

The help I've had from friends and colleagues has been immense. My enthusiasm for Lancashire and 'the common people' owes much to the late Ruth and Eddie Frow. I've had huge support from Linda

ACKNOWLEDGEMENTS

Nuttall who has spent hours reading through drafts and making informed and helpful comments. Andrew Rosthorn has fed me countless 'stories' about forgotten Lancastrians. Thanks to Janet Geddes for help with the technology and to Ibrahim Kala for his kind assistance with photographs of Bolton's Asian community. And many thanks to my publisher for all their help—from embracing the initial idea to seeing the job through to completion.

INTRODUCTION

LANCASHIRE—COUNTY, CULTURE AND IDENTITY

Lancastrians is about 'historic Lancashire'—the region stretching from the Mersey to the Lakes. It isn't a conventional history—there are plenty of those around already.[1] It's an excursion into Lancashire identity and culture, in the very broadest sense, aiming to shed light on neglected aspects of Lancashire history as well as looking forward to the future. Along the way, we'll meet a lot of Lancastrians, many of whom have been unjustly neglected or forgotten.

Lancashire has many great achievements to its credit, in culture and politics as well as industry. In 1892, at the zenith of its power, Ernest Axon wrote in *Bygone Lancashire*:

> The county is a sort of epitome of the whole country, embracing within its boundaries mining, commercial, manufacturing and agricultural districts; moorland, woodland, mountain and Lakeland, small hamlets, large towns and great cities. This may explain the position the county claims in most social and political matters, as summed up in the well-known phrase—'What Lancashire thinks today, England thinks tomorrow'.[2]

Few would recognise Axon's statement today. The county has been dismantled, leaving only a rump of the historic shire. The mining and manufacturing that Axon refers to has largely disappeared, replaced to some extent by new industries and 'the knowledge economy', but it could hardly be said that Lancastrians are leaders in the field. It could change.

It's a region with a strong identity, which overlays and complements many local identities. It has suffered in recent times through a combination of industrial decline and local government 'reform'. The combined effect of the two has been a fragmented region which

1

compares unfavourably with its neighbour and traditional rival, Yorkshire. True, the county of the white rose has experienced similar industrial decline, with the loss of its woollen textile industry, coal mining and engineering. The three historic 'ridings' have been re-structured into West, North and South Yorkshire. Yet it has survived much better than its Lancashire rival and neighbour. It still has its own paper, *The Yorkshire Post*, and its annual 'Great Yorkshire Show' outshines our 'Royal Lancashire' at least in terms of sheer size. Yorkshire even has its own political party which is starting to make modest progress in local and mayoral elections.

Much of the damage was done in 1974, when many of the recommendations of the Redcliffe-Maud Report were implemented.[3] Most of south-east Lancashire—Manchester and the 'cotton belt' towns—went into what became 'Greater Manchester'. To the west, Liverpool, St Helens and Southport became 'Merseyside', later to be re-christened 'Liverpool City Region'. That area of Lancashire 'North of the Sands' was placed into the newly formed county of Cumbria. At the same time, dozens of small but mostly very efficient local authorities with strong identities were abolished, merged into the new metropolitan councils.

* * *

I hope the publication of *Lancastrians* will stimulate ways of re-imagining what we want this part of the North of England to be. It's an exploration of Lancashire culture and identity, of how it has developed and changed and the influence and contributions made by the many 'New Lancastrians' through waves of migration, from the second half of the last century to the present. The focus is on the nineteenth and twentieth centuries, when what became one of the most powerful economic regions in the world rose—and fell.

Lancastrians is not an exercise in nostalgia; it's a work of history and contemporary politics that hopefully combines objectivity with passion (A.J.P. Taylor, historian and eminent Lancastrian, had that to perfection). There are plenty of books which yearn for 'the old Lancashire', complete with the smoking mill chimneys, men in cloth caps and women wearing clogs and shawls. This book is about its people, past and present, and how this part of Britain became not just an industrial powerhouse, but also a dynamic political, intellectual and cultural force. It's a reflection on 'how are the mighty fallen' and how Lancashire might rise again.

The sense of a 'regional patriotism' that emerged in the late nineteenth century is an example of a contemporary approach that could help bring people together rather than divide them. The idea of Lancashire as a 'cultural province' is developed, to sit alongside our historic friend, neighbour and rival, Yorkshire. As that proud Yorkshirewoman, the late Jo Cox MP, said, we have more in common with each other than what divides us.

Navigating the book

Why no chapter on 'women'? Each chapter of *Lancastrians* features women prominently. Some of them have been ignored by conventional histories. The work of Elizabeth Gaskell and Frances Hodgson Burnett is well known and rightly celebrated. I don't ignore them, and the figure of Gracie Fields ticks nearly every possible box— Rochdale through and through with a very strong Lancashire sensibility, and a former mill girl. She was adored by Lancastrians, never frightened to speak gradely (i.e. 'proper') Lancashire. But there are many more who have been forgotten. These include Mary Fildes, hero of Peterloo, and writers such as Ethel Carnie, Margaret Lahee and Sarah Robinson. Union and Co-op activists who helped shape Lancashire included Sarah Reddish, Selina Cooper and Alice Foley. Mary Higgs was a remarkable pioneer of community planning.[4]

Chapter 1 is a tour of 'historic Lancashire', starting from 'Lancashire North of the Sands' and ending at its southern-most tip, Hale, on the Mersey Estuary. It is the longest chapter and weaves in many of the themes which run through the book. I wanted to give space to the great cities but also feature the fascinating and too-often neglected or maligned towns. The chapter looks at distinct parts of Lancashire and their cultural achievements. Towns and cities developed their own 'feel' and characteristics, with a distinct politics and local culture.

Much of the 'tour' is by rail, my preferred form of transport and the industry I've worked in for all of my life. Lancashire's growth was underpinned by some visionary infrastructure—the

Bridgewater Canal, the Liverpool and Manchester Railway, the Manchester Ship Canal and more. Chapter 2 is about 'the shaping of Lancashire' and the men and women who had the vision to do it. It features early experiments in town planning such as the 'Beautiful Oldham' project and the influence of the garden city movement across urban Lancashire.

A fascinating, and neglected, aspect of Lancashire history is the development of a distinct 'Lancashire sensibility' which included the emergence of a regional intelligentsia during the second half of the nineteenth century, outlined in Chapter 3. The account uses Raymond Williams' concept of a 'structure of feeling' that is distinctly 'Lancastrian'.[5]

Chapter 4 is about what we ate and drank. Lancashire, like most parts of Britain, had a food and drink culture that continues today. Bury is of course famous for its black puddings which have an enduring popularity, which tripe perhaps doesn't enjoy. Lancashire has outstanding cheeses, simnel cake and hot pot. A new generation of brewers have revived some old Lancashire favourites such as 'dark mild', and 'whoam-brewed' (home-brewed) ale is celebrated in many dialect poems. Lancashire was where vegetarianism began and the Vegetarian Society still has its headquarters in the North-West. The 'New Lancastrians' have brought their own cuisine to Lancashire which crossed ethnic divides.

How did people *live* in Lancashire? Housing and healthcare were hugely important parts of life, and death. Chapter 5 looks at the housing of ordinary people, from farmers and handloom weavers to factory workers. Health, and healthcare, is also explored, particularly Lancashire's strong and distinctive herbal tradition.

The growth of educational provision in Lancashire was patchy; for the majority of the population in the nineteenth century and before, 'schooling' was minimal. Yet there was a tradition of working-class self-education through various institutions, not least the Co-op. Chapter 6 provides an overview of education in the county, using Lancaster as a case study, with a celebration of pioneering educationalist Teddy O'Neill.

Lancashire came to be largely defined by its industries. In Chapter 7, I look at the core activities which 'made' Lancashire—cotton, coal and engineering—and the men and women who were central to it. The role of the handloom weavers, the intellectual aristocracy of the working class in the early nineteenth century, is crucial. Many were highly literate, accomplished musicians, mathematicians and botanists. Their contribution to a Lancashire culture and sensibility cannot be exaggerated.

Lancashire developed a pioneering role in engineering, initially in relation to textile machinery, but broadened out into other fields and built a worldwide market. Engineers from Bolton and Oldham were instrumental in creating Russia's cotton industry and many stayed, marrying Russian women. The role of the British Empire is crucial in Lancashire's development and this was reflected in areas such as textile design.

Trades unions developed rapidly in Lancashire during the nineteenth century, emerging from illegality in the 1820s; most were local or regional in nature. For much of the century the main cotton towns had their own independent unions reflecting hierarchies within the industry—spinners, card room workers, weavers and others. The Lancashire miners' union remained independent throughout most of the nineteenth century and continued as a highly devolved regional body up to and after the Miners' Strike of 1984/5 when the Lancashire NUM took a different stance to the national (Yorkshire-led) leadership.

'Lancastrians at Play', Chapter 8, covers recreation, holidays and festivals. Lancashire people have an enduring love of the countryside; an important aspect of the handloom-weaving culture was an interest in botany and herbalism. This combined with an appreciation of the countryside which developed into the organised rambling and cycling movements of the late nineteenth century.

Sport was, and remains, a major part of Lancashire identity, highlighted in Chapter 9. There were few specifically 'Lancashire' sporting bodies, with the notable exception of county cricket. Towns had professional football and Rugby League clubs from the late nineteenth century and they became symbols of local pride. Chapter 10 features 'Lancashire at War' including the English Civil War, which had a major impact on parts of Lancashire. The county has a strong military tradition, with regiments including the Lancashire Fusiliers, the East Lancashire and the Duke of Lancaster's Regiments. The horrendous carnage in the First World War was highlighted by the wiping-out of the 'Accrington Pals' but the impact was felt in many more of Lancashire's towns and villages. Alongside the formal military tradition, many Lancashire men joined the International Brigades to fight in the Spanish Civil War and are celebrated with memorials in several locations.

Chapter 11, 'Co-operative Lancashire' highlights the unique role of Lancashire as the place where the world co-operative movement began. Lancashire's contribution to art, literature, journalism, drama and film is discussed in Chapter 12. It includes, but goes beyond, the remarkable achievements of Lancashire's dialect writers, from Tim Bobbin in the mid-eighteenth century, to the present day. The arts tradition is extensive and well documented. Lowry is important, but so too are his predecessors, such as Adolphe Valette and Walter Crane and his successors including Theodore Major, Helen Clapcott, Geoffrey Key and many others.

Lancashire has produced a wealth of musical talent. The focus of Chapter 13 is on the county's diverse musical heritage which helped to bolster a regional sensibility and identity, from the 'Larks of Dean' in the late eighteenth century to the Hallé Orchestra, Kathleen Ferrier and Gracie Fields, composers Arthur Butterworth and Tom Pitfield, and bands like The Fall in more recent times.

Chapter 14 considers how religion has helped shape Lancashire and continues to do so; 'Lancashire North of the Sands' and west Lancashire have kept an agricultural base, with their own distinctive cultural identities. 'Old Catholic Lancashire' retains its outposts in the west of the county whilst having experienced a series of revivals through successive waves of migration—from Ireland and more recently eastern Europe. Lancashire was the birthplace of Quakerism and has a strong Unitarian tradition. Spiritualism was enormously popular across industrial Lancashire in the late nineteenth and early twentieth centuries, and some chapels remain. Asian migration has brought the religious traditions of Islam and Hinduism to Lancashire, with large mosques and temples taking the place of many gaunt Victorian churches.

Chapter 15 looks at the politics of Lancashire, from the late eighteenth century to the present day. This includes the much-hyped fall of the 'red wall' constituencies such as Leigh and Burnley in the 2019 General Election. Religious identity was often reflected in political loyalties and through the nineteenth century there was a close correlation between church-going Anglicans and the Conservative Party, with various hues of Nonconformity tending strongly towards Liberalism.

Lancashire was at the forefront of the rise of the socialist movement in the last decade of the nineteenth century. This had a strong cultural element with the formation of socialist clubs with their own choirs, field rambling clubs and a distinct socialist literature, often using dialect. At the opposite end of the spectrum was the phenomenon of 'Clog Toryism' with some Lancashire towns retaining strong loyalties to the Conservative Party.

Both middle- and working-class women were actively involved in the campaign for women's suffrage; it was much more than a family campaign led by the Pankhursts. Mrs Marjory Lees, wife of one of Oldham's major cotton magnates, was a dedicated supporter, as was Farnworth's Margaret Barnes whose husband was the owner of several local mills. Many female cotton workers were involved in the campaign for the vote, organised by the North of England Women's Suffrage Society.

Chapter 16—'Lancastrians Abroad'—covers one of the most fascinating aspects of Lancashire's history: the thousands who emigrated from Lancashire in the nineteenth and early twentieth centuries, principally to the United States, Australia, New Zealand and Canada, but also to Russia. In some places distinct Lancashire communities were re-created, with the importation of customs such as 'Wakes Week'. Many of those who emigrated were 'economic migrants' who wanted to build a better life abroad. Others left home to set up cotton mills in America and Russia and decided to stay.

Lancashire is a region of immigrants, from the Flemish weavers of the fourteenth century to Syrians and Ukrainians today. Chapter 17 outlines the contribution of the 'new Lancastrians' and the 'push and pull' factors that brought them here. The Irish exodus of the 1840s, escaping famine, created large and often very poor Irish communities in many Lancashire towns; outbreaks of anti-Irish hostility were common. Jewish migrants arrived in Lancashire in the late nineteenth and early twentieth centuries, mostly settling in Manchester. Later refugees from war and oppression included German Jews in the 1930s through to post-war waves of immigration from eastern Europe, Asia and Africa.

The concluding Chapter 18 ends the book on a reflective note, with thoughts on whether a twenty-first-century Lancashire can be re-born, becoming the cradle of a new, green, industrial revolution. Manchester and Liverpool ought to be its twin capitals. Towns like Rochdale, Oldham, Bolton, Wigan, St Helens and further north Barrow and Ulverston retain a strong Lancashire identity. Can a new region be born that is forward-looking but celebrates its past achievements? Or are Lancashire towns doomed to be suburban outliers of the major cities?

In the preface to his book, written nearly 150 years ago, Ernest Axon modestly says that his "*Bygone Lancashire* is set forth in the hope that it will prove a not uninteresting addition to local literature and that it may encourage the local patriotism which is such a striking characteristic of the Lancashire lad."[6]

I hope mine does the same.

Lancashire Day, 27 November 2022
Bolton, Lancashire

1

THE SHAPE OF LANCASHIRE

'Gradely Lancashire', stretching from the Mersey to the Lakes, is a remarkable mix of town and country.[1] It includes some of the largest cities in the UK contrasting with miles of open countryside, large and small towns and remote villages. Today's 'shrunk' county is much more rural, having lost Liverpool, Manchester and their surrounding urban hinterlands. However, this book is concerned with the shape of Lancashire 'as was' around 1900 and could perhaps become once more.

This tour of 'historic Lancashire' is unbalanced, admittedly. It's more of an exploration of the less celebrated towns, without neglecting Manchester and Liverpool. Writing in 1936, the Bolton-born journalist James Haslam observed that "Lancashire life is such that there is a distinction between town and town, some touch of character and accent which indicates that Bob comes from Oldham, Dick from Bolton, Joe from Blackburn, and so on."[2] He goes on to say that, "Still, there is a salient characteristic somewhere that stamps us as Lancastrian, made up, probably, from a combination of native features, which makes Lord Derby as plainly a Lancashire man as it does factory operative. Hence, which particular Lancashire life must we take as a supreme example?"[3]

Haslam struggles to answer his question as to which town or city epitomised 'Lancashire life' when he was writing; but he is clear as to which parts of the county do not:

Manchester does not quite represent the life of Lancashire. A Manchester man in these days knows little about the outposts of Lancashire. Perhaps it was different when Elizabeth Banks gave us

Jabez Clegg as the 'Manchester Man'. Manchester, then, was more Lancashire than it is now … Liverpool is a great city, stirring with picturesque maritime life, but it is hardly Lancashire. It is in Lancashire, but not of Lancashire.[4]

Haslam's observations, if true in 1936 are much more so now, in the 2020s. Both Manchester and Liverpool have 'seceded' from their parent county to form 'Greater Manchester' and 'Liverpool City Region'.

* * *

The relationship between town and country in Lancashire was always close—economically, culturally and recreationally. While the growing industrial centres of south-east Lancashire had some migrant labour from Ireland, Scotland and Wales, many of the workers who swelled the ranks of the textile proletariat were relatively local, from surrounding villages and small towns. The sense of yearning for a lost rural lifestyle (undoubtedly seen through rose-tinted spectacles) was a recurring theme of much dialect poetry in mid-nineteenth century Lancashire.

The farms of west and north Lancashire fed the people of Manchester, Liverpool and the surrounding industrial towns. By the late nineteenth century there were daily trainloads of produce leaving small village stations for the major cities. Fish was transported by express goods trains from Fleetwood. The moors and Lake District were the 'lungs' of the factory workers of the major industrial towns and cities, within easy reach by train.

* * *

Let's take a look at the 'shape' of Lancashire and how it grew in the nineteenth century, taking the train (as much as we can) to get us around. Up to 1780, or thereabouts, it hadn't changed very much in centuries. Liverpool was the dominant port and already expanding, in part (but only in part) due to the growth of the slave trade. Manchester was smaller but already a significant mercantile centre. Preston and Lancaster were well established, with histories stretching back centuries. The surrounding towns—Wigan, Bolton, Bury,

Rochdale and many more—were small centres of trade with their own economic hinterland based on domestic cotton manufacture. Barrow-in-Furness, Blackpool and Morecambe hardly existed.

'Lancashire North of the Sands'

The area north of Morecambe Bay, traditionally referred to as 'Lancashire North of the Sands', encompasses a large area of the county that is geographically separate from the rest of Lancashire. It formed the old hundred of 'North Lonsdale'. Unless you took the perilous route 'over sands' to Lancaster, the traveller would have to pass through a small part of Westmorland, around Arnside. Today, the whole area is part of 'Westmorland and Furness'—a recent return to more traditional identities.

Present-day 'Lancashire' ends at the pretty village of Silverdale (see page 20); the railway from Carnforth to Barrow runs through it. The 'Furness Line' via Arnside, Grange-over-Sands, Ulverston and Barrow is one of the most scenic journeys in the North of England with magnificent views of Morecambe Bay on one side and mountains on the other.

Our journey across Lancashire starts at the 'Three Counties Stone', set high in the Lakeland fells at Wrynose Pass. It's where the historic counties of Cumberland, Westmorland and Lancashire meet. The stone was carved in 1816 by William Field, who had the title of 'Furness Roadmaster'. However, for about fifty years the stone languished in a yard at Cartmel. After his death, some of the villagers decided to erect it where he had wanted. Or maybe they just wanted shut of it. Whatever the reason, it was dragged up to the top of Wrynose—to a height of 393 metres—and has stood there to this day, though it was accidentally broken in 1998 and subsequently repaired.

The inscription on the stone reads "THREE SHIRES STONE: Three stones have traditionally marked the adjoining boundaries of Cumberland, Westmorland and Lancashire on this site. The Limestone monolith, carved in 1816, for the Furness roadmaster, William Field of Cartmel, was set up by friends, after his death. Repaired and re-erected by the National Trust in 1998, with local support."[5]

* * *

Barrow-in-Furness came to dominate this part of Lancashire; it's very much an 'outlier' of Lancashire industrial towns. In 1801 Barrow comprised a mere eleven houses and was far overshadowed by its larger and more historic neighbour, Dalton-in-Furness, with about 2,500 inhabitants.[6] Dominating the area and beyond was Furness Abbey, whose origins go back to the twelfth century. It was developed by Cistercian monks with the abbot becoming an enormously powerful figure.[7] The country surrounding Furness Abbey was rich in mineral deposits, mostly iron ore and lead. It began to be exploited in the early nineteenth century when Dalton and Lindal became major mining centres.[8]

Geography and geology helped determine the respective evolution of the Furness towns. Ulverston was just outside the iron mining area but was able to capitalise on its wealth, with the development of some fine mansions. Lindal and Dalton grew as working-class towns, with large concentrations of basic terraced housing. In the case of Dalton, this was overlaid on top of an historic town centre that was once 'the capital' of Furness, up until 1824.

The really explosive growth was around the small village of Barrow. Not only were rich deposits of iron ore discovered, but it was situated by the coast, offering access for shipping into and out of the port. The town's population expanded from about 500 in 1851 to 35,000 in 1874, a phenomenal rate of growth.[9] While the port grew, so did shipbuilding alongside it. This was initially served by locally sourced metal. Transport was central to the development of Barrow and the Furness area. The first railway opened in 1854 linking the iron ore centre of Kirkby with Barrow. It expanded eastwards to Ulverston and opened throughout to Carnforth in 1857, where it joined the London and North Western Railway's main line from London to Glasgow.[10]

The Furness Railway Company, owned mostly by local capitalists and led by James Ramsden, was the catalyst behind much of Barrow's development. It had its company headquarters and engineering works in the centre of Barrow; its locomotives were regarded as some of the most elegant on the British railway system.[11]

Migration to Barrow was from a variety of places, Scotland was certainly important, but the lure of good jobs brought miners from Cornwall, who mostly settled in the area around Roose, and also from Wales. Working-class housing clustered around the developing shipyard, iron works and railway yards. Unlike most of north Lancashire, Barrow developed a strong working-class political culture. By the end of the nineteenth century the Independent Labour Party was well established and trade unions in the shipyards, mines and railways were strong.[12]

In contrast to Barrow, Grange-over-Sands developed as a sedate resort for the Victorian middle classes, though its growth was also a result of the coming of the railway, in 1857. The Grange Hotel, overlooking the town, was built to exploit the railway and the tourists it brought in. Other hotels and guest houses developed, along with the large sanatorium which in later years became 'The Cumbria Grand'. The railway company had the good sense to build a promenade on the bay side of the railway, which in later years was enhanced by a lido (open-air swimming bath) and delightful gardens. While the gardens still look lovely, the lido itself has been derelict for many years and is the subject of a major restoration project.

Near to Grange is the small hamlet of Kents Bank, still served by regular trains. It was traditionally the northern starting point of the 'over sands' route to Lancaster (Hest Bank). Up to the coming of the railway, horse-drawn carriages made the perilous crossing of Morecambe Bay from here. Over the centuries, hundreds of people lost their lives making the crossing.[13] This led to the appointment of a 'Queen's Guide' who would escort people across the bay; in recent years the honour fell to Cedric Robinson, who became a local celebrity. Cedric died in 2021 and the mantle has been taken over by Michael Wilson. The guides have been appointed since at least the Dissolution of the Monasteries and probably earlier.[14]

These days, the only bay crossings are well-organised group events in aid of charity. Owing to changes in the tides the walking route has switched from Kents Bank to start at Grange-over-Sands. The Guide Over Sands Trust oversees the appointment of guides. It is a charity, set up in 1877 by the Duchy of Lancaster, which owns much of Morecambe Bay.

The Furness Railway was one of the most entrepreneurial regional railway companies of the Victorian era. Whilst its growth was very much down to transporting iron ore, it developed successful sidelines in areas such as tourism. The growth of places like

Coniston, Hawkshead and Ambleside was in large part down to the railway companies' marketing, with the London and North Western promoting its Lakeland terminus at Windermere. The marketing campaigns included combined train, steamer and omnibus excursions, which flourished up to the First World War. The lake steamers on Windermere and Coniston were, naturally, owned by the Furness Railway Company.

The railway never got as far as Hawkshead, with the tracks stopping at Windermere, in part thanks to opposition from William Wordsworth, which was a bit short-sighted. However, a branch line was opened in 1859 between Foxfield and Coniston. It didn't achieve the growth its promoters had hoped for and closed in 1962, though passenger services ceased in 1958.[15]

John Ruskin who, in his earlier years, together with Wordsworth, had opposed railway development, was a regular user of the branch, being taken from his home at Brantwood by his horse-drawn carriage. He became good friends with Coniston's stationmaster during the 1880s, Edward Woolgar.[16] Perhaps he would have been as vocal in opposing the line's closure as he was against the original railway's construction.

The branch from Ulverston to Lakeside, offering a direct connection to the Lake Windermere steamers, did slightly better. Like much railway development in the nineteenth century, tourism and 'hard-end' industry combined to make a railway just about viable. The Lakeside branch served the iron mines and gunpowder factories in the area, as well as tourists enjoying the pleasures of a trip on Windermere.

Some of the smaller towns and villages of Furness have kept their charm. Cartmel grew on the basis of its magnificent priory, though less-spiritual activities, such as horse-racing, add to its more recent charms. Racing began in 1856 and punters would arrive by train at Cark-in-Cartmel, just under a couple of miles away. Race-goers were met by horse-drawn 'charabancs' and paid a small extra fare to get them to the track. They had the option of walking back to the station if their bets didn't come off.

Race days remain major events along with the annual agricultural show which began in 1872. The show became an event for the whole of 'Lancashire North of the Sands' in 1928 when it was decided to include 'The Whole of the Hundred of Lonsdale North of the Sands'.[17] The village is famous today for its Michelin three-star L'Enclume restaurant, sticky toffee pudding and the longstanding Norman Kerr's bookshop.[18]

Cark station served the Devonshire estate at Holker Hall; the Duke was a regular traveller. The stationmaster during much of the inter-war years was Joe Brown, a well-known local character, who always made sure that he met his Lordship when he was returning from parliamentary business in London, usually arriving on the last train of the day, known as 'The Whip'.[19]

The station not only serves the small hamlet of Cark itself and Cartmel, but is also handy for Flookburgh—completely different in character from its posher neighbours. It is very much a working village, still making a living through fishing—including shrimps and flounders, or 'flooks'. The village has one of the North's most renowned brass bands. Flookburgh Band performs all across the region and performances are usually sold out quickly.

Ulverston is a short distance from Cark by train but a long way round by road. The Leven Viaduct was completed in 1857 and along with the Kent Viaduct between Grange and Arnside made the railway a strong competitor to the roads. Approaching Ulverston you can catch a glimpse of a branch line that went westwards to Conishead Priory. The original intention was to reach Bardsea and continue to Barrow, avoiding the steeply-graded route via Lindal, which was liable to mining subsidence. This was graphically demonstrated in 1872 when a locomotive disappeared down a forgotten mineshaft. It's still there.

Conishead Priory has gone through some fascinating changes over its long life. It became a convalescent home for the Durham Miners Association in 1929 and had the occasional through train from Durham, at least as far as Ulverston. After becoming derelict for several years it became a Buddhist monastery in 1976. I'm sure the monks would love to be able to reach the place of worship by train but they have to change at Ulverston and take the excellent local Blueworks community bus, partly run by volunteers.

Give yourself time to explore Ulverston, it's well worth it. *A Guide to Ulverston*, aimed at the 'respectable' tourist market, was published as early as 1904. It is addressed to a diverse audience, beginning with 'Mr. and Mrs. John Brown and family, of Work-borough', perhaps foreshadowing Bolton's later caricature as 'Worktown', applying to all of the south Lancashire industrial towns. A welcoming hand is also reached out to 'Mr. and Mrs. McSandy and their bairns' together with a warm 'cead mille failte' to 'Mr. and Mrs. O'Patrick and their little company of Home Rulers'![20]

The station is a fine example of Furness Railway architecture, designed by local firm Paley and Austin.[21] The town centre is a short stroll and for me the market hall is the place to head for, with book-shops, cheese stalls (the 'Lancashire creamy' is to die for) and lots more beside. None of the usual tat you often find these days on some markets. And just to prove you're still in Lancashire, there's a Red Rose Club close to the bus stops. Ulverston is well known for its 'Laurel and Hardy' connection and the comic couple are cele-brated in a statue by the Post Office. Towering above Ulverston is the Hoad Monument, erected in 1850 to celebrate Sir John Barrow, a founder member of the Royal Geographical Society. It is some-times known as 'the pepper pot' and during the Second World War the Nazi collaborator Lord Haw-Haw kindly informed the people of Ulverston that the Luftwaffe were going to bomb it. Fortunately, they never did.

A pleasant walk along the historic (and once heavily industrial) Ulverston Canal takes you to Canal Foot which has a popular pub, The Bay Horse, and fine views out to sea. Turn slightly to the left and you'll see the Leven Viaduct taking the railway across towards Cark. It was the scene of what might have been a catastrophic acci-dent in 1903 when strong winds derailed a train crossing the bridge. Amazingly, the train stayed upright and the passengers were rescued unharmed.[22]

Northward from Preston

One of the most interesting books about the country north of Preston was written at the turn of the last century by historian and antiquary Anthony Hewitson. *Northward*, subtitled 'historic, topo-graphic, residential and scenic gleanings etc. between Preston and Lancaster' was published in 1900 by George Toulmin and Sons of Preston.[23] It provides a good framework for our journey, perhaps best done by bike exploring some of the fascinating towns and villages on the way, calling at time-honoured Lancaster and then heading forward to Carnforth and Silverdale. If you're in more of a rush you can take the train and catch a glimpse of the sea at Hest Bank, the only part of the 'West Coast Main Line' where you can.

Preston is one of Lancashire's historic towns, elevated to 'City' status in 2002. It is the administrative centre of present-day Lancashire, with County Hall visible from the train on your left as you depart northwards. It's a 'two-tier' city with the county council responsible for most strategic functions and Preston City Council doing the more local, hands-on jobs. The city council has pioneered the 'Preston Model' of economic development, encouraging local investment and use of local businesses and services. It's had much success and the city has a vibrant feel to it.

Preston was the most important northerly outpost of 'Cotton Lancashire'. It formed the basis for 'Coketown' in Charles Dickens' *Hard Times* and had its fair share of industrial unrest in the 1840s. Several Chartist demonstrators were shot dead by soldiers in a confrontation in the city's market square in 1842. A fine memorial, inspired by Goya, was erected in 1991 to the victims. Edwin Waugh, best known for his dialect poetry, visited the town during the Cotton Famine of the 1860s and much of his *Home Life of Lancashire Factory Folk During the Cotton Famine* is based on his Preston visit.[24]

Some of the large spinning mills remain, such as Tulketh which stands out on the skyline as you approach the city from the north. It also had a significant engineering industry, with firms such as Dick, Kerr (famous for its ladies football team as well as locomotives!). It was fortunate in being close to the sea, with the Ribble creating the basis for a sizeable docks, though most cargo handling ceased in the 1990s. University of Central Lancashire is one of the most important players in the present-day economy.

The Ribble runs alongside the magnificent Avenham and Miller parks. Follow the river eastwards and you quickly reach fine rural scenery and eventually get into the Yorkshire Dales. If you head west along the south side of the river out of Preston you're into West Lancashire which we'll look at later. Penwortham, just a couple of miles out of town, once had its own castle but today is a large suburb. Sadly, the railway that once served it, from Preston to Southport, closed in 1966.

Rather than going north, let's deviate slightly and go in a north-easterly direction towards the interesting mill town of Longridge. This is another railway that closed well before Dr Beeching took his axe to lines such as Preston–Southport. The 'Longridge branch' was intended to be a through route into Yorkshire but it never happened. Longridge lost its passenger service in 1936 and goods traffic ended with a short stub serving the ICI factory which went in 1980.[25] It developed in the early nineteenth century as a small textile village with an agricultural hinterland. The coming of the railway didn't bring the hoped-for prosperity and plans to continue eastward into Yorkshire were abandoned.

Heading back towards our 'core route' from Preston to Lancaster, the roads take you through charming villages such as Chipping. Garstang is worth calling at, a small town bypassed by the M6 as well as the West Coast Main Line. Its station closed in 1967. Despite large-scale housing development, there seems to be no impetus to re-open it. Garstang has the honour of being Britain's first 'Fair Trade Town' and many small shops remain alongside the 'Lancashire Waitrose', Booth's. The former station at 'Garstang and Catterall', to use its full name, was the junction for an interesting railway byway: the Garstang and Knot End Railway (for many years it only gave Knott End a single 't'). This was an independent light railway (standard gauge though) which served the rural communities between Garstang and the small seaside town of Knott End, just across the Wyre from Fleetwood (see page 22). It went close to the former parish church of Garstang at Churchtown, which is notable for being the last resting place of six rebels from the 1715 Jacobite Rising. They were arrested, given a summary trial, and executed.

The journey north from Garstang can be made on the frequent Stagecoach bus or by waterway. The Lancaster Canal leaves the Ribble at Preston and meanders, lock-free, through pleasant countryside to Lancaster, with a branch to Glasson Dock, one of Lancashire's smaller ports but still doing some business. The former branch line into Lancaster is a cycleway, paralleling the River Lune.

This peaceful and expansive river was once the means to Lancaster's prosperity, which was partly down to the slave trade.

Looking across the estuary you can see the small (tidal) settlement of Sunderland Point which was a sister port to Lancaster in the eighteenth century. There is a touching memorial to a young black slave who died on arrival at the port. 'Sambo's Grave' is looked after by local children and it's worth paying a visit to leave a small stone on his grave.[26]

Lancaster itself is an attractive small city which today is very much dependent on its university, a couple of miles out of the centre at Bailrigg. In the nineteenth century it had some textiles but its main industrial base was linoleum and fibres.[27]

Much of the city—Shakespeare's 'time honour'd Lancaster' in *Richard II*—has remained unchanged. The castle is the 'jewel in the crown' but don't forget its history. It was the scene of frequent executions and many of Lancashire's working-class radicals of the early nineteenth century found themselves incarcerated there. Samuel Bamford, the famous Middleton radical, was imprisoned there after the Peterloo Massacre in 1819.

Legend has it that a Bolton handloom weaver was sentenced to a week's imprisonment at Lancaster for some minor offence, sometime in the 1820s. He had to make his own way to Lancaster and arrived at the gaol complete with his parcel of clothes which included two shirts. In those days one shirt was deemed sufficient for a week's stay as guest of the Crown and the gaoler expressed surprise to his two-shirted guest. He replied that, "Well aw'm only here for a week but aw meyt like it and stay on for another..."

North of the Lune the canal and railway continue towards Carnforth, with Morecambe and Heysham to the west. Carnforth was a major railway centre, where three major railway companies converged. It also had a large iron works, of which little remains. The West Coast Main Line from London to Glasgow was operated up to 1923 by the London and North Western Railway (LNWR). The railway to Barrow was, as we've seen, run by the Furness Railway while the line coming in from Wennington and Hellifield was owned by the Midland. Each railway had its own depot facilities and a large complement of staff. The station was used as the setting for David Lean's film *Brief Encounter* and a heritage centre on the station celebrates his work. Carnforth's West Coast Railway Co. still maintains a fleet of steam locomotives; the company operates over much of the UK including the popular 'Jacobite' from Fort William to Mallaig. Given that Carnforth would have been on the route of the Jacobite rebels marching south in 1715 and 1745, it seems very appropriate.

Going north, if you opt for the more sedate and highly scenic route from Carnforth towards Barrow you soon reach Silverdale, which provides access to the RSPB bird sanctuary at Leighton Moss. It's a very pleasant stroll from the station to the foreshore near Jenny Brown's Point. An ancient chimney serves to remind you that this was once a busy industrial area. There are various footpath options to take you into Silverdale which had close links to the novelist Elizabeth Gaskell. There's a Gaskell Memorial Hall in the village which is well used by local community groups and societies.

Walk out from Silverdale through Elmslack and you'll soon find yourself in old Westmorland, which, as noted above, has now reverted from being 'Cumbria' to 'Westmorland and Furness'. You won't find any border controls though, not even a sign saying 'Goodbye from Lancashire, hello Westmorland and Furness'. The train takes you across the Kent back into Lancashire—'North of the Sands'.

Seaside Lancashire

The major resorts of Lancashire deserve their own slot—Morecambe, Blackpool and Southport above all, but let's give a nod to Knott End, have a flutter in Fleetwood and a stroll around sedate St Anne's and Lytham, as well as Formby. This was, and still is, the playground of Lancashire and the development of the 'Big Three'—Blackpool, Southport and Morecambe—was very much a result of the growth of industrial Lancashire from the mid-nineteenth century onwards. The railways provided the means of getting large numbers there, with each of the towns getting rail-linked by mid-century.

Morecambe hardly existed before the coming of the railway in 1864. It was originally called 'Poulton-le-Sands' and comprised a few fishermen's cottages. It grew rapidly in the second half of the century, gaining a slightly different market to Blackpool's. It became known as 'Bradford-by-the-sea' as large numbers of West Riding textile workers took advantage of the railway via Bentham.

Morecambe was the nearest place to the seaside, competing with Scarborough on the east coast. It developed a small colony of Bradford textile magnates, echoing Blackpool's cotton manufacturers' desire to live at a respectable distance from their mills. Like Blackpool, it had its own train to take them to Bradford each morning and back home again at night.[28]

Morecambe's links with Yorkshire have continued. In the early 1970s I was looking for accommodation in Morecambe, having secured a place at Lancaster University. I bought a copy of what I thought was the local paper from a news seller on the promenade to search for a flat; it was *The Telegraph and Argus*. It was only when I started reading the small ads that I realised it was the Bradford paper. Cheated out of tuppence!

Today, Morecambe is experiencing a revival, thanks in part to the restoration of the magnificent art deco Midland Hotel and the coming of 'Eden North' which is to get £50 million of 'levelling-up' funding. The restoration of the fine Winter Gardens is well underway and will provide a superb venue for a range of events in Morecambe.

Just a couple of miles south is Heysham, an ancient village noted for its Nettle Beer, which is still available from local shops and cafes. St Patrick's Church is one of the most historic in the county and the nearby stone graves are amongst the 'wonders of Lancashire'. Heysham was developed as a port by the Midland Railway in the late 1890s; the ferries to the Isle of Man and Dublin continue to operate though all goods arrive by road. A small number of rail passengers use the single train a day, from Leeds, which connects with the ferry. The nights of 'The Belfast Boat Express', which used to leave Manchester Victoria at 20.55 to connect with the overnight Belfast sailing, are long gone.

Blackpool: jewel of the Lancashire coast

Some might detect a note of irony in the title but I would deny it. Blackpool remains very special and very popular. It has its social problems but show me a large seaside resort in the UK that hasn't. It is starting to bounce back. Alongside the historic trams that grace the promenade during 'the lights', it now has a fleet of modern trams that give the resort a European feel.

Blackpool's growth was spectacular. Before the coming of the railway it was a small village with a handful of cottages. Allen Clarke, with characteristic flair, described how it looked in 1750:

> Behold! Blackpool in the eighteenth century, about 1750, just a few dozen cottages, and the Gynn Inn, and the Fox Hall (then a farm) and two hotels, a couple of bowling greens, and an old barn used as a theatre ...[29]

Clearly, Blackpool was beginning to show signs of appealing to an emerging tourist market with hotels and a theatre, however basic. It was another hundred years before Blackpool's 'take-off' as a resort for mass tourism, though that needs treating with caution. For its first few decades, up to the 1870s, Blackpool was mainly patronised by the middle and lower classes.[30] The coming of the railway was crucial, but other factors were important, not least an industrial working class which was starting to achieve some degree of relative affluence and could afford a 'chep trip' to the seaside. Fleetwood got its railway before Blackpool with the first train arriving in 1840. They didn't reach Blackpool for another six years, with construction of a branch line from Poulton-le-Fylde to Talbot Road (now Blackpool North). Growth was astronomical, and Blackpool saw the emergence of a very distinctive cultural (and economic) icon—the Blackpool landlady.[31]

Neighbouring Fleetwood's development was much more problematic. William Hesketh Fleetwood had grand designs to develop the place as a major port. The naming of the 'North Euston Hotel' was anything but accidental. It was seen, for a few short years before the railway extended beyond Preston to Carlisle and Scotland, as the northern end of the West Coast Main Line. It was hoped that from there, Scotland-bound travellers could continue their journey by coastal shipping. Instead, Fleetwood became an important port, noted for its fishing industry. While that ended in the 1970s, the port still sees a substantial amount of 'roll-on-roll-off' freight to and from Ireland. Knott End-on-Sea is reached by ferry from Fleetwood and is well worth exploring; the former terminus of the Garstang and Knott End Railway is a cafe with lots of local memorabilia. Fleetwood is totally different in character to its more famous neighbour, Blackpool, with a popular market and some fine quayside buildings. There are plans to re-open the railway down to Poulton-le-Fylde, putting right one of the worst closures of the Beeching era. A local group also has plans to re-open part of the Garstang and Knot(t) End Railway.

Windmill land

Back in the early 1900s Bolton writer Allen Clarke moved to Blackpool. He already knew the town and its surrounding countryside, but quickly got acquainted with the area in greater depth. Always a great publicist, he coined the name 'Windmill Land' to cover the Fylde area, south and east of Blackpool. In 1916 he published *Windmill Land*, subtitled *Rambles in a Rural, Old-fashioned Country, with Chat about its History and Romance*.[32]

The area that Clarke chats about, in his highly engaging style, includes the coastline south of Blackpool, taking in Lytham and St Anne's. Clarke described Lytham as "an ideal place—a Garden of Eden for lovers and honeymooners".[33]

Both developed as much more 'genteel' resorts compared to their larger neighbour up the coast. Today they are full of up market cafes and bars but retain a sense of the past. Lytham Hall is a particularly fine place, once the home of the powerful Clifton family. Today, a charity is working hard to restore it and the grounds are open to the public. A highlight in the horticultural calendar is late February when the snowdrops are out in abundance. Travellers arriving by train at St Anne's are greeted by fine floral displays and artwork; the delightful park and cafe ('The Pavilion') in Ashton Gardens are a couple of minutes' walk. From there, why not pay homage to that great Lancastrian—and comic—Les Dawson, whose statue is on the front?

Further along the coast the land opens out into the Ribble Estuary and Preston. The coastline south of the Ribble did not lend itself to industrial development, though the village of Tarleton had its own small dockyard. This area, east of the coast, remains strongly agricultural, noted for its tomatoes, potatoes and other produce.

The next major resort development was Southport. Like Morecambe and Blackpool, it was 'summat o' nowt' before the railways came—from Liverpool in 1848 and from Manchester and

Wigan in 1855. It became a large but elegant resort, frequented by the middle classes of Liverpool, many of whom 'moved out' and built large villas around the edge of the town. The annual Flower Show began in 1924 on the initiative of Southport Council. It grew into a major regional event with dozens of special trains bringing visitors to view what remains a remarkable spectacle. However, it came very close to extinction in the 1980s. Small and large 'c' Conservative Southport was absorbed into solidly Labour 'Sefton' through local government re-organisation in 1974, with the further blow (to many) of being taken out of Lancashire and put into 'Merseyside'. Sefton councillors added yet more fuel to the fire by deciding in 1986 to end funding for the Flower Show. The Show's website tells the story of what happened next:

> Southport people have always shown an extraordinary passion for and love of gardens and horticulture and were not prepared to lose their famous show … [A] committee of local horticulturalists and business men was formed to negotiate with the council over the future of the Southport Flower Show. Tensions on both sides were running high when they met in December 1986 but the mood was lifted after a symbolic gesture by Carl McClure, the leader of the local committee. When he entered the meeting with Sefton Council's Resources Committee he placed a single orchid on the top table.[34]

This seemed to do the trick and a deal was struck. The council agreed it would work in partnership with the local committee in organising one more show, in 1987, but would not underwrite any losses the show might incur. Thirty years on, Southport Flower Show is the UK's biggest independent flower show.

Continuing along the coast, Formby, Birkdale and Ainsdale have developed into prosperous communities in their own right, separate but closely linked to Southport. The frequent Merseyrail electric service provides an important link between Southport and Liverpool, despite being threatened with closure by Beeching in the 1960s. It survived and prospers. The Formby area has long been famous for its red squirrels but more recently the metal sculptures of Antony Gormley—'Another Place'—have attracted thousands of visitors.

That's it for seaside resorts: New Brighton, on the other side of the Mersey, is in Wirral, historically part of Cheshire and a pleasant place to visit. But for the true Lancastrian it's worth carrying on through Liverpool, ignoring the Wirral's many charms, towards John Lennon Airport. Call in at Speke Hall, a fine Tudor manor house now owned by the National Trust. Continue on to the pretty village of Hale, comparing and contrasting with the large inter-war municipal housing estate at Speke. If you take the road past The Childe of Hale pub and the ancient church where 'the Lancashire giant' was buried, it peters out into a path which takes you down to the lighthouse.[35] This is the most southerly point of Lancashire, not that there's anything there to tell you.

West Lancashire has a 'feel' all of its own. It was, and to a degree still is, the salad bowl of Lancashire. Local farms still produce top quality new potatoes and salad tomatoes, though the days when trainloads of produce departed daily for the markets of Manchester, Birmingham and London are long gone. This is the heart of 'old Catholic Lancashire', once a bastion of both the old faith and royalism. The defence of Lathom House by the Countess Charlotte (wife of the 7th Earl of Derby) in 1644, when besieged by parliamentary forces, is legendary in Catholic mythology.

East Lancashire

The cotton towns east of Preston have a very different 'feel' to the big former mill towns of south-east Lancashire. Perhaps part of this is down to the specialisation that these towns developed in the mid-nineteenth century as weaving centres. The unit of production was generally smaller than in the 'cotton spinning' belt of Bolton, Rochdale and Oldham which evolved on the basis of large-scale enterprises employing thousands rather than hundreds.

The train from Preston is a good way to experience east Lancashire today. The first main stop is Bamber Bridge, a relatively small town but possessing some substantial mills, most of which have disappeared, in some cases quite recently. Bamber Bridge has become famous for its 'battle' during the Second World War, when Black GIs fought a pitched battle with US military police.[36]

Beyond Bamber Bridge the landscape becomes more rural, with Hoghton Tower just about visible to the right as the train reaches the top of the climb up from Bamber Bridge and the West Lancashire Plain. It stops (on request to the guard) at Pleasington and then reaches the outskirts of Blackburn, at Cherry Tree and then Mill Hill. This is urban Blackburn, and remains of the town's textile greatness are visible at Waterfall Mill, just beyond Mill Hill station.

Blackburn developed in the nineteenth century as the world centre of cotton weaving, dominated by family firms such as the Hornbys and Feildens. Today, the local authority covers both Blackburn and its historic rival, Darwen. Blackburn-with-Darwen was imposed on Blackburn's smaller neighbour through local government re-organisation in 1974 and many 'Darreners' still resent it.

It's worth hopping on a Manchester-bound train to the next stop, Darwen, to see something of this fascinating town which once had its own local administration which ran the trams (later, buses), gas supply, libraries, art gallery and council housing. Darwen had a thriving civic culture, exemplified by the Darwen Literary Society. As well as textiles—mostly weaving—it developed a thriving wallpaper and paint industry. The Market Hall (1882) has been restored to its Victorian splendour and the hideous 1970s excrescence nearby has been demolished. The Carnegie Library of 1908 has a well-resourced Local Studies Room as well as a small art gallery.[37]

Darwen is always worth a visit and you can take a well-earned drink in The Old Chapel—the magnificent Wetherspoons pub just across the road, described as 'the finest building in Darwen'. It was built in 1866 and designed by Edward Bates who was also responsible for India Mill and its amazing tower, which thankfully still survives. Another notable landmark is Jubilee Tower, completed in 1897 to mark Queen Victoria's Golden Jubilee but also to celebrate 'the free-ing of the moors' in 1896.[38]

The train back into Blackburn will take you past Ewood Park, home of Blackburn Rovers since 1890 but with a history going back fifteen years earlier. It crosses the Leeds–Liverpool Canal on the Blackburn outskirts, which the railway will follow through east Lancashire to Colne.

However, another railway divergence is required at Blackburn to see Whalley and Clitheroe. Whalley, reached by an impressive twenty-eight-arch viaduct, is an historic religious settlement. The Abbey, visible from the train as you cross the arches, was established by Cistercian monks in 1296. A few miles further up the line is Clitheroe, with the remains of the castle visible from the train. It was the seat of Roger de Poitou, who was gifted 'the Honour of Clitheroe' after the Norman Conquest. This bizarre example of feudalism still remains and comprises sizeable chunks of land across Lancashire. Since 1945, the 'Barons Clitheroe' have styled themselves *Lords of the Honour of Clitheroe*; more formally, their legal style of address being 'Lords of the Various Manors and Forests within the Honour of Clitheroe'.

The coming of the railway transformed Clitheroe from a small market town into something bigger, with some textile manufacturing.[39] More recently it has diversified into cement production, with the large Ribble Cement factory just north of the station providing considerable local employment.

Returning to Blackburn to continue our journey eastward, the railway, following the Leeds–Liverpool Canal, takes you through the heart of industrial east Lancashire: Rishton, Accrington, Burnley, Nelson and Colne. These are all fascinating towns in their own right and were once the heart of Lancashire's weaving industry, along with Great Harwood and Padiham which are no longer rail connected.

Accrington is a particularly interesting place. A 1962 report in the Lancashire Authors' Association *Record* said that, "in spite of modern developments ... Accrington is a town of stone, and the Town Hall, with its classical porch and the massive market hall blend in with the general character of the town, strong and enduring like the surrounding moors".[40]

Alongside its weaving sheds the town once hosted the mighty engineering firm of Howard and Bullough, whose Globe factory survives as part of the local college. The public architecture of the town is impressive—the town hall and adjoining market hall are magnificent and the Post Office Arcade, nearby, would be thriving with artisan shops and cafes if it was further south. Hopefully, its time will come—the buildings are listed so there is some protection. I like the open market with its local produce, including tripe and excellent Lancashire cheese. The nearby library is a fine building which opened in 1908 in the former Mechanics' Institute. It's worth a visit to admire the decorative tile work and the stunning stained-glass window. Give yourself time to look through its well-stocked local history library, the staff are really helpful. The Haworth Gallery, with its outstanding collection of Tiffany glassware, is a mile out of town on the Baxenden road.[41]

Accrington station is a modern building and a showpiece for eco-friendly railway architecture. It is also home to Community Rail Lancashire, a pioneering community project which links schools and local community groups with the railway. Up until 1969 there was a direct line from Accrington to Manchester via Bury, up the steeply graded Baxenden Bank. Special locomotives were built by the Lancashire and Yorkshire Railway to assist heavy freights up the climb.

The train continues through the former brick-making village of Huncoat (locally pronounced as 'Uncoyt') and Hapton before reaching Rose Grove. The M66 motorway has smashed through what was once a thriving railway centre with a locomotive depot (one of the last steam depots in Britain, closing in August 1968) and marshalling yards which handled coal from Yorkshire, serving the local mills and more recently power stations at Padiham, Huncoat and Whitebirk. The former 'Great Harwood Loop' line branched off at Rose Grove and dropped down a steeply graded line to Padiham. It's a fascinating and very historic town, once an important weaving centre. The original Weavers' Institute remains, with lettering in the windows denoting its union origins. Gawthorpe Hall is nearby, the historic home of the Kay-Shuttleworth family. It is now a textile and dress museum and hosts a range of events including open-air theatre in the summer. It belongs to the National Trust and is co-managed with Lancashire County Council.

Burnley is close by, with a grand view of the town as the train leaves Burnley Barracks station and crosses the viaduct to Central station. Although the 1960s shopping precinct is much like anywhere else, the town has kept some fine stone buildings, above all 'The Mechanics' on Manchester Road. It's a reminder of the strength of local culture in east Lancashire, when each town had its mechanics' institute alongside the Co-op. Today, The Mechanics is at the heart of the town's cultural activities. Burnley was second only to Blackburn for the size of its weaving industry. Queen Street Mill at Harle Syke has survived as a museum of cotton weaving with 300 Lancashire looms preserved.[42]

Brierfield is the next stop, another former weaving community. The mills of Smith and Nephew have been extensively refurbished and now house a mixture of apartments and offices. Nelson, a couple of miles further east, was known as 'Little Moscow' because of its left-wing politics. Today, it seems like a town looking for an identity. It was a nineteenth-century 'new town', hardly existing before the textile boom of the early 1800s.[43] It was named after the local pub—the Lord Nelson—and spread out over the older settlement of Marsden. Many of the late-nineteenth-century stone buildings survive, including the recently restored Unity Hall, opened in 1908 as 'The Socialist Institute'. Another remnant of Nelson's working-class history is the splendid Weavers' Institute.

Part of Nelson's socialist culture was the 'Clarion' movement and its promotion of cycling and walking.[44] There was once a network of around twenty Clarion 'club houses' across Lancashire, offering cultural and sporting activities such as tennis, billiards and football and overnight accommodation. Thankfully, one has survived thanks to the efforts of Nelson Independent Labour Party members. 'Clarion House' is near Roughlee, a 3-mile walk from the centre of Nelson. It opens each Sunday and is staffed by volunteers. The house, opened in 1912, is adorned with images of Labour pioneers like Keir Hardie and Nelson's own Selina Cooper. A summer Sunday afternoon at 'Clarion House', listening to stories from old Clarion cyclists, is one of life's pleasures.

Nelson and Colne were once almost like brother and sister, sharing a common textile heritage, similar stone terraces running up the hillside and the characteristic single-storey weaving sheds with their sky-lit windows. They have drifted apart, with Nelson having a larger Asian population and looking more down-at-heel than its neighbour. Colne—known as 'Bonny Colne upon the hill'—feels like it is becoming a bit more gentrified and prosperous.[45]

Colne is the end of the line from Preston, thanks to Dr Beeching. The line beyond, to Earby and Skipton, closed in 1970. Local campaigners are mounting a determined campaign to re-open the missing 10-mile link and have had encouraging messages from the government.

It's worth taking a couple of hours to explore Colne. From the station, walk up the hill into the town centre, passing 'The Muni', or Municipal Hall, built in 1902 and a venue for everything from the annual Rhythm and Blues Festival to pantomime. The magnificent Co-operative store, opened in 1907, stands nearby and is now used for shops and offices. The former mill village of Trawden has developed as a centre of modern-day co-operation thanks to enterprising local people. The village pub is run as a co-operative together with the shop. Any further and you're in Yorkshire.

Rossendale

In many ways Rossendale epitomises 'old Lancashire'—its industries, stone terraces and fine municipal buildings, open moorlands and a strong independent spirit. It really begins at Ramsbottom, now part of Bury Metropolitan Borough, and continues to Rawtenstall and Bacup, which are the main towns making up the present-day Rossendale Council, a two-tier authority within Lancashire County Council. The preserved East Lancashire Railway will take you, steam-hauled, from Bury to 'Rammy' (Ramsbottom) and on to Rawtenstall but the scenic route beyond, to Bacup, has gone, as Stanley Accrington so poignantly sang. And it really is 'scenic'—the section of railway that ran through the steep gorge between Waterfoot and Bacup and plunged into Thrutch Tunnel reminds me of the Welsh Highland Railway's Aberglaslyn Pass. It was a heavily industrialised valley, with a succession of weaving sheds and also shoe factories linking communities such as Clough Fold, Waterfoot and Stacksteads, which still has its band room.

Ramsbottom, Rawtenstall and Bacup are all richly endowed with fine municipal buildings. Of the three, Rawtenstall has probably most to offer, with 'The Whitaker' being outstanding. The art gallery and museum has undergone a major renovation and is set in a fine park just on the outskirts of town. The municipal library is another example of late-nineteenth-century municipal pride. Rawtenstall is noted for having Lancashire's last-remaining temperance bar. Fitzpatrick's has become an iconic place, retaining its late-Victorian 'feel'. The home-made sarsaparilla would slake the thirst of even the most hardened boozer.

Today, Ramsbottom seems to be the most prosperous of the three towns, with several high-quality restaurants and bars. The steam railway runs through the town centre, unlike Rawtenstall where it terminates on the wrong side of a major road junction. The old 'Picture House' cinema in Rawtenstall is a magnificent building that has lain derelict for some time though there are plans to convert it into apartments. Bacup also has a fine art deco cinema in need of repair, along with quite a few more buildings including the market hall. It has its own Natural History Museum, whose history goes back to 1877 and is still thriving. 'The Nats' occupy a small building on the Todmorden Road and should be at the top of the list of places to see in any tour of Rossendale.

The other great institution around here is the Britannia Coconut Dancers. Britannia is a small village on the way out to Rochdale, once a centre of mining and quarrying. The Lancashire Sock Manufacturing Co. remains, having adapted to modern-day markets. The Coconut Dancers—they're happy just to be called 'The Nutters'—are a troupe of dancers whose history stretches back to the early nineteenth century. They have caused some controversy over the tradition of blacking their faces, but it is fairly certain that the origin of this custom is either to do with coal mining, or arose from the dancers wishing to evade recognition. Whatever, the controversy seems to have been effective in raising their profile and the Nutters are in demand across Lancashire. Their 'big day' is Easter Saturday when they parade the streets of Bacup accompanied by Stacksteads Band, calling in at numerous pubs on the way. The 2022 event, after a two-year Covid-enforced gap, was blessed with fine sunshine and large crowds.

The railway from Bacup to Rochdale closed to passengers in 1947—a pity. Had it survived it would have offered a fast link into Manchester, maybe even with a tram extension from Rochdale. As it is, the old railway makes for a pleasant walk, particularly across Healey Dell Viaduct which ranks as one of the North's most beautiful structures.

The moors above Britannia, Facit and Whitworth were once hives of industry, with coal mining and quarrying linked by a network of tramways, many of which can still be traced. Some quarrying remains, and it is large-scale stuff. The former Lee Moor Quarries above Bacup have been landscaped with some historical interpretation.

To get a real sense of contrast, take the bus from Bacup over the tops through Sharneyford to Todmorden—or just 'Tod'. This is a thriving town with a fine covered market supplemented by an open market several days a week. It's next door to the Grade I listed town hall. These days Todmorden is part of West Yorkshire but historically half of it was in Lancashire, the area south of the Calder.[46] The old county boundary runs through the middle of the town hall. It's the only place in Yorkshire where Lancashire county cricket is played. The Centre Vale ground was historically in Lancashire and the local team still forms part of the Lancashire Cricket League, though the flags of both the red and white rose are flown around the ground. This was once a textile town though few if any of the weaving sheds have survived. However, the old Weavers' Union offices remain—substantial buildings tucked away down a side street next to the canal.

Tod has re-invented itself as a bohemian sort of place, noted as the first 'incredible edible' town. This was the brainchild of Pam Warhurst who coined the idea of 'Incredible Edible Todmorden'.[47] Like all the best ideas it's very simple. Get people growing their own vegetables wherever you can find the space. The railway station was an early target and you can still pick herbs on the platforms. As the idea caught on other bits of unused land, public or private, were taken over for planting. And if you are getting the train west back to Lancashire, the Platform Gallery is definitely worth a visit, with several artists based in the station buildings. The booking office has its own community-run lending library if your train is late; it also has its own resident cat, as all stations should.

The great mill towns

To me, 'Cotton Lancashire' is really four main towns—Rochdale, Bury, Oldham and Bolton. These were cotton spinning towns, dominated by huge, multi-storey brick-built mills. Whilst Blackburn, Accrington and Burnley were enormously important as textile centres—mainly weaving—the domination of cotton was not so physically obvious.[48] Weaving sheds were usually single-storey buildings (the floors couldn't handle the weight of hundreds of heavy looms).

The four big towns had smaller, but still substantial, neighbours such as Heywood and Middleton for Rochdale, Failsworth, Royton and Hollinwood alongside Oldham, Radcliffe next to Bury, and Farnworth adjoining Bolton. Each of those smaller towns once had their own local authorities and a strong sense of civic pride and independence. This was sometimes reflected in a degree of rivalry towards their larger neighbours which in recent years has exploded, in some cases, into very successful independent political parties such as Farnworth and Kearsley First, Radcliffe First and Failsworth First.

Let's start with Rochdale. It's on the busy Calder Valley railway from Leeds and Bradford via Hebden Bridge, Todmorden and Littleborough—a small town within Rochdale Borough notable for its excellent bookshop and station heritage centre. Up the road from Littleborough or Smithy Bridge stations is Hollingworth Lake, known as 'The Weavers' Seaport'. Before people went off to Majorca or even Blackpool, Hollingworth Lake was a cheap alternative. Today it still has pubs, cafes and a fairground.

Just before you get to Rochdale you glimpse Clegg Hall, alongside the canal. The historic building is noted for its 'boggart', though I've never spotted it. A 'boggart' is a very Lancastrian type of hobgoblin, a truculent character not to be messed with; many spots around Lancashire still, so visitors will be told, still have their resident boggart. In the 1920s Allen Clarke wrote a dialect story called 'The Clegg Hall Boggart' which features the Chartist leader Ernest Jones.[49]

The station is about a mile out of town but you can hop on a tram and get into the town centre if you'd rather not walk. Before you do though, call in at the excellent museum in the old Fire Station. It tells the story of the fire service in the area. Just opposite is the impressive St John the Baptist Catholic church with its huge basilica.[50] Rochdale, as we'll see in Chapter 11, was 'the cradle of co-operation' and the original Toad Lane shop is part of an attractive conservation area facing the parish church and adjoining the excellent Baum pub. The Co-op store includes a museum and is a venue for meetings and events. The town has a particularly fine town hall, designed by Pugin. In the same area is the gallery and museum—'Touchstones'—built in an attractive art nouveau style, contrasting with the more gothic town hall. Broadfield Park, just above the gallery, is home to the Lancashire Dialect Writers' Memorial, erected in 1900. It commemorates three men and a woman, Margret Lahee.[51] Dialect enthusiasts should also pay homage to the

33

nearby grave of Tim Bobbin, or John Collier, 'the father of Lancashire dialect'. His grave, protected by metal fencing, is in the graveyard of Rochdale Parish Church.

From Rochdale I'd recommend getting a tram to Oldham. It takes you through places such as Milnrow (birthplace of Tim Bobbin) and New Hey with its magnificent goods shed, still emblazoned with the words 'Lancashire and Yorkshire Railway Cotton Warehouse'. Shaw, or 'Shaw and Crompton', or just 'Shay', still has some fine mill buildings next to the line. Crompton was home to dialect writer, cartoonist and mill lad Sam Fitton.[52]

Royton was once served by a branch line from the Rochdale–Oldham line at Royton Junction but this closed in 1970. Royton itself has been undergoing something of a revival, with its street market prospering. The fine town hall stands half-empty; some major mill buildings have managed to survive demolition.[53]

The tram takes you through the centre of Oldham and you get a feel that the town has been experiencing a revival. There is a fine statue of women's suffrage leader Annie Kenney in the town square. The library and art gallery has some fascinating material on the town's history as well as exciting contemporary art. The Coliseum Theatre managed to survive Covid but in 2023 the Arts Council of England withdrew its funding and the theatre is set to close.

There used to be a railway that headed east to Greenfield, joining the main Trans-Pennine route taking you into Saddleworth—an area sometimes described as a mini county ('Saddleworthshire') by its laureate Ammon Wrigley. Sadly the branch line to Delph—known locally as 'The Delph Donkey'—has disappeared and is now a bridleway (suitable for donkeys). Mossley, today part of 'Tameside', is the only town in England that straddled three counties: Lancashire, Cheshire and Yorkshire. The restored Huddersfield Narrow Canal runs east from Ashton via Stalybridge, Mossley and Greenfield to Diggle where it enters Standedge Tunnel, alongside the more recently constructed railway.

Head back to Oldham and get the tram towards Manchester; you'll get a magnificent view of the south Lancashire plain as you descend through Hollinwood towards Failsworth, past the Ferranti factory. Back in the early 1900s a film was made from a train carriage window along this line. One mill after another dominated the view. A few remain, but not spinning cotton.

Failsworth was once very much its own place, the birthplace of dialect writer and politician Ben Brierley, who popularised 'Daisy Nook' as a local beauty spot. 'Failsworth Pole' remains, at least the most recent one. The town has had a succession of poles going back to the early eighteenth century. The one erected in 1793 was intended by local 'Church and King' loyalists to 'overawe the Jacobins' who were quite a force in the area at the time. It blew down in 1849. Other poles were erected, the most recent in 1950.

If you're feeling adventurous, you could get a bus from Failsworth to Middleton. They are of a similar size but Middleton has more of an 'old town' feel compared to Failsworth which seems more suburban. There's quite a lot to see in Middleton, including the grave and memorial to Samuel Bamford, hero of Peterloo and star of the Mike Leigh film made in 2019. There are some ancient buildings and historic pubs, as well as a modern theatre. Perhaps the most exciting building in Middleton, at least potentially, is Warwick Mill. It's a classic 'late generation' spinning mill on seven floors. It has been empty for some time but is to be developed in a partnership between Rochdale Council and private developers.

From Middleton you can get a train from nearby Mills Hill into Manchester or do a bit more exploring. Go for the latter option. Close to Mills Hill station is 'The Rose of Lancaster' pub, celebrating the area's historic identity (who would imagine calling anything 'The Rose of Greater Manchester'?) and also a meeting place for radicals at the time of Peterloo. From here, you can stroll down the Rochdale Canal towards Manchester and see the old brewery of John W. Lees at Middleton Junction, where the branch line once diverged from the Manchester–Leeds line. It's a short walk from here to Foxdenton Hall, a fine Georgian house currently empty but, hopefully, soon to be renovated. The famous women's suffrage leader Lydia Becker often stayed at the house, owned by her parents. A community group runs 'Lydia's Tea Rooms' which celebrate her memory, set in a pleasant park.

It's never easy getting between these smaller towns, transport planners prefer you going into city centres and out again. But persevere and get the 163 bus that will take you via Heywood, where you can get more frequent services into Bury. Heywood is home to the gigantic 'Mutual Mills', proposed for conversion into apartments; they are absolutely stunning. The name itself is a giveaway to the 'mutually owned' company structure that developed the mills, rather than the more conventional family business model.

Heywood is the current terminus of the East Lancashire Railway, which continues via Bury to Ramsbottom and Rawtenstall. There are hopes to extend to Castleton and join up with the Calder Valley Line. As it is, Heywood doesn't really benefit from the railway, with the station about a mile from the town centre. It's worth making the effort to walk into town and have a drink in 'The Edwin Waugh' pub, celebrating Lancashire's most famous dialect writer and a noted drinker. Queen's Park is one of Lancashire's most pleasant municipal parks, though sadly it's many years since the boating lake was in use. Heywood Library is yet another 'Carnegie' library and a very fine one indeed.[54]

Bury is a short bus ride away, via 'Summit' and past Heap Bridge, once the home of Yates and Duxbury Paper, one of Lancashire's largest paper mills which closed in 1977. It is now the base for the Bury Black Pudding Co.[55] The paper works had its own railway with three delightful steam locos, two of which sound like they inspired 'Thomas the Tank Engine'—Annie and May.

There's a lot to see in Bury. It has done well out of the East Lancashire Railway, which has its main base there, with the 'Trackside' pub and shops. It's in the heart of the town centre, close to the Lancashire Fusiliers Museum which is opposite the excellent art gallery and museum. But, with all respect to my railway friends, the jewel in Bury's crown is the market. Coach parties come from far and wide to visit the market—and hopefully see the museums and take a trip on a steam train. An essential souvenir of any visit to Bury is a brace of black puddings; several stalls sell them. Unlike haggis, nobody has yet come up with a vegetarian alternative, which is perhaps just as well.[56]

From Bury, take the 524 Bolton bus which meanders via Radcliffe and Little Lever. Bury is the northern terminus of the highly successful Metrolink tram system and you could be clever and hop on a tram to Radcliffe and have a look round the newly refurbished market hall before continuing to Bolton. The business model is innovative—when it was under local authority ownership the market hall was on its uppers and needed major investment. The council assisted with the capital investment but helped set up what is in effect a local co-operative of traders who run the hall.

The bus takes you via the busy village of Little Lever to Moses Gate. Instead of carrying on to Bolton, walk back along Manchester Road into Farnworth. Like Heywood and Radcliffe, it was once very much its own place—a municipal borough from 1939 until 'Year Zero', 1974. It's where I spent much of my childhood, being looked after by my grandma while Mum worked at Burton's factory. It has fared worse than most Lancashire towns, which is saying something. Most of the huge mills, some of which specialised in the West African trade, have disappeared. Bentinck Mill, once managed by Whitmanite, socialist and town planning enthusiast Charles Sixsmith, does still stand. I've heard stories of African chiefs arriving at Moses Gate station and walking up Egerton Street in full tribal costume to visit the mill management.[57]

Farnworth's Library, yet another Carnegie job, remains in use with some fascinating local displays. A proposal by Bolton Council to build a new 'multi-purpose' library and close the old one met with howls of protest. The proposal was dropped. Next to the library is the fine town hall where 'the dictator of Farnworth', the Rev. John Wilcockson, once held sway. He was a very benevolent dictator, it has to be said.[58]

Opposite the library is Farnworth Park, opened by Gladstone in 1864 and still a delight. It was gifted to the town by mill owner Thomas Barnes who was concerned about the loss of open spaces in the town as the population boomed in the 1850s.

Could I tempt you a bit further? The Moses Gate Country Park is in the Croal-Irwell Valley, on the site of former chemical and paper-making factories. On the other side of the valley is the remaining part of the Bolton–Bury Canal which takes you past Nob End and the amazing derelict flight of locks down to Prestolee, where the main branch of the canal once continued to Manchester. It's a pleasant walk and you can get well into urban Salford before it peters out.

But if you've had enough of Farnworth, get a number 8 bus to Bolton, passing the site of the former Bolton Wanderers football ground at Burnden Park; they now play three miles north-west of Bolton at Middlebrook. The area is given over to ugly out-of-town retail developments now. I can say that because I'm Bolton born and bred, and I am ultra-critical of anything that has happened in the last forty years, or so. But I exaggerate, it's not all bad, although most local people would agree that Bolton has not fared too well in recent years. There is still much to be proud of. The town hall and the cobbled Civic Centre Crescent are magnificent, and always in demand for filming. The library, art gallery and museum are splendid, with some particularly good twentieth-century art depicting aspects of Lancashire by painters such as Julian Trevelyan. Bolton's links with Walt Whitman are commemorated in the priceless Whitman archive and also several Whitman artefacts including his stuffed canary and 'loving cup'.[59] Just across from the art gallery and library is the Octagon Theatre, opened in 1967 and still at the forefront of Northern drama.

Bolton town centre isn't blessed with many good places to eat but for a good hearty meal try 'The Olympus' fish restaurant, run by a lovely Greek Cypriot family. It's a Bolton institution. The market is nearby, trying its best to compete with Bury but with some way to go yet. We do very little to celebrate Bolton's status as the former world leader in fine cotton spinning, home of Samuel Crompton, inventor of the spinning mule. Hall i' th' Wood is on the outskirts of town, a short walk from the local railway station of the same name. Just on the other side of the railway is Firwood Fold, where Crompton was born. Both are well worth a visit. We owe it to William Hesketh Lever for the restoration of Hall i' th' Wood, without whose intervention in 1900 the place would probably have fallen down. It's now a small museum, in the ownership of Bolton Council.

Bolton was originally called 'Bolton-le-Moors' and it's easy to see why. Much of the town is surrounded by moorland, particularly on the north side. If you get a bus out of town up Halliwell Road you can visit Smithills Hall, dating back to the fourteenth century and the interesting mill village of Barrow Bridge, popularised by Allen Clarke in the 1890s. The mill to which it owed its development wasn't a great success, closing in 1877. It stood derelict for many years despite attempts to sell the buildings to varied potential buyers such as The Salvation Army. It was demolished in 1913 and the remaining clock tower and engine house was pulled down twenty-one years later.[60]

The attractive rows of stone cottages, rather unimaginatively named First, Second, Third, etc. Terrace, remain—as does the original educational institute, now apartments. Beyond Barrow Bridge you are into attractive moorland countryside, with a network of good footpaths. It wasn't always so and in 1896 Colonel Ainsworth, the local landowner (and occupant of Smithills Hall) closed off several footpaths, leading to the famous 'mass trespass' in September of that year.[61] Eventually the estate was passed on to Bolton Corporation, and it was sold to The Woodland Trust, an environmental charity which manages a total of 1,700 acres. They are gradually transforming the area with footpath improvements and signage.

To the west of Winter Hill is the slightly lower Rivington Pike with its tower, a traditional place of pilgrimage by generations of Boltonians each Good Friday. The land was purchased by William Hesketh Lever in 1900 and he set about transforming the area into a surreal playground, with Chinese gardens, a castle 'folly' and other features. His endeavours included restoration of the two historic barns. Much of the land he bequeathed to the people of Bolton. His own residence (one of many) was called The Bungalow and was burnt down by a suffragette activist, Edith Rigby, in 1913. The house was rebuilt, with Lever this time avoiding too heavy a dependence on highly combustible timber.

Horwich sits at the foot of Rivington Pike, a growing town that has finally weathered the closure of its large Locomotive Works in 1983. There is an excellent community museum—Horwich Heritage Centre—which celebrates its railway history as well as the town's other industries which included textiles, quarrying and aircraft engineering.

From Rivington it's an attractive walk via Anglezarke Reservoir, constructed by Liverpool Corporation between 1850 and 1857, towards Chorley. This is a town that has managed the transition from textiles to a more diverse economy very well. The town centre has a flourishing market and theatre together with some 'big name' shops and many small independent retailers including a bookshop. It runs an annual literature festival, 'What's Your Story, Chorley?'

Coal Lancashire

The West Coast Main Line from Preston south via Wigan and Warrington to Crewe effectively separates 'Cotton Lancashire' from 'Coal Lancashire'. That's an over-simplification, but there's an element of truth in it. Wigan was the centre of Lancashire coal mining, our equivalent to Yorkshire's Barnsley. That isn't to say that Bolton, or Salford, didn't have coal mining—the Lancashire miners had their union headquarters in Bolton, and the building still stands on Lower Bridgeman Street. Parts of Rossendale also had smaller pits which became exhausted by the 1950s or earlier. But the sheer scale of coal mining across parts of west Lancashire stands out. The main centres were Wigan, Leigh, Ashton-in-Makerfield and St Helens, though smaller towns including Coppull, Atherton and Westhoughton were significant coal mining centres, as we'll see.

If you take the train from Bolton to Wigan you will pass through Westhoughton with its gaily decorated and planted station, the work of the local station friends group. The town had a number of collieries which expanded during the late nineteenth century. One of these was Pretoria Pit, close to the boundary with Atherton. On 23 December 1910 the pit blew up, as the morning and afternoon shifts were changing. A total of 344 men and boys died and scores of families were devastated. There is a memorial close to where the disaster happened, as well as a large monument in the Parish Churchyard, and another more recent memorial in the nearby park depicting a Lancashire miner, against the names of the victims.

Westhoughton is known locally as 'Keaw Yed' though some call it 'Howfen'. The 'Keaw Yed' title is dialect for 'Cow Head', after the legend about a farmer sawing his cow's head off after the beast had got stuck in a gate. Funny lot in Howfen. And Keaw Yed.

Nearby Atherton combined both coal and cotton, with some very large spinning mills alongside some substantial collieries such as Gibfield and Chanters. The Atherton Collieries combine, owned by Fletcher, Burrows and Co., was amongst the first companies to introduce pit-head baths and provide good quality housing for their workers with recreational facilities. Some of their houses can be seen at Howe Bridge on the road between Atherton and Leigh, with a small monument to the area's mining heritage at the road junction.[62]

Westhoughton marks the easterly boundary of the Wigan coalfield. The next station on the line is Hindley; it served a bigger mining area and the station, through its own very active 'station friends' group, commemorates the Ladies Lane pit which was nearby. Close to Hindley was the enormous Kirkless ironworks, developed by the Wigan Coal and Iron Company in the early nineteenth century. In 1900 it had six blast furnaces in operation and employed 10,000 men. By 1930 it had closed.[63] Today some of the buildings survive in industrial use and remains of the slag heaps are visible.

Wigan itself grew rapidly in the nineteenth century as coal mining took off. The earliest pits were in the Orrell area. One of the main coal-owning dynasties were the Balcarres family whose residence was Haigh Hall, some 3 miles from the centre of Wigan and now owned by Wigan Council, which is bringing the hall back to life. Within the hall grounds are the remains of the historic Haigh Foundry, one of the earliest locomotive builders in Britain. Wigan is proud of its heritage and the museum is well worth a visit. I suppose I should mention 'Wigan Pier', the butt of thousands of jokes and the title for Orwell's classic. *The Road to Wigan Pier* was one of the first political books I ever read and I like to think Orwell's democratic socialism, combined with some healthy scepticism, had a lasting influence on me. He is commemorated by the 'Moon over Water' pub in Wigan and there is an interesting display about his time in Wigan in the Museum of Wigan Life on Library Street.

Ashton-in-Makerfield is an unpretentious town with an attractive town centre. Nearby is Haydock, another former mining community but more famous for its racecourse. St Helens is the next main stop if you're on the train from Wigan. It's a town that is quite different to any of its neighbours. Whilst coal mining was important in its early industrial development, it was glass making, and to a degree chemicals, that really made the town what it is today. Pilkington's Glass became a world-famous brand and the Glass Works museum is a fascinating story of the growth of the industry. The St Helens (or 'Sankey') Canal, opened in 1757, was one of the first canals in the country and makes for an interesting walk through to Earlestown, once an important railway engineering centre, named after Sir Hardman Earle, a director of the London and North Western Railway.

The collieries to the south of St Helens—Bold, Sutton Manor and Parkside—were amongst the last survivors of the Lancashire coal mining industry.

Chemical Lancashire

This doesn't have quite the same nostalgic ring to it as the 'Coal' and 'Cotton' Lancashires, but it's apt, even if not as extensive as its two neighbours. St Helens is a bit of a hybrid, having a traditional coal mining history and later chemicals, but we've already been there. However, there are two towns of special importance close to St Helens. The first is Prescot. A new theatre—'Shakespeare North'—opened in 2022, celebrating the historic links between Shakespeare and the area.[64] Its industrial development was largely down to wire-making and coal mining but it was also home to a community of highly skilled watch-makers.

To the south of St Helens, once connected by the St Helens and Runcorn Gap Railway, is Widnes. The frequent bus service takes you past the site of Sutton Manor Colliery and the *Dream* memorial which celebrates the area's mining heritage. The council and local residents, including former miners from the colliery, were involved in the consultation and commission process through which *Dream* was selected. The sculptor was Catalan artist Jaume Plensa.

Widnes grew thanks to its position on the Mersey Estuary. It had an extensive network of railways which fed the chemical factories from adjoining collieries, as well as serving the docks. It had the unenviable reputation for being 'the dirtiest, ugliest town in England' in the latter years of the nineteenth century, though there would have been no shortage of competition across the North at the time.[65]

Today, Widnes is part of Halton Council, which includes Runcorn, across the Mersey in Cheshire. It has a pleasant pedestrianised main street and a sizeable covered market. Its MP, Derek Twigg, remains 'a true Lancastrian' despite everything. The town is still served by rail, though it's a bit of a way out of town and was originally named—more accurately—'Farnworth'. It is reputed to be where Paul Simon wrote 'Homeward Bound' in 1964, a song which famously begins with the singer sitting in a railway station.

Apparently he was on his way to Hull for another 'one-night stand' which would have made sense, with a change of train at Manchester. Controversy still surrounds the claim. Could he have been at Widnes Central station, which closed in October 1964, rather than waiting at what was re-named 'Widnes' shortly after?

Folkies and rail cranks will continue to argue it out but my money is on 'Widnes North' (the station that is still open).

Warrington sits between Liverpool and Manchester, just on the north side of the Mersey, making it unquestionably 'Lancashire'. It was famous for its wire industry, which the rugby club was originally named after (now 'The Wolves', enough said). Crosfield's chemical works is still active, part of the Unilever empire. It's the first thing you see when you arrive in town, at Bank Quay station. Very near is the old town hall with its magnificent gates. Dave Hadfield, on his trek through the North in search of Rugby League shrines, commented that "they would look more at home in Versailles than in industrial Lancashire", and he's right.[66] Warrington once promoted itself as 'The Athens of the North', and why not? It had a very lively arts scene in its day, explored in Chapter 12. The nearby art gallery and museum is worth a few hours of anyone's time; look out for the mural celebrating Warrington's history, just behind it.

The two great cities

I've tended to focus on the less-well-documented towns of Lancashire but the role of its two great cities, Liverpool and Manchester, cannot be stressed too much. Both grew on a very different basis, Liverpool as a port and Manchester as a business centre, with substantial industries. Traditionally, people talked of 'Manchester men—and Liverpool gentlemen'. The cities were linked by the world's first inter-city railway, the Liverpool and Manchester, in 1830.

If you're travelling to Liverpool you'll most likely arrive at Lime Street. It's a grand station, enhanced by statues of Bessie Braddock and Ken Dodd, though I was never a fan of the latter with his ridiculous 'Diddy Men'; his stock sank even lower when he came out as a Thatcherite in the 1980s. You emerge to the magnificent sight of St George's Hall.

Liverpool developed as a major port in the eighteenth century. The docks stretch from Garston, south of Liverpool up to Seaforth, part of Bootle, in the north. Widnes and Runcorn both developed as major ports just a few miles up river. Part of Liverpool's historic dockland now forms the Tate Liverpool. When it was a derelict wreck it featured in *Boys from the Blackstuff* as a metaphor for the city's decline. Characters such as 'Yosser' Hughes ('Gis a job') symbolised the fall of what was once a great city.

It's on its way back. The development of the 'Liverpool ONE' shopping centre has brought new life back to the city and it has capitalised on its heritage through several outstanding museums. It has re-captured its position as a major arts centre with the Walker Art Gallery being just one of the great galleries in the city. The city's former wealth, some of it 'slave money', is demonstrated today by the fine Georgian buildings that abound in the city centre.

Liverpool has always been a radical, independent-minded city. It was probably one of the few places in the UK, alongside Glasgow, that had a significant anarchist movement in the early twentieth century. Its political influences were truly international: Ireland being first and foremost, but also Europe, Asia and America. 'The International Club'—long gone now—was a meeting place for revolutionaries from all over the globe, many of them seafarers making brief calls in Liverpool.[67]

In more recent times, Liverpool became famous for its musicians and notorious for the political machinations of the 'Militant Tendency' which gained a strong base in the city, personified by the deputy leader of the council, Derek Hatton. What became 'Merseyside' in the 1974 re-organisation is now the 'Liverpool City Region' led by an elected mayor.

Manchester's history stretches back to at least Roman times. Its growth in the seventeenth and eighteenth centuries was based around textiles and the city was at the heart of Lancashire's 'take-off' as an industrial superpower in the 1780s. Although the city developed as the commercial heart of the cotton industry, with the Cotton Exchange at the centre of things, it also had substantial cotton spinning factories close to the city centre and an expanding engineering industry which grew off the back of cotton. Mather and Platt, originally of Salford, later moved to the east of Manchester and developed as a great world business. It was one amongst many. South of the city Beyer Peacock developed as a major locomotive engineering works, with the Great Central Railway's Gorton works just opposite. Crossley's, Gardiner's and many others grew into worldwide prominence. Trafford Park grew as Manchester's industrial growth area in the twentieth century with major companies such as Metropolitan Vickers and many more being based there, close to the Ship Canal.

It was at the heart of many political struggles, not least the campaign for democratic reform in the early years of the nineteenth century. Its Liberal politicians championed the anti-Corn Law League and it was the scene of the Peterloo Massacre in 1819. In the 1840s it was a major centre of Chartism. The city can justly claim to have been at the heart of the women's suffrage movement, with the Pankhursts based in Manchester, and many other key figures in the women's movement being Mancunians. It has been home to dozens of major artists, musicians and writers.[68]

Perhaps the city's crowning glory is its music, with a great tradition stretching back to the mid-nineteenth century when Charles Hallé rode into town. The tradition was kept alive by the Hallé, the Free Trade Hall and its Bridgewater Hall successor, the Royal Northern College of Music, Chetham's School of Music and several more orchestras and choirs.[69]

Like Liverpool, it has supported several major galleries including the City Gallery on Mosley Street and the Whitworth. Part of its interest is in the smaller galleries which continue to spring up around the rapidly changing Ancoats district.

The city's transport network developed rapidly in the 1840s, but in an unplanned way. For well over a century the two major stations served separate routes, with a third (Central) a terminus for the Midland and Cheshire Lines services. Victoria was the main station of the Lancashire and Yorkshire Railway, with its headquarters at Hunts Bank, just opposite (the site now forms part of Chetham's College). The London and North Western Railway had a 'secondary' facility at Exchange which was actually in Salford (see below) linked to Victoria by Platform 11—the world's longest platform, at 670 metres or 2,200 feet in old money.[70] The London and North Western's main station was London Road, which became Piccadilly in 1964 and sees trains to London, Birmingham and the south-west. If plans come to fruition it will be the city's 'HS2' station.

While Liverpool languished during the harsh Thatcher years, Manchester was gradually re-inventing itself under the creative combination of its dynamic chief executive Howard Bernstein, leader Graham Stringer and his successor Richard Leese. The IRA bomb of 1992, which destroyed much of the city's centre, led to a remarkable regeneration during which the Labour-run city council collaborated with the Conservative government, particularly through Michael Heseltine, to rebuild the city. I think they succeeded beyond their wildest dreams.[71]

Salford

I bet you thought I'd forgotten Salford. Many people do, which is inexcusable. The city's identity, in many outsiders' minds, has become submerged within Manchester, its historic rival. To me it's every bit as interesting as its more famous neighbour, and very different. It doesn't have a grand station, like Manchester's Piccadilly or Victoria. The Lancashire and Yorkshire Railway provided a modest facility at what is now called Salford Central, but the London and North Western Railway, whose tracks passed next to it, didn't feel it was worth the bother of providing platforms. Instead, it built what it mistakenly called 'Manchester Exchange' at the eastern extremity of Salford, but on the north bank of the Irwell, ensuring it was well and truly within the city of Salford. Just thought I'd let you know. Manchester Exchange closed in May 1969 though some of the platform (which joined it to Victoria, making it the world's longest station platform) can still be seen.

Before the Railway Age, Salford had already developed as a substantial settlement. It was given 'Free Borough' status in 1844 and became a county borough in 1889. It received 'City' status relatively recently, in 1926. Today it has an elected mayor, currently (2023) Paul Dennett who has done much to put Salford back on the map. It should never have fallen off—its history, ancient and modern, is fascinating. It can claim to have the first free public library in the country, a pioneer of gas lighting, and much more. Not much of the 'ancient' has survived, although Ordsall Hall remains and is open to the public.

For Lancashire Catholics, at least east of Warrington, Salford is the 'Main HQ' with the not-especially-imposing cathedral forming the heart of the Salford Diocese. The Bishop of Salford was a man of great standing in the British Catholic hierarchy and would appear, in a suitably elevated position, to inspect the crowds of thousands of processionists on the annual Whit Walks, a feature of most of the large Lancashire towns up to the 1970s. As a boy I used to walk with my local church and school, St Williams, in the Bolton procession. Each year my parents would pack me off to the local tailors to get my uniform, probably money they could ill afford and essentially just for a single day. The local (Catholic, of course) tailoring firm did very well out of us.

To a degree, Salford has tended to define itself in relation to its neighbour, Manchester, on the opposite bank of the River Irwell. Attempts to unite the two, going back to 1830, have foundered on a combination of local pride and political complexities. Hampson, writing in 1930, contemptuously dismisses the idea, saying that "Those who chatter so blithely of joining Salford and Manchester into one community should be interested to know that this proposal is as devoid of originality as it is of practicability."[72]

It's much more of a 'Lancashire' city than its neighbour. The 'Salford Hundred' ('Hundred' was the original unit of local government) legally still exists as part of the historic county and my own anecdotal experience suggests that many 'born and bred' Salfordians still see themselves as 'Lancastrian'.

The city of Salford stretches a long way out, taking in former mining communities such as Walkden and Little Hulton, which grew enormously in the 1960s and 70s with large 'overspill' housing estates. From being examples of good quality housing, removing Salfordians from appalling housing conditions which almost equalled Liverpool's, some of the estates became havens for drug dealing and crime. They are picking themselves up now, but it has taken a long time.

Today, the city's jewel in the crown is the Royal Horticultural Society's Bridgewater Gardens. It was developed on the site of the original Bridgewater Hall and opened in 2021. It is close to what can be justly described as one of Lancashire's 'Great Wonders'—the underground canal system which emerged into daylight at Worsley Court House.[73] The network of underground canals covered a route mileage of about 30 miles and extended out as far as Bolton.

The River Irwell traditionally provided recreation for many Salfordians. The Salford Regatta was a major event across Lancashire and "crowds would line the river on both sides of the course between Regent Bridge and Throstle's Nest and watch with keen enthusiasm the best oarsmen of the country in competition, and afterwards join with true Lancashire vim in the revels of the Fair on Sunnyside Fields".[74]

Salford is a Rugby League city, though Manchester United's ground at Old Trafford is a stone's throw the other side of the Ship Canal. It had a diverse industrial base. During the nineteenth century it developed some textile manufacturing as well as coal mining on its periphery. Swinton and Pendlebury, which up to 1974 did of course have their own local administration, were major mining centres. The city's coat of arms depicts a weaving shuttle, a ship and engineering. Strangely, it doesn't feature the pickled onion factory which once stood on Bolton Road, Pendlebury. Pilkington's Lancastrian Pottery and Tiles was located at Clifton Junction and examples of its 'Lancastrian Lustre' glazed pottery were exhibited at international exhibitions in the early 1900s. A superb collection of artefacts in Salford's Museum celebrates its achievements.[75]

Salford grew dramatically during the nineteenth century, yet it seems to have declined in affluence, if not industry. Hampson mentions streets of Georgian elegance in the 1780s which were swept away as the city developed, leaving squalid cramped housing in their place. An industrial 'outlier' within Salford was the former Irlam Steel Works which closed in 1972. Close to the steelworks was the Co-op Soap Works which had its own passenger train service linking it to the mainline at what is now the finely restored Irlam station.

The coming of the mis-named 'Manchester Ship Canal' in 1894 ought to have transformed the fortunes of Salford and it's odd that it didn't. The main docks were very much in Salford and were generally referred to as 'Salford Docks'. The main dock gates were along Trafford Road and as a boy in the early 1960s I can remember wandering in to marvel at the ships loading and unloading from destinations around the world.

The docks closed in 1982 and became derelict. However, in a renaissance spearheaded by Salford City Council, which purchased the site in 1984, the former docklands area has been transformed. The re-christened 'Salford Quays' has seen the coming of the Lowry, MediaCity and a host of other activities, connected by the Metrolink tram network. Yet somehow it all seems like a huge bubble, disconnected from the city of Salford as a whole and more a part of Manchester. As an added slight, the Metrolink tram runs into Manchester city centre and Trafford, rather than going into the heart of Salford itself, with a branch fizzling out at Eccles, not even reaching the railway station. Its main saving grace (there are others) is Peel Park and the excellent art gallery and local studies library— within a few minutes of Salford Crescent station and opposite the equally wonderful Working Class Movement Library, housing the huge collection of the late Ruth and Eddie Frow, to whom I am grateful for their advice, inspiration and Ruth's tea and cakes.

Conclusion

'Historic Lancashire' remains a viable, though fractured, regional entity. It was founded on a complex unity which took in the great world cities of Liverpool and Manchester; its industrial towns were linked by commercial, professional and transport connections whilst the wider agricultural hinterland fed the towns and cities. Today, Lancashire has a much more diverse industrial base, weaker in some ways than in the time of cotton and coal, but in other ways potentially stronger, without dependence on a single industry. The 'knowledge economy' is one of the region's strongest assets, with major universities and colleges that rival the best in the world. In more rural parts of Lancashire, tourism is a bigger employer than agriculture, though the latter remains important—potentially more so in the future. As climate change forces us to re-think unsustainable leisure travel, many parts of Lancashire and the Lake District will become more popular.

Good transport links will be key to making a new Lancashire work and that must be based on a sustainable hierarchy, with rail at the top, making the most of electrification and modern forms of traction, with feeder bus and light rail connections. Many of the 'second tier' towns we've visited need to re-imagine themselves with strong local governance and a vibrant local economy, and avoid the fate of becoming cheap dormitory suburbs for Manchester. Part of a greater region, yes, but we should re-discover the local patriotism and energy which drove the success of places like Bolton, Blackburn, Wigan, Barrow, St Helens and Burnley.

2

SHAPING LANCASHIRE

To us 'old 'uns' the Lancashire youth is a new creature. How it will shape the Lancashire of the future we can hardly know. It would be encouraging to see it shaping a little better.[1]

Journalist James Haslam was writing in 1936 when Lancashire, or at least parts of it, was still struggling to emerge from depression. War was only two years away. This chapter looks at how Lancastrians have helped 'shape' their county over the last 250 years or so. It's about how our towns and cities have grown and attempts to create 'the city beautiful'. This goes back to 'model villages' at places such as Calder Vale and Barrow Bridge, as well as more urban development based on Ebenezer Howard's garden city concept. Oldham's 'garden suburb' is a good example from the twentieth century. Skelmersdale, developed in the 1960s, was a brave attempt at a Lancashire 'new town' which has had its problems, not least poor transport links, the arteries that any healthy town, or region, needs.

The Council for the Preservation of Rural England (now CPRE— the Countryside Charity) has always had a high profile in Lancashire. The figure of Charles Sixsmith, the Lancashire Whitmanite and 'ethical socialist' figures prominently in its work (see below). He was a member of the CPRE's regional executive and was closely involved in the production of *Buildings in Lancashire*, published by the CPRE in 1937. The Earl of Derby wrote the foreword, urging that: "Lancashire people should support and encourage the efforts of the CPRE, and the local authorities in safeguarding what remains of beauty in the country. It is a heritage we should jealously guard."[2]

* * *

Lancastrians: Charles Sixsmith 1870–1954

Charles Sixsmith was a man of many parts. He was elected to Chorley Rural District Council in 1917 and served for thirty-seven years, rising to become chairman in the 1940s. In 1915 he played an active part in the defence of local footpaths when Liverpool Corporation attempted to close some of the reservoir paths around Rivington. He was actively involved in preserving local landmarks and was a member of the North-West committee of the Council for the Preservation of Rural England.

He was a key part of the Bolton Whitman group, becoming involved in their activities from the early 1890s. He built up a large collection of Whitman artefacts and letters which are now available in Manchester's John Rylands Library. As well as fellow Whitmanite Dr John Johnston, he was a close friend of the socialist and sexual radical Edward Carpenter and was a frequent visitor to his home near Sheffield. He contributed to Edward Carpenter: In Appreciation, *after Carpenter's death.[3]*

He rose to a senior position in the Lancashire cotton industry, managing Bentinck Mill in Farnworth, which specialised in the West African trade. He was an authority on textile design and had progressive views on industrial relations in the textile industry. He was a founder member of the Manchester branch of the Design and Industries Association and of the Red Rose Guild, formed in 1921. In the late 1920s he was thanked "for his zeal in organising two expeditions" to Smithills Hall and Rivington Hall, and again for the "visit to Bentinck Mills where Mr Sixsmith received and showed the party the dyeing and weaving of stuffs for the West African market". He became chair of the Red Rose Guild holding that post for most of the 1930s.[4]

He chaired the panel of councillors and officers that produced the Advisory Plan for Lancashire in 1946 (see pp 70–3). He died at the age of 83 and is buried in Rivington Unitarian churchyard.

* * *

Building Lancashire: architects and architecture

Most books written about Lancashire which touch on architecture and building design focus almost entirely on what was built before 1850, typically the mansions of the wealthy. Occasionally a farmhouse might feature or perhaps a weaver's cottage. Yet Lancashire has an architectural tradition that is distinctive and more 'democratic'. It includes the great industrial buildings that incubated Lancashire's economic growth, but also the tens of thousands of terraced cottages which mark out Lancashire towns as distinctive.

Each town, from relatively small places such as Farnworth, Darwen, Radcliffe and Bacup to the great towns such as Blackburn, Wigan, Bolton, Rochdale, Oldham and Bury had substantial public buildings, most of which were built in the late nineteenth century—town halls, libraries and art galleries. Most of them were designed by local firms, such as Stott's, Bradshaw Gass and Hope, and George Woodhouse. In addition, there was a substantial number of 'statement' buildings by working-class organisations—primarily the Co-ops, but also trade union buildings, many of which survive but nearly all put to alternative uses. Nelson's magnificent Unity Hall is an exception—in 2021 the building was restored to use as a community centre with its links to the socialist movement of the early 1900s celebrated.

To do justice to this architectural heritage—and nobody really has done, yet—requires a book in its own right. For our purposes, what is interesting about this tradition is firstly the fact that it was largely home-grown and secondly that it has been treated with neglect, bordering on contempt, by historians.[5]

Even among Lancashire historians, its mills have been derided as ugly, re-hashing and misquoting William Blake's reference to 'dark, satanic mills'. Yet the mill buildings that survive can be impressive. Girouard refers to the chimney (mistakenly referring to it as 'the tower') of India Mill, Darwen, as 'sensational', which it undoubtedly is. Yet it isn't typical, and it is buildings such as Swan Lane (Bolton), Mutual (Heywood), Tulketh (Preston), Warwick (Middleton), Lees Brook (Lees, Oldham) and Trencherfield (Wigan) that are exciting reminders of what was once typical and unexceptional. Does age make a building change from being dull and ordinary into something of awe? Or its relative scarcity? Perhaps both. I grew up in the shadow of the now-demolished Beehive 1 and 2 Mills and didn't think anything of them when I was a child. I was outraged when what I came to recognise as fine Grade II listed buildings were demolished. Undoubtedly, nostalgia plays a part.

Today, in the first quarter of the twenty-first century, the image of the cotton mill has acquired a new status in Lancashire identity.

It is no longer an object of dislike or shame but increasingly an iconic structure which encapsulates a sense of Lancashire identity, or perhaps even further, 'Northern-ness'. A lively new online magazine of contemporary culture and current affairs published in Manchester chose *The Mill* for its title.

Oldham, at the height of its greatness as a cotton-spinning centre, had 300 mills in operation; Bolton lagged behind with a few less. The total number of large mills, spinning and weaving, across Lancashire would have exceeded a thousand in, say, 1900. The larger mills were constructed in a series of 'waves', which culminated in a spate of mills constructed around 1900–10, with a final burst in the short-lived boom period after the First World War. Unsurprisingly, it is the later ones that have survived and been made into stylish conversions, such as the former Sir John Holden mill in Bolton and Deakin's at Egerton. However, many languish in multiple-use occupation, slowly decaying despite listed status.

The most prolific mill architects were Stott's of Oldham. Abraham Stott and his brother Joseph established rival firms which dominated contracts for mill design in the Oldham area in the second half of the nineteenth century.[6] Abraham's son, P.S. Stott, continued the family business as Stotts and Sons of Manchester and designed some eighty mills in the south-east Lancashire area.[7]

George Woodhouse designed a number of mills in Bolton including the surviving (and listed) Gilnow Mill. Bradshaw and Gass, still trading in Bolton as Bradshaw Gass and Hope, were responsible for a number of mills in the Lancashire region as well as municipal buildings such as Bolton's fine civic centre and several municipal libraries and town halls. Bradshaw and Gass had a link to another byway in Lancashire cultural history, as the employer of J.W. Wallace, the main figure (or 'master' as friends half-jokingly described him) in the Bolton Whitman group. Wallace was classed as an 'architect's assistant' but is credited with the design of a number of buildings himself, including Great Lever public library in Bolton.[8]

There is an interesting aspect to the story of textile architecture. Alan Fowler and Terry Wyke have outlined the history of textile union buildings across 'Cotton Lancashire'. These were built as statements of union power, echoing the much more prevalent Co-operative Society buildings.[9]

Bolton and Oldham each had an impressive Spinners' Hall. Bolton's was re-built in 1912 replacing an earlier building which was originally the Bolton Junior Reform Club. The new building was designed by William Potts, of Bolton and Manchester-based Potts and Hennings. It was opened by the Labour MP A.H. Gill at an impressive ceremony. As well as providing offices for its own organisation the union rented out space to other textile unions in the town. Both the Oldham and Bolton halls were ostentatious statements of the power of the 'operative cotton spinners' of Lancashire in its heyday. The weavers' associations had equally impressive buildings in Burnley, Nelson and Todmorden. Bury was a rare demonstration of workers' unity: the Bury Textile Operatives Hall, opened in 1894, provided a home for the three main cotton unions in the town, covering weaving, spinning and card room workers. David Hardman of Bury was the architect. Alan Fowler and Terry Wyke commented that the hall "articulated solidity and respectability; a declaration in stone that the cotton trade unions were no longer marginal institutions in the town. From a distance it might have been mistaken for a bank."[10] Bolton, as we've seen, was the base of the Lancashire and Cheshire Miners' Federation; Bradshaw Gass and Hope designed the impressive Miners' Hall, which still stands on Lower Bridgeman Street.

Several architects, and architectural practices, deserve mention. The Lancaster practice of Sharpe, Paley and Austin was responsible for many fine buildings across Lancashire, particularly in Lancaster and 'North of the Sands', though the firm won commissions across the North of England. Most remain, including The Grange Hotel of 1866 and the nearby railway station.[11] James Price was surely right in his assessment that the firm "has left a legacy of superbly designed buildings across the North of England".[12]

Edgar Wood, the Middleton-born architect and artist, has been a neglected figure in British architecture for many years. His reputation is gradually being re-established, helped by the Edgar Wood Society.[13] His work was influenced by William Morris and the Arts and Crafts Movement and later by the work of Charles Rennie Mackintosh. Wood has been called 'The Lancashire Rennie Mackintosh' and there is something in that. Keith Parry notes Wood's "sympathy for the local style" and refers to his designs for Rochdale pubs—The George and Dragon at Castleton and The Victoria on Spotland Road—as being influenced by domestic architecture common in Lancashire in the early nineteenth century. He went into partnership with Oldham architect James Henry Sellers. As Parry says, "together they designed some remarkably advanced buildings. Two schools in Middleton (Durnford Street and Elm Street) illustrate a style that was clean, clear, almost ascetic, relying heavily on proportion and almost devoid of unnecessary ornament."[14]

* * *

Lancastrians: Charles Holden 1875–1960

Holden is fascinating, one of the key figures in British architecture of the twentieth century. He was born in Great Lever, Bolton, in 1875, the son of Joseph Holden, an iron turner, and Ellen, who ran a provisions store in Bolton.

He served his apprenticeship ('articled pupilage') as an architect with the Manchester firm of Everard William Leeson. He returned to Bolton and worked for the Bolton architect and close friend of William Hesketh, Jonathan Simpson. He attended the Municipal School of Art in Manchester, at a time when Walter Crane was Director of Design. Holden's biographer, Eitan Karol, commented that "Holden was there for only one year and was not taught by Crane, but he, like many others in the Lancashire artistic community, felt the effect of Crane's influence and the precepts of the Arts and Crafts movement reflected many of Holden's socialist ideals."[15] He was later employed at Bradshaw Gass and Hope, where he worked alongside the Bolton Whitmanite J.W. Wallace. He became close friends with fellow Whitmanite, mill manager and socialist Charles Sixsmith and later designed his house, Brownlow, near Adlington ("a Whitmanesque house for a Whitmaniac").[16]

Holden was hugely influenced by Walt Whitman, a passion which remained with him throughout his life. He wrote two articles (anonymously) for The Architecture Review *in 1905 in which he celebrated the poet and mystic.[17] Holden is best known for his work with Frank Pick at London Transport in the 1930s. Many of his magnificent art deco stations are still very much in use and several are listed. He also designed the grand Senate of London University. He said that some of his 'grand designs' were influenced by the mills and warehouses of Lancashire amongst which he grew up.*

He was awarded the Royal Institute of British Architects' Royal Gold Medal for architecture in 1936 and was appointed a Royal Designer for Industry in

1943. He twice declined the offer of a knighthood. He died in London, in 1960. His biographer said that "he created an exceptional architecture, inspired by the poetry of Walt Whitman and the search for the elemental".[18]

* * *

Beauty in civic life: radical town planning

Town planning is a relatively new profession, emerging from the work of socialist planners such as Raymond Unwin and Ebenezer Howard in the late nineteenth century with strong encouragement from William Hesketh Lever (see below and pp. 169–70). Edward Carpenter wrote essays and gave lectures on themes such as 'Beauty in Civic Life' and at a local level many voluntary associations emerged which promoted radical town planning—such as the 'Beautiful Oldham Society' (see page 60) and the Bolton Housing and Town Planning Association.

By the 1880s many towns and cities had grown rapidly, with pollution, poor sanitation and consequent ill health. Workers' housing had been thrown up, mostly very cheaply, with little thought to even basic amenities. The infrastructure of Northern towns and cities simply could not cope with the demands being placed upon them and by the late nineteenth century there was a growing awareness amongst many socialists that something must be done to improve the basic fabric of towns and cities.

One option, pursued by Ebenezer Howard and others, was to create entirely new communities. Whilst Letchworth is well known, there are other examples of similar schemes in Manchester, promoted by the City Council (in Burnage, Blackley and Fairfield). Several enlightened industrialists had created their own communities going back to the 1820s, and some survive—and indeed prosper—today. Barrow Bridge, near Bolton, and Calder Vale between Preston and Lancaster are excellent examples of good quality housing provided by employers. A bigger challenge was to re-structure and rebuild existing towns and cities.

William Lever and his visions

William Hesketh Lever (later to become Lord Leverhulme) was an enthusiast for town planning and 'garden cities'. His garden village at Port Sunlight was a fascinating example of applying arts and crafts concepts to an industrial community. He also developed a visionary plan for his home town of Bolton, through Thomas Mawson (see below). He commissioned Mawson to develop ideas around 'beauty and civic life' which were presented in a series of lectures to the Bolton Housing and Town Planning Society. A few years later, at the height of the First World War, Mawson produced more detailed plans for 'Bolton as it is and as it might be'. The plan involved the creation of a new town centre, based around the fine town hall that had been completed in 1873, with boulevards extending to the parish church and the public park. Brian Lewis commented that Lever "wished to impose a Beaux-Arts/City Beautiful town plan on the incrementally grown, haphazard mess that was Bolton. He sketched out his ideas on Ordnance Survey maps of the town and handed them in 1910 to Mawson to work up into something achievable."[19]

* * *

Lancastrians: Thomas Hayton Mawson 1861–1933

Thomas Mawson was born near Garstang and left school at age 12. His father was a warper in a cotton mill and later set up a building business. He started work in the building trade in Lancaster, then worked at a London nursery where he gained experience in landscape gardening. In the 1880s he moved back north, where he and two brothers started the Lakeland Nursery in Windermere. Mawson's first commission was the garden at Graythwaite Hall. He went on to design other gardens in the North-West including Langdale Chase, Holehird, Brockhole, and Holker Hall around the turn of the century.

From the 1890s he became a well-known landscape designer, doing work in the Lake District but also in Wales. He was the landscape designer for Glyn Cory Garden Village, the first garden suburb in Wales. In 1908 Mawson was commissioned to design the main public park in the new town of Barrow-in-Furness. In 1900 he wrote The Art and Craft of Garden Making.

Mawson was commissioned by Lever to produce a radical plan for Bolton which was published in 1916 as Bolton As It Is and As It Might Be, *following on from a series of lectures he gave to the Bolton Housing and Town Planning Association.*

His first project for Lever was his garden at The Hill, in Hampstead; it was the beginning of a long-lasting but sometimes tetchy relationship. He went on to design Rivington Gardens and Lever Park in Lancashire for Lever and his home at Thornton, Cheshire. Padiham Memorial Park (1921) was another commission in Lancashire. From 1910 to 1924 he lectured at the School of Civic Design, Liverpool University, which had been endowed by Lever.

In 1923 he became president of the Town Planning Institute and in 1929 the first president of the Institute of Landscape Architects. His later work included the Fazl Mosque in London. He died at Applegarth, the house he designed at Hest Bank, near Lancaster. He is buried in Bowness Cemetery, overlooking Windermere.

* * *

Little of his monumental vision saw the light of day, though in the late 1920s the Civic Centre, a crescent of exceptionally fine buildings acting as a girdle to the rear of the town hall, was designed by Bolton firm Bradshaw Gass and Hope (see above). Lever himself was invited to become Mayor of Bolton in 1918, a unique position as the role was normally taken by an elected councillor.

Bolton seems to have been a ferment of ideas around town planning and design in the first two decades of the twentieth century. As well as Mawson's work, ideas for community building were prevalent within the local socialist movement. Dr John Johnston, the 'Whitmanite' GP,[20] chaired a meeting of Bolton's Progressive League and Housing and Town Planning Society at New Spinners' Hall (St George's Road) in October 1912 when Edward Carpenter spoke on 'Beauty in Civic Life'.

While there were similarities between the ideas of Carpenter and Lever (and garden city pioneer Ebenezer Howard), there were significant differences; Lever was essentially a paternalist with strong dictatorial tendencies. Jane Jacobs, the New York community activist, said of Ebenezer Howard many years later, "his aim was the creation of self-sufficient small towns, really very nice towns if you were docile and had no plans of your own … As in all Utopias, the right to have plans of any significance belonged only to the planners in charge."[21] Perhaps she was being a bit unfair on Howard, but the comments applied to Lever.

Lever was keen to promote the new town planning discipline and worked with Charles Reilly, Professor of Architecture at the University of Liverpool, who had aspirations for a Department of Civic Design. Lever funded a 'school of Civic Design' out of his libel winnings in a case he brought against the *Daily Mail* in 1910. A 'City Beautiful' conference had already been held in Liverpool in 1907 and Reilly sought help from Lever to realise his dream. He responded quickly and positively, telling Reilly that, "I have felt for many years that some help is necessary to be given both in educating the public on the matter and also in providing the requisite knowledge available for Towns and Cities in the near future to be able to deal on broad lines with their suburban areas." He endowed a Chair in Town Planning and Civic Design, a research fellowship and a journal, the *Town Planning Review*.[22]

Beautiful Oldham—a model for today?

The most significant urban 'garden village' development was in Oldham. Its creation was very much down to the efforts of two remarkable women—Sarah Lees, daughter of the Oldham mill owner Charles Lees and wife Marjory, and Mary Higgs. Mary Higgs had the vision and drive and was ably supported by the Lees family; Sarah became a Liberal councillor in 1910, Oldham's first female elected member. They were directly influenced by the ideas of Ebenezer Howard and his book *Garden Cities of Tomorrow*, published in 1898.[23]

Mary Higgs established The Beautiful Oldham Society in 1902 after an energetic campaign promoted by the local paper. An article appeared in the *Oldham Chronicle* proposing 'Beautiful Oldham! Why not?' It was unsigned but written by Mary Higgs. She contrasted pre-industrial Oldham, "a place possessed of considerable beauty", with the present-day town at the turn of the century. However, she doesn't labour the current state of the town with its factories, pollution and slum housing. She says,

> There is in the character of Oldham people a love of having things about them nice ... in no other town are greater pains taken to have a clean and tidy doorstep, pavement and window sill ... the Co-operative Stores have done their best to beautify the town with

handsome buildings. Why not set before ourselves the noble ambition of making our town again a 'Beautiful Oldham'? What is wanted is that every citizen, every householder, should become ambitious.[24]

Reading Mary Higgs today is inspirational. So many of the ideas that have been adopted by the green movement, 'Incredible Edible' and community rail groups are to be found in her work. She identified railway cuttings and embankments for possible planting; she advocated the adoption of 'spare land' as public gardens, even mills could be transformed: "plant the reservoirs with trees, throw down ugly fencing and hideous hoarding, grow creepers up the sunny side and even a mill might be beautiful".[25]

The Beautiful Oldham Society was formed in October 1902. Its objects were:

a. To preserve existing features which add, or may be capable of adding, to the attractiveness of the town
b. To utilise waste and open spaces for tree planting, gardening, etc.
c. To encourage the cultivation of shrubs, flowers, &c, in the spaces adjoining public buildings, schools, mills, houses etc.
d. To cultivate the love of nature and gardening in school children
e. To prevent and punish the wanton destruction of trees and shrubs and the uprooting and theft of flowers
f. To encourage and provide facilities for the cultivation of plants and flowers in window pots and boxes
g. To urge the erection of varied and picturesque architecture and the laying out of building plots to provide groups of cottages with common gardens or grass plots.[26]

The objects of the society were radical and ambitious, though with a good combination of short- and longer-term objectives. The society reached out into the town establishment: it was strongly supported by the editor of the *Oldham Chronicle*, had the enthusiastic backing of some of the main employers, particularly the Lees family, and its vice-presidents for 1904–5 included several aldermen, the mayor and 'Winston S. Churchill Esq. M.P.'

* * *

Lancastrians: Mary Higgs 1854–1937

Her obituary in The Record *described her as "mystic, social reformer, poet-ess, authoress, lecturer and preacher".[27] She was all that and more, one of Lancashire's most remarkable figures of the twentieth century. She was born in Devizes where her father was a Congregational minister. The family moved to Bradford and at the age of 17 she won a scholarship to the newly formed College for Women at Hitchin, which shortly moved to Girton. Her good friend Marjory Lees said she was "one of the Girton pioneers, taking 2nd class honours in the Natural Science Tripos", noting that women were not awarded degrees, a position not corrected until 1928 when Mary received certificates for her BA and MA degrees.[28] She married the Rev. T.K. Higgs, also a Congregational minister and lived in the Potteries for ten years before arriving in Oldham in 1893.*

She was horrified at the poverty she found in towns like Oldham and decided to go 'on tramp' to see what conditions were like at first hand. Her experiences were published as Glimpses into the Abyss *and led her to giving evidence before a Parliamentary Inquiry into vagrancy.*

Mary's experiences were described in fictionalised form in Allen Clarke's novel The Red Flag *where she appears as Mrs Wilkinson. Marjory Lees was her friend and co-worker; they were both actively involved in the women's suffrage movement in Oldham. Between them they developed the 'Beautiful Oldham' movement: "The City Beautiful was an ideal to be striven for and so she evolved the Beautiful Oldham Society with its Spring Flower Show, its practical information on the possibilities of town gardening and its Junior Section amongst the school children, nearly 3000 of whom visited the last Show. Out of these meetings sprang the first Garden Suburb to be laid out in Oldham, which was opened in 1909.[29]*

Mary joined the Lancashire Authors' Association in 1915 and became a member of the Society of Friends (Quakers) during the First World War. She was awarded an OBE shortly before her death.

* * *

Unlike many similar bodies it put down deep roots in the town, largely thanks to Mary's organising abilities. Children were encouraged to get involved and there were annual flower competitions. Carol Talbot commented that, although the idea of a 'Beautiful Oldham' was ridiculed by many, the Society undoubtedly achieved some measure of success. Many Oldhamers will remember the annual shows and competitions with affection. Schools encouraged children to plant spring bulbs and to draw and colour pictures of plants to enter the yearly competitions … the Beautiful Oldham Society introduced countless children who lived in houses without gardens to the pleasure of planting bulbs and waiting for them to flower into a thing of beauty.[30]

A plot of land was gifted by the Lees family to create a 'garden suburb' and building commenced in 1908. The following year the first phase was completed and a gala event was held on Saturday 7 August. Howard was a guest. He said that he believed Oldham could become "a town of beautiful and peaceful homes and dwelling places, a place which they could find refreshing to come to from the outside world, a place of intimate associations of sound friendships and good memories."[31]

Today's 'garden suburb' remains an attractive community, though most of the homes are now in private ownership. The *Oldham Chronicle* reported on the centenary of the project in 2009, emphasising the work of the tenants in creating an active community, "…now called the Garden Suburb Association, which started an amateur dramatic society, dances and whist drives, in a wooden community centre. In 1929 the centre was replaced by the current brick building." The *Chronicle* quotes Barbara Fell, the association's honorary secretary for fifteen years, who said:

In the past there were heralds, page boys and sword carriers in powdered wigs accompanying the rose queen, who was the best behaved girl on the estate. We still use the same sword and a red velvet and turquoise blue train for the queen and retiring queen, and there is still a sword carrier, and one page who carries the tiara and another who carries the badge awarded to the rose queens. The spirit of Garden Suburb is still going strong 100 years after it was founded and that is the achievement of everyone over the last 100 years.[32]

Athens of the North—Warrington

Warrington grew rapidly in the nineteenth century, on the back of chemicals and wire-making. It was also an important railway centre, with the world-renowned Vulcan Foundry nearby (which led to the creation of a classic 'industrial village' which mostly survives). In the early years of the twentieth century the town had a particularly active group of creative people, led by a Conservative politician and chartered accountant, Arthur Bennett. *Manchester City News* said that Warrington "was to him a place of enchantment because of its numerous literary associations. He revelled in its past history, and made it his joy as well as his business that famous houses should bear tablets, for they were all shrines in his sight."[33] However, Bennett was much more than an antiquarian; he was at the forefront of radical ideas to transform Warrington into a garden city. Despite his Conservatism, he edited the far-from-conservative local paper *The Dawn* (subtitled 'A Monthly Magazine of Progress'). The paper quoted Edward Carpenter on its first page: "Arise, O England, for the day is here."[34]

In many ways, Bennett was a Tory Edward Carpenter. On the one hand he was an imperialist, on the other he had radical ideas about municipal ownership, well to the left of the Labour Party. The origins of his paper went back to 1885 when a Mr William Heap Butler arrived at Bennett's office "to propose that we should start in Warrington a gratis weekly, devoted to the cause of social progress, on the lines of 'The Football Record'".[35] The title originally proposed by Heap Butler was *The Herald of Progress: A Weekly Paper for the People*, though this did not go down well with others. The title of *Sunrise* was chosen and the first issue appeared on 1 September 1888; it ran until the end of 1899.

The 'business model' of *Sunrise* (and that of *The Football Record*) was based on advertising revenue; a familiar model nowadays but less so in the 1880s. Bennett and his colleagues hoped to spread the business to Rochdale and elsewhere, harbouring "dim ambitions of eventually flooding England with our golden beams". They succeeded in reaching Widnes and Runcorn, but went no further.

After a twelve-month gap, a new paper, very much modelled on *Sunrise*, appeared—*The Dawn*. The paper was really quite remarkable, succeeding in promoting visions of 'the city beautiful' and priding itself on "never containing a single Limerick competition or a line of betting news" since it began. The publishers also produced one-off publications with Morris-inspired titles like *Warrington As It Was, As It Is, and As It Might Be*,[36] followed by *The Dream of a Warringtonian*.

Bennett accepted much of the 'ethical socialist' approach exemplified by Robert Blatchford and stated that, "we have never changed our early notion that co-operation is better than competition, and brotherhood than laissez-faire, or in the municipalisation and nationalization, by cautious and well-considered stages, of suitable industries..."[37] He said that, "you cannot set a limit to the possibilities of collective control. These ideas, then, have all along been fundamental—a Beautiful Warrington and a Merrie England."[38]

The paper carried an article by W.H. Woodcock called 'Warrington: a Utopia', in which the idea of a 'utopian town' is promoted. He stressed the importance of not only being concerned with 'the obvious' frontages but also "the slum and alley, back yard and court ... for it is well that all should live within the public eye; and, on the site of dismantled dove-tailed hovel, and of sunless court, the free and open air must once again be breathed".[39]

In the same issue, 'Fulmen' wrote about 'Our Municipal Progress' in which he applauded Warrington's municipal electricity generation, tramways, waterworks and the new Technical Institute. He also praised the council's policy of 'open spaces and municipal bowling greens' and the development of public parks. The author paid tribute to the success of the Sanitary Works Committee, "the most successful of all" of the council's departments, and the development of new municipally run schools. On the downside, the "inadequate railway station facilities" were an ongoing sore, despite "pious resolutions" by the council and Chamber of Commerce. The author concluded by lamenting "the disappearance of 'The Dawn' from our midst", and her hope that "we should be mindful not only of the Fatherhood of God but the brotherhood of men, and strive to bring about that state of things of which we daily pray, 'Thy Kingdom come on earth, even as it is in Heaven'".[40]

The group around *The Dawn* acted as a catalyst for promoting 'City Beautiful' ideas and putting them into practice. They succeeded in getting the council to acquire or extend public parks and open spaces and formed a 'Beautiful Warrington Society'.

Colonies and communes

Examples of community building continued throughout the nineteenth century, but the pace accelerated in the 1880s and 1890s.

Starnthwaite, near Kendal, was the location for another community which, though relatively short-lived, was used as a base for 'rest and recreation' by itinerant socialist propagandists, particularly from nearby industrial Lancashire. It was the creation of Kendal-based Unitarian minster Rev. Herbert V. Mills in 1892. The young and idealistic Katharine St John Conway was persuaded by Mills to act as secretary and became responsible for the recruitment of 'colonists' which included well-known socialists such as Enid Stacy and Dan Irving, later to become the leader of Burnley's socialist movement and ultimately its MP. Mills made few concessions to democratic control and the end result was an insurrection, graphically described by Katharine's biographer:

> They (the colonists) presented Mills with a long list of demands, including the right to appoint or dismiss their own foremen by democratic vote. Mills told them, in effect, to go to blazes, and matters proceeded by way of summonses at Kendal police court to an eviction party, 'led by Mills on his charger' and including according to the scarely unbiased Miss Stacy, twenty assorted roughs hired from Kendal beer-shops at three shillings apiece...[41]

Allen Clarke became one of the most devoted apostles of alternative living. He summed it up in a pamphlet, *Can We Get Back to the Land*, published in 1904:

> Certain circumstances have created an anti-natural, absurd and ailing state of things and today we are confronted with two great problems, insisting on a solution—the unemployed question and the physical (which also means mental) deterioration of the nation. Both these problems can be resolved by getting back to the land, and returning to that labour which nature meant should be the fundamental of every man's occupation...[42]

He tried to put his Tolstoyan vision into practice with the 'Daisy Colony' Scheme ('Daisy', as he explained to Tolstoy, because the daisy is the most communistic of flowers). It is a story which has echoes of the experience of most attempts to build 'communist colonies' at the time. It was fairly common for a group of enthusiastic socialists to get together to attempt to create a socialist utopia, but often found that the realities of human nature and economics conspired to wreck the hopes of the idealists.

Clarke launched his appeal to create a Tolstoyan community in his *Northern Weekly* of 4 July 1903. A meeting took place at Bolton's Vegetarian Restaurant, Newport Street in September and attracted thirty people from all over Lancashire. Branches of the 'Daisy Colony' scheme were formed in Bolton, Blackburn, Stockport, Manchester, Reddish, Tottington, Heywood, Burnley and Rawtenstall. Eventually they totalled thirty-one branches, with outposts in Marsden, Bradford and even Glasgow. The agreed objects were, "To form a communistic colony and natural holiday resort, as soon as enough money is raised to purchase land, in the North of England (near Blackpool if possible) to start market gardening etc. and then develop hand industries and a college of agriculture."[43]

His 'Teddy Ashton Picnics' helped bolster support for the plans and numerous fund-raising concerts were held. In February 1905 Clarke announced that some land and a house had been rented at Carleton, near Blackpool. William Addison, vice-president of Bolton Labour Church and a former activist in the agricultural workers' union in East Anglia, was appointed manager, a move which caused some jealousy among some of the scheme's members. However, some people moved into the house and the colony attracted a lot of visitors who purchased produce from the colony.

By July 1906 problems were mounting up and there were reports of squabbles among the colonists. Clarke admitted that "brotherhood, so sweet in the mouth, proves very bitter in practice". Clarke concluded the scheme could not work on 'communist' lines and suggested a co-operative allotments scheme, similar to that run by Blackpool Clarion. By 1907 the scheme was declared a failure and the colonists had departed. The lease was surrendered to the landlord, leaving Clarke with substantial debts.[44]

The Daisy Colony, like most others, was short-lived. However, what these experiments showed was people's willingness to challenge the natural order of things and attempt to create a socialist 'heaven on earth'. Nobody imagined that would be easy, but their efforts should not be quickly derided. Israel's kibbutz movement has many similarities, and the commune movement of the 1960s—and today—is about the same desire to live in a better and more sustainable way.[45]

* * *

A very different attempt at creating an alternative community came in the 1930s through the formation of the Liverpool Catholic Land Association. Archbishop Downey of Liverpool suggested that, "far better than huge barrack-like tenements would be the sight of a pleasant landscape, dotted with homesteads, real houses on country lanes".[46]

Establishing a community in West Lancashire was seen as a practical solution to unemployment, which was particularly high in the Wigan area. The intellectual influences came from the Catholic tradition of social action—Belloc, Chesterton and Fr McNabb. Downey supported the project which took over Prior's Wood Farm at Parbold, near Wigan. Dom Gregory Buisseret was appointed warden, vacating his post as parish priest at St Benedict's, Hindley.

On Sunday 12 May 1935, over twelve hundred people from around the archdiocese attended the opening and blessing of the farm by Downey. In his speech the archbishop, perhaps optimistically, claimed that with proper cultivation of the land the country could support a population of 70 million. The event, and Downey's speech, received widespread publicity. The association took over a similar project in Salford and renamed it The North of England Catholic Land Association Ltd. However, the project struggled to attract sufficient people and resources. It was unclear whether the objective was to create a single community or train men to run their own smallholdings. The emphasis changed to training young men for farming but the project closed in 1943. The association continued as a charity until 1969.

Peter Doyle comments that, "as with other schemes up and down the country, the initial hope of being any sort of solution to the severe unemployment of the 1930s was unrealistic".[47]

Industry and prudence: the case of Accrington

Many Lancashire local authorities had visions to 'build back better' after the depression of the 1930s, focusing on existing towns. Accrington had been badly affected by the economic slump. Its textile industry and associated engineering, as well as coal mining and brick-making, were very hard hit, leading to a substantial population decline. Accrington was only out-stripped by Darwen which suffered a 2.3% drop between 1931 and 1937 compared with a 2.1% reduction in Accrington.

Much of its housing stock was in poor condition with a large area of slums in the central area. In 1949 Accrington Borough Council commissioned a substantial report called *Industry and Prudence: a Plan for Accrington*. It was prepared by Professor J.S. Allen of King's College, Newcastle-on-Tyne and Robert Mattocks, a past president of the Town Planning Institute. There are several aspects which make it something of special interest. Firstly, a borough council (supported by Lancashire County Council it should be said) had the imagination to take a holistic view of the borough which took in the local economy, housing, transport and the wider 'public realm'. Also of note is the obvious engagement of the council and its elected members at a time when it would have been easy to assume that the town would bounce back through post-war recovery and its textile and engineering industries would revive. The foreword by the Mayor of Accrington, Alderman W.W. Cocker, recognised the town's heritage but stressed the need for radical change:

Accrington is proud to be one of the first industrial towns to have sought the advice of town planning consultants regarding the future of the borough. A town which grew with remarkable speed during the nineteenth century was inevitably faced with unusual problems of reconstruction in order to meet present day and future conditions. Because of the radical economic changes of recent years its problems are not merely physical and the report presented by the consultants indicates the close relationship between economics and civic design. Much of Accrington is out of date and will have to be replaced if the borough is to maintain its proud position. It is vitally important that these changes shall be made in the right way and at the right time. For these reasons alone the value of a comprehensive plan cannot be over-emphasised.[48]

The Plan proposed a staged re-development which would lead to "an efficient social organism in which industry, education, commerce, leisure, transport, architecture may all make their due contribution to the total well-being".[49] The Plan proposed a mix of new development, including a cultural centre and new town hall, with road schemes which included some pedestrianisation and sealing-up 'rat runs'. The Plan also included developments in local centres including Altham where a new 'neighbourhood centre' was proposed. It was inevitably strong on road development, with the railway and its station receiving little attention, though the report did recommend a new approach to the station and a new concourse area.

The Plan's authors concluded with the observation that,

> Britain's future lies not so much in her new towns—excellent though these may be—but in the successful maintenance or rebuilding of the many existing industrial towns. If this is fully appreciated and action taken these robust nineteenth century towns may be visited in the future because of their contribution to progress in industry and in the art of living.[50]

What became of the Plan? And what would a visitor think of Accrington today? Inevitably, much of the Plan's vision never saw the light of day. The town's main industries—cotton, engineering, brick-making and coal mining all went into decline in the decades after the Plan's publication. Some of the road schemes were implemented and the area around the town hall and market hall have been pedestrianised. A new 'eco station' was constructed in the early 2000s to replace the very basic structure that British Rail provided in the 1960s, following closure of the Accrington–Bury route. A new bus station was provided in 2020. Many of the fine Victorian buildings remain, not least the Post Office Arcade, populated by low-cost shops and empty spaces.

Post-war optimism: the *Advisory Plan*

Towards the end of the Second World War, when an Allied victory seemed virtually certain, local authorities in south-east Lancashire began to turn their minds to post-war reconstruction. A South Lancashire and North Cheshire Advisory Planning Committee had been formed and established a Technical Sub-Committee to prepare a strategic report that could form the basis for a 'new Lancashire', building on a previous strategic plan published in 1926. The result was An Advisory Plan, published in 1947. It was prepared by two highly experienced town planners, R. Nicholas and M. J. Hellier and included a foreword by Charles Sixsmith, chairman of the Advisory Committee, Chorley borough councillor and also admirer of Walt Whitman and a close friend of Edward Carpenter (see p. 52). His comments in the foreword are characteristic, making the point that,

> we now deplore the lack of foresight of earlier generations who, while leading the world in industrial development, gave no thought to human considerations, this contributing to an almost insoluble social and economic problem which faces the generation. This report ... should prevent a repletion of this error and promote for future generations a more healthy and pleasant way of life.[51]

The make-up of the Advisory Committee which Sixsmith chaired is interesting. The area covered was vast, with a population of 3,243,246 people and having every local authority represented on the committee would have been unwieldy. Instead, sixteen 'regional planning committees' were formed which grouped local authorities. For example Rossendale Regional Planning Committee (RPC) comprised Bacup, Haslingden and Rawtenstall municipal boroughs. Wigan included the county borough itself plus twelve urban districts. Representation on the Advisory Committee was based on population size, so Wigan had five elected representatives as well as several officers providing technical support. Rossendale had two elected representatives but four officers, mostly senior planning officers. Lancashire and Cheshire county councils had additional representation at elected member and officer level.

The context of the *Plan* was the Town and Country Planning Bill that was currently going through Parliament and was enacted in 1948. A concern of the Advisory Committee was that the 'region' they covered required a more co-ordinated planning approach, rather than each county borough and county council (Lancashire and Cheshire) having separate planning powers. The committee hoped that by creating a voluntary system this would lay the basis for a more formal regional planning framework. The authors of the *Plan* recognised the challenging circumstances of post-war England, but stressed that,

> the difficulties of the times are in themselves a challenge, and the authors make no apology for submitting in this report an outline plan and a series of recommendations for the use of land in the Advisor

Area which imply a gradual revolution in conditions accepted for generations as unavoidable features of the industrial North.[52]

The choice of the area covered by the Advisory Committee is important. Superficially, it looks similar to present-day 'Greater Manchester' but was in fact much bigger. To the north it included Rossendale and Chorley, to the west Warrington and to the south of Manchester it took in Macclesfield, Congleton and Sandbach. Manchester was clearly at the heart of this embryonic region. As the Plan's authors said:

> There are two distinct senses in which Manchester may be described as a regional capital. The policy of national decentralisation is giving the city a growing importance as the headquarters of many Government offices for the North-West region, which stretches from Crewe to Carnforth. But it is also a regional centre in a more local and native sense. Within the Advisory Area there has developed, since the early industrialisation of this part of the country, a close association for industrial, commercial and social purposes between Manchester and the surrounding towns. The development of this region into one of the largest concentrations of population and industry in the country has made Manchester the recognised economic and cultural centre for North-East Cheshire no less than for South and South-East Lancashire."[53]

Merseyside, and north Lancashire, had separate advisory committees with some local authorities having overlapping membership of two regional advisory committees.

The recommendations of the Plan seem modest, though the authors, and Councillor Sixsmith, would have argued that they were preparing the foundations for major changes in society. The proposals for what was in effect stronger regional planning had limited acceptance. *The Plan* proposed developments in communications, with a new airport at Unsworth, near Bury, two new rail routes across Cheshire with extension of rail electrification to most of the network and investment in new roads. An important feature of the recommendations was a clear rejection of high-density housing, arguing that, "the barrack discipline which has to be applied in large blocks of flats is foreign to the traditions of Lancashire". It also emphasised the importance of social infrastructure in any new housing development, including "community and health centres, churches, schools and recreation areas, shops and places of entertainment".[54]

Lancashire under the hammer

Whatever the good intentions of post-war planners, Lancashire went into a seemingly terminal economic decline during the 1960s, worsening in the 1980s. The collapse was more than economic; it took on political and social aspects too. Cotton, coal and engineering had developed together and it was broadly true that their decline was simultaneous, though some aspects of engineering diversified. Many of the railways that had supported the development of industry closed during the Beeching era of the 1960s.

The break-up of the historic county of Lancashire in 1974 stimulated a loss of the 'local patriotism' that was a feature of late-nineteenth-century Lancashire. The merging of small local authorities with a strong sense of civic pride, into larger, more centralised units was a further blow to an over-arching Lancashire pride. The movement of capital out of Lancashire, with small, long-established local firms being taken over by large, often multi-national, companies was another aspect of the decline. With the destruction of traditional industries went that of the trades unions and their own strong identities. Local co-operative societies, which once dominated not only the retail sector but often the cultural life of Lancashire towns, disappeared as most of the societies merged into a large, less locally rooted, organisation.

The geo-political shape of Lancashire, with its separate 'North of the Sands' has always been odd, an accident of ancient history and the Norman conquest, with land handed out to favourites. However, over the centuries Lancashire developed an identity and that strong sense of 'patriotism' that many Lancastrians cherish. To a degree, change was inevitable though the scale of it took many by surprise; perhaps we've still not recovered from it yet.

Lancashire's golden age was in the years before the First World War. The cotton industry was at its peak, local government was strong and confident, a multitude of creative ideas and projects took root. The First World War changed so much. Apart from the sheer carnage and shattered lives, Lancashire was never the same again. After a couple of years of relative prosperity, economic depression—'collapse' isn't too strong a term for some parts of Lancashire—struck hard. In east Lancashire particularly, dependence on one industry, cotton, had disastrous consequences and many towns experienced dramatic falls in population, as we have seen with Accrington and Darwen. Not only cotton, but coal and engineering suffered huge drops in production. One of the most telling books to come out of that period was Bowker's *Lancashire Under the Hammer*.[55]

It took another war to end unemployment and give Lancashire's staple industries another stay of execution. Yet the writing was on the wall for cotton, despite the post-war boost. Whether the industry could have been saved if more investment had been made, replacing some of the ancient spinning mules and looms, is a moot point. Historians have argued that the owners were slow and complacent, but my own assessment is that whatever had been done, the heyday of Lancashire cotton had passed and competition from the Far East was unstoppable. It was a long and painful decline. By the mid-1980s we can say that the Lancashire cotton industry was finished, and with it coal and much of engineering.

The 're-structuring' of local government took place almost simultaneously. It was all in the name of efficiency but identities were trashed. It started with the recommendations of the Redcliffe-Maud Report of 1974. Historic Lancashire was to be broadly divided into three. The cotton belt of south-east Lancashire, and Merseyside were removed with a rump based on Preston, east and north Lancashire remaining. Warrington was to transfer to Cheshire whilst some rural areas, including Saddleworth and some country areas north of the Ribble, went into Yorkshire.

Keith Parry, writing a few years after the changes, observed that "there was no logical name for the new county based on Manchester and the working title 'South-East Lancashire–North-East Cheshire' was adopted. Mercifully, this was shortened to SELNEC which prompted one Saddleworth character to remark, "I don't like th'idea o' goin' in wi' Oldham, I don't like th'idea o' leavin' Yorkshire. But I'll be buggered if I'll be tekken over bi a set o' bloody initials!"[56]

Before long 'SELNEC' was changed to 'Greater Manchester' which was hardly any more popular than the set of initials it replaced. Keith Parry again put his finger on the issue when he commented that "the new counties were perhaps logical administratively, but emotionally—particularly in the case of Greater Manchester—they were anathema to the local people".[57]

At the same time as the creation of the 'metropolitan counties' of Greater Manchester and Merseyside, second-tier re-organisation was no less drastic. The old county boroughs disappeared, forming the basis of metropolitan districts. Some had a degree of logic to them, such as Wigan, Bolton and Salford, but 'Tameside' and 'Trafford' seemed artificial creations. More controversially, many proudly independent boroughs such as Radcliffe, Farnworth, Leigh and Stalybridge were merged into the new 'metro' districts.

To the west of the county 'Merseyside' arguably made more sense, with the Wirral forming part of the metropolitan county. Southport's transfer into the Merseyside metropolitan borough of Sefton has never been well received by some Southport people who have felt politically and culturally remote from solidly Labour and working-class Bootle, the administrative centre of the borough.

'Lancashire North of the Sands' was transferred into the new county of 'Cumbria'.[58] Again, looked at from a bureaucrat's desk in Whitehall it might have made sense. But the people of Ulverston, Grange-over-Sands, Dalton and Barrow-in-Furness begged to differ. Further changes were to come with the creation of larger districts absorbing neighbouring authorities. Perhaps the most controversial has been 'Blackburn-with-Darwen', with Blackburn effectively absorbing its neighbour and historic rival. Yes, on paper it looks fine, but ignores centuries of (usually friendly) rivalry in politics, religion and sport.

Whilst the momentum for 'One Yorkshire' is growing, on the west side of the Pennines there is a sullen resignation about traditional identities being trashed. The most tangible sign of the latent discontent has been the growth of 'hyper-local' political parties mentioned in the introduction. They have been highly successful and captured several council seats from the traditional parties whom they perceive as having neglected their towns and merged strong identities into a monolithic 'big brother'. These are 'people from somewhere' but who feel they now belong to 'nowhere'. Their Lancashire identity, nurtured over centuries, has been taken from them, submerged into 'Greater Manchester' which is increasingly shortened to just 'Manchester'. Their local identities as Farnworth, Failsworth or Radcliffe have been absorbed into Bolton, Oldham and Bury. No wonder they're cross.

A remarkable feature of these drastic changes was the almost complete lack of debate or 'consultation'. People in Bolton, Oldham, Bury or Wigan were not asked if they'd be happy losing their Lancashire identities and becoming part of 'Greater Manchester'; we were told it was merely an 'administrative' change. There was a token consultation on the Local Government Bill but the full implications of the proposals hardly registered with people outside the political networks before the act was implemented the following year. The same went for people in St Helens, Southport, Widnes and Prescot. They were presented with no option other than to become part of 'Merseyside'.

If you lived in somewhere like Farnworth, Radcliffe, Failsworth, Leigh, or Widnes, you had the added indignity of losing your own local council and getting swallowed up into a new authority dominated by a larger neighbour (with whom you might not have always got on).

There remains a sense of loss, a nostalgia for the 'old Lancashire' which feeds into a yearning to restore Lancashire's traditional borders, at least among older people. The irony is it all happened by a sleight of hand. We were told that the Local Government Act of 1972 'did not abolish traditional counties' such as Lancashire, only 'administrative' ones.[59] Yet in reality, an 'administrative county' provides the basic political framework. What we have seen has been the gradual 'withering away' of historic Lancashire, unlike its Yorkshire neighbour which has generally managed to maintain most of its traditional identity and most of its institutions.

* * *

Is any of this important? Some of my friends tell me to forget all this 'Lancashire' stuff and move on. There are bigger things to worry about, like climate change, war in Europe, the cost of living and our crumbling transport system. Fair enough, these are important. But we cannot ignore 'identity' and when people feel that their traditional identities are being trashed or ignored, they get upset.

There is a class dimension here. I've been struck by the divergence between the feelings of left-of-centre, liberal, middle-class people, often university educated and to an extent 'rootless', compared with working-class people (regardless of ethnicity) who have a strong sense of belonging and 'place'. David Goodhart made some very astute observations in *The Road to Somewhere—The Populist Revolt and the Future of Politics*,[60] identifying a growing divergence between 'people from somewhere' and 'people from nowhere'. The latter category includes much of the 'metropolitan intelligentsia', perhaps personified by Tony Blair more than anyone. But it crosses political divides. Goodhart argued that,

> anywheres dominate our culture and society. They tend to do well at school … then usually move from home to a residential university in their late teens and on to a career in the professions that might take them to London or even abroad for a year or two. Such people have portable 'achieved' identities based on career success which makes them generally comfortable and confident with new places and people.[61]

This isn't new. Back in the 1980s, Raymond Williams raged against the 'metropolitan provincialism' of the London-based left.[62] In contrast, Goodhart's 'somewheres' "are more rooted and usually have 'ascribed' identities—Scottish farmer, working class Geordie, Cornish housewife—based on group belonging and particular places, which is why they often find rapid change more unsettling".[63] He might have added it's usually those who come off worst from rapid economic change.

For Goodhart, the 2016 vote to leave Europe was the defining moment of these changes that had been taking place beneath the surface of British, and particularly English, politics which exemplified the 'populist revolt' of the 'somewheres'. That said, I suspect this revolt is far from over and may well find expression in other causes; a 'regionalism' based on historic identities not technocratic boundaries could be one of them.

Brexit was not the only example of where there was a massive kick-back against the liberal middle-class consensus. In the last few years there has been the rise of what have been termed 'hyper-local' parties in towns such as Farnworth, Radcliffe, Horwich and

Failsworth, which have won spectacular victories against the established parties and forced political realignments. Their main campaigning issue has been the historic neglect of their towns since their forced marriage with their bigger neighbour (Bolton, Bury and Oldham). They also feel upset about losing their 'Lancashire' identity, but that's a bigger and more complex problem. As noted above, Yorkshire has been ahead of Lancashire in setting up its own regionalist party which came a respectable third in the mayoral elections for South Yorkshire. Whether a new political party is the answer to re-creating a strong, united Lancashire is debatable.

During the writing of this book I came across many people, of different generations and ethnicities, who regarded themselves as 'Lancastrian' but were exiled in 'Greater Manchester', 'Merseyside' or 'Cumbria' (which itself has been abolished and split into 'Cumberland' and 'Westmorland and Furness'). They are not narrow-minded racists or anti-European (or anti-London) bigots, but they feel neglected and sometimes despised; and politically homeless.

As Colin Speakman has argued, "the really important debate still to be had is the future of the structure of Regional Government in the English Regions...", and I would add the future of genuinely local government.[64]

3

A LANCASHIRE SENSIBILITY

What is a 'Lancashire sensibility'? It's a central part of regional identity and can take in speech, dress, manners, diet—every aspect of how we live. The (Labour) Minister of Education, George Tomlinson, wrote the foreword to the journal of the newly established Lancashire Dialect Society, in 1951:

> I have a feeling that we cannot afford to lose the characteristic features of our County, which are bound up in no small degree with the accents of its people and our own particular dialect ... were I in any doubt as to the value of these Lancashire characteristics, my experience in the last few years would have resolved the doubts, for since I became a Minister of the Crown, in every part of the country people have come to me at the end of a meeting, shaken me by the hand and said, 'I too come from Lancashire,' and it was grand to hear the accent again.[1]

The Marxist literary critic Raymond Williams developed the concept of 'structure of feeling' which is very close to what I mean. Williams was no typical Marxist, if there is such a thing, and was very aware of the complexities of class and regional identity. The Lancashire sensibility was very much a part of the social and intellectual make-up of the Lancashire middle class, and some 'respectable' working men in the mid-nineteenth century. It would include membership of 'learned' societies, a reverence for the Lancashire dialect, combined with an ability to speak it when appropriate, and patronage of the arts and local publications.

* * *

Lancastrians: Allen Clarke ('Teddy Ashton') 1863–1935

Allen Clarke embodied the 'Lancashire sensibility' and spent his life promoting it—through dialect sketches, novels and non-fiction works. He was born into a working-class Bolton family in 1863, but most of his later life was spent in Blackpool. He followed his parents into the mill, starting as a 'half-timer' at the age of 11.

He went on to write over twenty novels, dozens of short stories and poems as well as factual accounts of life in the factories, one of which was translated into Russian by Tolstoy, whom he greatly admired as a writer and political thinker. He was deeply spiritual and wrote several books on philosophy, strongly influenced by Hindu and Buddhist thinkers. In his later years he wrote extensively on spiritualism and his book The Eternal Question *was one of his most popular works. He was passionate about the environment and his book* The Effects of the Factory System *(1895) is a social and also environmental critique of the Lancashire cotton industry.*

His sketches in Lancashire dialect (written as 'Teddy Ashton') "poked sly fun and undermining sarcasm" at the social evils of the day and sold over a million copies. His newspapers, like Teddy Ashton's Northern Weekly, *were read and passed around mill and factory by the thousands. His book* Windmill Land *popularised the Fylde countryside and is a mix of history, folklore and roadside chats. Alongside his Christmas* Lancashire Annual *he published a* Blackpool Annual *in the 1920s aimed at summer visitors.*

As well as his own work, Clarke encouraged other working-class men and women to write for his newspapers and was instrumental in forming the Lancashire Authors' Association in 1911. His 'readers' picnics' attracted hundreds of visitors, often arriving by train or bicycle. One, at Barrow Bridge near Bolton in 1901, was held to raise funds for the locked-out quarry workers at Penrhyn, Wales; it was attended by several thousand and the Clarion Choir provided the entertainment. He mobilised his child readers to raise funds for the starving families and organised cycle trips to the quarry villages.

After his move to Blackpool he created the Blackpool Ramble Club, one of the biggest walking groups in the country. He died in December 1935 and is buried at Marton Cemetery, close to the windmill that is now a shrine to his memory.

* * *

The idea of a 'Lancashire patriotism' emerged in the 1880s and was distinct to the nationalistic patriotism which became virulent during the Boer War and reached its apogee between 1914 and 1918. Speaking in the middle of the First World War, local Liberal politician and Lancashire historian Samuel Compston said that, "if patriotism is a virtue, especially in these days, surely county clanship, in no narrow sense, is a virtue also".[2]

* * *

Lancastrians: Gracie Fields 1898–1979

Grace Stansfield was born in Rochdale, above the shop owned by her grandmother, Sarah Bamford, in Molesworth Street. She made her first stage appearance as a child in 1905, joining children's repertory theatre groups. Like most Rochdale girls, her first job was in a local mill, working as a half-timer. Her professional debut was at the Rochdale Hippodrome theatre in 1910, and she soon gave up her mill job to become a professional singer. She appeared in several local venues in 1913 and 1914, including Todmorden, Milnrow and Burnley. After the end of the First World War her career took off, with appeareances in London's West End.

Her most famous song, 'Sally', featured in her first film, Sally in Our Alley, *in 1931. One of her classic 'Lancashire' films was* Sing As We Go, *produced in 1934. She was appointed a Commander of the Order of the British Empire (CBE) for her services to entertainment in the 1938 New Year Honours and was granted the Freedom of the Borough of Rochdale in 1937. She helped Rochdale Football Club in the 1930s, when they were struggling to pay fees and buy sports equipment.*

She was enormously popular with troops during the Second World War, performing at 'front-line' locations in France and as far as the South Pacific. During the war, she paid for all servicemen and women to travel free on public transport within the boundaries of Rochdale. During 1947 she gave a series of broadcasts from Lancashire towns as 'Gracie's Working Party' where she championed local artists and writers. All her fees were donated to the orphanage she supported at Peacehaven.[3]

In 1978, she opened the Gracie Fields Theatre, near Oulder Hill Leadership Academy in her native Rochdale, performing a concert to open the show. Seven months before her death in 1979, she was made a Dame

Commander of the Order of the British Empire (DBE) by Queen Elizabeth II. Gracie was a member of the Lancashire Authors' Association and used her fame as a singer and actor to promote a positive image of Lancashire and its dialect. She wrote the foreword to George C. Miller's More Lancashire Yarns, *published in 1959, stressing the historical validity of dialect, saying that "our dialect has its roots in good broad Saxon, expressive of our wild moorlands and grey northern skies".*[4]

On 3 October 2009, the last train to run on the Oldham Loop Line before it closed to be converted to a tramway, was named in her honour. In September 2016, a statue of Gracie was unveiled outside Rochdale Town Hall, the first statue of a woman to be erected for over a century in Lancashire.

* * *

Badges of identity—dialect speech

Lancashire speech—from 'accent' to full-blown dialect, or 'broad Lancashire'—forms an important part of Lancashire identity. Debates over its use, among Lancastrians, highlight some of the wider issues around Lancashire identity. There is a difference between dialect speech and literature. The latter is explored more thoroughly in Chapter 12 as part of a body of distinctive regional literature. Whilst dialect speech is, at least normally, a spontaneous, 'unconscious' form of speech, dialect literature was a created form—an 'invented tradition', with its origins in the writings of John Collier ('Tim Bobbin') in the late eighteenth century, but more popularly through the work of Edwin Waugh, Ben Brierley and Samuel Laycock in the second half of the nineteenth century.

An historic meeting took place in 1868 involving Samuel Bamford and a number of his friends, at his home in Moston, on his 80th birthday. The event was reported in *The Ashton-under-Lyne Reporter* and covers a number of themes that Bamford was closely associated with, not least parliamentary reform. Bamford raised the issue of Lancashire dialect, and the need to preserve it:

> [T]he veteran also gave expression to his opinion on the importance of preserving all that was good and pure in the Lancashire dialect, believing that a glossary of great value might be collated by the

Literary Club at Manchester of which he and Mr. Benjamin Brierley, who was present, were members.[5]

There was a major debate in Rochdale in the early 1890s following the suggestion of a school inspector, a Mr Wylie, that dialect speech should be encouraged, rather than actively discouraged, in local schools. This brought a negative response from Rochdale dialect writer John Trafford Clegg, who urged, "Keep th'od Lanky eawt of'th'schoo's Mesther Wylie, for aw want my childer to talk smart when they grow up."[6]

The historian, journalist and leader of the 1896 Winter Hill Trespass, Solomon Partington, fought a one-man campaign to preserve dialect and opposed attempts by teachers to prevent its use amongst Lancashire school children. It seems that Mr Wylie was a lone voice as far as school inspectors were concerned in their campaign against 'vulgar' speech. Partington wrote:

> Ever since 1870 the Education Board has done its utmost to kill dialect ... the reader may have seen Professor Moorman's illuminating statement of how Government inspectors complimented teaching staffs having eliminated all trace of dialect from their scholars' mode of speech.[7]

During the late 1920s and early 1930s there was an ongoing debate, particularly within the Lancashire Authors' Association (LAA), about whether dialect speech should be encouraged, or allowed to die. The popular dialect writer T. Thompson, who had a regular column in *The Manchester Guardian*, spoke in defence of dialect speech at a meeting of the Manchester Literary Club in 1938. He argued against attempts to 'standardise' English and stressed that,

> language is a living thing, always changing, and if they standardised it, it became a dead thing. He agreed that dialect was vulgar, but it was vulgar in the very fine sense in which the word was used in the seventeenth century, when the Bible was authorised to be published in the vulgar tongue—the tongue understood by the common people.[8]

Use of dialect in advertising remained common during the 1930s and 1940s. The Co-op ran adverts in *Teddy Ashton's Lancashire Annual*, using Lancashire dialect, to promote their services. A report in the LAA's *Record* noted that,

it would appear that dialect is coming more to the fore in the advertising world. A short time ago Mr. T. Thompson wrote a series of
domestic dialect sketches for one firm's advertisements ... another
Lancashire firm are inserting, in their weekly advertisements in the
evening papers, stories from Edwin Waugh's works.[9]

Members of the LAA were pushed into a spirited defence of dialect
writing following an intervention from association member James
Haslam, former president of the Manchester Press Club and editor
of the National Union of Journalists' magazine *The Journalist*, in *The
Manchester Evening Chronicle*. Haslam described Lancashire dialect as
"uncouth, a confounded social disadvantage, a thing that should be
kicked out of existence".[10]

Major David Halstead, president of the LAA, read a lengthy
paper at the association's Manchester meeting on 12 December
1931 on 'Our Lancashire Dialect'. After pointing out the literary
uses of dialect, he asked, "where has the dialect proved a drawback?"
and went on to point out that, "There are at the present time more
dialect societies and more dialect writers, not only throughout
Lancashire, but throughout the country than ever before." He drew
similarities between the revival of interest in Irish, Welsh and Scots
Gaelic and claims,

> similar respect and regard for our Lancashire dialect. We do not urge
> it to be taught in our schools or that it should supplant literary English.
> We say there is room and scope for both, to be used on suitable occa-
> sion; that use and love of the dialect is not and should not be any
> hindrance to the student in college, to the workman in street or work-
> shop and field, to the professor or even the politicians.[11]

Allen Clarke commented on Lancastrians' ability to 'switch' from
standard English to dialect, as the occasion required it:

> Just as in Wales, I suppose, they talk both Welsh and English,
> what's wrong about Lancashire using its dialect as well the English
> language? (Which, indeed, is what is done today.) As it is not so
> much the tool as the man who uses it ... so it is not the mere words
> but the thoughts and sentiments that make the power and beauty
> of a language. While the Lancashire dialect is equal to any other
> language in pathos, its fundamental characteristic is its humour,

mostly cheery and kindly, and in that respect it is first and foremost in the world.[12]

Further debates took place in the *Manchester City News*, *Manchester Evening Chronicle* and the Manchester-published *News Chronicle* during 1933. Riley Stansfield, a former member of Southport Town Council and a member of the LAA, spoke 'In Defence and Appreciation of the Dialect' at the LAA's Southport meeting of 24 June 1933.[13]

Many other well-known figures in the Lancashire Authors' Association rallied in 'defence of the dialect' (and Haslam subsequently moderated his position). These included Gracie Fields, who said that, "without use of the dialect my performances would not have been so successful. People like to hear a dialect—Lancashire or any other, but I think Lancashire particularly. It was George Formby's quaint, quavering dialect—his Lancashire drawl—that made him the successful comedian he was."[14]

The debate re-ignited towards the end of the Second World War. *The Daily Dispatch* of 17 April 1944 carried an article by the Rev. Herbert Stonely on 'How does dialect stand to-day?' The article asked for readers' views on whether it is worth preserving dialect speech, whether it precluded reaching a wider audience and what are the general strengths of spoken dialect. After the discussion had closed, the editor said that 65% of responses wanted dialect "as abounding with pearls worthy of a better fate than being trampled underfoot".[15]

However, dialect came under increasing pressure as the 1950s wore on. Salford librarian, A. Longworth, gave a talk to the LAA at their Bolton meeting on 4 March 1961 on the subject of 'Is the Lancashire Dialect Still in Significant Use?' His comments made for uncomfortable listening for the members:

> Mr. Longworth said he had no expert credentials, but had been brought up in the Rossendale Valley and grew up in an atmosphere of dialect. Once, older people spoke nothing but dialect but it would be difficult to find such now. In defining dialect we must separate 1) dialect—use of words, 2) accent—way of speaking and 3) sloppy speech. Lancashire dialect was a form of old English which had grown up in the cotton towns when they were isolated

communities and had to develop and alter. Tim Bobbin had his own form of dialect, later writers had theirs. Dialect in his view had been broken down mainly by the growth of railways and the development of education, mass media of communication such as cinema, radio and television, and two world wars which had scattered Lancashire men all over the world. The common use of dialect is dying out, and interest now was mainly academic. Young people seemed more interested in 'beat' language. In conclusion, Mr. Longworth said that whilst a universal language was a good thing, the loss of dialect indicated a loss of individuality.[16]

The report in the LAA newsletter commented that "it can hardly be said that any of the members who spoke in the ensuing brief discussion crossed swords with our speaker", although some referred to isolated pockets of rural Lancashire where dialect was still spoken by older people.[17]

Yet five years later, at least the debate around dialect was alive and well. The BBC ran a series of programmes on 'The Other English' and Lancashire had a session to itself. Joan Pomfret and other members of the LAA selected some readings and Harry Craven spoke about 'What's to Come?' He shared Herbert Kirtlan's critical view of much contemporary dialect writing, but noted that there was,

> a tremendous upsurge of interest in dialect at present and an anxiety to preserve it ... it was no longer regarded as a mark of social inferiority to use dialect ... As to the future, Harry Craven thought that our dialect would disappear as our teenagers are being influenced largely by the language of the 'pop' world which is overloaded with American speech-forms.[18]

A Lancashire intelligentsia

An essential part of Lancashire's economic and political development, particularly from the onset of the Industrial Revolution, was the creation of a distinctive 'intelligentsia' which could provide a network, or networks, of influential figures. It's an area that has been given insufficient importance, yet it underpinned the county's growth. Its relative weakness, as the twentieth century wore on, parallels and reinforces Lancashire's decline in political, economic and intellectual influence.

Britain, England particularly, has never celebrated its intellectuals in the way that other European countries have. Perhaps Lancashire, with its customary down-to-earth pragmatism, could be said to be even less inclined towards 'intellectualism', at least for its own sake. Antonio Gramsci, the Italian Marxist thinker, wrote extensively on the role of intellectuals in the development of capitalism, and what he saw as its antithesis, the 'revolutionary workers' party' with its intellectual cadre. He wrote:

> Every social group, coming into existence on the original terrain of an essential function in the world of economic production, creates together with itself, organically, one or more strata of intellectuals which give it homogeneity and an awareness of its own function not only in the economic but also in the social and political fields. The capitalist entrepreneur creates alongside himself a higher level of social elaboration, already characterised by a certain directive and technical (i.e. intellectual) capacity...[19]

Gramsci's observations throw up some interesting questions regarding not only the role of intellectuals in the development of capitalism but also the issue of regional and local intelligentsias, which became a feature of nineteenth-century Lancashire. It should be emphasised that the development of Lancashire industry—particularly cotton, but also engineering and to a lesser extent coal mining—was initially very much a home-grown exploit, at least in terms of the driving forces behind those industries.

Manchester, and in different ways Liverpool, were the regional 'intellectual hubs' each with their own organisations—learned societies, libraries, clubs—which formed the institutional bases for a regional intelligentsia. The Manchester Literary and Philosophical Society was formed in 1781, mirroring almost exactly the 'take-off' of Manchester as an industrial city. Its library today forms the basis of the John Rylands Library on Manchester's Deansgate, part of the University of Manchester. John Dalton was an early member of the society and served as secretary and then president from 1817 until his death in 1844.[20]

It remains today and is the second oldest learned society in the world. Manchester's Portico Library, also still in existence, was established in 1806 (see pages 153–4). In Liverpool, a Literary and Philosophical Society was formed in 1779, three years before Manchester's equivalent. However, it only survived for four years. Other 'learned societies' were subsequently formed, appealing to Liverpool's growing mercantile class. However, this development of societies aimed at a middle-class elite was not confined to the two cities. Similar bodies had been formed in Warrington (1760), Lancaster (1770), Rochdale (1770) and other Northern towns and cities in the second half of the eighteenth century.[21]

Liverpool's intellectual life during the eighteenth century had been led and dominated by its merchant elite and the voluntary cultural organisations and institutions which they had been instrumental in founding. Arline Wilson commented that:

> Although the creation of such associations was not a new phenomenon in the first half of the nineteenth century, the increase in their number, variety and public importance has been seen as remarkable, especially after 1780. For the urban male middle classes, cultural societies in particular provided a means of asserting power, status and identity, and played an important role in helping to forge a sense of class solidarity amongst urban elites, otherwise sharply divided by their political and religious convictions. In Liverpool such organisations also made a vital contribution to the redefinition of the image and identity of the town itself. The eighteenth century had witnessed a rapid rise in Liverpool's fortunes, from an insignificant seaport at the opening of the century to a position at its close where the town was vaunting its position as Britain's second city.[22]

In 1853, delegates from four of Liverpool's learned societies, the Liverpool Literary and Philosophical Society (the 'Lit. and Phil'), the Historic Society of Lancashire and Cheshire, the Liverpool Polytechnic Society and the Liverpool Architectural and Archaeological Society, met to consider the feasibility of union. They were not able to agree on a merger. Wilson commented:

> The failure to bring this initiative to fruition, at a time of growing municipal involvement in cultural and educational provision, was indicative of the passing of an age in which Liverpool's intellectual life had been led and dominated by its merchant elite and the

voluntary cultural organizations and institutions which they had been instrumental in founding.[23]

The network of societies is interesting in several ways. Firstly, Liverpool's elite comprised merchants and professional men, rather than manufacturers. The old Lancashire saying of 'Manchester men and Liverpool gentlemen' is underlined. Also, some of the societies were clearly of a directly professional nature. In the case of the above four, the Architectural and Archaeological Society was at least in part a professional network of practising architects. The city also had its Chemical Society, reflecting the growth of the chemical industry along the Mersey. Finally, it is noteworthy that Liverpool was home to 'The Historic Society of Lancashire and Cheshire', vying for a position as the regional capital of Lancashire (and perhaps Cheshire as well) over its inland rival, Manchester. For many years the *Liverpool Post*, and its sister *Liverpool Weekly Post*, aimed to gain a Lancashire-wide readership.[24]

* * *

Lancastrians: William Roscoe 1753–1831

William Roscoe, dissenter, radical politician and abolitionist, was the architect and embodiment of Liverpool's cultural aspirations. Born in 1753, the son of a Liverpool innkeeper and market gardener, Roscoe rose to become a renowned historian, botanist, minor poet, artist and art lover, Member of Parliament and opponent of the slave trade. But he was also a lawyer, banker and businessman, and as such involved in and committed to the commercial success of the port. The publication of Roscoe's biography of Lorenzo de' Medici in 1796, highlighting the Anglo-Florentine entente between commerce and culture, has been cited as 'a turning point, if not the starting point of Liverpool's intellectual life'. Roscoe portrayed Florence and its ruler as the apotheosis of the union between culture and commerce, and although he insisted that his interest was literary and cultural rather than political, denying that the book had any relevance for contemporary problems, it was here that Roscoe looked for a role model for his native town. His belief in the efficacy of Lorenzo's academies, schools, libraries and associations provided him with the blueprint for the construction of a similar cultural infrastructure in Liverpool. The analogy of Liverpool and Renaissance

Florence proved particularly appealing to his fellow townsmen. Roscoe had succeeded in rewriting history in a way that allowed Liverpool's merchants to celebrate themselves, and they were now willing to accept Roscoe, the man of letters, as their cultural icon, whilst at the same time rejecting Roscoe, the Radical politician and abolitionist.

Roscoe was elected Member of Parliament for Liverpool in 1806, but his tenure was short-lived. During his brief time as an MP he was able to cast his vote in favour of the successful abolition of the slave trade.

In the early 1800s, he led a group of Liverpool botanists who created the Liverpool Botanic Garden, initially located near Mount Pleasant, which was then on the outskirts of the city. In the 1830s the garden was moved to Wavertree Botanic Gardens; remnants of the collection can still be found in the walled garden at Croxteth Hall. Roscoe was also closely associated with the formation of the Liverpool Royal Institution in Colquitt Street, first as chairman of the General Committee and subsequently as its first president.

* * *

When the Roscoe circle regrouped to establish the first of the enduring nineteenth-century cultural institutions, their efforts received a very different reception from that which had accompanied their earlier efforts. The first evidence of the merchant elite's willingness to eschew religious and political animosities in the cause of cultural re-definition came in 1797 with the founding of the Athenaeum, one of the largest and most impressive of the urban gentlemen's libraries founded in Britain at this time. Useful as the Liverpool Library was in providing current publications, it was inadequate to meet the demands of a scholar such as Roscoe, the library being considered 'not sufficiently select in its choice of books' and to have too many subscribers. Proposals for the new institution were drawn up and circulated to the town's leading five hundred male citizens (women were not granted full membership until 1996), eliciting an immediate and favourable response. Although the majority of the founders were men associated with reform and dissent, the oligarchic and staunchly Tory common council recognised the new foundation as a potential ornament to the town and looked on it with approval, granting it the reversionary interest in its premises. The mayor was elected an honorary member and the first president, George Case, was a member of the council.

Liverpool's early literary societies brought together key elements of the city's elite who were to take the lead in the cultural advancement of Liverpool: in politics they were reformers; in religion, predominantly Unitarian or Quaker. Wilson makes the point that in the case of Liverpool, by the second half of the nineteenth century, Liverpool's merchant elite was "legitimated and secure and its concern lay more in reinforcing individual status rather than in asserting a group identity through joint cultural enterprise". She observes that several members re-directed their energies towards co-ordinating municipal cultural provision and the establishment of a university.

If Liverpool's elite—in business, culture and politics—was dominated by the city's mercantile sector, Manchester was different, tending to have a stronger manufacturing element, leavened with a varied range of professionals. In the case of Lancashire, Gramsci's description of 'capitalist intellectuals' being predominantly 'technical' in their interests is only partially true.

* * *

A group of radicals came together in 1796, when 'freedom of speech' was effectively forbidden, to form 'The Manchester Thinking Club'. William Axon quotes from a contemporary newspaper account:

> On Monday evening (28th December 1796), the members of The Manchester Thinking Club commenced their first mental operation by beginning to think, or in other words, submitting themselves like good subjects to a constitutional numbness. The number of thinkers was not less than 300, and many of the thoughtful actually came from Liverpool, Stockport, and other remote places to witness this novel spectacle. The members were all muzzled, and such an imposing silence prevailed as would have done honour to the best thinkers that ever adorned assemblies of a more dignified nature ... the word 'Mum' appeared in large characters on every muzzle...[25]

The article went on to inform readers that "the members of this truly constitutional society continue to meet for the intellectual purpose of silent contemplation every Thursday evening, at the Coopers Arms, Cateaton Street, where strong constitutional muzzles are provided at the door by Citizen Avery, a tailor to the swinish multitude".

The 'Thinking Club' was a clever piece of political theatre, poking fun at repression and intolerance. What became of the club is not recorded, but many of its members would have coalesced into the networks, mostly operating in the shadows of legality, which grew into the great reform movements of the 1820s and 1830s.

The Manchester Literary Club was founded in 1862 and was described as possessing a "subtle charm, which arises from the combination of a love of literature and art with a 'clubbable' spirit of fellowship and sympathy". George Milner served as president between 1880 and 1914. With J.J. Nodal he edited *A Glossary of Lancashire Words*.[26]

The aims of the club were to "encourage the pursuit of literature and art; to promote research in the several departments of intellectual work and to protect the interests of authors in Lancashire; to publish from time to time works illustrating or elucidating the literature and history of the county and to provide a place of meeting where persons interested in the furtherance of those objects can associate together".[27]

The subscription rates in the 1870s were 15 shillings a year, which would have been beyond the means of most working men. A typical member was Samuel Barlow, a partner in a bleach works at Stakehill near Middleton. As well as being an active member of the Manchester Literary Club he was a founder of the city's Arts Club, an artist and botanist and had a strong interest in Lancashire dialect.[28]

* * *

Lancastrians: William E.A. Axon 1846–1913

Axon was born in Manchester and became a central figure in the Manchester intellectual circles towards the end of the nineteenth century. His first job was with the Manchester Free Libraries in 1861 and in 1874 he joined the staff of The Manchester Guardian *as its librarian. He had already been writing for the Guardian, and used his pen in support of the anti-slavery cause during*

the American Civil War. "His eloquent pen gave their cause great aid, being enabled to do so because the Guardian, always to the forefront in humanitarian work, provided him with a medium through which a wide and influential audience could be reached." In 1899, the all-black Wilberforce University in the United States, made Axon an honorary LL.D. His poem 'Lincoln and the Brown Thrush' was published in his collection:
The Ancoats Skylark and includes the lines:

> *When Lincoln freed the slave*
> *The brown thrush sang its loudest strain,*
> *A joy that thrilled from heart to brain,*
> *A melody full strong and brave,*
> *When Lincoln freed the slave.*[29]

Axon was a progressive Liberal and also an enthusiast for Lancashire culture. He published a short book on Folk Song and Folk Speech of Lancashire *as well as writings on folklore. He was an active member of the Manchester Literary Club. Other works include* Lancashire Gleanings *(1883) and* Annals of Manchester *(1886).*

* * *

Middle-class sponsorship—'The Subscriber's Edition' in local publishing

The tradition of 'subscribers' editions' in local book publishing in the nineteenth century is an important indicator of local cultural elites. William Alexander Abram's *Blackburn Characters of a Past Generation* was published by the author's son in 1894, shortly after his father's death. There were three separate subscribers' editions, ranging in quality from a 'large paper impression' of just thirty-nine copies, to the small paper version 're-bound in half-calf' to the basic 'small paper impression'.

Abram, although progressive in his politics, ensured that the three editions reflected a hierarchy in Blackburn society. Taken together they form a roll-call of Blackburn's cultural (as well as economic and political) elite. Of the thirty-nine 'de luxe' copies, subscribers include William Ashton, one of Darwen's large mill-owners and Edgar Appleby JP of 'The Grange' in leafy Wilpshire. Sir James Hoghton, of Hoghton Tower, was another of the thirty-nine, as well as William Henry Hornby, Lieutenant-General Feilden CMG and MP of Witton Park and the Duke of Devonshire. A total of twenty-seven out of thirty-nine subscribers had addresses in the Blackburn area. The 'middling' paper edition had forty-three subscribers, including thirteen JPs; and most of these subscribers had addresses in the Blackburn area too. The 'small paper impression' received over 200 subscribers including several public libraries, mechanics' institutions, and Blackburn Conservative Club. An interesting 'foreigner' is Mr W.H. Ratcliffe who ordered his copy from 'Fabric Raboff', in 'Serpuchoff, Moscow', almost certainly one of the many Russian cotton mills which employed Lancashire engineers and managers. The 'small paper impression' would still have been a substantial publication, probably beyond the reach of many Blackburnians. The addresses of the subscribers were in predominantly middle-class parts of the town, including Wilpshire, Shear Brow and Preston New Road.[30]

Another example of local sponsorship through a 'subscribers' edition' was Henry Cunliffe's *A Glossary of Rochdale-with-Rossendale Words and Phrases*, published 1886. It was written at a time when dialect was popular amongst middle-class antiquarians and the quality of the book is very high. The list of subscribers (as far as I know, there was only one edition) totals 220. Most of them are local, with several 'esquires' ('Esq.') and local councillors, JPs and public libraries. Several co-operative societies subscribed, including those at Bacup, Bury, Waterfoot, Heywood (specifically, the 'Co-operative Society Library') and Rochdale Equitable Pioneers' Society Library.

Burnley poet Henry Houlding produced a collection of his poetry in 1895. It was published by the 'Joint Committee of Literary and Scientific Club and the Literary and Philosophical Society' of Burnley and had over 350 subscribers.[31] The overwhelming majority of the subscribers were local to Burnley, with once again a good number of councillors and JPs. Sir Ughtred Kay-Shuttleworth of Gawthorpe Hall subscribed, as well as Lady O'Hagan of Towneley Hall. The local police station, through an offficer described as 'D. Bond' also contributed, in addition to the public baths. Several pubs were listed, including The Fighting Cocks Inn, Mereclough, The Mason's Arms, The Commercial Hotel and J. Pletts of 'The Borough Brewery'. These were balanced by The Temperance

Hotel, Bridge Street and a similar establishment in Leyburn, Yorkshire. Two subscribers' addresses were in the United States—Colorado and New Jersey.

Regional associations

Lancashire developed a number of cultural associations which provided a network for the county's intellectual communities. The Historic Society of Lancashire and Cheshire was founded in Liverpool in 1848. The three founder members of the society were Rev. Abraham Hume (1814–84), Henry C. Pidgeon (1807–80) and Joseph Mayer (1803–86). The public meeting, held at the Collegiate Institution in Shaw Street, was called "for the purpose of establishing a society for collecting, preserving, arranging and publishing such Historical Documents, Antiquities, Objects of National History, Specimens of Ancient and Mediaeval Art, etc. as are connected with the Counties Palatine of Lancaster and Chester".[32]

By October 1848 the society had nearly 200 members, although full membership was restricted to men. Early members of the society were issued with a diploma designed by Joseph Mayer. On his earliest trade card Mayer styles himself as designer and heraldic engraver as well as goldsmith and jeweller, occupations which he practised at 65 Lord Street, Liverpool, from around 1844. The first volume of the annual *Transactions*, including some of the first session's lectures, was published in 1849. The society is now one of the oldest historical or archaeological societies in the country in continuous existence. Early members were drawn from the clergy, professional and commercial classes and country landowners from all over the two counties.

* * *

Lancastrians: Alice Collinge 1885–1957

Alice Collinge was a poet and teacher, of Scottish parents. She lived at Riding Gate, Harwood, near Bolton, for most of her life and was a talented poet and inspirational teacher. She crossed many divides, between literature, politics and education.

She was active in the women's suffrage movement and, like her friend Sarah Reddish, the Independent Labour Party. She was the resident organist at Bolton Labour Church in the early 1900s when Allen Clarke was involved, and met 'the rebel countess' Constance Markievicz, the first woman elected as an MP to the UK Parliament. As a Sinn Fein member she did not take her seat. Alice also met leading national figures such as Edward Carpenter, Eva Gore-Booth and Adela Pankhurst through her political activities. She became one of the first women members of the Bolton 'Walt Whitman Fellowship' which venerated the great American poet and mystic.

In her autobiographical notes, she tells this charming story of the Bolton Whitman group and its leader, J. W. Wallace, in particular:

> *As a counter-attraction to those hectic days, there was the restful contemplative influence of the Whitman Fellowship behind it all, and in that influence alone, I owe an eternal debt to Bolton. To hear the late J.W. Wallace read a paper on Whitman, in a Whitman atmosphere, either at Rivington, Walker Fold or The Haulgh, was a perfect inspiration, and one of those special privileges that one cannot account for.*

Alice won several poetry prizes and lectured for the Workers' Educational Association on English Literature. She was an active member of the Lancashire Authors' Association, and was elected deputy chair of the association. In her later years she was appointed a governor of Bolton School. She made a great contribution to Lancashire's political, social and cultural life, dying in 1957.

* * *

The Lancashire Authors' Association (for 'writers and lovers of Lancashire literature') was established in 1909 on the initiative of Allen Clarke. It developed into a substantial organisation with a membership, at its inter-war peak in 1930, of 266.[33] The LAA Library was created in 1921 from members' donations and is now the largest collection of regional literature in the UK. It is housed as a special collection in the University of Bolton Library.

The association did not try to be an exclusive body beyond the reach of working-class writers. Pearce notes that at the inaugural meeting in 1909, "a few simple—very simple—rules were fixed, and its modest annual subscription decided upon—mere males half-a-crown, lovely ladies one shilling. Its whole membership of twenty was constituted the committee."[34]

Women, lovely or not, played an active part in the association's proceedings from the start, though despite the financial inducements, men remained the majority of its members. By 1930, the executive committee of thirteen included only three women. Edith Pearce (wife of Alfred) played a prominent role, editing *The Record* and *The Red Rose Circulating Magazine*, over many years.

The early years of the association were, as Pearce notes, chequered. Allen Clarke was elected chairman but his organisational skills left much to be desired. Eventually, his friend Alfred Pearce staged what amounted to a coup and Clarke stood down as chairman. The changes that ensued enabled the LAA to develop and prosper. Pearce observed:

> At the end of ten years' existence—November 1919—the Association was able to congratulate itself that it had paid a really wonderful series of public visits to Lancashire cities and towns, mostly at the invitation of their respective Mayors ... Municipal librarians had willingly displayed to us their treasures of local literature, many learned gentlemen had read to us papers on Lancashire authors and their books, ministers of religion had delighted to show us over and to explain the historical edifices in their care, civic authorities had exhibited to us their town halls, libraries, art galleries, museums ... there can be no doubt that our travellings to Lancashire cities, towns, shrines of county literary and historical interest, had focused attention upon them, creating deeper and truer recognition of their value in the minds of the general public.[35]

The 'operating model' of the LAA proved, as Pearce claimed, highly successful. Rather than being centred on one locality, it spread itself across the county as a whole, with, typically, four meetings a year held at different towns across Lancashire. There were sporadic attempts made to establish local branches but they were mostly short-lived. The association managed, to a degree, to gloss over differences in politics and social class. The Pearces, Allen Clarke, R.H. Brodie (its first secretary) and Sam Fitton were socialists from modest backgrounds. Other founder members such as Henry Brierley were middle class and Conservative. The 'travelling' meetings offered opportunities to engage with local literary societies and similar bodies. The programme of most of the meetings, after a welcome from the town's mayor, would include a lecture on the history of the town they were visiting, often with detailed literary information.

There was considerable collaboration between Lancashire's literary bodies. In the early 1930s the LAA held some of its meetings in the rooms of the Manchester Literary and Philosophical Society and many had joint membership of the two bodies. Allen Clarke resigned from the LAA in 1918. A report in *The Record* says that he departed "owing to lack of time and other reasons". The report added that, "In the early days of the LAA Mr. Clarke, who was one of its founders, took a deal of active interest in its welfare; and though in later years he could not see eye to eye with the rest of the executive in matters of policy, still the Association is much his debtor for services rendered, and we are sorry to lose his membership." It was a generous comment, and sadly it has never proved possible to find out what the precise 'other reasons' for his departure were. It may have been political differences, though several remaining members of the LAA executive were on the left, including the Pearces and W.H. Jenkins. Clarke did, eventually, rejoin the LAA, to a friendly welcome, in 1926.[36]

A special feature of the LAA's work was its *Circulating Magazine*, edited for many years by Edith Pearce and started in 1917. Harry Craven took over as editor in 1943. This was a single volume of members' work, often comprising cuttings or sometimes original work, pasted into the book. It was circulated to a list of members who were registered as 'subscribers' who added their own comments to the particular stories, and then mailed it on to the next person on the list.

* * *

Lancastrians: Edith Pearce 1886–1963

Edith Pearce was one half of a powerful literary and political couple; both she and her husband Alf ('Lord Knowsho') playing active roles in the Lancashire Authors' Association (LAA) over many years. Edith was born in Birmingham and moved to Droylsden in 1904 when she met Alf. She had broad interests. She was an active member of the Independent Labour Party (ILP) and edited its children's paper, The Young Socialist, *for many years. She wrote for Allen Clarke's* Teddy Ashton's Northern Weekly *and was a founder member of the LAA in 1909. Her biography in Swann's* Lancashire Authors *says, "her writing has a wide and versatile scope, ranging from dainty fairy stories of children to labour songs and deep essays on various social and psychical subjects for adults".[37]*

She was fascinated by eastern religion and was active in the Theosophical Society. In 1952 she was reported giving a lecture on 'Karma' at the Theosophical Lodge Room, Blackburn.[38]

She edited the LAA's Circulating Manuscript Magazine *between 1917 and 1943 and its printed magazine Red Rose Leaves.*

* * *

The Lancashire Authors' Association is no longer the large-membership organisation it once was, but retains an active profile and *The Record* is still published, as a quarterly magazine. The Lancashire Dialect Society was formed in 1951, mainly on the initiative of Professor G.L. Brook who was based at the University of Manchester, where most of the early meetings were held. It aimed to be a more academic body focusing on dialect rather than literature, though in effect the two went hand in hand. Membership peaked in 1953 with a total of 319, including thirty-one public libraries. The society was wound up in 1992; the society had found it increasingly difficult to recruit officers and there was a clear duplication with the work of the LAA. Members were offered a reduced rate membership of the LAA which several took advantage of. The society's library collection was transferred into the LAA's.[39]

A local intelligentsia

Most large and medium-sized towns in Lancashire had at least one, often several, 'learned societies' which provided a meeting place for members of the local middle-class elite. The Radcliffe Literary and Scientific Society collaborated with other local societies to stage an exhibition to mark Queen Victoria's Diamond Jubilee in 1897. The catalogue describes "pictures, curiosities, natural history and other specimens" together with "home work and local industries". It was held in the town's Technical School over a four-week period from 21 June 1897. Local companies such as Tootal, Broadhurst Lee and Co., H. Morris and S. Walker loaned items, including a model loom and historic mill machinery for the exhibition.[40]

The East Lancashire Review ('A Literary, Social and Antiquarian Magazine for Bury, Heywood, Radcliffe and Rossendale') helped to promote the work of local learned societies, including those of Radcliffe, Bury and Greenmount. Its April 1890 edition mentions a visit of the Bury society to local collieries. Its Register of Events for May 1890 mentions an excursion of members of Bury Fine Art Society to nearby Ringley and a visit by Heywood Literary Society to Blackstone Edge.[41]

Burnley had an active literary culture, which included members of the town's elite. Henry Houlding was president of the town's Literary and Scientific Club. Lady O'Hagan, the last of the Towneley family line, was a prominent member of the local literary scene, as were successive generations of the Shuttleworth (later Kay-Shuttleworth) family at Gawthorpe Hall.

* * *

Lancastrians: George Hindle 1852–1916

Hindle was born in Helmshore but the family moved to Burnley when he was four. He was a mill engineer and in later life became secretary of the Burnley and District Enginemen and Firemen's Association. He played a very active role in town affairs, "his name being associated in no little degree with various political, religious, literary and trade union matters".[42]

He stood for Burnley Council on three occasions, as the Independent Labour Party candidate, but failed to get elected. He was a keen antiquarian and dialect enthusiast. In 1894 he helped found the Burnley Literary and Philosophical Society and was also a member of the Burnley Literary and Scientific Club. A collection of his poetry was published as Tales of the Brun *(Burnley, 1906). It was dedicated to his fellow Burnley writers and friends, Henry Nutter and Henry Houlding.*

He edited The Burnley Monthly Co-operative Record *and contributed both prose and poetry. He published several local guides including a description of Towneley Hall and its park.*

He died on the day that the Burnley Literary and Philosophical Society was about to elect him president. He left a wife and nine children.[43]

* * *

As well as having a flourishing co-operative society, which encouraged literary and artistic activity, Leigh had its own Literary Society. J.H.H. Smith, a local businessman, helped to found it in 1878 and remained prominent in the group until his death in 1931. He was also an active member of the Lancashire Authors' Association. The Literary Society grew to be one of the largest bodies of its kind in Lancashire, a remarkable achievement for a relatively small town sandwiched between Wigan, Bolton, Warrington and Salford.[44]

Darwen was a medium-sized weaving town, slightly overshadowed by its larger neighbour, Blackburn, but was still able to develop a strong local intellectual community which was very much part of the town's professional and commercial elite. It had several 'learned societies' which functioned as informal networks for the local middle-class elite. Darwen Literary Society was formed in 1882 and it seemed almost *de rigueur* for the society president to be 'a man of substance', a JP at least.

However, the impetus for the formation of the society came from a series of lectures arranged by the Darwen Industrial Co-operative Society, which were "appreciatively received by all classes in the town, and many of the representative townsmen conceived that the time was opportune for the founding of scientific classes for young people. On further consideration, however, it was felt to be of equal importance that the adult section of the community should be afforded opportunities of bettering their literary and scientific knowledge."[45]

The embryonic body quickly took the form of a middle-class group. An invitation was sent to "some sixty or seventy gentlemen in the town" and the Darwen Literary Society was formed in late 1882. Membership was set at 5 shillings per annum, which clearly indicated the demographic to which it was pitching. It was increased to 7/6d in 1883, but was reduced back to 5 shillings in 1886 'owing to commercial depression'. Women do not seem to have been admitted. Some early lecture topics included, 'Civilization, its origin and progress', followed by 'Modern Education', 'The Dynamo Machine and Its uses in Electric Lighting and the Transmission of Power', with the session closing in April 1883 with a lecture by Rev. W.C. Russell MA on 'The Relation of Brain to Mind'.[46]

Most of the speakers were local. The Rev. Russell was the Pastor of Duckworth Street Congregational Church. Another local clergyman who contributed a number of lectures, including the delightfully-titled 'A Picnic Among Words' was Rev. H. Bodell-Smith who went on to play an important role in municipal reform.[47] Subsequent lectures maintained the diversity of the original session, with topics including, 'Among the Alps on a Bicycle', 'Walt Whitman', and 'The Thames'. A number of lectures had 'health' themes including, 'Food and Its Relation to Health', 'Exercise', and 'Sanitation in its relation to Health'.[48] The society was conscious of its Lancashire heritage and several talks, over many years, reflected this. The history of Darwen was a popular and recurring topic. Mr. J.J. Beckett contributed a lecture on 'Edwin Waugh and Other Lancashire Dialect Writers', whilst the economic historian J. Jewkes, of Manchester University, spoke on 'The Industrial Future of Lancashire' in 1932.

The society reflected and reinforced the town's elite, in which Liberalism and Nonconformity predominated. The 'popular Toryism' of neighbouring Blackburn, with its attendant vulgarity, would not have been countenanced. The society developed close links with larger bodies, above all the Manchester Literary Club. Its president, George Milner, was a frequent guest to Darwen events. The proceedings of the society were meticulously reported by *The Darwen News*, whose editor J.J. Riley was a prominent member of the society in its first few decades. Membership grew steadily from around sixty in the early years to nearly 200 by the time of its fiftieth anniversary.

A sense of community: the voluntary tradition

Lancashire has a rich heritage of voluntary activity, stretching back to the eighteenth century through literary societies and subscription libraries, which were very much the preserve of the rising middle class. Working-class voluntary activity came shortly after, with the growth of friendly societies, burial clubs, trades societies and co-operatives early in the nineteenth century. A later addition was the working men's social club, some but not all of which sold alcohol.

A number of 'female unions' were established in some of the Lancashire cotton towns in the early nineteenth century, to the horror of some men. These were primarily 'discussion groups' rather than unions as we understand the term today. During the nineteenth century some of Lancashire's 'aristocracy' sponsored voluntary activity at a community level.

Informal networks: the Bolton Whitmanites

Less than 10 miles to the south of Darwen, Bolton had a larger and more complex network of learned societies, including less formal bodies such as the 'Whitman Fellowship'. Towards the end of his life, the American poet Walt Whitman (1819–92) developed a close friendship with a small group of admirers in the town. They jokingly called themselves 'The Eagle Street College' after the modest two-up two-down terraced house on Eagle Street, off Bury Road. The group's mentor, J.W. Wallace (see biography below), an architect's assistant, lived there with his parents in the mid-1880s.

* * *

Lancastrians: J.W. Wallace 1853–1926

Wallace, as he liked to be known, was the centre of the Bolton Whitman group. He was often called—only slightly tongue in cheek—'The Master'. His early years in Bolton were spent with his parents, living in a small, terraced house at 14 Eagle Street. He later moved to 40 Babylon Lane, Anderton. He is commemorated by blue plaques at both locations.

He worked all his life for the Bolton firm of Bradshaw Gass and Hope which designed many of the town's finest buildings.[49] He was particularly close to his mother whose death in 1885 affected him deeply, triggering a spiritual crisis which led him to what he called a higher level of spiritual awareness. He was described by R.M. Bucke as an example of someone possessing 'cosmic consciousness'.

He corresponded with Walt Whitman on an almost daily basis in Whitman's final years, between about 1886 and 1892. He visited Whitman at his New Jersey home in 1891.

Some members of the group took certain aspects of the Whitman 'creed' with a healthy pinch of salt whilst enjoying the intellectual comradeship and sense of fun which pervaded many aspects of the group's activities. Not so Wallace, who applied missionary zeal to his work and that of the group.

He was a member of the Independent Labour Party and served on its National Administrative Council. He was a close friend of John Bruce Glasier and his wife Katharine, as well as Robert Blatchford and Keir Hardie. He was active in the Bolton Labour Church during the 1890s.

He was an enigmatic character. His public writing suggests a didactic person. However, the people who came into contact with Wallace loved him. The term 'guru' could be accurately applied to Wallace and the role he had within the group. Another early member of the group, Wentworth Dixon described him as, "the very embodiment of the perfect friend", adding, "I only wish I had the ability to portray to you the almost unique man he was—the nobility and beauty of his personality, his loving kindness, sympathy and helpfulness to everyone regardless of condition."

* * *

Its membership comprised clergymen, mill managers and other members of the 'professional classes'. Allen Clarke wrote:

> It is fitting that Bolton should be distinguished above all towns in England by having a group of Whitman enthusiasts, for many years in touch by letter and visit, with 'the Master', for I am sure Walt Whitman, the singer of out-door life, would have loved to ramble our Lancashire moorlands…[50]

The friends who gathered at Eagle Street at this time were described by Wentworth Dixon as Wallace himself and "Fred Wild (cotton waste dealer), Dr John Johnston (GP),[51] Richard Greenhalgh (bank clerk), William Law, Sam Hodgkinson (hosiery manufacturer), William Pimblett (engineering employers' federation secretary), Rev. Tyas (Curate, Bolton Parish Church), Rev. F.R.C. Hutton (St. George's Church), Richard Curwen, Thomas Shorrock (magistrates' clerk), William Ferguson (bank clerk), Fred Nightingale (clerk), myself (lawyer's clerk)."[52]

Fred Wild described the Bolton group them as young men, "… all from the Parish Church and for the most part were engaged as

clerks or minor gaffers and were attracted to Wallace by his personality and intellectual powers, but not one of them except
Dr Johnston and myself could be called 'Whitmanites'".[53]

The highlight of the group's year was Whitman's birthday,
31 May. Members of the group took the train out from Bolton to
Adlington and walked up to Rivington for a garden party hosted by
the Unitarian vicar, Samuel Thompson. Readings from *Leaves of
Grass* were followed by a speech from Wallace. A 'loving cup', a gift
from Whitman's American friends, was passed around the assemblage, containing 'spiced claret'. Members of the party sported
lilacs in their jackets, Whitman's favourite flower immortalised in
his elegy on the death of Lincoln, 'When Lilacs Last in the Dooryard
Bloomed'. Another member of the group was Charles Sixsmith,
textile manufacturer and town planning advocate.[54]

The group built up a strong relationship with many of Whitman's
American friends which continued decades after the poet's death. It
is perpetuated in the links today between Bolton and American
Whitman scholars who are regular visitors to the town.

Intellectual influencers: Whitman, Ruskin and Morris

The Bolton Whitman group was a unique development. However,
the influence of Whitman, as well as Ruskin and William Morris, was
more general and their ideas had a particular resonance in the North.
Let's continue with Whitman for a while. What made him so popular? He cut a striking figure, with a shock of white hair and beard,
wearing a cap perched at a jaunty angle. He was almost sanctified by
the early socialist movement in England, particularly in the North.

Whitman had a wider influence on the intellectual life of
Lancashire, particularly amongst some of the pioneering socialists.
The magazine of the Labour Church—*The Labour Prophet*—featured
regular articles on Whitman, whose portrait adorned the front
cover of the February 1895 issue with an accompanying article by
John Trevor, founder of the Labour Church movement.

A fascinating insight into socialist activists' 'hall of fame', and
Whitman's standing within it, is contained in *A Comrade's Garland—
Woven by The Fellowship*, subtitled '*a keepsake from the International
Bazaar, held in the Exchange Hall, Blackburn, by the Blackburn Independent*

Labour Party, March 1908. Attendees and supporters of this major event, from local activists to international figures, were invited to send in greetings to form a part of *The Comrade's Garland*—either a personal message or a quote from an influential figure. Of the local respondees, the most popular quotes were from Whitman, Omar Khayam and Shakespeare followed by Burns, Morris, Blatchford, Lowell and Ruskin. The magazine of the Labour Church—*The Labour Prophet*—featured regular articles on Whitman, whose portrait adorned the front cover of the February 1895 issue with an accompanying article by Trevor.

There is a well-known reference to Ruskin's influence on the twenty-nine Labour MPs elected to Parliament in 1906. They were asked by a literary magazine which book had most influenced them and most said John Ruskin's *Unto This Last*. Jonathan Glancey commented that, "*Unto This Last* is one of the most far-reaching books published in Britain in the past 150 years. It inspired the foundation of the welfare state and was translated into numerous languages, including Gujarati by Mahatma Gandhi."[55]

Ruskin, it could be argued, was at least partly 'Lancastrian'. He lived in Coniston for almost the last thirty years of his life. Ms Daisy Brown delivered a lecture to the LAA's Accrington meeting in 1941 titled 'Can Lancashire Claim Ruskin?' She argued that while Ruskin's message was universal, Lancashire has a special claim to him, as the report of her talk in the LAA's *Record* revealed:

> Beneath all the teaching of Ruskin lay the fundamental conception of the beauty of human life, dignity of human work, the desire that all men should be able to live peacefully, fulfilling the noble functions of man. Ruskin indeed had a message for today. Though most of his teaching was universal and not to be confined to the limits of any one county, Ruskin she considered had a place in Lancashire. He praised our beauties and did not hesitate to criticise what he considered our blemishes. Ruskin honoured Lancashire even though he criticised. Our County could claim and honour Ruskin, not perhaps by merely advertising on railway posters Coniston as the home of Ruskin ... but rather by encouraging sincere thinkers to approach his works with a spirit of fresh enquiry, rejecting the ideals that seemed unreasonable and selecting those universal principles which

were applicable in the world of today, principles, too, which might serve as a guide in post-war reconstruction.[56]

Ruskin inspired several societies across England including a Ruskin Society of Manchester. Its programme for Autumn 1901 included lectures on Tolstoy by his biographer Aylmer Maude, 'Ruskin's Attitude towards Democracy' by J.A. Hobson, Ebenezer Howard on 'Garden Cities of Tomorrow' and Edward Carpenter on 'Social and Political Life in China'.

Professional bodies

Lancashire had several professional associations based on the cotton industry. One of the most interesting professional societies was the Gas Institute, not least because its one-time president was Thomas Newbigging, the Lancashire historian. He personifies Gramsci's concept of the 'technical' intellectual but is much more than that, combining high-level professional knowledge with literary, social and political interests. Newbigging's professional career was that of a gas engineer and he rose to international status. He was elected president of the Gas Institute in 1885 (formed in Manchester in 1864). During the course of Newbigging's 'Inaugural Address' on becoming president, he emphasised Lancashire's pioneering role in the development of the gas industry. He said that "it was peculiarly appropriate that Lancashire and Manchester should have been the birthplace of the Gas Institute", pointing out numerous technical innovations, including that the "first application of gas to the illumination of large premises was made by Murdoch, in the sister borough of Salford", in 1804.[57]

The Manchester Section of the Society of Chemical Industry seems an unlikely body to take a broad view of culture in Lancashire. However, in 1928 the society was instrumental in commissioning *The Soul of Manchester* to mark the society's Manchester meeting the following year. The Earl of Crawford and Balcarres (also vice-president of the Lancashire Authors' Association) contributed the introductory essay on 'The Soul of Cities' and other prominent figures contributed essays on a range of subjects including 'Music' (Neville Cardus), 'Art' (F.W. Halliday), 'Recreation' (W.P. Crozier) and 'Manchester and Its press' (W. Haslam Mills). The collection was published by Manchester University Press.[58]

Working-class intellectual networks: the botanists

Some early associations of working men deserve more recognition than they have had from historians. As Manchester writer Leo Grindon commented in 1858:

> The history of these men is peculiar. It is not simply that of individuals, but inseparably identified with that of the botanical societies of South East Lancashire and the neighbourhood, without question the most remarkable in England. Every man of course has had his own private and personal history, but the energies and activities of each have been so closely intermingled with those of his companions that the history is essential like that of a tree or a corporate body—not so much of many things as an organic whole. Many persons have never as much heard of these societies, though assembling almost at their very doors. While the learned and wealthy have been holding brilliant soirées and conversazioni in lecture halls and royal institutions, meetings have been going on among weavers and other craftsmen, quietly and unostentatiously, with aims exactly similar, and success not inferior ... because of its simplicity and earnestness.[59]

Lancashire has a rich heritage of botanical societies. However, these societies were more than purely botanical bodies, important though that was. There is evidence that they functioned as community-based discussion groups where the major issues of the day were debated and discussed.

Samuel Bamford paid tribute to the great number of botanists and horticulturalsts amongst the Lancashire handloom weavers.[60] A strong local network of weaver-botanists developed in the Prestwich and Whitefield area during the early years of the nineteenth century. John Horsefield, a handloom weaver, founded a Prestwich Botanical Society in 1820 which met in local pubs including one named 'The Railway and Naturalist'. They developed an extensive library; Horsefield has a plant named after him—a dwarf daffodil called *Narcissus Horsefieldii*. He became good friends with Richard Buxton, a shoemaker and they collaborated in botanical projects. Other botanist friends at the time included John Mellor of Royton, Jethro Tinker of Stalybridge and John Martin of Tyldesley.

Working-class intellectuals and politics

Gramsci's concept of the 'working-class intellectual' was linked to his notion of the Communist Party functioning as an 'organic' intellectual, a collective body. In Britain, the Communist Party provided a home for working-class intellectuals from the 1920s and encouraged some talented writers and artists.

Lancashire does not stand out as having many examples, though Harry Pollitt, general secretary of the Communist Party between 1929 and 1939 and again from 1941 to 1960 was a true Lancastrian who 'served his time' as an apprentice at Gorton Locomotive Works; he was fond of reciting Samuel Laycock's poem 'Welcome Bonny Brid' at party socials and I once heard a story he performed it before Joseph Stalin during a trip to Moscow.

Bob Davies, of Westhoughton, was a talented writer whose work did not get the exposure it deserved. His work on local history was of high quality.[61] Mick Weaver, a leading figure in the National Union of Mineworkers in Lancashire, was encouraged by his party to write his autobiography, published as *Michael's Story*, which describes his early life in the West of Ireland and his work in the Lancashire pits.[62] Sol Garson, a product of Manchester's Jewish community and a committed communist, was a talented sculptor whose work includes the International Brigades' memorial to Spanish Civil War veterans, in Manchester Town Hall.[63]

The Labour Party, and its predecessor and political companion the Independent Labour Party, was less interested in promoting cultural activity though the arm's-length Clarion movement spawned a number of cultural organisations. These included choirs, naturalist groups and others. The British Socialist Party, which merged into the Communist Party in 1921, published Allen Clarke's novel *The Red Flag* in 1908.[64]

Perhaps the co-operative movement came closest to providing an intellectual framework for working-class men and women in the years between the 1850s and 1960s. As we see in Chapter 11, the co-operative movement was a network of local, independent societies. The larger ones had substantial libraries, reading rooms and lecture theatres, with frequent talks by eminent speakers. Some of the societies would run formal educational classes before these were absorbed by municipal colleges towards the end of the nineteenth century.

A surviving sensibility—or something different?

One of the problems facing Lancashire regionalists (there aren't that many of us) is that 'Lancashire' as a brand tends to be seen as archaic and backward, as noted above. It's a particular millstone that Yorkshire has largely managed to shake off. Lancashire-themed events inevitably roll out tired clichés of flat caps, clogs and potato pie.[65] Contemporary writing in Lancashire dialect is mostly backward-looking, harking back to the days of mills, cobbled streets and smoking chimneys. In contrast, 'the North' is developing with a more modern sensibility that is forward-looking, diverse and inclusive—but still distinctive.

The post-war years saw the coming of mass entertainment, particularly television—which was less suited to dialect. The demographic stability which had been a feature of Lancashire for over a century started to change as a result of large-scale immigration from Asia and the Caribbean, with people bringing their own dialects. Was it, finally, the beginning of the end that had been forecast for so long?

Actually, no. Go to schools in many parts of Oldham, Rochdale or Bolton and you will hear young Asian as well as white English children speaking 'broad Lanky'. Many of the expressive 'gradely' dialect words may not be used but the basic form is still there. Social attitudes have changed and the world is far more accepting of regional accents; what was once a stumbling block can now be an advantage. I suspect the next fifty years will see a dialect that is different, but recognisable to our forebears.

In Ruth Cockburn's *Miss Nobodies*, modern Lancashire women give their view on what makes them special.[66] The comments make for a fascinating profile: strong and to the point, hard-working, community-minded, homely; and a bit weird! I'd also add hugely talented and principled, and also perhaps having a stronger 'Lancashire sensibility' than men. Lancashire women have always been at the forefront of change, including at work, in politics and culture.

Take the 'Lancashire Nanas'! They are a great example of modern campaigning, creatively incorporating aspects of traditional Lancashire identity. *The Guardian* reported:

In August 2014, gangs of older women in yellow tabards and heads-carves started to become a common sight on Preston New Road in Lancashire. They call themselves the 'Nanas', though not all are grandmas. They took the name as a nod to trust, family and tea, leaning into stereotypes of northern matriarchy.[67]

In actions recalling Parkside's Women Against Pit Closures, they occupied some of the land proposed for fracking by the firm Cuadrilla. They climbed over the fence, set up tents and claimed squatters' rights, staying for three weeks. By the time they left, the Nanas had earned the support of 14,000 local residents and appointments at Manchester's High Court. Yet their action led to Lancashire County Council rejecting Cuadrilla's planning application and ultimately changed government policy towards fracking.[68]

There is a sense that Lancashire identity is disappearing and some of today's young people, particularly in areas such as Bolton, Bury and other towns outwith what remains as 'Lancashire' have little or no identity with it. Horwich local councillor Kevin McKeon wrote to me describing his fond memories of a Rochdale childhood, but said, "I look back at this nostalgically but to my three grown sons it is a foreign country. To my five grandchildren the term 'Lancashire' is a totally unknown quantity."[69]

Kevin is right to point this out, though some young people in towns like Bolton would say they are proud Lancastrians; it's not uniform. I would argue that a modern sense of 'Lancashire' can be created. The 'Nanas' highlight a modern, radical Lancashire sensibility. It's there for the building. The 'Lancashire sensibility' has not gone away, neither has Lancashire. It took a Yorkshireman, the late Bill Mitchell, to tell us that:

> The monarch is still 'Duke of Lancaster'. And some old people still think of the county as extending from The Three Shires Stone on Wrynose to the sandbars at the mouth of the Mersey. Squabbles over boundaries are but a wink in the long story of this part of England.[70]

A new regional politics could chime with a revived Lancashire sensibility. Yorkshire has been quicker off the mark and the Campaign for a Yorkshire Parliament has won wide cross-party support; the Yorkshire Party has made several local gains. The Yorkshire-based 'Same Skies Collective' has developed some fresh new ways of thinking about regionalism; the Yorkshire society brings together a wide range of people and groups who are passionate about their region.

Here, there's a Friends of Real Lancashire, and a smaller 'Lancashire Society'. A campaign to re-unite and re-imagine Lancashire needs a higher profile and cross-party support; and it needs allies across the Pennines. The Chartists of the 1840s called for a 'Republic of Lancashire and Yorkshire'; maybe they had a point.

A reformed Lancashire that includes Greater Manchester and Merseyside makes sense as an economic unit, but also chimes with people's identities—in a way that artificial 'city regions' never will. 'Greater Manchester' has reduced the once proudly independent county boroughs to the status of satellites—commuter suburbs of Manchester (or 'Manctopia' as it was described in a TV programme). Nearly fifty years on from the creation of 'Greater Manchester' our 'city region' still has precious little legitimacy. Alternatives are explored in the concluding chapter.

4

FEEDING LANCASHIRE

FOOD AND DRINK

What was distinctively 'Lancastrian' about what we ate and drank? Quite a lot; Lancashire has one of the strongest regional food traditions in England—including offal-based dishes, cheese and of course fish and chips with mushy peas (never, ever, with gravy). Lancashire was at the forefront of the vegetarian movement. Lancastrians are also fond of their drink; this was where the Temperance Movement took off.

Writing in 1998, food historian Matthew Fort said:

Lancashire, like other counties, has remained true to its own regionality. You can still quite readily find Manchester pudding, Manchester tart, Ormskirk gingerbread, Preston parkin, Morecambe Bay shrimps, Bolton brewis, Goosnargh cakes, Eccles cakes, Bury oatcakes, Bury simnel cake. Modern tastes and abundance may have dented the popularity of traditional cooking of economy and thrift—cow heel pie, tripe and onions, weasand, black puddings, hot-pot, brawn, meat and potato pies, but not to the extent that these dishes have become as rare as the bittern or the natterjack toad. They survive because they are an expression of place and community.[1]

His points are well made and go to the core of what this book is about. Matthew Fort's book is a conversation with Lancashire chef Paul Heathcote who did much to re-popularise Lancashire cooking, opening top-of-the-market restaurants which specialised in local cuisine. He makes the link with other regional culinary traditions, suggesting that Heathcote is doing what French chefs have done for generations, renewing the cooking of his region—*la cuisine du terroir*, as the French would say. He added that a number of younger chefs are turning back to their own culinary culture, learning from it and finding new ways to express it.[2]

Since Matthew Fort published *Rhubarb and Black Pudding* some of the 'younger chefs' he refers to have developed a distinctive Lancashire cuisine, stretching from Manchester northwards to the Ribble Valley and 'Lancashire North of the Sands'.

* * *

I love black puddings but I'm less keen on tripe and trotters; fish and chips naturally. But there's more to it than just the most obvious delicacies, though let's start with them and visit some literary connections on the way.

* * *

Lancastrians: Elizabeth Raffald 1733–81

Elizabeth Raffald was described by Lancashire chef Tom Bridge as 'the mother of Northern English Cookery' and Lancashire has good cause to claim her.[3] She was born in Doncaster in 1733, the daughter of Joshua Whittaker. She married the head gardener of Arley Hall (Cheshire), John Raffald and they moved to Manchester in 1763.

Elizabeth opened a confectionery shop in Fennel Street, Manchester, complementing her husband's florist and market gardening business. She opened a pioneering employment agency in Manchester, supplying catering 'servants' near and far, ran what Tom Bridge suggests may have been Britain's first 'take-away' and managed to have no less than fifteen children. She provided cookery lessons and in 1769 published a selection of Northern recipes. She died in 1781 and is buried in Stockport Parish Church graveyard.

* * *

If you mention 'food' and 'Lancashire', two particular dishes often spring to mind—tripe and black puddings. Unlike black puddings (our next course), tripe has suffered a fall in popularity in recent years though some market stalls dotted around the county still offer it. It has experienced a cult revival through the ironic exploits of the 'Tripe Marketing Board', a very cleverly executed spoof organisation which combines promotion of tripe with entertaining swipes at modern-day corporate culture.

'Tripe' is the lining of an animal's stomach, typically the ox, though in some countries sheep's stomach linings are favoured. The profession of 'tripe dresser' was a skilled occupation with a lengthy apprenticeship. As tripe increased in popularity tripe dressers formed their own associations. Tripe, and its near-neighbour cowheel, was popular with factory workers—cheap, nutritious (so it was said) and easily available. Marjory Houlihan, through careful perusals of trade directories for the early 1920s, found twenty-one tripe dressers in Burnley, thirty-five in Preston, forty in Bolton and over fifty in Stockport.[4]

Tripe was promoted as an authentically Lancashire dish. This included a remarkable photo in Marjory Houlihan's booklet showing a group of Lancashire soldiers in North Africa during the Second World War with a banner proclaiming, 'When in Lancashire—Eat Entwistle's Tripe'. Entwistle's was a well-established tripe firm based in Ashton-under-Lyne. Another piece of unsubtle marketing was the advice that, 'If you would live to an age that is ripe, Eat plenty of Entwistle's Wholesome Tripe'.

Most Lancashire towns had tripe restaurants where you could enjoy a proper 'sit-down meal' of tripe. Hiley's Restaurant in Eccles opened a new outlet in 1937 and described the fine art deco eating place as 'a poem in green and silver'. United Cattle Products (UCP) developed a chain of tripe restaurants across south-east Lancashire. It was formed in 1920 following the merger of fifteen Lancashire tripe dressers. The UCP's most popular restaurant was Hill's on Market Street, Manchester. Houlihan quotes an account from the *Manchester Evening News* in 1964 which conjures up a delightful image: "Soft music and pleasant surroundings induce a relaxed atmosphere. With the accent on comfort you can enjoy a three-course meal for only 4s".[5]

The adjoining 'Coniston Suite' could cater for over 120 guests. The UCP shop downstairs sold the full range of UCP products.

* * *

Our Lancashire gourmet trail continues to the noble black pudding. Black puddings remain popular, with an expanding market. Richard Morris, former Bolton School lad, is now MD of the Bury Black Pudding Company. He comes from a family of butchers, Morris's, originally of Farnworth. He developed the 'black pudding' side of the business very successfully and now employs over a hundred staff at its Heap Bridge works. As well as feeding the 'greater Lancashire' market, Richard's company supplies restaurants in London and the south-east and even New Zealand, America and continental Europe.

Potato cakes are an Irish import of the nineteenth century. My grandmother's 'prato cakes' were the best in Lancashire and she bequeathed the recipe to me, but I'm honour-bound not to reveal it. However, Allen Clarke came close to the recipe in one of his novels. *Driving—a Tale of Weavers and Their Work* is one of Clarke's finest achievements, but sadly was never published in book form. It is set in 'Drivenden', loosely based on Darwen. The heroine is Bertha Lindley, a weaver who stands up to the inhumane 'driving', or harassment, of her sisters by the villainous tackler, Lot Ruff. She falls in love with the middle-class socialist journalist, Haddon Peer, who visits Drivenden to report on working conditions. When Haddon is brought round to the family home to be introduced to her parents, Bertha's mother bakes him some potato cakes and Haddon is delighted with them. Mrs Lindley proceeds, in considerable detail, about how to make them. Best served warm, with melted butter.[6]

Clarke manages to weave potato cakes into another of his stories, set in Barrow Bridge during the visit of Prince Albert (the Prince Consort) in 1863, accompanied by Disraeli, then Chancellor of the Exchequer. His royal highness is taken for a tour round the model industrial village whilst the missus is off visiting the gentry in nearby Worsley. He gets a delicious whiff of some cooking and enquires as to what it is. The Prince Consort and Chancellor are introduced to Mrs Billing and they are offered one of the freshly-baked delicacies each.

"Sublime!" said Disraeli. "How magnificently it melts in the mouth. It is like eating glory!"

"The 'prato-cake' is the king of cakes," said the Prince. "I could eat another!"

"I could eat a dozen!" said Disraeli.

Mrs Billing smiled. "That would never do," she said. "You would have indigestion".

Another potato cake is offered to Disraeli, leaving just one, which is taken away by Disraeli to be presented to the Queen. The narrator comments at the end of the tale, "in his brilliant career, Disraeli gave many things to his Queen, but—and on this both political parties will agree—he never gave her anything better than the Barrow Bridge 'prato-cake'."[7]

It would be remiss of me to ignore fish and chips. Arguably, it isn't specifically 'Lancashire' but most Lancastrians would concur in the belief that you won't get better fish and chips anywhere. Lancashire has a solid claim to the first fish and chip shop in the world. It opened in Mossley around 1863. John Lees sold fish and chips from a wooden hut in the market and he later transferred the business to a permanent shop across the road which had a sign in the window proclaiming, "This is the first fish and chip shop in the world." So let's not get into arguments about whether it was in the 'Lancashire' bit of Mossley and just accept that it was. There is a suggestion that a fried chip shop opened on Tommyfield Market, Oldham, in 1860, but did they sell fish as well? I'm inclined to stick with Mr Lees' claims.[8] Just to settle one other point, fish and chips should be served with salt and vinegar, never gravy. Mushy peas are a tasty extra but not essential and difficult to eat outside with your fingers.

* * *

Lancashire was the world pioneer of vegetarianism. It started in Salford in 1809. The Reverend William Cowherd established the Bible Christian Church as a breakaway from the Swedenborgian New Church; his congregation had to take a vow not to eat meat. Other chapels were soon established in Ancoats and Hulme.

Nineteenth-century Salford was ripe for vegetarianism for a number of reasons. When Cowherd died in 1816, his mantle was taken over by the ideals of his successor as Pastor, Joseph Brotherton, who became Salford's first MP in 1832. In 1847 Brotherton presided over the meeting that created the Vegetarian Society. It elected

James Simpson, a deacon of the Bible Christian Church, as its first president. When Simpson died, his father-in-law, William Harvey, then mayor of Salford, took over as president until his own death in 1870. Harvey's sister, Martha, married Brotherton and wrote the first vegetarian cookery book, in 1852. The original copy is in the University of Leeds Library.

The Church continued to provide the Vegetarian Society with its leadership. The Reverend James Clark succeeded Brotherton after his death in 1857 and served as secretary of the Society and also helped to found the International Vegetarian Union. The Vegetarian Society still has its headquarters in the North-West, in Altrincham.[9]

There was a close connection between herbalism and a vegetarian diet. Charles Abbott of Leigh campaigned strongly against meat eating, on both moral and health grounds. Not one to mince his words, he said that "if your medical adviser tells you to keep your body nourished with plenty of flesh foods and meat extracts which contain concentrated sweat and urine, sack him and die a natural death. You will live longer for it."[10] Abbott's book *A Legacy of Health* was not only a tirade against the medical profession and its advocacy of meat eating; it contained many useful recipes for meat-free meals, including common staples of today like nut roast and leek and lentil pie, as well as the less appetising 'tomato mould'. The book concluded with suggested breakfast, lunch, tea and supper menus for each day of the week.

Allen Clarke was a vegetarian for most of his life and advised in *The Eternal Question* to "kill no beast, bird or other living thing, for food, sport or science. Live on vegetables and fruit."[11] He wasn't so strait-laced not to see the amusing side of things and wrote a 'Tum Fowt' comic sketch called 'Bill Spriggs as a Vegetarian' which commented on the current fashion. Bolton had its own vegetarian restaurant in the early 1900s and it was a popular meeting place for local radicals. Clarke held his first meeting to promote his 'Daisy Colony' scheme at the venue, on 4 July 1903 and attracted a sizeable crowd. Vegetarianism was common amongst socialists in Lancashire in the early 1900s, particularly the 'ethical socialists' of the Independent Labour Party.

* * *

Today, there is a growing number of food events across Lancashire, perhaps the most exclusive being the Aughton Pudding Festival which only takes place once every twenty-one (or twenty-two) years in Halton-with-Aughton. The last one took place in 2013. Legend has it that the festival has been in existence since 1782 after the village took delivery of a boiler to help strip the bark from willow growing along the banks of the Lune. Someone commented that it looked like a pudding could be cooked in it and the rest is culinary history. The festival stopped in 1886 amid claims it had caused 'rancour in the village' and only started again in 1971. Ramsbottom has its annual 'Black Pudding Throwing' contest which attracts a growing crowd of contestants. Bolton hosts one of the biggest regional food festivals in the country, taking place over the August bank holiday weekend. Clitheroe's is usually at the end of July.

Lancashire has retained a large number of markets, many of which have their origins in the seventeenth century or earlier. Bury has managed to fight off competition to retain several top prizes for its market. Other large markets include those at Bolton, Preston and Warrington. Vibrant, smaller markets are held at locations including Chorley, Todmorden, Gorton, Earlestown, Ormskirk and Garstang. Both Liverpool and Manchester have a growing number of smaller street markets.

Booth's is a company with a strong sense of Lancashire identity, which does much to promote Lancashire produce. From its origins in Blackpool in 1847 the company has expanded and now has over twenty stores, nearly all in Lancashire, or very close.

Perhaps the most distinctive 'fine dining with a Lancashire accent' experience is the 'Lancastrian' Sunday lunch on the East Lancashire Railway between Bury and Rawtenstall. The railway invites you to enjoy "fresh local produce and a plate that celebrates the best of Lancashire ... a steam journey through the Irwell Valley that includes one of the best three-course Sunday lunches in all of Lancashire".

What we grew

In 1895, Allen Clarke mused about the possibility of Lancashire growing its own cotton in large 'hot houses', where tropical fruits could be grown, transforming factories into "delightful gardens, as well as useful growing grounds, for the inhabitants to stroll in during the natural winter of their own climate".[12] Climate change hadn't been heard of but I suspect Clarke, an environmentalist well before its time, would have recognised the danger, but maybe also some of the opportunities.

Lancashire was, up to the middle of the nineteenth century, a predominantly agricultural county. Much of it still is. West Lancashire, the Fylde and north Lancashire retain a strong agricultural sector which includes sheep and dairy farming as well as market gardening. West Lancashire has by far the largest amounts of land allocated to cereal and arable production in Lancashire. Livestock and dairy farming represent the major agricultural land use in the county. Livestock and dairy farming is far more important than arable production in the broader Lancashire area. The top-grade farming land in West Lancashire means that the area is a significant producer of field vegetables and crops under glass/plastic. In terms of employment, the Lancashire workforce involved in farming totals about 10,000 people, around 3.4% of the England total. If Greater Manchester and Merseyside were included, the total would be nearer 15,000.[13]

Lancashire (historic Lancashire at any rate) was the birthplace of one of the most exciting community-based developments in the last twenty years—the 'Incredible Edible' movement, which grew from small beginnings in Todmorden. It was the brainchild of Leigh-born Pam Warhurst and is based on the elegantly simple idea of growing food wherever there's space to do it.[14] In Bolton, housing provider Bolton at Home is encouraging its tenants to develop community-based growing projects where people learn basic skills in food production and cookery.

* * *

Lancashire, in common with its neighbours, has a tradition of agricultural shows. These include local events such as Cartmel, Chipping, Coniston and Bury. The Cartmel Agricultural Show, since 1928, has covered the area of 'North Lonsdale—North of the Sands', keeping the 'Lancashire North of the Sands' tradition very much alive, with attendance numbering over 10,000. The Royal Lancashire Agricultural

Society's main aim is to promote Lancashire and raise money for charity—done by hosting a show once a year in the heart of the Ribble Valley at Salesbury Hall. The event dates back to 1847 and in 2022 attracted 10,000 visitors over a three-day period.

What we drank

Lancashire has a rich tradition of locally brewed beer, though it has gone through some major changes over the last fifty years. Traditionally, Lancashire's 'pub culture' was based on locally based breweries which typically owned several tied houses within their area, usually capable of being served by horse-drawn drays. Breweries which became well known in their towns included Thwaites of Blackburn, Magee's in Bolton, Hartley's of Ulverston, Yates and Jackson in Lancaster and dozens more. Many disappeared in the 1970s, closing down as the thirst for keg beer took over.

The industrial towns of Lancashire had a problem with drink. Beer was cheap and the quickest way out of Oldham, Bolton, Wigan and other similar towns was to get completely legless on a Friday night. Domestic abuse by drunken husbands was an all-too-common phenomenon. There was a reaction against this violent drink culture. Preston was the birthplace of the temperance movement, with Joseph Livesey creating the 'teetotal movement' of the 1840s. Livesey was a political radical, a strong supporter of working-class causes and the fight to extend the suffrage. His biographer observed that,

> his labours in various fields of philanthropic effort were so extensive, that had he never been involved with the Temperance Movement, it might still have been said of him that his long life was devoted to the service of humanity … His active labours, however, in the promotion of Temperance, extending as they did over a period of fifty-four years, were of a character which fully entitle him to be regarded as the Father and Founder of the Total Abstinence movement.[15]

The movement which Livesey did so much to create is often dismissed today as a crank's cause, depriving working men of 'an honest drop' of ale. Yet the scale of alcoholism in nineteenth-century Lancashire (as well as other industrial centres) required action which was often unforthcoming from the powers-that-be. There was often a close relationship between the brewing industry and Toryism, with towns such as Blackburn being not untypical.[16] The early socialist movement, dating from the mid-1880s, had a strong anti-drink culture and many of the early socialist clubs of Lancashire and the West Riding had a strict 'no alcohol' rule. In some cases these restrictions were not dropped until decades later.

An alternative that developed across 'Cotton Lancashire' was the temperance bar, one of which survives. Fitzpatrick's in Rawtenstall has managed to keep going when others succumbed and has become an iconic visitor attraction. Traditionally, temperance bars would offer a range of 'botanical' non-alcoholic drinks, including sarsaparilla, 'blood tonic' (raspberry) as well as lemonade. Tea would also be served.

The decline of the small local brewery has been reversed and all of the Lancashire towns now have several micro-breweries which often celebrate a local or regional identity. Lancaster Brewery ('Lancashire born and brewed') is a good example of a modern brewery that is expanding its range of good quality beers. It owns three pubs—in Lancaster itself, Barrow-in-Furness and Ulverston. Clitheroe-based Bowland Brewery is another Lancashire success story, having taken over the derelict Holmes Mill and transformed it into a pub, restaurant, hotel and food hall. Northern Monkey is a growing Bolton-based artisan brewery.

* * *

Lancashire, particularly the south-east part, has a rich ethnic diversity which is reflected in its food. Chinese restaurants have been a feature of Liverpool's dining scene for a very long time, reflecting the city's long-established Chinese community. The first (Indian) Asian restaurants appeared in Blackburn, Bolton and Oldham in the late 1950s or early 1960s, mainly catering for an Asian clientele. Non-Asians soon took a liking to curry, confirming Allen Clarke's reference to Lancashire culinary taste in the 1890s, when people liked something 'with a bit of taste', to overcome the deadening of tastebuds as a result of working in polluted industrial environments. By the early 1970s, going out 'for an Indian' became a common pursuit, often as a late-night meal after the pubs had shut.

The quality of Asian food in Lancashire has always been high, even if the original restaurants themselves may have left a bit to be desired. Today, even the smallest town has at least one Indian. What is perhaps surprising is that we haven't seen a growth of eastern European restaurants, supporting the culinary needs of Poles, Hungarians and Czechs who now represent a sizeable part of Lancashire's ethnic mix. Maybe it will come; I'd love to have somewhere within reach of home where I can enjoy a good Hungarian meal, not the awful 'goulash' slop which is sometimes offered by British restaurants who know nothing better, but a real Magyar pőrkőlt or lecsó.

5

LIVING IN LANCASHIRE

HOUSING AND HEALTH

An unhealthy place

Industrial Lancashire was a dangerous, dirty and unhealthy place in which to live and work. Most Lancastrians in the nineteenth century could not afford professional medical care and relied on community-based herbalists; a tradition that continues to the present day. Lancashire produced some notable figures in the medical world, including Thomas Barlow, son of a handloom weaver who became Queen Victoria's private physician. Many working-class communities benefited from the unpaid support of local general practitioners, such as Dr James Dorian of Bolton, commemorated by a statue in the town's Queen's Park. Not far from the park, in Bolton's Victoria Square, Samuel Taylor Chadwick, the public health reformer, is celebrated by a fine statue. His Manchester-born namesake, Edwin Chadwick, led the fight for improved sanitation in working-class areas.

We'll never know the true toll on people's lives as a result of atmospheric pollution but it must have been enormous. Allen Clarke, in his *Effects of the Factory System* (1895), makes a useful comparison of death rates in the industrial towns of Lancashire with nearby rural towns and villages. The annual death rate in Bolton per thousand of population was 23.49 while it was 10.7 in Lytham and 7.3 in nearby St Anne's. Bolton was a deeply unhealthy place to live and the cost of medical treatment was prohibitive. And for 'Bolton' read Oldham, Rochdale, Salford and Manchester.[1]

There was no NHS. If you were ill you had to pay, unless you were lucky enough to be protected by a friendly society or trade union, for which of course you had to pay contributions. Working in mill, mine or factory didn't just expose you to physical injury from machinery, but more insidiously the long-term risks to health from airborne pollution. Allen Clarke highlighted the appalling results of industrialisation. After pointing out the physical dangers of factory work, he asks, "What wonder then, that after such wearying, worrying days, continued from year to year, coupled with having to live in packed streets and vitiated air after leaving work, the cotton operatives are not healthy."[2]

Alternative medicine: the Lancashire medical herbalist tradition

An alternative to the high fees charged by 'professional' doctors was to go and see the local herbalist. Herbalism has a history stretching back centuries, practised in many parts of the world amongst what we were taught as being 'primitive' societies. They were anything but! From the middle of the nineteenth century 'medical herbalism' took root in Lancashire's industrial towns. For many years Bolton was the regional headquarters of the National Association of Medical Herbalists, at number 53 Manchester Road.

* * *

Lancastrians: Richard Hool 1847–1920

He was born into a working-class family at Whittle-le-Woods, near Chorley, on 24 November 1847. His father was part of the 'aristocracy' of the cotton industry, a mule spinner, though his family were probably handloom weavers originally. As well as being avid readers, philosophers and political radicals, the handloom weavers took a keen interest in botany. The young Hool accompanied his dad on 'botanical rambles' and learnt his expertise and knowledge of plants from his father and fellow-botanists.

He moved to Bolton as a young man and spent much of his life in Farnworth, living at 26 King Street. He became a well-known figure amongst Lancashire medical herbalists and was in great demand as a speaker. One of his students, Mr T. Ramsden, recalled Hool's lectures in 1890: "I first became acquainted with Mr. Hool thirty years ago, when he came to Hindley to lecture at the Star Botanical Society, and he opened my eyes to the wonders of the botanical kingdom in every direction, and gave a joy to life, and a love of the plant world that will remain with me until the end."[3]

Hool and his friends combined the collection of plants with their use for medicinal purposes. Typically, groups of them would walk miles into the surrounding countryside to identify and collect herbs. Hool would often act as a group's informal teacher, helping his students to discover unusual plants. That same evening the group would study their 'finds', name and classify them and identify their possible medicinal uses.

Hool was much more than a local specialist. His fame grew nationally and internationally. He became one of the leading figures in the National Association of Medical Herbalists and was well known and respected in the United States as well as in British universities, including Oxford. He became editor of the national journal of medical herbalists, The Herb Doctor.

* * *

Hool's wife Margaret was also a professional herbalist. Unlike in 'official' medicine, women were not excluded from the profession, though they seem to have been a minority amongst herbalists up until recent times. It was common for working-class 'wise women' to act as community midwives as well as herbalists but they received scant recognition other than from their own communities.

Scores of working men were indebted to Hool for training them in the skills of medical botany. One was George Worthington, a young miner in Atherton at the turn of the last century. In 1908 his sister was taken seriously ill with a form of dysentery and the doctor had told the family she had no chance of survival. In desperation he went to see the local herbalists who were meeting in the upstairs room of a local pub. He was given a specially prepared remedy which did the trick within a matter of days. This stimulated Stanley's interest in herbalism. He soon met R.L. Hool himself and became his part-time student while still working down the pit. By 1913 Stanley had become a full-time practitioner in Atherton. His three sons each followed in Dad's footsteps as practising herbalists. The eldest, Stanley, moved to Davenport, near Stockport, in 1935, where he continued to practise until the early 1980s.[4]

Hool began a family tradition which continued for nearly a century after his death. His nephew inherited the business when Richard Lawrence died in 1920. Many generations of Boltonians will remember the stall in Bolton's Market Hall, and more recently on the open market, which kept the Hool family tradition alive until its final demise in 2022.

R.L. Hool was not the only prominent medical herbalist in the Bolton area. Charles H. Hassall practised for many years in Farnworth and was nationally respected; he established his Farnworth business in the 1870s. The firm packaged 'D.W. Herbs' which became popular locally and nationally, by mail order. Following his death, the business was continued by his son, Charles Vincent Hassall, who maintained the tradition of advertising in Allen Clarke's *Teddy Ashton's Lancashire Annual*. Frank Horridge took over the business in 1947 and ran it until 1959. It seems it ceased trading in 1960. For many years, the lettering on Hassall's shop at 11–13 Longcauseway survived, advertising herbal products including 'D.W. Herbs'.

Herbalism remained popular after the First World War and hundreds of working men and women would go out 'herbing', sometimes chartering 'charabancs' to get out into the country. As herbs became ever more popular, firms were established to supply local herbalists' shops in Lancashire. Potters, until recently located in the former Haigh Foundry near Wigan, became a popular choice.

The coming of the NHS in 1948 posed a challenge to medical botanists. They were not permitted to practise within the NHS and many felt that this had more to do with the middle-class medical profession wanting to protect their own fiefdom than any objections based on scientific evidence. It should be stressed that practising medical herbalists had to go through a rigorous training and assessment process. This was managed by the National Association of Medical Herbalists. Hool's books, such as *Health from British Wild Herbs* and *Common Plants and Their Uses in Medicine*, have long been regarded as almost biblical texts.[5]

Yet despite treatment now being free on the NHS, many working-class patients of established herbalists stayed loyal to their 'community doctor'. Occasionally, tensions between the 'medical profession' and the medical botanists spilled out into open war. The highly respected Leigh herbalist, Charles Abbott, was dragged through the courts in what became known as 'The Black Box Trial'. The box in question was a diagnostic tool used by Abbott but it was sensationalised by the media of the day. Several doctors testified against him but Abbott was acquitted at Manchester Assizes of the manslaughter of a boy who was taken to him for treatment. Thirty years later he commented that "all the doctors who gave evidence at his trial were dead, but the patients who gave evidence were still alive and he made his living out of doctors' failures!"[6] The case was made into a play written by Neil Duffield and performed by Leigh's Pit Prop Theatre.

Medical herbalism declined in popularity during the 1960s and 1970s but has had a new surge of popularity through interest in 'alternative medicine'. One medical herbalist practising in Lancashire today is Edwina Hodkinson of Darcy Lever. She was delighted to hear about R.L. Hool having lived in the same area and collected herbs in Darcy Lever over a century ago. The National Institute of Medical Herbalists, descended from Hool's association, has several practising members in the county.

The Whitworth Doctors

The story of the 'Whitworth Doctors' is one of the oddest tales of Lancashire medical history. In about 1760 John Taylor, a young man of 20, arrived in the small village of Whitworth, between Rochdale and Bacup. He had been apprenticed as a blacksmith and farrier; his father was a herbalist and had imparted for of that knowledge to his son. Local journalist John Broderick wrote that, "besides fabricating metal and showing horses John applied his knowledge of herbal remedies to ailing animals, as well as resetting their broken bones … [H]e became an accomplished vet.[7] Taylor was able to use 'transferable skills' and applied his medical talents to men and women who could not afford doctors' bills. Taylor himself had little time for the medical profession who regarded him as a crank. Yet his popularity locally, and further afield, grew. And Taylor became known simply as 'Doctor John'.

The doctor's methods were simple and sometimes effective; they could also be brutal. A misplaced hip would be remedied by a smart thump from Dr John's knee. Patients were often tied to the iron railings outside the house and a flying kick would remedy a badly set bone. The Taylor family were also famous for their treatment of cancers using an ointment called 'keen' which seemed to have mainly resulted in extreme pain when administered. Robertson, the historian of Rochdale and the Vale of Whitworth, gave a thorough account of Taylor's activities and his brusque manner with patients, observing that by 1800 his reputation had extended all over England and Ireland. His sons were trained up by Taylor and 'the Whitworth Doctors' became legendary. Robertson wrote:

> About the year 1820 William Howitt, the author of *The Rural Life of England*, visited Whitworth for the purpose of ascertaining the truth of the often-told tales of the 'Whitworth Doctors'. He ascertained that John Taylor had been a curious compound of rude impudence and good nature. Whoever had visited him, lord or labourer, were treated just in the same way … the standard price was eighteen pence a week for medicine and attendance.[8]

* * *

Lancastrians: Dr John Johnston 1852–1926

One of the most remarkable figures in Lancashire medical—and cultural— life in the years before the First World War was Dr John Johnston. He was a man who wore many hats—doctor, poet, cyclist, traveller, photographer and more. He was one of the main figures in Bolton's 'Walt Whitman Fellowship' known colloquially as 'The Eagle Street College', along with his good friend J.W. Wallace (known as 'The Master').

He was a proud Scot, born in Annan, Dumfriesshire, in 1852. He moved to Bolton in 1876 as a GP, after having qualified as a doctor at Edinburgh in 1874 followed by a two-year stint as hospital surgeon at West Bromwich. He lived initially at 2 Bridgeman Street before moving to 54 Manchester Road.

Johnston was a highly skilled physician, trained at Edinburgh where he gained his MD. As well as his 'day job' as a GP he found time to be an instructor for the Lancashire and Yorkshire Railway's ambulance classes. This brought him into direct contact with the realities of daily life on Britain's railways, and the dangers faced by railwaymen. In his diary for 1887 he records the death of a shunter at Trinity Street station, William Davies. He fell off a truck and was run over—both his legs were broken and his left foot was cut off. He died from his injuries: "The poor fellow was one of the members of my ambulance class and has left a wife and five children. Alas! Alas!"⁹

In addition to his work as an instructor for the railway ambulance classes he acted as a judge at many railway ambulance competitions, including those of the London and North Western and Great Central Railways. These contests were major events which continued well into the 1960s but have sadly died out.

During the First World War he served at the vast Whalley (Calderstones) Military Hospital before moving on to Townley's Hospital where he was appointed Medical Superintendent in September 1917. In Moorlands and Memories Allen Clarke writes of Townley's Hospital during the First World War, still a very recent memory, and how "many boys in the characteristic blue suit of the wounded and invalid soldier have sat on the seats at the Great Lever tram terminus, close to Townley's Hospital".¹⁰

Johnston's poetry was published in 1897 as Musa Medica. The book of poems was dedicated to "The Master and the boys of The Eagle Street College, from whom so many of these songs and verses received their initial impulse..." The collection included 'The Song of The Eagle Street College' written in Scots dialect. Like Wallace he was involved in the early Independent Labour Party but also played an active role in a range of local institutions, including the Bolton Lads' Club, the Bolton Housing and Town Planning Society and numerous medical associations. During the First World War he served at both Townleys (now Bolton Royal) and Whalley Military Hospital, lamenting the appalling injuries of soldiers returning from the trenches. His diaries, kept in Bolton Library, are a fascinating resource about life in early twentieth century Bolton. Rev. Hutton was part of the 'inner circle' of 'eminent Boltonians' which included senior political figures and major employers. He was president of the prestigious Bolton Literary Society¹¹ and didn't hide his Whitmanite sympathies.

In Johnston's diary there is a particularly moving entry where he describes a soldier pleading with him to amputate his hand so that he wouldn't have to return to his regiment. Johnston records that, "We decided that to attempt its removal might involve some risk to the future usefulness of his hand and we therefore counselled it being left alone. 'Danger or no danger,' said the soldier to me, 'I want you to do the operation, I'd rather lose my hand than go back yonder'. He meant The Front—'it's Hell!'"

131

As well as a practical way of getting around, he recognised cycling as a means to health and well-being. His poem 'Doctor Air' tells us:

There's Dr. Blister, Dr. Bleed, and old-fashioned Dr. Pill,
Who with mixtures, potions, draughts, will cure your every ill;
And Dr. Sanitation will with wonder make you stare,
But the king of all the doctors, new or old, is Doctor Air.[12]

The name of Dr Johnston crops up in many accounts of 'civic' activities in Bolton between the 1880s and First World War. He was active in the early Independent Labour Party and Labour Church but also played high-profile roles in a range of local institutions, including the Bolton Lads' Club, civic societies and numerous medical associations.

He was strongly opposed to child labour, sharing Clarke's outrage at the half-time system which still operated in the Bolton mills at the turn of the century. His book Wastage of Child Life *(1909) was a denunciation of child labour, using his home town as an example.*

He was a man of advanced 'liberal' views and became a close friend of the gay socialist Edward Carpenter, becoming his (unpaid) physician. The two, with Carpenter's lover George Merrill, went on holiday together to Morocco.

* * *

Taylor himself died in 1802, and his son James, assisted by his brother's two sons, continued the practice. James seems to have inherited his father's eccentricity and regaled his patients with entertaining anecdotes.

The business was lucrative and the family amassed a fortune of £30,000. Their patients included the Archbishop of Canterbury and—according to anecdote—Princess Elizabeth, daughter of George III. The Taylors used to dispense a noxious substance known as 'Whitworth Red Bottle', which was still being produced and sold in Whitworth forty years ago. The last Taylor to practice at Whitworth was James (1823–76). He had a formal medical education and was apprenticed under Mr Field of Charterhouse and studied with the president of the Society of Apothecaries. He also spent some time at King's College London, and qualified in 1845 before returning to Whitworth. He adopted a more orthodox approach, but still used the traditional skills of the family and gained a reputation as a bone-setter.[13]

* * *

Lancastrians: Arup Banerjee 1935–

Arup Banerjee's career is an example of the achievements of South Asian medical professionals who came to Lancashire in the 1960s and 1970s. He helped to found the geriatric speciality and in 1996 became president of the British Geriatric Society, the first South Asian doctor to hold that post.

Arup was born in Calcutta (now Kolkata) in 1935, into a traditional Hindu family. His father was an electrical engineer; his mother was home educated but responsible for Arup and his brother's early education. He started school at the age of 8, matriculating in 1950 with distinction. After attending Calcutta Presidency College he joined the prestigious Calcutta Medical School and qualified in 1957 at the age of 21, staying on as House Physician. A year later he moved to Mangalore Medical College and then to medical school in Pondicherry, as a tutor.

Arup and his wife Aleya decided to move to Britain to pursue their medical careers; they travelled by boat in the cheapest possible class, then by train from Genoa to Calais, locked in 'like cattle'. They arrived at London Victoria in September 1960. They had no money, no place to stay, no job and nobody to guide and help them.

He found work in several hospitals before leaving the UK to teach in the medical school in Kuala Lumpur. After three years they decided to return. In 1971 Arup joined the new field of geriatric medicine as a senior registrar in the south of England.

In 1973 Arup took up his first consultant post at Bolton Hospital. He set up 'case-finding clinics' in the community and was involved in the management and delivery of services at both district and regional levels. Arup became an honorary lecturer at the University Hospital of South Manchester where he taught clinical students, junior doctors, nurses and therapists and at the same time conducted research.

He became chair of the regional consultants and specialists committee of the BMA and was chair of the North-West geriatrics training committee. He was appointed as a member of the North Western Regional Health Authority, eventually becoming vice-chair as well as president of the Manchester

Medical Society. While president of the British Geriatric Society he was awarded an OBE and was Medical Director at the newly formed Bolton NHS Trust between 1994 and 1998.

Arup retired from the NHS in 1999. Since his retirement he has continued to develop elderly care in other districts—in South Manchester, Wigan and Leigh and in Barnsley. He lectures to health visitors and community nurses at the University of Bolton where he has an honorary professorship.

His three sons are all senior medical professionals while two of his grandsons are studying medicine at Cambridge. He has always fought for better education, training and research in elderly care. He still writes regularly and lectures on ageing.

* * *

Lancashire and mental health

I've dwelt on the herbalist tradition as it offers an alternative to conventional narratives about working-class health—and there is something distinctly 'Lancastrian' about it. Can the same be said of the modern NHS, almost by definition a centralised service, with common standards and approaches—for all the right reasons? Notable in Lancashire healthcare was mental health. Lancashire developed several enormous mental hospitals which became almost like medieval cities, being virtually self-sufficient—growing their own food, providing housing for hospital staff and laying on a wide range of cultural events. Some even had their own railways connecting them to the national network.

The Regulation, Care and Treatment of Lunatics Act of 1845 required the provision of 'asylums' for the care of pauper lunatics. Lancaster Moor Hospital was first to open. Although it has long since ceased to have a health function, the Gothic buildings remain as apartments and are a very visible landmark from the M6 motorway. Prestwich followed, serving the Manchester conurbation, then Rainhill, having a similar function for Merseyside.

The last major mental hospital to be built in Lancashire was at Calderstones, near Whalley. It opened in 1915 as Queen Mary's Military Hospital during the First World War. Nearly 57,000 servicemen were treated at the hospital between April 1915 and June 1920.

A 1,000-bed hospital at Whittingham, near Preston, was projected in the late 1840s but the first patients were not admitted until 1873. It had its own telephone exchange, post office, reservoirs, gas works, brewery, orchestra, brass band, ballroom and butcher's shop. By 1939, the number of patients had reached 3,533, with a staff of 548, making it the largest mental hospital in Great Britain.[14]

It got its own independent transport service, the Whittingham Hospital Railway, in 1889. The line connected with the Preston to Longridge branch at Grimsargh and used a mixture of second-hand locomotives acquired from as far afield as the London, Brighton and South Coast Railway![15] Both Whittingham and Calderstones played major roles in the First World War, receiving thousands of wounded soldiers. Calderstones also had its own railway which was able to accommodate trainloads of wounded troops at its purpose-built station.[16]

Housing: from slums to garden suburbs

Workers' housing in the early nineteenth century was devoid of most creature comforts, but handloom weavers' cottages may have had space for a small garden and room to grow vegetables. In some places they would be three-storey, making good use of natural light for the detailed work involved in specialist weaving. In some semi-rural parts of Lancashire some handloom weavers' cottages have survived and are now desirable properties.[17]

Housing in the industrial towns developed in a haphazard manner, often reflecting fragmented land ownership patterns and a desire to build housing quickly and cheaply to cope with a burgeoning population. We've seen how rapidly towns such as Barrow grew, from next to nothing to a large town of over 40,000 in thirty years. Whilst that was exceptional, towns such as Oldham, Bolton, Wigan and St Helens all experienced rapid population growth in the mid-nineteenth century. Between 1801 and 1851 Manchester's population more than quadrupled, whilst the rate of Liverpool's growth was even more rapid.[18] This led to some of the worst slum housing in Britain. Until the first quarter of the twentieth century, local authorities had little power to make improvements and the examples of good quality workers' housing tend to be scattered in more rural industrial villages such as Calder Vale near Garstang, Barrow Bridge, Eagley and Egerton near Bolton, Spring Vale, Darwen—products of philanthropic employers who needed employees to be located close to the workplace.[19]

There were examples of some good quality housing grouped around factories in more urban areas—but this was the exception to the rule. Fletcher, Burrows and Co. created good quality houses and community facilities close to its pits at Howe Bridge, on the edge of Atherton. The company, owners of the Atherton Collieries, expanded the village in the late 1860s and 1870s to house their growing workforce, building 200 cottages for their workers, but also shops, including a fish and chip shop, schools, adult education facilities, a bathhouse and a club. Recreational facilities included football and cricket.[20]

Wythenshawe, technically within the historic county of Cheshire, was developed by Manchester Corporation as a major housing scheme modelled on 'garden city' lines. The council commissioned architect Barry Parker to create Britain's third garden city, following Letchworth and Welwyn Garden City. Wythenshawe Amateurs FC's website tells us that: "It was to be the largest Garden City in the world, the concept being it was to be self-sufficient, houses with gardens, surrounded by greenbelt."[21] Shena Simon, a key figure in progressive Manchester politics in the inter-war years, chaired the city's Wythenshawe Estate Committee, and said "it was the boldest scheme that any municipality has yet embarked on" and represented "a century's progress".[22] However, Wythenshawe was not without its problems. Tenants complained about a lack of shops, unmade roads and poor public transport.[23]

Inter-war municipal housing: Farnworth and Nelson

The example of Wythenshawe (see above) was the most ambitious municipal housing scheme in the North of England. Several other local authorities promoted smaller, but significant, schemes. Farnworth, a relatively small local authority on the southern edge of Bolton, was one of the earliest. The driving force behind Farnworth's housing programme was the council leader, the Rev. John Wilcockson, a fascinating figure, very much on the left of the

Labour Party.[24] In 1939 the town celebrated the granting of its incorporation as a borough. The commemorative souvenir brochure grandly states:

> Although the town's cotton trade has suffered depression in common with the whole of Lancashire, a vigorous civic policy has been pursued. Where parts of the old township have shown decay the municipality has pruned with wisdom … The town has no slums today, for with great concern for the health and comfort of the working people, the District Council has transplanted the poorer classes from ill-conditioned cottages to delectable dwellings in ideal surroundings. Figuratively they have, as Suetonius said of Caesar Augustus, attempted to rebuild their city of marble.[25]

This relatively small authority built 2,000 homes between 1919 and 1939. As the council proudly said of itself, "the Housing Committee of the Council have shown wisdom and vision in planning on broad attractive lines. The new Farnworth which has thus appeared a goodly town of nearly 2,000 houses, all owned by the authority—is not only composed of workers' homes which are attractive in internal planning and external design, but gives each house an attractive setting on the latest 'garden city' lines."[26]

One of the estates, probably at Wilcockson's instigation, had streets named after famous Labour movement figures—Keir Hardie, Ramsay MacDonald and William Stewart. They survive today as examples of good quality social housing, in the ownership of Bolton at Home—a charitable company which inherited Bolton Council's housing stock.

Nelson had Lancashire's first Labour council, elected in 1905. After the First World War it embarked on an ambitious house-building programme following the passing of the Housing and Town Planning Act of 1919. A total of 271 houses were built in the period up to 1924 when additional legislation encouraged further municipal house building. The council built the Marsden Park and Hodge Housing Estates with 776 houses. They also embarked on a major programme of slum clearance and constructed several 'aged persons' homes'. The authority experimented with new materials, building 100 prefabricated aluminium homes.[27]

The new framework for social housing

British council housing has gone through a traumatic period of change. The Thatcher government 'right to buy' policy saw thousands of council tenants buying their own homes, with strong inducements from government. Local authorities were starved of resources and many once immaculate and well-maintained housing estates degenerated.

A new approach towards social housing evolved during the 1980s and 1990s which saw many local authorities setting up their own 'arm's-length' housing bodies. In some cases these have become fully independent charitable 'community benefit' companies, such as Bolton at Home which owns a stock of over 18,000 properties, mostly in the Bolton area. Its homes include the housing estates built by Farnworth Council in the inter-war years. First Choice Homes is also a community benefit society, owning properties across Oldham. It is the descendant of Mary Higgs' vision of co-operatively owned housing for the people of Oldham.

6

EDUCATING LANCASHIRE

The development of an educational 'system' in Lancashire was a slow and disjointed process. Up until the mid-eighteenth century most children would have had little in the way of formal education other than what they were given at church, assuming they attended. Most didn't.[1]

The picture in the nineteenth century prior to the passing of the 1870 Education Act, which formalised primary education, was complex, with much local variation. Typically, schools would be provided privately, sometimes through charitable bodies. The most basic form of education, reserved mainly for working-class children, was the 'dame school' usually run by a woman from her own living room, often with little formal education herself.

Allen Clarke, writing in 1920, recalls what passed for his own education when he was a young child in the mid-1860s, when he and his pals were looked after by Mrs English who used to peel her potatoes and do other domestic chores while her charges learnt their ABC. He was able to move on to something more resembling a school environment when he was a few years older, at Hulton School, where he became a pupil-teacher. The school was endowed from a charity established by Nathaniel Hulton in 1691 and the head teacher was Mr J.T. Simpson who also taught evening classes at the mechanics' institute. Clarke described him as "a kind man but he could use the cane eloquently on occasion".[2]

Schooling in a Victorian community

Clarke's experience of school life was not untypical. A glimpse of school life in Lancaster during the nineteenth century was offered by the National Union of Teachers in their souvenir book published when they held their annual conference in nearby Morecambe in 1909.[3] It notes that a school had been in existence as early as 1472 when a schoolmaster was appointed in Lancaster under the authority of the mayor, though it had ceased to function by the 1570s. However, Lancaster Corporation seems to have created a new school by 1615 which they ran until local government reform in 1896. The 'Free Grammar School' was free 'for the sons of freemen' until 1824 when charging was introduced for all pupils. One of its most illustrious pupils was Dr William Whewell, who became Master of Trinity College. It seems that by the 1820s there were other primary schools ('Blue Charity' institutions, for boys and girls) available within Lancaster which did not charge. The grammar school developed a good reputation. A Charity Commissioners' report from 1865 described it as 'one of the most prosperous in the county, or indeed the North of England, a state of things ascribed to the management being in the hands of the town council, and therefore really public, and to the large number of boarders'.[4] Lancaster Corporation handed over the school's administration to a Board of Governors but they retained a strong influence. Other schools in the area included one endowed by the Society of Friends (Quakers).

* * *

Lancastrians: Hannah Lightbody 1776–1828

Hannah Lightbody was an early champion of education and welfare reform. She was born in Liverpool in 1766 to a wealthy family. She was a free-thinking, liberal woman whose work centred around the rights of women and the abolition of the slave trade. Throughout her life, she shunned advice to become 'less bookish' and attended debates and lectures and participated in a wide range of Liverpool's cultural activities. She was an active Unitarian.

At the age of 21 she married a powerful textile merchant, Samuel Greg, and lived with him at Quarry Bank Mill, Styal, Cheshire. Hannah introduced education, healthcare and music to workers at the mill, before campaigning for the adoption of her practices nationwide.

As a well-educated and highly intelligent young woman she also had a wide circle of literary and artistic friends and attended discussion groups with men of power from Roscoe to Rathbone.

David Sekers, a former director of the National Trust which owns Quarry Bank Mill, uncovered her diary. He told The Liverpool Post: *"I found Hannah's diary whilst sifting through a wealth of archive material left at the mill by descendants of her family. The diary is of course in Hannah's own words—so we read and understand it very much through her eyes. Even at this early stage in Hannah's life, she comes across as a free-thinking young woman, ahead of her time, very much concerned with the role of, and enlightenment of, women in society."*

* * *

He added: "She missed Liverpool and compared the increasingly elegant and cultured world of Liverpool with the grimy centre of Manchester. It's then that she turned her attention to the pauper children in the mill factories. Her passion for education meant she started teaching the children and introduced thinking, music and better diets for the mill families. Hannah is thought to have been instrumental in the establishment of a Women's Club and Sick Club for the growing community of families in the mill's factory community."[5]

Like other towns in the late nineteenth century Lancaster was empowered to establish an elected School Board. It was formed in 1893 with representation from local clergymen and town councillors and embarked on a programme of school building. Its work was absorbed in 1903 by the creation of a Local Education Authority which formed part of Lancashire County Council.[6]

Adult education

Most of the industrial towns of Lancashire had a 'mechanics' institute' by the middle of the century, often endowed by a local philanthropist. The Barrow-in-Furness institute was funded by industrialist H.W. Schneider at a cost of £3,450.[7] It had 600 members with access to a lending library of 1,500 volumes. Bacup Mechanics' Institute opened in 1846 and included a lecture theatre capable of holding a thousand people. J.W. Hudson, writing in 1851, listed mechanics' institutes at major towns such as Bolton, Oldham, Accrington, Blackburn and Wigan but also smaller centres including Clitheroe, Colne, Heywood, Farnworth, Lees and Tyldesley.[8] A Lancashire and Cheshire Association of Mechanics' Institutes was established in the early 1850s.

Manchester and Salford had their own mechanics' institutes from the mid-1820s, though Manchester tended to dominate.[9] As well as its own mechanics' institute, Lancaster had a School of Science and Art and a 'Merchant's Subscription News Room'. In 1887 the mechanics' institute became absorbed into the new Storey Institute, which comprised a technical school, school of art, public library, news room and art gallery. It was endowed by the local linoleum entrepreneur Thomas Storey. 'The Storey', now owned by Lancaster City Council, remains a vibrant part of the local arts scene.[10]

The co-operative movement was a major provider of adult education facilities in the nineteenth century. The doyen of co-operative societies, the Rochdale Pioneers, had a library of several thousand volumes. By 1870, Lancaster and Skerton Co-operative Society had a collection of 4,000 books. Over Darwen Industrial Co-operative Society provided a large meeting room for lectures and a reading room available to members and their children aged 13 or over.[11] Nelson Co-operative Society had a substantial lecture theatre and meeting room.[12]

Larger towns, such as Oldham, had several institutions. They included a Lyceum, Literary Institute, Werneth Mechanics' Institute and also the Hollinwood Working Men's Club which offered educational facilities, and the Glodwick Mutual Improvement Society.[13]

The Workers' Educational Association was formed in 1903 by Albert Mansbridge. It developed a strong presence in the North of England, with offices in Liverpool and Manchester. The WEA has survived a difficult time over the last 30 years and today focuses mainly on skills and employability. A complementary development has been the University of the Third Age (U3A) which has several very large branches across Lancashire, offering courses on a wide range of subjects. Its work is very much in the tradition of Northern 'self-help'.

The technical and art schools

One of the most important developments in nineteenth-century Lancashire education was the 'technical' school. One of the earliest examples was The Wigan Mining and Mechanical School, opened in 1858. It aimed to provide the technical skills for the town's rapidly expanding coal mining industry and was endowed in part by Edward Cardwell, a local mine owner.[14] Initially, the school rented space in the public hall but the expected support from the local mining interests was not as great as had been anticipated. After numerous difficulties the school won support from what was one of the biggest mining companies in Lancashire—the Wigan Coal and Iron Company, led by its managing director Alfred Hewlett. He became chairman of the school board and launched an energetic campaign to raise funds for a brand-new purpose-built building.[15]

Whilst Wigan was the undoubted centre of Lancashire mining, several towns in 'Cotton Lancashire' laid claim to being major players in textiles, usually with their own specialism. Oldham concentrated on coarser yarns while Bolton spun the finest. They increasingly required a trained workforce in a number of areas, including design, engineering and more specialised spinning and weaving techniques. To a degree, the technical schools took over the role of the mechanics' institutes. An account of the Lancashire textile districts, produced by the large textile manufacturer, Bannerman, said:

> In our peregrinations among these manufacturing towns we have often had occasion to note the existence of the Technical School. As an educational medium it has taken the place of the old Mechanics' Institution ... in its instructive purpose it assumes to deal technically and therefore practically with the arts and crafts and sciences; and as a rule the best materials available are forthcoming.[16]

The history of Bolton School of Art, now part of the University of Bolton, bears out the above comment. Bolton had a mechanics' institute from 1825, using rented accommodation. A new purpose-built building was opened in December 1868 by the famous novelist Anthony Trollope and took over the role of the mechanics' institute in arts subjects. The school had a chequered career in the following decades but seems to have put down firm roots by the

1890s, in response to growing demand 'by organised labour' for classes in weaving and other subjects. The running of the school was taken over by Bolton Corporation and new premises were provided in the palatial (and locally designed) Pupil Teachers' Centre on Hilden Street, from 1901.[17] Alongside the more arts-related subjects, a Textile and Engineering School opened in nearby Bridgeman Place in 1891. The institution was re-named The Municipal School of Art in 1928.

Bury had one of the most well-regarded technical schools and the building survives as part of the town's museum and art gallery. It was described as "a handsome stone-fronted building, with carvings in relief thereon".[18] It was mainly used for evening classes and offered courses in chemistry, geometry, cotton spinning, French and German, dressmaking, mechanical engineering and weaving. The school had its own weaving shed equipped with modern Lancashire looms as well as an original timber-framed handloom dating back to the eighteenth century. The top of the building provided space for the art studios where life classes and sculpture were practised.

Smaller towns such as Darwen had their own technical and art schools and nurtured some talented students. James H. Morton attended Belgrave British School as a young boy and benefited from their stress on art education, with a Mr Jackson of Manchester School of Art teaching part-time there. Morton moved on to Darwen's Municpal Technical School, "where art was pursued with vigour and exactness, as witnessed by the subjects examined by the Department of Science and Art: Drawing in light and shade, Modelling, Geometrical Drawing, perspective, freehand Drawing and Model Drawing".[19] In 1899 Morton won a fellowship at the Royal College of Art in London, with a scholarship funded by G.P. Holden, owner of Bank Top Mill. He went on to become Assistant Art Master at Darlington Technical School but returned to Darwen in 1905 to pursue his own painting career.

Centres of learning

Lancashire's university sector is relatively new; we do not have anywhere that could compete, in terms of longevity, with Oxford, Cambridge and the Scottish universities although a public meeting held in Manchester in 1640 called for the establishment of a 'Northern University' in Manchester.[20]

However, some of the Catholic schools, particularly Stonyhurst have a long and distinguished history. Several of the old Lancashire families, such as the Towneleys, encouraged the pursuit of knowledge and became informal centres of intellectual activity. Towneley Hall became the focus of the 'Lancashire Renaissance' in the seventeenth century.[21]

Stonyhurst, near Ribchester, has a history dating back to the late sixteenth century. The school was originally founded in Saint-Omer, near Calais, in 1593 by Fr Robert Persons SJ under the patronage of Philip II of Spain and is the oldest continually active Jesuit school in the world. The college had to 'up sticks' from revolutionary France and move en bloc to Lancashire. The transition seems to have worked remarkably well. Today, the college is home to 800 pupils, comprising children from over 28 countries.[22]

The story of Up Holland School is more chequered, reflecting the decline of Catholicism in England. St Joseph's College was founded in 1880 by Bishop Bernard O'Reilly to be the seminary serving the North-West of England. It was a large and impressive structure. However, it never quite lived up to expectations and numbers declined in the later years of the twentieth century. The college closed in 1996 and has since been converted into apartments.

Lancashire's first university was Owen's College, Manchester, established in 1851 following a bequest by John Owens of £100,000 "for providing or aiding the means of instructing young persons in such branches of learning and science as are usually taught in English universities".[23] Its early history was difficult, with student numbers falling to just thirty-three in 1856. However, it succeeded in establishing itself on a firm footing and by the beginning of 1900 it had over a thousand students enrolled. In 1903 it became the Victoria University of Manchester. Lord Morley of Blackburn became the first cancellor, "of whom all Lancashire is proud as one of her most distinguished sons", in the words of Professor F.E. Weiss.[24]

The Earl of Crawford and Balcarres, one of the great Lancashire landowners, industrialists and antiquarians, succeeded Morley in 1923. The governance of the university reflected a strong Lancashire influence. The Court of Governors included the chairman of

Lancashire County Council, the Lord Mayor of Manchester and representatives from several county and borough councils across the county.

The University of Liverpool was founded in 1881 as 'University College, Liverpool'. It established the University of Liverpool Press in 1899, becoming only the third university press in the country. It received its Royal Charter in 1903, becoming the University of Liverpool.

Its first chancellor was 'the uncrowned king of Lancashire', Edward Stanley, the 17th Earl of Derby. Many years later, in 1980, Philip Lever, the 3rd Viscount Leverhulme—and grandson of William Lever—was appointed Chancellor. The first Lord Leverhulme had strong interests in the university. After winning a libel case against the *Daily Mail* in 1910, he gave his substantial damages, totalling £91,000, to the university to found schools of Tropical Medicine, Russian Studies and Civic Design. He also endowed a chair in Town Planning. He developed friendship with the Professor of Architecture, Charles Reilly, whom he commissioned to design the centre of Port Sunlight.[25]

Primary school with a difference: the remarkable Teddy O'Neill

One of Britain's most remarkable educationalists spent most of his working life running a small primary school on the banks of the River Irwell at Prestolee, Kearsley. He transformed an ordinary, run-of-the-mill school into a national showpiece of what progressive education could achieve. Teddy O'Neill served as head of Prestolee School from 1918 until his retirement in 1953. He was loved by his pupils and their parents, but some critics called him 'The Idiot Teacher'. The name stuck and he regarded it as a badge of honour.[26]

* * *

Lancastrians: Teddy O'Neill 1890–1975

O'Neill was born in 1890, into a working-class environment in Salford. His mother ran a pub and his drunkard father was absent much of the time, leaving mum a single parent with a busy pub to run. It wasn't an environment in which a young lad would be expected to thrive. But Teddy was no ordinary child and his mother was no ordinary pub landlady. Before he was born she'd visited Jerusalem, travelling much of the way on the back of a donkey! At the age of 16 he was appointed as a 'pupil-teacher' at Ordsall Lane School in Salford. This involved spending half your time as a student and half as a 'teacher', without formal qualifications. It was a traditional school and most teachers ruled with 'the stick'. His biographer, Gerard Holmes, says that "children found him interesting ... he often reached school with a pocket full of strange exhibits, some beetles maybe, or a mouse".[27] Yet he didn't fit in with the school ethos and at the end of his two years' apprenticeship was deemed unsuitable.

He went back to helping mum in the pub and earned a few bob by going round bars singing popular songs and gave piano lessons. Fortunately for his future pupils, he wasn't prepared to accept the negative report on his teaching potential. He was given another chance. He taught the basics but encouraged a love of nature and literature to the sixty-plus pupils in his class.

By a few lucky breaks he was admitted to teacher training college at Crewe, where he excelled. New ideas in education were gaining ground and O'Neill embraced them. His principal at the college commented, "no new developments in Education will find Mr. O'Neill unprepared".

In 1951 he was awarded an MBE in the New Year's Honours List. The Farnworth Journal commented on his 'surprise' at the honour, given his impatience with authority!

* * *

He inspired the children with a love of nature, music and dance. It got results, recognised by a visiting schools inspector who encouraged him further. Over the next forty and more years he transformed Prestolee School, winning national and international accolades and being featured in the popular magazine *Picture Post*. It wasn't plain sailing and he faced determined opposition from some of the school governors. Two of the most prominent were managers of the local mills who just wanted an obedient, punctual labour force to work in their factories. The school's job was to produce them.

This was anathema to O'Neill, who gradually introduced a very different regime into the school. Traditional classrooms were abolished along with timetables. Open-plan use of space was encouraged.

It became known as the 'do as you please' school by its detractors but there was a structure, albeit a subtle one, which ensured children got 'the basics' but were able to opt for more creative subjects as well, including gardening, music, cookery and other arts- and crafts-based subjects.

O'Neill encouraged staff and pupils to change their surroundings. A report in the local press for 1937 said that "in one month a waste plot of ground adjoining the Prestolee Council School has been converted into a children's paradise".[28] The former waste ground included a paddling pool, fountain and 'Japanese' style bridges. The children also constructed a fairytale 'castle' and the paper reported on future plans to construct a windmill, which would have the very practical function of pumping water into the paddling pool. In 1950 Teddy O'Neill decided to outdo Blackpool by creating the 'Prestolee Illuminations' as part of a 'Festival of Prestolee' in and around the school, attracting over 20,000 visitors from far and wide.

O'Neill decorated the school with his favourite 'proverbs' including:

'Impossible' is the slogan of a fool
The Cranks of today are accepted tomorrow
Let teachers be spacious
Real poverty is lack of imagination
... and many more.[29]

Lancashire's libraries and librarians

Lancashire has a rich collection of public libraries and some outstanding private subscription libraries such as Manchester's Portico which welcome members of the public. They range from the palatial Manchester Central and Liverpool's with its stunning Picton Reading Room to substantial libraries in towns such as Wigan, St Helens, Warrington, Preston, Accrington, Bolton and Blackburn. There are less grand but still impressive libraries in Darwen, Farnworth, Heywood and Chorley. Many of the smaller libraries were funded by the philanthropist Andrew Carnegie. The high tide of library building in Lancashire was between 1900 and the outbreak of the First World War. The Public Libraries Acts, passed between 1892 and 1901, provided the impetus for the phenomenal growth across Lancashire and the North, at a time of growing optimism within local government.[30]

Many of the buildings reflect a strong sense of municipal pride and achievement. Reading rooms were established in many villages, often supported by public subscription. Examples of reading room buildings survive at Haggate and Worsthorne (Burnley), Withnell Fold, and Stalmine—which is now the village hall. The Reading Room at Pilling survives as a bowling club, while Coniston's Reading Room forms part of the John Ruskin Museum. Some libraries were first established as mechanics' institutes, such as Lytham, which opened in 1876, and Accrington which was established two years later.

The role of librarian was crucial in the effective development of Lancashire's library sector but also, more broadly, in nurturing a distinct Lancashire literary culture and historical awareness. The Chief Librarian became, by the beginning of the twentieth century, an important figure in town life and was usually supported by a Libraries Committee, chaired by a senior member of the council. Some boroughs added the job of looking after the town art gallery and museum to the Librarian's job description. With some exceptions (e.g. St Anne's, see below) they were men; they built powerful attachments to their communities and to Lancashire as a whole. For example, Bolton's Archibald Sparke wrote and published his encyclopaedic *Bibliographia Boltoniensis* in 1913 which reflected his deep knowledge, and love, of Bolton literature.[31]

The Lancashire Authors' Association provided a useful platform for the talents of the country's librarians. On the occasion of an LAA visit, it was traditional for the borough librarian to deliver a paper on aspects of local history and literature. For example, Gilbert Bland, Lancaster's Borough Librarian and Curator spoke at the LAA's June 1932 gathering on the 'The Local Record Room and its Treasures'. A.C. Fairhurst, Assistant Librarian at Bolton, gave a paper on 'Bolton Centenary Authors' to the association's meeting in Bolton in April 1940.[32]

Joseph Pomfret was particularly active in the Lancashire Authors' Association. He was Darwen's Borough Librarian before taking the Chief Librarian's job at Preston. In 1927 he delivered a paper to the LAA on 'The Literary Associations of Darwen', noting that "Darwen is not without romance or material for the novelist or poet … there is romance in the stories of local success and failures in industry … then again the wild beauty of the moors, their ever-changing colour and mood…"[33]

* * *

Lancastrians: Joseph Pomfret 1878–1944

Joseph Pomfret was born in Blackburn and in his early teens was appointed 'Junior Assistant' at Blackburn Library and Museum where he trained under Richard Ashton. He left to become Borough Librarian for Darwen in 1905 and remained there until 1928 when he was appointed Chief Librarian at Preston. He established a young people's library and reading room and introduced free public lectures. He wrote a history of Darwen and of Holy Trinity Church and Parish in Darwen. A biographical sketch in the LAA Record *notes that "he has given numerous lectures on literary, historical, and antiquarian subjects, including the dialect in which he is particularly interested". He was prominent in the professional librarians' networks and was president of the North-West Branch Library Association in the early 1930s. At Preston he built up a nationally important collection of private press books which is often referred to as the Pomfret Collection. Dr Cynthia Johnston notes that, "Pomfret's curation of the private press collection has resulted in an internationally significant legacy for Preston including books produced by William Morris's Kelmscott Press, Doves Press, Essex House, Golden Cockerel and Gregynog Press".[34]*

He served as president for the Darwen Literary Society and after his move to Preston became the first president of the Preston Dickens' Fellowship, vice-president of Preston Drama Club and Preston Shakespeare Society and a prominent member of the literary and antiquarian section of Preston Scientific Society. He retained a close bond with Darwen and continued to be involved in various societies and organisations including the Darwen District Nursing Association. He was an active member of the Lancashire Authors' Association for many years as well as the Lancashire and Cheshire Antiquarian Society.[35]

* * *

Speaking not long after the end of the Second World War, Preston librarian Ms Jane A. Downton spoke to the LAA on 'The Book and

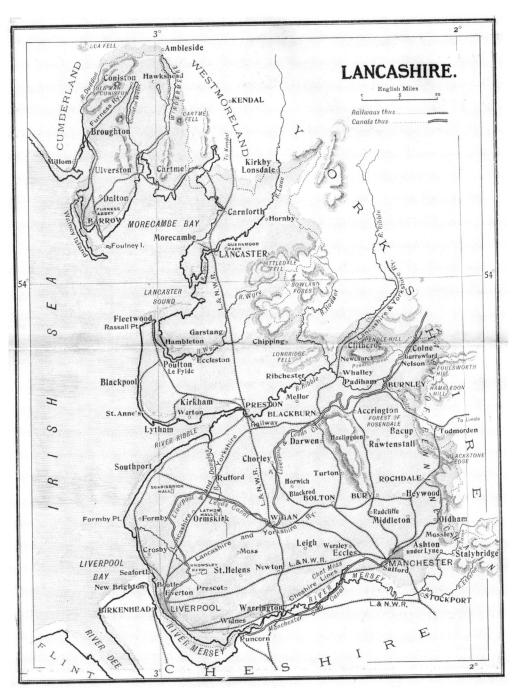

1: Map of Lancashire, c. 1900.

2: Map of Lancashire from *A History of Lancashire (Oxford County Histories)*, E.G. Hewlett, Oxford at The Clarendon Press, 1913 (Reprinted 1934).

From Farnworth's Smoke and Grime
It's a welcome change for Thee and Thine

3: From Farnworth's grime to seaside pleasure: holiday postcard, c. 1900.

4: Awaiting new uses—or demolition? Mutual Mills, Heywood.

5: Opening of Farnworth Park, 1864.

6: The Three Counties Stone, Wrynose Pass: Lancashire, Westmorland and Cumberland.

7: Commemorating Gandhi's visit to Lancashire, 1931: plaque at Garden Village, Darwen.

8: Weaving shed: Queen Street Mill, Burnley.

9: Furness Abbey.

10: Memorial to the Pretoria Pit Disaster, 1910: Ditchfield Gardens, Westhoughton.

11: Textile students study handloom weaving: Bolton Technical College, c. 1960.

12: View across Burnley towards Pendle and Ingleborough, from Crown Point.

13: No takers? Cotton mill for sale, c. 1980.

14: The Spinning Room, Falcon Mill, Bolton, 1982.

15: Astley Green Colliery still in production, 1969. The colliery now forms the Lancashire Mining Museum.

16: Oldham Lyceum: once at the heart of Oldham's cultural life.

TRADE UNION SECRETARIES—
Send Your Printing
TO THE
"Cotton Factory Times"
MARKET SQUARE, ASHTON-U-LYNE

Cotton Factory Times

VOLUME LI   FRIDAY NOVEMBER 1, 1935   PRICE ONE PENNY

o 2,646

"In things essential, Unity; in things doubtful, Liberty; in all things, Charity."   "Give me above all other liberties, the liberty to know, to utter, and to argue freely, according to conscience." — Milton.

DISEASES FROM DUST

ave the Tests on Grinders Been Adequate ?

POSITION EXPLAINED

we published a letter from
on ... controversy concerning
tude of ... cardroom officials
spect to medical investigation
plaints arising from the in-
... of cardroom dust. He hoped
... ... cotton dust. There
... ... light for the removal of this
... disease and expressed sur-
... ... reported in the
... ... denture of results and
... ... tained from ... tests that had
do hitherto.

Roberts the secretary of the
amalgamation replies this
... ... the points raised by
Consumption in order, for
... of others, to call atten-
... situation as it now appears.

... ... with interest the letter
... under the above head-
... of October 20th.
... desire nor intent to enter
... controversy on this
... feel that some of the points
... comment and explanation
... out in your preface to
... correspondent. ... Cardroom
... ... misunderstood ... the
... phrase from our point
... ... results have been

No Interference with Compensation

"It is important to remember, and
should be obvious to anyone who takes
an interest in this vital problem, that the
workers and the independent scientists
and was carried out for the primary
object of finding methods of prevention
and cure. It does not affect or interfere
with any attempt to obtain compen-
sation for our disabled operatives.

"The officials have done, and are doing,
all they can to arrive at a satisfactory
solution of this problem and are getting
tired of the constant criticism, which,
oftener than not is based on misappre-
hension and without regard to the difficulties of the situation. I would remind
tives have some responsibility for the
present position, as was pointed out in
the C.F.T.' Insurance Notes of last week
... should not be unmindful of the fact that
... advice has been given by the officials
... which they have ignored.
... In the ... ... last paragraph
of your correspondent's letter, he states
that two grinders have been treated very
... reasonably (sic), and goes on to say that

Misunderstanding

any possibility of future
... ing, I will explain, in the
... manner, that was the
that our position is as this

Presently was appointed by
... ... on Country conduct
... on Respiratory disease of
peratives in the cotton in-

... and have abundant proof

Weaving Mills' Dispute

Ancilliary Workers' Wages

Sir John Grey presided at a meeting
of representatives of the Northern Counties Textile Trades Federation and the
Wages Committee of the Cotton Spinners and Manufacturers' Association in
Manchester, on Tuesday, to consider
wages questions surrounding the work
of employes in connection with weaving
sheds not covered by the new schedule
list. These include loom oyer-lovers,
warehousemen, beamers, tapers,
drawers, warpers, sizers and others.

The meeting was adjourned till 29th
November to give the workers' organisations time to consider the views of the
ployers which appear to be for a general
alteration in rates of pay, probably
meaning a reduction for most employes
included in the above list. It is the
and with independent scientific figures
or any other matters submitted at the
meeting, have to be kept secret for the
present. The operatives' representatives have to await the decisions of the
various districts which will be asked to
discuss the proposals of the employers
and it is stated that about 20,000 workers
are affected.

Weavers' Troubles

Complaints About New Wage List

The committee of the Bolton Weavers'
Association is most having quarterly report, with as follows:

In the Heart of Anglezark

Our picture shows two keen Bolton mill girls who cycle all the year round. Like many others of their sex,
they like a spin along country roads and over open moors after their week of hard work in the shed.
And a fine tonic it proves; body and mind, a prophylactic against chills and colds. Here,
during a brief spell of sunshine, they are seen resting on the Anglezark Moors, round by Rivington Pike.

17: *The Cotton Factory Times helped popularise cycling and walking around Lancashire.*

18: India Mill, Darwen.

the Child', which provided an overview of children's literature and also the impetus given to work with children by the passing of the 1944 Education Act. The borough librarian of Preston, Joseph Pomfret (see above) supported his Lancaster colleague by chairing the meeting.[36] The talks were an opportunity for Lancashire's towns to promote themselves and redress what they sometimes saw as a negative image for their towns. Speaking to the LAA at its Oldham meeting in October 1936, Stanley Deem, the town's Assistant Borough Librarian, said in his paper on 'Old Oldham':

> I think sufficient has been written to prove that Oldham and its people are by no means of the backwoods. Many more favoured places produce pageants and endeavour to impress their wealth in historical background. By what I have said and what I have implied it will, no doubt, be obvious that if some gifted pen were exercised in similar fashion, Oldham could provide a pageant which would astonish even Oldhamers themselves.[37]

* * *

St Anne's Library is a little gem. It was designed by local architects and opened in 1905. The first Librarian was Mr T.P. Thompson who was previously in charge of Bolton Free Library. He was succeeded in the following year by Miss Bertha Barrow. The local paper reported that, "Miss Barrow was an applicant when the council advertised last year, but the committee had, at that time, resolved to appoint a male librarian. The committee therefore knew her qualifications and for that reason the vacant post was not again advertised. The council, we believe, will not regret their choice."[38] *The Express* also commented that as 70% of those who attended St Anne's Library were women the appointment was 'especially appropriate'. She remained in post until retirement in 1939.

Darwen was the first 'non-borough' to adopt the Public Libraries Act in 1871 and was the first in the North of England to adopt the 'open-access' system—the borrower could browse through the books rather than have to request them being brought out by a member of staff. It was preceded by the mechanics' institute which had opened in 1839. The first library (1871) moved in with the Technical School which opened in 1895. The current library, a very fine art nouveau building, opened on 27 May 1908. Andrew Carnegie had donated £8,000 towards the building and he attended the opening event in person. The 'stars and stripes' flag flew over the library for the occasion and Carnegie was made a freeman of Darwen.[39]

Heywood was a Carnegie library, opening in 1906. However, its roots lay with the Heywood Free Library, established in 1874. Rev. Richard Storry was the key figure in its early years; he had been a member of Heywood Mechanics' Institute Library which dated back to 1840. The Heywood Industrial Co-operative Society had its own library, founded in 1863, with a very active librarian, John Albert Green. When the new Carnegie library opened, the Co-op shut down its own facility and transferred its entire stock to the new municipal library, which remains a well-used community facility to this day.[40]

In 1846 a mechanics' institute was founded in Rawtenstall, complete with its own library attached. Forty years later the local Co-operative Society also established a librarian in their large town-centre building. In 1902 Andrew Carnegie offered a grant of £6,000 to the borough council towards the building of a new library, which seems to have been a typical sum he granted towards capital works for new libraries. The design of the building was by Crouch, Butler and Savage of Birmingham. A ceremony to mark the laying of the cornerstones took place on 15 September 1904; Councillor Samuel Compston[41] applauded Rawtenstall people's desire "...to secure for our children, and their children to the third and fourth generation, the blessing of a free lending library and reading room, to be their own, which they will appreciate and be grateful to its founders for in years to come".[42]

Hargreaves Wilkinson from Burnley was appointed as Librarian and it opened for business in 1906 with 6,000 volumes. The official opening the following year was, as with Darwen's, attended by Andrew Carnegie.

Accrington got a larger library befitting a town of its size. It was built between 1906 and 1908. The 'Amazing Women by Rail' website tells us that "the library has five bays in a Cinquecento style with upper pilasters and arched windows. Inside, look for the green art nouveau tiles and huge stair window with stained glass."[43] The library developed from the Mechanics' Institution of 1878 which is next door and now forms part of the library. There is an excellent

Local Studies collection upstairs and the library was once home to the extensive collection of the Lancashire Authors' Association, now part of the University of Bolton's special collections.

Like so many others in Lancashire and Yorkshire, Accrington's library owed much to the financial help of Andrew Carnegie. In 1904 he offered £7,500 to the town for the building of a new library but it seems that Accrington Corporation felt it was not enough. Following an application for more funds the offer was increased to £10,000. The building was opened in January 1908 and was designed by the Borough Engineer William Newton, when local authorities were able to do such major works. The ground floor contained a reading room, children's room and lending department; the first floor housed the reference library, librarian's office and a lecture room which could hold 500 people. Several gifts of books were made including the 4,000-volume library of William Ashworth and the Mechanics' Institution Library of 5,000 books. A souvenir brochure was produced to commemorate the opening of the library, which explained that the 'Safe-guarded open access' system used in the previous library premises was to be maintained and that there were 11,000 volumes available to the public in the lending library as well as 2,000 volumes in the children's library. The library also worked with the Blind Society to provide books, presumably in Braille. The library continues to provide sterling service to this day. The magnificent stained-glass window is its crowning glory.[44]

Manchester city centre has three magnificent libraries—the refurbished 'Central Ref' in St Anne's Square, John Rylands Library on Deansgate (part of the University of Manchester) and the Portico. The Portico Library is one of the hidden gems of Manchester. The modest doorway on the corner of Mosley and Charlotte Streets does not prepare you for the magnificent domed interior once you negotiate the flight of stairs. It was established in 1806 by 400 subscribers, drawn from Manchester's emerging middle and upper classes. Early readers and associates included world-famous authors, future prime ministers, leading scientists, and educators. The history of the library tells us that: "built with wealth derived from the Industrial Revolution, British empire-building, and colonial expansion, the library amassed a collection that reflects the innovations, but also the exclusions and inequities of its time".[45]

The library's early members were all men until the Married Women's Property Act of 1870. These included people of all political persuasions, from Radical and Liberal abolitionists and anti-poverty campaigners to Tory factory owners and textile traders. Elizabeth Gaskell used the library while her husband William acted as its longest-serving chair.[46]

Today, the Portico is run as a charity with a board of trustees. Whilst members are able to borrow from the collection it is open to all members of the public to visit—and enjoy lunch. The library sponsors the annual 'Portico Prize' which promotes literature reflecting 'the spirit of the North'.

The Working Class Movement Library, in Salford, is housed in a former nurses' home and is opposite the excellent municipal art gallery, museum and library in Peel Park. Its origins go back to the 1950s and the work of Edmund ('Eddie') and Ruth Frow, both dedicated activists in the Communist Party and avid book collectors. Their semi-detached house at 111 Kings Road, Stretford, developed into an extensive 'domestic library' with many extremely rare labour-movement books and pamphlets. It became a charitable trust in 1971. By the 1980s the Frows' house was at bursting point and Salford Council agreed to house the library in the former nurses' home on Salford Crescent.

The library "tells the story of working class activism, protest and campaigning through its extensive archive and library collection. The collection explores how working people have and continue to work collectively to make change and records over 200 years of campaigning by ordinary men and women."[47] The work of the library is supported by 'Friends of the Working Class Movement Library' and it hosts a regular programme of talks, events and exhibitions.

Liverpool has a number of outstanding libraries with pride of place going to the magnificent Central Library on William Brown Street. The 'William Brown Library and Museum' was completed in 1860 to the designs of John Weightman, Surveyor to Liverpool Corporation, and has always shared with the city's museum, now known as World Museum Liverpool. The library was then extended with the addition in 1879 of the Picton Reading Room and to the rear with the Hornby Library in 1906. All three are Grade II* listed buildings. The Lyceum (or Liverpool Library) was England's first subscription library opening in 1758 but destroyed in the 1942 Blitz. Arline Wilson wrote of Liverpool's early libraries:

> An increasing demand in Liverpool for the 'amenities of civilized life' was also reflected by a growing demand for books, newspapers and periodicals. In 1758 the Liverpool Library was founded; it survived until 1941. This was not the first subscription library in the British Isles (precedence in the matter goes to Scotland), but it was the first of the English gentlemen's subscription libraries, and was widely imitated in other provincial towns. The entry fees ensured exclusivity, initially set at one guinea with an annual subscription of five shillings, they rose steadily as the century progressed, and exclusivity remained a feature in the nineteenth century. The opening of the Free Public Library in 1852 served to ensure that membership of the Liverpool Library was somewhat less of a privilege. It is interesting to note that in contrast to the early learned societies, the library was open to ladies as well as gentlemen. Towards the end of the eighteenth century the library acted to some extent as an informal literary club when committee meetings took place, generally in the Star and Garter Hotel in Paradise Street. Here, men such as William Roscoe, Dr. James Currie, the fourth William Rathbone (merchant) and Dr. John Rutter met together for business, dinner and conversation.[48]

The Athenaeum is a delightful haven in the heart of Liverpool, "offering a distinguished setting and an atmosphere unrivalled in the city".[49] It was founded in 1797 to provide a meeting place where ideas and information could be exchanged in pleasant surroundings. Today the Athenaeum continues to provide this facility in the elegant building erected near the Bluecoat Chambers in Church Alley. In addition to its newsroom the Athenaeum has a library, dining room and a smaller meeting room. The heart of the Athenaeum is its library. In 1848, Washington Irving wrote, "One of the first places to which a stranger is taken in Liverpool is the Athenaeum; it contains a good library and a spacious reading room and is the great literary resource of the place".[50]

The library has approximately 60,000 volumes dating from the thirteenth century to the present. Most of the material may be borrowed by members. The collection is particularly strong in classical and other literatures, theology, history, biography and travel. There is a good section on local history which includes manuscripts, maps, playbills and some prints and drawings. Areas of note are books from the library of William Roscoe, eighteenth-century plays, bound volumes of economic and other pamphlets and local directories.

The Lancashire Authors' Association (LAA) Library

The Lancashire Authors' Association (LAA) was formed in November 1909,[51] but it wasn't until after the First World War had ended that serious thought was given to creating a collection of books on or by Lancashire authors. The association's Southport meeting, on 25 June 1921, devoted some time to discussing the need for a library. The LAA's vice-president, Major David Halstead, initiated a discussion on the need to "devote attention to the collection and compilation of historical and literary data", for the benefit of future historians. His comments were echoed by Thomas Phillips of Southport, "who urged the Association to form a Library of Lancashire books, pamphlets, etc. written by LAA members and others". The executive decided to pursue the library project "with vigour".[52]

The next full meeting of the association, held at the Railway Mechanics' Institute, Horwich, on 17 September, formally agreed to establish an LAA Library. R.H. ('Harry') Isherwood was elected as Librarian. In Mr Isherwood's report to the committee he said that the main objectives of the library would be: "To provide a collection of the literary and artistic work of L.A.A. members (past, present and prospective) for the interest and inspection of their fellows" and "To provide a collection of books, prints, cuttings etc., on matters distinctly pertaining to the literary, artistic and historical aspects of Lancashire, whether written by LAA members or others."[53]

He added an appeal for the donation of books and other manuscripts. He said that the LAA Executive Committee was keen to celebrate the works of the classic dialect writers such as Tim Bobbin, Waugh and Brierley, but that other writers including Harrison Ainsworth, Mrs Gaskell and Stanley Houghton should also be included.

The library was to be located at the librarian's home, which was then 29 Greenside Lane, Droylsden, literally a few doors away from

Alf and Edith Pearce, who were at number 23. Alf was editor of *The Record* and Edith was 'editress' of the association's *Circulating Magazine* and the LAA magazine *Red Rose Leaves*.[54] By early 1922 the library's collection comprised over 200 books. This was augmented further by the donation of fifty books from the late J.T. Baron's collection. These had been purchased from Baron's estate by LAA member J.W. Cryer who then donated them to the library.

By the following year the library had increased to 350 volumes. Getting a comprehensive catalogue of the collection had become a major challenge, but one was issued in May 1923. From then on, the story of the library is one of incremental growth, with donations of books by authors of their own work, and other contributions. The librarian brought a 'touring library' to each meeting of the association, using his car. However, it was becoming increasingly difficult to keep the growing collection in a private home and the association was on the lookout for suitable premises.

The breakthrough came during 1932. At the Manchester 'business meeting' held on 10 December 1932, Harry was sad to report that borrowings had been even fewer. However, there was a glimmer of hope. A new reference library was under construction in central Manchester and was due for completion in 1934. The new facility would house many special collections which, Harry suggested, he hoped would include the LAA's. The ensuing discussion showed strong support for the move to Manchester 'Ref'. However, it was hoped that members would still be able to order books by post as well as borrow them from the library.

The next year's business meeting, on 9 December at Pegg's cafe in Manchester, heard some positive news. Manchester's Library Committee had approved the move and had allocated space for the LAA collection in the new reference library, which was approaching completion. The collection would be housed in its own room, which members would have full access to and could be used for meetings. Manchester Reference Library would provide the necessary shelving and tables at its expense. At the next year's business meeting, Harry was able to report that the collection was now housed in Manchester Reference Library. He reported that "all the books are accessible to the general public on the same conditions as other books of the reference library, but are not loaned out, except to LAA members upon showing the recognised ticket. Should at any time the Association be dissolved the books would become the property of the Libraries Committee who also undertake to insure and keep in good repair all deposited books."

The annual report of the Manchester Public Libraries Committee for 1934–5 was able to report that, "important additions to the department this year include … the Lancashire Authors' Association Library: a deposit collection of 898 volumes mainly concerned with the literature (particularly the dialect) of the county". Crucially, it went on to add that "those libraries which have been deposited as a permanent loan are still the property of the respective Associations, and members of these Associations have the special privilege of being able to borrow books from their own collections for home reading, even if they are not residents of Manchester".

The successful transfer of the LAA Library to Manchester Reference Library in 1934 was a major step forward for the association. Members were able to borrow books from the collection on proof of membership and members of the public were allowed to consult the collection on a 'reference only' basis. Books could be posted to members on payment of postage, and members could borrow books at local libraries through 'inter-library loans'. Harry Isherwood, the Librarian since the very beginnings in 1921, had much to be proud of. A collection of regional literature totalling nearly 900 items was without parallel in the UK.

At the Bolton meeting on 4 December 1936, George Wormleighton was elected Librarian to succeed Harry Isherwood. George was stepping into some very large shoes but he carried out his duties with great verve and enthusiasm. He was a Salford lad, born in 1909, and left school at the age of 14 to work in an accountants' office.[55]

Despite the horrors of the war, which included heavy bombing of Manchester, the library continued to function—a remarkable testament to the staff of Manchester Central Library. Some duplicate copies of books in the collection were donated to Liverpool's Central Library to replace stock which had been destroyed during the city's Blitz. The LAA also agreed that where books were in triplicate the third copies would be offered to the Lancashire Library in Preston.

During 1953 the association met in Manchester Public Library. The large gathering, numbering over a hundred, was received by the Lord Mayor, Alderman Abraham Moss, and took time to visit the LAA Special Collection, which now comprised over 1,300 volumes. However, the arrangement with Manchester Central Library came to an end and the collection was moved to Accrington Public Library, which formed part of Lancashire County Council's library service. The numbers using the collection dwindled.

In early 2020 the possibility of locating the collection at the University of Bolton was raised and the LAA recognised the advantages of being part of an academic community that could encourage students to make use of the collection, which by now stood at over 2,000 books and manuscripts. The LAA's annual meeting, held in Chorley in March 2020, voted to transfer the collection, and its ownership, to the University of Bolton. Despite the difficulties of Covid-19, agreement was reached between Lancashire Libraries, the LAA and the University of Bolton and several boxes of books were transferred across to Bolton during 2021. The legal agreement transferring ownership to the University of Bolton, and protecting the integrity of the collection, was signed in March 2022. It is now open to members of the LAA, university staff and students, as well as the general public by appointment. After the decision taken in Horwich in 1921 to create the library, it is now 'back home' in Bolton, as a special collection that constitutes the largest archive of regional literature, as well as dialect writing, in the UK.

7

LANCASTRIANS AT WORK

King Cotton

It all started here. Lancashire became the powerhouse of the British Empire. Cotton dominated Lancashire for the best part of two centuries and its legacy is still clearly felt. The Lancashire 'cotton story' was taught to most Lancashire school children as a list of inventions, great men, the fact it rained a lot, and we were near the sea to export finished cotton and import raw.

Some 'facts' are of course undeniable, but the story is much more complicated, and still hotly debated—both why the cotton industry grew so massively and why its decline was so rapid and complete. It's worth looking at the arguments without dwelling too much on them—there are important stories to tell about the people who worked in the industry and the 'culture' it gave rise to, which has been far less written about.

Lancashire had a textile industry as far back as the sixteenth century, possibly even earlier. It was a domestic industry, often carried on alongside farming. It involved all members of the family—typically the man doing the weaving, the woman spinning and the children helping out.[1] It supplemented the meagre earnings to be made from the land. Something started to happen in the mid-eighteenth century when demand within England grew for textile goods. This may have been a result of the restrictions placed on Indian imported textiles.[2]

The availability of capital was critical in the growth of a Lancashire cotton industry. Again, we have to be careful about over-playing the 'self-made man' thesis. Many of the early cotton manufacturers were already rich landowners with spare capital to invest. The number of truly 'self-made' artisans was really quite small, though there are always exceptions to every rule.[3] Certainly, the availability of skilled labour was of great importance.

Technology did play an important role. The spinning inventions of Hargreaves, Arkwright and Crompton revolutionised the spinning process, but weaving lagged behind. A huge labour force in the weaving sector rapidly emerged and declined with equal speed, between around 1780 and 1850. This, however, masks the specialisation within weaving. Highly decorative cloth was still being woven on handlooms at the end of the nineteenth century, though the weavers were a rapidly diminishing band, down to two or three individuals in places like Bolton and Darwen.

A corps of highly skilled handloom wavers emerged in the second half of the eighteenth century, proficient not only in specialised weaving using Jacquard and Dobby looms, but often well-versed in mathematics, botany, music and literature. Spinning evolved, based on Samuel Crompton's 'mule' which was originally designed to be operated by hand—relying not only on skill, but strength. By the middle of the nineteenth century, gender roles had been reversed, with women coming to predominate in weaving, once it had been mechanised. Men reigned supreme in the spinning room; mule spinning became the preserve of a distinct class of men—the spinners who built up a highly privileged position based on strong trades unions. This wasn't to the cotton manufacturers' liking and they encouraged the development of the 'self-acting' spinning mule which was easier and lighter to operate. Potentially, the work could be done by women, at lower wages. Yet through determined collective action the men retained their supremacy in cotton spinning, creating a 'closed shop' that was extremely difficult to penetrate without the agreement of the men who became known as 'minders'.

Queens of cotton

In 1930 the most widely circulated regional newspaper in the country, the Manchester *Daily Dispatch*, launched a competition to find the first 'Cotton Queen of Great Britain'. The title was created to improve the fortunes of the ailing British cotton trade through the selection of a 'beautiful young woman' as an official representative of the industry.

Rebecca Conway researched the history of the industrial 'queens': "The Cotton Queen was carefully constructed to embody both the mill girl and the modern young working woman as a spokesperson for her industry, a fashion expert, and as a figure that could be deployed by advertisers to connect with consumers in Lancashire. This study provides valuable new insight into the significance of beauty contests in inter-war England and makes a new contribution to the body of research on the young fashioned female worker in this period."[4]

Between 2019 and 2020 The University of Bolton, Blackburn College and Bolton at Home developed a community arts project to explore a forgotten part of Lancashire's history. The *Cotton Queens* project included the production of a film and other stories about the lives of women cotton workers—both in the mills and also on holiday in Blackpool during the 1920s and 1930s.[5]

Women find their union voice

Women had been almost entirely excluded from trades unions up until the emergence of 'new unionism' in the 1880s and had virtually no involvement in formal politics. We have already come across Margaret Lahee of Rochdale, who clearly had a strong interest in radical politics and wrote a biography of the Rochdale Chartist Tom Livsey; but there are few other examples of working-class women being politically active much before the 1880s, following the end of Chartism.

Women textile workers were amongst the first to become organised, notably the weavers in east Lancashire, many of whom joined their local associations as early as the 1870s. Alice Foley, a Bolton weaver and socialist of the 'Clarion' generation, was one of the first to 'make it', after a long struggle against male prejudice. She was appointed to the staff of the powerful Bolton Weavers' Association in 1930. From 1949 until 1961 she was secretary of the association, one of the most powerful jobs in the textile unions.[6]

* * *

Lancastrians: Alice Foley 1891–1974

Alice was born in 1891 in Bolton. Her family, of Irish working-class origins, were poor but were keen readers. She learned to read at an early age and retained a great interest in learning and adult education throughout her life. Her father's belief in education meant that she did not become a half-timer but remained in school until 13 when she left for a full-time job. After trying shop work she went into the mill as a tenter (a weaver's assistant).

Like Alice Collinge and Sarah Reddish, she was involved in the socialist movement of the town, including the Labour Church and the Socialist Sunday School. In the years before the First World War she joined the Clarion Cycling Club. As she recalled, "I joined the Clarion Cycling Club and a new era of fun and comradeship opened out. In merry company we slogged up hills and freewheeled joyously down them thrilling to the beauty and excitement of a countryside as yet unspoiled by the advent of motor transport."

In 1912 Alice got a job with the Amalgamated Weavers Union as a 'sick visitor' for union members. Five years later, the assistant general secretary of the union resigned. The executive decided not to replace him but made Alice a temporary clerk doing the job normally done by the assistant secretary. This involved helping members to understand their wage packets, based on highly complex calculations, as well as negotiating with employers.

When the war ended in 1918, the executive decided that they needed to appoint a permanent assistant general secretary. The recruitment procedure was based on a demanding written examination; out of six candidates, one got 72%, the nearest rival managed 38%. The executive never revealed who got the highest score but decided not to appoint! The suspicion was that Alice got the top score but wasn't appointed because she was female. The following year the executive again raised the issue of an assistant general secretary. This time they announced that no applications would be accepted from women members! Alice, in her own words, "plodded on".

She was elected to Bolton Trades Council, became a magistrate and was active within the Co-op and the Workers Educational Association. In 1942 the Assistant position became vacant again. This time, rather than appoint her, the committee made her 'Chief Women's Officer'. Finally, in 1948, the retirement of the then general secretary resulted in the appointment of Alice to the top job. Her persistence finally paid off, but what a wait! In 1950 she was awarded an MBE and ten years later Manchester University honoured her with an MA for her contribution to adult education.

* * *

The transition to 'the factory system' was prolonged and difficult for many of those affected. The huge army of handloom weavers that had emerged following the rapid growth of demand through the abundance of spun cotton was plunged into abject poverty by the 1840s. Those who could, escaped to other jobs. Many survived on the brink of starvation whilst a very small number of skilled handloom weavers carried on, often providing highly specialised weaving for major firms well into the late nineteenth century, if not after.[7]

The story of how the male mule spinners succeeded in heading off this threat is fascinating. They ensured that women were kept out of mule spinning and, with only minor exceptions,[8] that stayed the position until the ultimate end of mule spinning by the early 1970s.[9]

The half-time system

If you were a boy or girl growing up in Rochdale, Bolton, Oldham or Blackburn in 1900, there would be a strong chance that from the age of 12 you'd go to work as a 'half-timer' in the mills. The other half of the day would be spent at school. It was widespread across many industries but was most endemic in textiles.[10]

The system came into force in the 1830s, as a progressive measure to limit the employment of children as young as 5 or 6. Child labour was particularly prevalent in the booming industrial towns of Lancashire and Yorkshire. It was not uncommon for children to work 12-hour shifts or longer and the accident rate was horrific. The government stepped in to regulate child labour with legislation in 1833 and then by the Factory Act of 1844. The hours that a child could work were dropped to eight hours a day. Children between the ages of 8 and 13 would be expected to attend school for three hours each weekday, either before or after lunch.

Although the half-time system applied to the country as a whole, it was most widespread in Lancashire. In 1892 Lancashire had 93,969 children working half-time, compared to less than a hundred in Bedfordshire, Berkshire, Middlesex, Norfolk and Shropshire. Yorkshire had the next highest total with just under 45,000, followed by Cheshire (including the cotton towns of Stalybridge, Stockport and Hyde) having nearly 10,000. Bolton had just under 6,000 half-timers, accounting for about half of all the children aged between 8 and 13. Blackburn had nearly 8,000 and Oldham just over 6,000. Most worked in the cotton industry. Lancashire (and the textile districts of Cheshire) dominated the figures for children's employment in the 1890s. The report of the Schools Inspectorate for the year ended 31 August 1892 showed that out of a total of 172,363 children working half-time, no less than 93,969 were in Lancashire and 9,684 in Cheshire. Yorkshire had the next largest concentration with 44,791 'half-time scholars'.[11]

The half-time system was not compulsory; parents had the option of keeping their children at school full-time until they reached 13—or longer if they could afford the fees. In reality, most Bolton working-class parents valued the extra income which their sons and daughters brought—in the 1890s a half-timer's weekly wage was about 10 shillings (or 50p in today's money). A feature of employment in cotton spinning was that 'the minder'—the 'operative' cotton spinner who managed the spinning mules—was the employer of the half-timer. Typically, a 'minder' in one of the big Bolton mills would employ a 'side piecer' (sometimes called a 'big piecer') and a little piecer, who would often be a half-timer; the little piecer's job was to help the minder 'piece up' broken threads but also to keep the machinery clean. Sometimes the three-person team would be a family unit, with dad employing his sons. In weaving sheds, most of the workers were women, apart from the overlookers (or 'tacklers').

Mule spinning remained an exclusively male preserve well into the twentieth century, though Heaton's Mills in Lostock was the exception to the rule, employing women in spinning from the early 1900s. In the weaving sheds, an experienced weaver, usually tending four looms, would have the help of a tenter—often a young girl. The relationship between the weaver and her tenter was often a close one, almost a mother-daughter relationship, which in some cases it actually was. However, many girls were less fortunate and suffered from bullying and sexual harassment by the male overlookers.

Life for a half-timer was not easy, though if you were part of a family unit it helped alleviate some of the worst features. But there was no getting away from the punishingly long hours children had to endure. Dr John Johnston, the Bolton GP,[12] described a half-timer's day in *The Wastage of Child Life*:

> Let us look at the day's work of a little 'half-time' girl. It begins at five o'clock in the morning with the ran-tan-tan of the 'knocker-up' with his long wand on the bedroom window. 'It's five o'clock Mary Jane', calls the father; 'get up!' Reluctantly and with a struggle against Nature's demands for a little more rest, Mary Jane tumbles out of bed and gropes her way down the dark stairs into the cold kitchen where she picks up her meagre breakfast of tea and sugar screwed up into a smoke-grimed can. But not now may she have breakfast—that is yet nearly three hours off, and will be taken in the mill. Throwing her shawl over her shoulders she hurries out into the street where she meets her companions … now the streets are alive with men, women and children hurrying along to the calls of hooters, sirens, bells and whistles all clanging and shrieking to them to make haste—for steam is up and it is nearly six o'clock; and woe betide the half-timer if, by the overseer's watch, she is a few minutes late![13]

Work stops for a half-hour breakfast and then the grind continues until 12.30. Mary Jane and her friends rush home for a quick dinner before going to school. "And this," says Dr Johnston, "with weekly alternations of work and school, is the daily life of the little 'half-time' child of twelve."

Conditions inside the mills and weaving sheds were physically dangerous, noisy and extremely hot. Children were expected to crawl under moving machinery, even though it was technically illegal. The practice of 'sweeping under' was described by Allen Clarke in *The Effects of the Factory System*:

> It consists in sweeping, with a short brush, the space between the advancing and receding mule-carriage and the base-work creel. The mule carriage slowly draws out for two or three yards, then suddenly rushes back like the shutting of a lid, and the piecer has to slip out of the way in 'half a jiffy'.[14]

167

Accidents while 'sweeping under' were common. Clarke notes that 172 serious accidents occurred in the Bolton mills alone for the first quarter of 1890.

As well as the risk of physical injury—typically the loss of an arm or hand through to death—there was the longer-term impact of working in the hot stifling atmosphere of the spinning room or weaving shed. Many local doctors, including Johnston as well as colleagues in neighbouring towns, pointed to the literal stunting of growth of children working 'half-time' in the mills, compared with their pals who were at school full-time. Half-time children's performance at school was noticeably worse than their full-time colleagues.

From the early 1890s there was a growing clamour to end the system. The National Union of Teachers was at the forefront of the campaign, led by Richard Waddington, headmaster at Bolton's St James' National School. They were supported by the fledgling socialist parties—the Social Democratic Federation and the Independent Labour Party. In 1892 Joseph Shufflebotham was elected to the Bolton School Board on a socialist ticket and campaigned to improve conditions for half-timers at school. Mary Haslam, one of the first female Poor Law Guardians in Bolton and wife of a wealthy cotton spinner, was a vigorous opponent of the half-time system.

Some of the strongest opposition to ending the system came from the textile unions. The loss of the children's earnings would have affected the family income, though it has to be said that a 'minder' was one of the most highly paid workers in British industry, earning (in Bolton) 38 shillings a week in the mid-1890s. Some of the half-timers themselves preferred working in the mill to school, though few liked getting up at five in the morning!

The system was finally abolished by the Education Act of 1918, bringing a long, sad episode of Lancashire's history to a close. Several half-timers went on to become nationally famous politicians. The Oldham 'little piecer' J.R. Clynes became a cabinet minister in the 1924 Labour government. George Tomlinson, who spent part of his childhood working half-time in a Rishton mill, was elected MP for Farnworth in 1938 and became Minister of Education in the post-war Labour government. He was commemorated by the naming of 'George Tomlinson' school in Kearsley after his death in 1962. It is now called 'Kearsley Academy'.

Where is the monument to 'the poor little half-timer'?

* * *

Lancastrians: William Hesketh Lever 1851–1925

William Hesketh Lever—later to become Baron Leverhulme of Bolton-le-Moors—is one of the most important figures in Lancashire history. There is no doubt that he was a great benefactor to Bolton and a pioneer of good quality 'social housing', the six-hour working day and a strong believer in women's equality. But there was a dark side to his career, most obviously in his company's activities in the Belgian Congo, but also his attempt to eradicate the way of life of the crofting people on Lewis and Harris.

He was born at 16 Wood Street, just off Bradshawgate, in 1851. The fine Georgian building remains and has been home to the Bolton Socialist Club since 1905, ironic in view of Lever's lifelong Liberal beliefs. He inherited the parental Nonconformity and was a member of Bolton Congregational Church. He went into the family grocery business and quickly excelled as a businessman and marketeer, expanding the family business to Wigan and elsewhere. He developed the 'Sunlight' brand of soap which became a household name. Its fame spread from Bolton to the whole of the British Empire. It made him enormously rich. He developed his own garden city on the banks of the Mersey, which he called 'Port Sunlight'. It was a model community with good quality housing and social and educational facilities for his workers and their families.

There was a price to pay if you were one of Lever's employees. The secretary of the Bolton Engineers' Union wrote to him saying, "no man of an independent turn of mind can breathe for long the atmosphere of Port Sunlight ... the profit-sharing system not only enslaves and degrade the workers, it tends to make them servile and sycophant, it lowers them to the level of machines tending machines".

There is no doubt that Lever expected complete subservience from his workforce, though he did accept trades unions in his factories. One union negotiator described him as a 'martinet' while other colleagues quickly realised that there was only one right way of doing things—his way.

This inability to compromise was to cost him dearly, with his ill-conceived plans to transform the Hebridean islands of Harris and Lewis into modern industrial communities, dragging the crofting people out of poverty and providing them with good housing and sanitation. He purchased the two islands in 1918 and set about his ambitious plans with gusto. The only problem was that the crofters were quite happy with their traditional way of life, and just wanted to own their own small plots of land—which they resorted to guerrilla tactics to achieve. Within five years his plans were in tatters and the huge investment was wasted. The irony was that if Lever had listened to what the islanders were asking, his own ambitions could probably have been reconciled with theirs.

Lever's role in the Belgian Congo and Solomon Islands was even more problematic, where the same tendency to exert total control—even if it was 'for your own good', as he would have seen it—caused him to become embroiled in the use of forced labour to coerce African workers to produce the palm oil essential for his soap manufacturing process. The coercion involved violence and imprisonment of workers and their families, leading to questions being asked in the Belgian Parliament, which had initially welcomed Lever's investment.

At home, Lever—Baron Leverhulme of Bolton-le-Moors from 1917—never lost his links with Bolton. He was elected mayor of the town in 1918 and a few years earlier produced a remarkable vision for 'Bolton as it is and as it might be', crafted by the landscape architect Thomas Mawson.[15] Most of his ideas never saw the light of day, but what did was his lasting legacy to the people of Bolton: the Rivington Estate and Lever Park. He saved Hall i' th' Wood, where Samuel Crompton invented the spinning mule, from decay and probable destruction and gifted it to the people of Bolton. He died in 1925 and in his will provided for the establishment of the Leverhulme Trust, which continues to support a vast range of research and educational projects.

William Lever: saint or sinner? Let history judge.

* * *

Queen Coal

Coal mining was an important Lancashire industry, an integral part of the Industrial Revolution in the North. It fed the mills, factories and loco sheds when steam power drove industry. Coal mining in Lancashire goes back centuries. In some of the big cotton spinning centres of south-east Lancashire coal mining was important but not dominant. In 1538 the traveller John Leland commented on the burning of coal and turf in the area. Wigan was the centre of

Lancashire mining. Major companies such as Wigan Coal and Iron dominated the industry.

In east Lancashire and Rossendale the pits were small and served a mainly local market—typically the local weaving sheds which had a voracious appetite for coal to feed the boilers which powered the mills.

As Lancashire's mills and factories expanded in the early nineteenth century, the demand for coal was insatiable. Lancashire's first public railway, the Bolton and Leigh, opened in 1828 and one of its main functions was to bring coal from the Leigh and Atherton pits to Bolton. The bigger collieries were owned by major landowners, such as the Duke of Bridgewater, the Earl of Balcarres, the Hultons and Fletchers. Andrew Knowles, born in Turton, started his mining career running the small family pit near Edgworth but expanded into large-scale deep-mining in the richer coalfields around Farnworth and Salford in the mid-nineteenth century. Many of the coal companies merged in 1929 to form Manchester Collieries Ltd.

In 1880 the Mines Inspector reported a total of 534 coal pits in the Lancashire coalfield. Mining was concentrated in the 'Greater Wigan' area, including Leigh, St Helens and Ashton-in-Makerfield. However, there were outliers in the Bolton area, Oldham, Rossendale and north-east Lancashire. Coal mining survived at Bank Hall Colliery, Burnley, until the early 1970s.

Life down the pit was hard and dangerous. Explosions and roof collapses were frequent and conditions were appalling. Children and women were still working underground until it was outlawed in 1842. Women continued working on the surface—the 'pit brow lasses'—until much later (see below).

Lancashire experienced one of the worst disasters in British mining history. On 21 December 1910, the Pretoria Pit, Westhoughton, blew up. A total of 344 men and boys perished. An earlier disaster on 12 March 1878 occurred at Unity Brook Colliery, between Kearsley and Clifton, when 43 miners were killed. Both events are commemorated to this day by their local communities and schools. These were not isolated incidents; the Unity Brook tragedy was the third of a series of major accidents occurring in the Bolton area in the mid-1870s. The Pretoria disaster is commemorated with a monument close to where the pit was. Each year there is a memorial event in Westhoughton.

Some of the companies were better employers than others. Atherton-based Fletcher, Burrows was one of the more progressive and was the first mining company in Britain to introduce pit-head baths.

One of the most remarkable engineering achievements of the industrial revolution was the network of underground canals developed in the 1760s to serve the pits on the south side of Bolton. The entry point into the system was at Worsley Court House and 'the delph' is still visible. The canals, on different levels, extended as far as Daubhill and Farnworth and are still there, abandoned, today.

After the Second World War the demand for coal continued to be high. In 1947 there were fifty-two collieries working in the Lancashire coalfield employing approximately 38,000 people.[16] The National Coal Board was formed in 1947. Several collieries had major investment, including Mosley Common, Agecroft and Parkside, near Newton-le-Willows. The older pits were closed. Astley Green Colliery, sunk in 1908, shut in 1970, is now a museum. It's well worth a visit.[17]

Industrial relations in mining improved following nationalisation. However, the industry was hit by major strikes in 1972 and again in 1974 which led to the toppling of the Heath government. It was a dress rehearsal for an even bigger conflict in 1984–5. The issue wasn't about pay, but the National Coal Board's pit closure programme, spurred on by the Thatcher government. The National Union of Mineworkers leadership voted to strike but not all of the districts went along with the decision, the traditionally moderate Lancashire area being one that didn't.[18] The strike was long and bitter. Ultimately the Coal Board, backed by the Thatcher government which demonised the miners as 'the enemy within', won.

The programme of pit closures accelerated and by January 1986 only six pits were left in the Lancashire coalfield, employing 5,500 workers. The last were Agecroft, Bickershaw, Parsonage, Golborne, Parkside and Sutton Manor. Bold Colliery closed in November 1985. However, within a few miles of Bolton and Salford some of the biggest and most modern pits of the Lancashire coalfield (Agecroft, Parkside, Sutton Manor, Bickershaw/Parsonage, Golborne) lasted into the early 1990s.

The pit brow lasses

Women's employment in the pits was made illegal in 1842. However, in some areas it remained common for women to be employed as surface workers. This excited the interests of some middle-class philanthropists such as Lionel Munby.[19] A fascinating account of life as a 'pit brow lass' in 1900 has survived from Mrs P. Holden who worked at Duxbury Park Colliery near Adlingon from the age of 13:

> I had three miles every morning to go to my work, so it tied me to get up every morning at 4 o'clock, as I did odd jobs about the house, before setting off for my work, at 5 o'clock. I had to travel down Hoggs Lane, and it was very unpleasant to travel alone … I met other Pit Brow lasses for company, at bottom of Hoggs Lane to Pit as there was about ten lassies from Chorley. I did it for ten years, in all sorts of weather … I set off with my basket on my arm, and a full can of tea in my hand. I wore a red head-wrap, tied around my head, to keep the coal dust out of my hair, then a nice shoulder shawl thrown over my head wrap. I wore a black velvet blouse, and a blue striped Pit Skirt. I made my own Pit brat (apron) out of Irish linen. I wore a man's jacket to come home in, also pit breeches as well. I took a pride in my clogs, they shone like a raven.[20]

It's a very moving and important story. I find it particularly emotional as my own family were miners in Adlington, slightly earlier than when Mrs Holden was a pit brow lass, but they lived nearby.

Lancashire women against pit closures

Perhaps the most dramatic postscript to the final end of coal mining in Lancashire was the Parkside pit camp between 1992 and 1994. 'Women Against Pit Closures' emerged during the 1984–5 miners' strike. WAPC included partners of striking miners and many other women, from the trades union movement and Left, who supported the strike. Following the end of the strike, Lancashire had only a handful of pits remaining—Parkside, near Newton-le-Willows, Agecroft in Salford and the Leigh pits of Bickershaw and Sutton Manor near St Helens. By 1992 only Parkside remained—a modern pit that only a couple of years earlier had been described by the leader of the local council as "rich and efficient and will continue to provide employment for our people and energy for our country".[21] Only weeks before the closure, Parkside had broken output records.

The Lancashire area of the National Union of Mineworkers staged demonstrations against the closure, but it was not until early in 1993 that Lancashire Women Against Pit Closures set up a 'Greenham Common-style' protest at the colliery entrance. The camp had two caravans with modest catering facilities, portable toilets and running water. The camp aimed to draw attention to the fight to keep the pit open (one of thirty-one threatened with closure across the country) and build support.

On 9 April 1993, four members of the camp decided to take the protest further—and deeper. Elaine Evans, Dot Kelly, Leslie Lomas and Anne Scargill started a four-day underground occupation. They went down the pit quite officially, as members of a school visit. They refused to return to the surface and stayed below ground for four days, emerging to a heroes' welcome. Some weeks later, on 28 May, four more women occupied the 260ft high no. 1 winding tower. They continued their protest for five days, withstanding heavy rain and high winds. Further action took place during the year and in October fifty women chained themselves to the pit gates.[22]

The Parkside women featured in a play, *Queens of the Coal Age*, performed at Manchester's Royal Exchange Theatre in June/July 2018. It was written and performed by Lancashire actor and writer Maxine Peake:

> I wrote *Queens of the Coal Age* because I wanted to shine a light on Anne, Lesley, Elaine and Dot's determination and bravery, their ingenuity and passion. These four extraordinary women did something ... they took direct action. I didn't want their protest to be forgotten. I wanted to celebrate their efforts ... We still have a fight in us and we won't roll over, and the Queens are for me champions of that—four fearless women who stood up to be counted.[23]

The engineers

While coal mining in Lancashire initially developed to serve the steam-powered mills in nearby towns, Lancashire's engineering industry was similarly indebted to 'King Cotton' for his largesse. All of the main engineering concerns that emerged in the early nineteenth century were based on textile machinery for the home market. And 'home' was very close to home indeed, with the biggest engineering companies being based in Oldham (Platt Brothers), Manchester (Mather and Platt) and Bolton (Dobson and Barlow).

Just as cotton quickly became a world industry, helped by Britain having the most powerful and extensive empire in the world, so too was engineering able to expand abroad, though some of its main customers were outside the empire—Russia and the United States in particular.

Platt's of Oldham became the largest textile engineering company in Lancashire by the end of the nineteenth century. It's a story of very humble beginnings on the rural outskirts of Oldham in the late eighteenth century. It starts with Henry Platt, a blacksmith who started manufacturing carding equipment, in Dobcross, Saddleworth. His grandson Henry founded a similar business in Uppermill before moving to larger premises on Huddersfield Road, Oldham, going into partnership with Elijah Hibbert. The firm became Hibbert Platt and Sons, and later Platt Brothers and Co. By 1872 the company employed 7,000 men and had established itself as the world's largest textile machinery manufacturer. They produced thousands of the ubiquitous Lancashire Looms which wove cotton in weaving sheds not just across Lancashire but all over the world. Ironically, when the Lancashire cotton industry went into decline many of the looms were exported to developing countries to further undercut Lancashire cotton.

By the 1890s it was estimated that the works supported 42% of Oldham's population. The company expanded to become a worldwide business, dominating textile engineering in Russia and having major markets in the USA and elsewhere. They also owned coal mines in the Oldham area. The company reached its peak shortly before the First World War, with its workforce numbering more than 15,000 people. Hartford Works was the largest employer in Oldham and the largest maker of textile machinery in the world. The works were visited by George V and Queen Mary on the first day of their eight-day 1913 Royal Tour of Lancashire on 7 July 1913.

The unusual structure of the Oldham cotton industry, based on joint stock companies, gave encouragement to many of Platt's employees to take shares in local mills and use their power as share-holders to encourage the mills to buy Platt's machinery!

Mather and Platt (not to be confused with Platt's of Oldham, above) was another major textile engineering company. Its origins go back to Salford in 1817 when Peter Mather set up shop making textile machinery, specialising in bleaching. He went into partnership with John Platt and established a factory at Newton Heath in 1845 and began developing overseas markets, particularly the United States and Russia. Towards the end of the century they expanded into electrical engineering and built one of the earliest underground locomotives in 1890. The firm moved to what became its permanent site at Park, near Newton Heath a few years later. The first machine shop was originally the Machinery Annexe of the Paris Exhibition of 1900. Mather and Platt's staff dismantled it and shipped it to Manchester via the Manchester Ship Canal, then re-erected it. The site expanded over the years, eventually incorporating a research laboratory, an iron foundry and a sports ground.

Dobson and Barlow became the predominant engineering company in the Bolton area. However, other companies such as Hick Hargreaves were major players in what became a world market for textile machinery. In the north-east of the county, several major textile engineering firms developed. The most notable was Howard and Bullough in Accrington. However, Burnley and Nelson had major engineering firms which supplied both the local mills and further afield in what was a highly competitive market.

Lino and sailcloth: rivalry and retribution

Lancaster had a flourishing linoleum industry, developed by James Williamson, who became Lord Ashton. There was a related business in fabric and sail cloth which was owned by the Storey family; therein hangs a tale.

Storey worked for Williamson for a short time before the two parted company, with William Storey starting his own company, Storey Brothers. They became sworn rivals of the Williamsons, latter-day Montagues and Capulets. It was economic, political, and, it seems, very personal.

By 1894, Williamson was employing 2,500 men and Storey about 1,000. Both saw themselves as philanthropists, though in the case of Lord Ashton it came at a price. In 1909 the Independent Labour Party put up a candidate against him in the Skerton ward and came very close to winning. Two years later, at another municipal election in the same ward, there was a tied vote between the ILP and Lord Ashton's Liberal nominee, John Turvey. The mayor, as the returning officer, gave the casting vote to Turvey. Less than a week later, notices were posted at the works, saying that advances in wages that had been agreed would not now take place. The notice also stated that: "in future employees would not be kept on at times of coal or railway strikes…" and "…that when times were bad, only men loyal to the firm, would be kept on and we shall not, as in the past, keep those who are bereft of all sense of what is due not only to their employer, but to themselves".[24] Lord Ashton also declined to make any further contributions to Lancaster charities, buildings or public events.

When I was a student at Lancaster I remember being told by an elderly former employee that Ashton gave his employees a celebratory tin of chocolate on a special occasion. Some of the workers scoffed the chocolates and then defecated in the tins which they threw over the wall of his lordship's residence.

The Storey family has a less controversial history. They helped to fund several projects around Lancaster including the Westfield Memorial Village, for First World War veterans. Thomas Storey provided the funding for the Storey Institute, opened in 1891 for 'the promotion of art, science, literature, and technical instruction'. It continues to the present day as a lively and progressive arts venue.

The union made us strong

It's surprising that a regional history of trade unionism in Lancashire has never been attempted. Perhaps the subject is too big, but it would lend itself well to a collaborative project. It's easy to forget that most trade unions, particularly in Lancashire and Yorkshire, were primarily regional, and sometimes local, organisations. This was particularly true in textiles but also in coal mining.

The Lancashire miners made spasmodic attempts to form unions from the 1830s. The Friendly Society of Coalmining was formed in Bolton in 1830. Unions were strongly resisted by the owners and it wasn't until the second half of the nineteenth century that trade unionism put down lasting roots. One of the most outstanding figures in Lancashire mining trades unionism was Thomas Halliday, a Little Lever miner who struggled to bring together a number of small, localised unions into one strong body. Eventually, the Lancashire and Cheshire miners became part of the Miners' Federation of Great Britain, later the National Union of Mineworkers. They chose Bolton as its headquarters, with a fine building designed by local firm Bradshaw Gass and Hope and opened in 1914 on Bridgeman Place. The building survives, owned by Greater Manchester Chamber of Commerce.

The railway workers were organised into national unions, partly on sectional lines. There were early attempts to combine amongst workers on the Liverpool and Manchester Railway. A strike for better pay in 1836 led to a brutal crackdown on the strikers with several being imprisoned in Kirkdale jail and forced onto the inhuman treadmill.

It was not until the 1870s that unions put down roots and Lancashire was one of the first bastions of the Amalgamated Society of Railway Servants, formed in 1873. The locomotive drivers and firemen created their own society—the Associated Society of Locomotive Engineers and Firemen (ASLEF)—at a meeting in Leeds in 1880. Manchester was quick to establish a branch, followed by Liverpool and other centres.

As we've seen, women were largely excluded from trades unions up until the emergence of 'new unionism' in the 1880s. Women textile workers were amongst the first to join unions, notably the weavers in east Lancashire, many of whom joined their local associations as early as the 1870s. The card room workers quickly followed suit.

* * *

The Lancashire cotton industry became Britain's most highly unionised industry by the end of the nineteenth century. It was highly segmented, through both craft and gender. The well-paid 'operative cotton spinners' were exclusively men and they created a powerful organisation. By the 1880s, the predominantly female weaving sector was also unionised. The less-skilled card room workers, with a mix of men and women, were unionised by the 1880s.

Strikes took place but often tended to be local, reflecting local patterns of wage bargaining. The most significant early strike took place in Preston in 1842. This led to a riot in which several strikers were shot dead by the military—the event is commemorated by a fine statue in the centre of Preston, erected in 1991.

Strikes tended to be few and far between. However, the highly organised and generally stable pattern of industrial relations in the Lancashire engineering industry was rent asunder in 1887 when a relatively small dispute in Bolton escalated into a major confrontation between strikers and police when strike-breakers were brought in by train, leading to the army being called into quell further disturbances. Strike-breakers were known in Lancashire as 'knobsticks' and the events around the 1887 strike formed the basis of Allen Clarke's novel *The Knobstick*, published in 1893.[25]

In the textile industry, 'turn-outs' were not uncommon but were often confined to a particular sector and quickly resolved. However, a strike in Blackburn in 1887 over wage cuts led to serious rioting which culminated in the house of one of the employers being burnt down.

Attempts to speed up production centred on the weaving sector. From the early twentieth century, manufacturers attempted to get weavers to tend more than the standard four looms they had in their charge. A major dispute took place at Sunnyside Mills, Bolton, in 1905. The mostly female weavers struck against attempts to bring in 'patent automatic looms' that would have led to a greatly intensified process, involving one weaver minding eight looms.

The strike was long and bitter but not without its entertaining side. The Bolton-based *Teddy Ashton's Northern Weekly* ran regular stories about the dispute by 'Billy Pickinpeg' which poked fun at the attempts of the employees to bring in the hated 'knobsticks'. A short story, in dialect, was written by Allen Clarke and published as 'Th'Patent Automatic Cemetery Looms'.[26] It was a rare (but not unique) example of dialect being used to promote the workers' cause in a strike. The Sunnyside dispute was a foretaste of further conflict, particularly in the predominantly weaving districts of east Lancashire. Attempts were made to bring in more automation in the early 1930s leading to the 'More Looms' strikes of 1932 which centred on the Nelson area.

Liverpool's role in trade union history has been mixed and sometimes explosive. While the Lancashire cotton towns generally settled into a well-ordered system of industrial relations, Merseyside was largely characterised by casual labour which was usually unorganised. In 1911 what amounted to a general strike swept through Liverpool, beginning with the transport workers and extending to the docks. Large numbers of police were drafted in and a pitched battle took place in St George's Square.

During the post-Second World War years, strikes tended to be few and far between. Unions were generally successful in negotiating improved conditions and wages, on the back of post-war prosperity. While it was clear that the days of the cotton industry were coming to an end, this did not lead to any major strikes. Perhaps there was a sense of resignation that decline was inevitable and the most the unions could do was to negotiate the best redundancy terms. A similar attitude applied to the rail industry following the publication of the Beeching Report in 1963.[27] This led to the closure of much of the rail network across the North of England and the loss of tens of thousands of railway jobs. Again, the sheer scale of the cuts made a fight-back futile. As a young trade union activist in the National Union of Railwaymen, I can remember a debate in 1976 over proposals to close the large railway goods depot at Oldham. A strike was proposed but was vetoed by the union members; they just wanted their redundancy money.

There were other relatively minor disputes but the National Union of Mineworkers' struggle against pit closures was on an entirely different level. By 1984, when the strike erupted, the Lancashire coalfield had shrunk to a handful of pits. Most miners made redundant from the closure of pits, such as Mosley Common, Astley Green, Bradford and Bank Hall, had been re-deployed to the remaining pits and there was the sense that there was 'nowhere else to go' once they had closed. Despite the threat to the remaining jobs in Lancashire, the traditionally moderate Lancashire NUM, led by Sid Vincent, was against a strike. Once the national executive, led by Arthur Scargill, called the miners out, the Lancashire miners mostly went along with their area's position and stayed at work.

However, the coalfield was split with several miners at each of the pits deciding to strike. The bitterness between strikers and non-strikers was immense, though the violent scenes on the picket lines witnessed in some areas were not repeated at the Lancashire pits.

By the early 1990s all the remaining pits had gone. The Lancashire Mining Museum at Astley Green remains as a powerful reminder of an industry that helped make Lancashire a world power.

The Cotton Famine

The Lancashire Cotton Famine (1861–5) was a catastrophic event that reverberated amongst Lancashire people throughout the rest of the nineteenth century. Thousands of cotton workers were thrown out of work due to the combined effects of the American Civil War and a cyclical depression which made for a 'perfect storm'. Much has been written about the Cotton Famine (or 'Cotton Panic' as it was called at the time) and people's reactions to it. In brief, the most noticeable impact was the blockade of the American southern ports by the anti-secession forces led by Abraham Lincoln. The supply of American cotton to Lancashire dried up forcing many mills to cease production or use highly inferior Indian cotton. The effects varied in their intensity with some Lancashire towns being particularly hard hit, including Ashton-under-Lyne and Stalybridge, as well as Preston and most of the east Lancashire towns.

By November 1862, 330,759 cotton workers had been laid off and were seeking relief. One of the most important and sometimes neglected aspects of the period was that the victims were not the marginalised 'lumpen proletariat' but often relatively affluent, highly unionised spinners and weavers who were suddenly thrown into destitution. Whilst some had savings, those did not last long. Attitudes of the local Poor Law Guardians varied considerably; the most humiliating tasks given to those on relief such as oakum picking were a cause of particular resentment.

Some of the local Poor Law Guardians forced those seeking support to give up their shareholdings in co-operative societies before they could get assistance and issued relief tickets that could not be used in co-op stores. Nick Matthews said: "In many ways these slights hardened the positions of both workers and co-operators, enhancing their support for the union and accelerating progress towards the formation of the CWS to enhance the commercial strength of co-op societies."[28]

Overall, the reaction to the 'distress' was relatively muted. It was seen as an event beyond anybody's control so there were few of the collective expressions of anger that had been a feature of Chartism in the early 1840s. There were riots in Ashton and Stalybridge but they were quite localised. The middle class, or at least a section of them, organised relief schemes and sewing classes, immortalised in the poetry of Samuel Laycock and Joseph Ramsbottom (see below).

Edwin Waugh's account of life during the Cotton Famine was commissioned by the *Manchester Examiner and Times* and later published in book form as *Home Life of the Lancashire Factory Folk During the Cotton Famine*.[29] His account is in standard English though the dialogue of his characters is in the local dialect of the places he visited—Blackburn, Preston and Wigan. This use of language emphasises the social differences between Waugh, writing for a Liberal middle-class newspaper, and the subjects of his writing. His image of being a homespun, down-to-earth countryman is replaced by that of the earnest, albeit sympathetic, outside observer. His escorts during his visits tend to be of a higher social status than the unemployed workers, usually members of the relief committees, or the boards of guardians, rather than representatives of the workers themselves, such as union officials or community figures. He is clearly writing for a different type of reader from the one who devoured his dialect sketches and poems during the factory lunch break, or at working-class social events. The direction of his writing is towards the educated, middle-class Liberal whom Waugh was anxious to persuade that the Lancashire workers were decent and respectable men and women who needed all the help they could get—and, in time, greater political rights. One of his first descriptions is of a local quarry where many out-of-work textile workers were employed as stone-breakers:

> I got into talk with a quiet, hardy-looking man, dressed in a soil-stained corduroy. He was a kind of overlooker. He told me that there were from eighty to ninety factory hands employed in that quarry. 'But,' said he, 'it varies a bit, yo known. Some on 'em gets

knocked up neaw an' then, and they han to stop awhoam a day or two; an' some on 'em connot ston gettin' weet through—it mays 'em ill … We'n a decal o'bother wi 'em abeawt bein' paid for weet days, when they couldn't wortch … at last th'Board sattle't that they mut be paid for weet an' dry—an' there's bin quietness sin.'[30]

This exchange brings out the severe jolt to workers who had experienced 'leet wark, an' a warm place to wortch in', in the spinning room who now found themselves doing heavy, outdoor labour. The trade unionism of the cotton workers did not disappear when they became unemployed, for as the account shows, they were prepared to 'cause bother' when they felt they were being unfairly treated—in this case, not being paid when they were rained off.

Waugh also describes, censoriously, bricklayers going on strike in the town, and weavers refusing to go on to three, instead of two looms—with a reduction of price per piece. In Waugh's words, "some of the old blindness lingers amongst them". During Waugh's visit to Preston, he also encountered strong feelings amongst textile workers labouring in a stone yard, who demonstrated their poverty—and anger—to Waugh: "'Look at these honds!' cried another; 'We'n they ever be fit to go to th'factory wi' again?' Others turned up the soles of their battered shoon, to show their cut and stockingless feet."[31]

Attitudes towards the American Civil War varied. The myth that all of Lancashire backed the anti-slavery cause of the North has been superseded by another myth that the majority supported the South. The reality was far more complicated. In the early months of the war, and the ensuing blockade and 'famine', it's likely that most Lancashire workers initially backed the South. This began to change, spurred on by Lincoln's decree to free all American slaves. Some freed black slaves visited Lancashire on speaking tours.[32]

The Cotton Famine stimulated a huge surge of poetry and some prose, mostly in dialect. Samuel Laycock wrote his famous 'Bonny Brid' about a father addressing his newborn 'brid' (bird), born at the height of the distress:

Tha'rt welcome, littly bonny brid,
But shouldn't ha' come just when tha did;
Toimes are bad.

We're short o'pobbies for eawr Joe,
But that, of course, tha didn't know,
Did ta, lad?[33]

In Laycock's poems there are glimmers of hope. For instance, the simple pleasures of gardening are praised in 'Aw've Turned Mi Bit o' Garden O'er'. However, there was little optimism in Joseph Ramsbottom's collection of poems in *Phases of Distress*. 'Philip Clough's Tale' was one of Ramsbottom's most poignant works. An out-of-work cotton worker, clearly a part of the 'respectable' working class, is forced to demean himself by oakum-picking with less respectable members of society:

Eh! dear, what wary toimes are these,
There's nob'dy ever knew 'em wur;
For honest-wortchin' folks one sees
By scores reawnd th'Poor-law office dur.
Aw hate this pooin oakum war,
An' brekin' stones to get relief;
To be a pauper—pity's mark –
Ull break an honest heart wi grief.
We're mixt wi' th'stondin paupers, too.
Ut winno wortch when wark's to be had;
Con this be reet for them to do,
To tak no thowt o' good or bad?

Unlike Laycock's unemployed worker who still has the pleasure of turning 'his bit o' garden o'er', Ramsbottom's character has nothing to compensate poverty:

Aw've gan mi little garden up,
Wi' mony a pratty fleawr an' root;
Aw've sowd mi gronny's silver cup
Aw've sowd mi uncle Robin's flute[34]

However, the Blackburn poet William Billington did write some poetry which gave clear support for the anti-slavery North. 'Aw Wod This War Wur Ended', written in 1863, makes clear his support for the North:

Some factory maisters tokes for t'Seawth
Wi' a smooth an' oily tongue,

But iv they'd sense they'd shut their meawth,
Or sing another song;
Let liberty nod slavery
Be fostered an' extended –
Four million slaves mun yet be free,
An' then t'war will be ended.[35]

Another feature of the period was the large number of singing groups which congregated in the towns and cities, hoping to gain a few pence from those better off. In the history of co-operation in Darwen the author looks back on the Famine years and remembers a song, sung by school children coming home from class:

We're warkin lads frae Lanysheer
An' gradely daycent fooak:
We'n hunted weyvin far an' near,
A' couldn't ged a strook;
We'n sowd booath table, clock an' cheer,
An' popt booath shoon an' hat,
An' borne wod mortal man could bear,
Affoorr we'd weyve Surat![36]

In another co-op history, of the Oldham Equitable, there are similar references to the Cotton Famine and numerous quotes from Laycock's poems in which the author says: "Nowhere are these hardships and sufferings, and the fortitude and heroism they brought forth, so powerfully brought home to us as in the verses of … Samuel Laycock."[37]

Another broadsheet which appeared during the Famine was 'Short Time Come Again No More', or, 'Hard Times Come Again No More'.[38]

The mills gradually came back into production as the blockade was broken and supplies of raw cotton could get through. Yet memories lingered for decades, as shown by the co-operative society histories. The Famine, or 'Cotton Panic', continued to feature in Lancashire literature. Allen Clarke, born in 1863 at the height of the Famine, wrote a serial novel about the distress, called *The Cotton Panic*, appearing in *Teddy Ashton's Northern Weekly*. It ran for several months during 1900 and 1901.

Clarke begins the novel philosophising on how the destinies of widely differing nations and peoples are intertwined, using the example of the American war. He then goes on to relate the story of his own life, and those of other Lancashire people:

> This terrible time of starvation is not forgotten by those who endured it ... Amongst the children born in that period of poverty and suffering was the author of this story; who presents this picture of Lancashire's 'hard times' in the hope that its like may never be known again.[39]

The bitter memories of the 'cotton panic' faded in the twentieth century. Lancashire endured more 'hard times' during the depression of the 1930s and in the years after the final demise of the Lancashire cotton industry.

The University of Exeter initiated a project on 'The Poetry of the Lancashire Cotton Famine' in 2017. It has developed a database of poems written in response to the Lancashire Cotton Famine of 1861–5, along with commentary, audio recitations and musical performances drawing directly on these poems. The poems were largely sourced from newspapers—local, regional, and national—based in Lancashire, around the UK, and America. Material has also been gathered from Australia and France.[40]

The Lancashire hunger march

Many parts of Lancashire were hard hit by the depression of the 1930s, though even within 'Cotton Lancashire' the impact varied massively. Some towns within a few miles of each other fared very differently depending on their specific roles in the cotton industry. Great Harwood, which specialised in low-quality mass-produced cloth was particularly hard hit, whereas Nelson, specialising in higher-quality cloth, was less hard hit. Public assistance was organised on a county basis, by the Public Assistance Committee—a sub-committee of the county council based in Preston.

The political response from the Left was led by the Communist Party, but very often in alliance with the Independent Labour Party (ILP). The Lancashire 'hunger march' took place in 1933, organised jointly by the two parties. It was a rare example of concerted political action across Lancashire, with a precise target, the Conservative-dominated Lancashire County Council. A joint statement by Rose Smith of the Communist Party and Bob Edwards of the ILP stated:

> From 'Bonny Colne' to 'Proud Preston' they have taken the road to protest against starvation and misery, against the infamous Means Test ... Slowly the protesting masses of Youth, Women and Men, have gathered their forces along the line of the 'All Lancashire March' until they have become a mighty army assailing the County Public Assistance Committee in Preston.[41]

The marches were joint initiatives but with a strong input from the Communist Party-led National Unemployed Workers' Movement (NUWM). A deputation of sixteen, plus the Marchers Council secretary Phil Harker, were elected. They were drawn from many of the towns that had been hardest hit by unemployment: Fleetwood, Bryn, Rishton, Accrington, Haslingden, Nelson, Darwen, Oswaldtwistle, Bamber Bridge, Chorley, Tyldesley, Farnworth, Prestwich, Ashton-under-Lyne, Eccles, Heywood and Bolton.

The first march set off on 22 July and made its way through the north-east Lancashire cotton towns towards Preston, in sweltering heat. Several separate sections of the march originated in different parts of the county before two of the largest marches (from Merseyside and south-east Lancashire) joined together in Chorley. Some 600 marchers left Chorley to cheers from a large crowd with the band striking up 'The Internationale'. Two hundred marchers from east Lancashire set off from Blackburn to rally with the other marchers in Preston on Sunday 23 July.[42] The 68-year-old Selina Cooper, veteran of countless strikes and women's marches, joined the march as far as Burnley.

The previous year east Lancashire had experienced several strikes against the 'More Looms' system which led to further job cuts in weaving, as fewer weavers were required. Selina Cooper marched under a banner proclaiming 'Lancashire Hunger Marchers: Nelson and Colne. More Looms Means More Means Test; Down with the Means Test'.[43]

The account of the march stressed its broad basis, including "unemployed weavers from Nelson, Cole and the Rossendale Valley, spinners from the south-eastern cotton towns; miners from the coalfields; dockers of Merseyside bearing their glorious tradition of struggle".[44]

The march arrived in Preston to strong local support though sections of the police displayed considerable hostility. Some of the marchers' food was destroyed and a huge urn of tea was over-turned! The marchers met members of the Public Assistance Committee, which promised to form a committee to look into the marchers' grievances. Outside County Hall, a demonstration of some 15,000 unemployed and factory workers rallied in the town square. The inquiry was inconclusive, but in 1934 cuts in public assistance rates were restored; the march had achieved at least a partial victory. There were signs of improvement in the economy, though places like Great Harwood and Darwen continued to suffer. Not until the outbreak of war did jobs start to become plentiful in parts of east Lancashire.

8

LANCASTRIANS AT PLAY

RECREATION, HOLIDAYS AND THE COUNTRY

Will yo' come o' Sunday mornin'
For a walk o'er Winter Hill?
Ten thousand went last Sunday
But there's room for thousands still!
Oh there moors are rare and bonny
And the heather's sweet and fine
And the roads across the hilltops —
Are the people's—yours and mine![1]

I've always loved the moors and was lucky enough to be within cycling distance from built-up, industrialised Bolton to the Rivington and Belmont moors. I could even catch a direct bus to lovely Barrow Bridge, immortalised by Allen Clarke in *Tales of a Deserted Village* who wrote the above lines to rally support for the Winter Hill Mass Trespass of 1896. I think love of the moorlands is something that's really in the DNA of all true Lancastrians—and a willingness to fight against any incursion on our 'right to roam'. So access to the countryside is a big chunk of this chapter. So too is public parks. Again, it's personal. I used to play with mates in the tiny Great Lever Park, the only bit of green space between densely packed terraced housing, mills, mill lodges and the loco sheds. On a grander scale was Farnworth Park where my Grandma Molyneaux used to take me when Mum was working at the clothing factory.

I can accept the beauties of the Lakes, particularly 'our' part, the South Lakes. And I love municipal parks. You never know what you're going to find—small memorials to unknown 'local heroes', often middle-class philanthropists but not always. Bolton's Queen's Park has a statue to Doctor Dorian, an Irish doctor who was much loved by poor working-class people in the 1860s. There's also a monument to the union leader, John Fielding, looking suitably dapper. Women (Victoria excepted) are few and far between, but Rochdale's Broadfield Park has one side of the Lancashire Dialect Writers' Memorial dedicated to Margaret Rebecca Lahee.

People's parks

Let's start with Farnworth Park, where I spent some of my early childhood being wheeled around by my grandma. It had a boating lake and paddling pool and a rather austere war memorial to which all paths led. The land on which it stands was gifted by local mill owner, Thomas Barnes, early in the 1860s. It was a job-creation project at the height of the Cotton Famine, and opened on 12 October 1864; a red-letter day in the history of Farnworth. William Ewart Gladstone, then Chancellor of the Exchequer, was guest of honour. The town was decorated with flags on public buildings and mills. A procession started in Darley Street and proceeded to the park; the presentation ceremony was followed by a banquet held in a pavilion.[2]

Thomas Barnes spoke about his reasons for gifting the park to Farnworth:

> I have looked with considerable interest on the extension of trade but while I have seen two or three mills erected yearly, cottages springing up on every hand and the price of land rising from three farthings to two pence or three pence per yard I have felt some uneasiness as to the future state of the place and of the health of the people. I have asked myself whether it was right that we should have every inch of ground built over and not a single place left, where the tired and weary artisan could resort, to breathe the fresh air. With children growing up, with the increase of population which is taking place, I have asked myself the question, shall there not be some place for the little ones to play in safety—some place for recreational purposes? I have made up my mind—and I now make the declaration—in commemoration of my son's coming of age and

in memory of his grandfather, to lay out a portion of the Birch Hall Estate as a park and to dedicate it for these purposes and present it to the people of Farnworth for their benefit for ever.

He was careful to ensure that no unscrupulous people would try to subvert his mission, stating that, "Of course I must have some security that the land will be held in perpetuity for the enjoyment and recreation of the people and for no other purposes."

William Gladstone then told the gathered crowd that he felt it was important that people who "spend the great bulk of their time within the walls of the factory or tool shop, or any other of our great industrial establishments should have the means when their labour is done of innocent, healthful and useful recreation".[3]

* * *

Queen's Park in Heywood was created in 1879 as the result of a gift from Queen Victoria, who was, of course, head of the Duchy of Lancaster. Local landowner Charles Martin Newhouse died in 1873 in a railway accident and did not leave a will. His money and land was handed to the Duchy of Lancaster, which asked the Heywood Local Board (the local authority at the time) if it wanted to accept the land 'as a gift of the Queen'. The chairman of the Local Board, Captain Hartley, believed that the money should be spent on a 'high class school for the town of Heywood'. It was his successor, William Bell, who persuaded the Duchy to present the legacy to Heywood as a public park, to be maintained at the expense of the ratepayers of Heywood.

The park originally covered 20 acres of land, pleasantly situated adjacent to the old Heywood Hall and overlooking Crimble in the Roch Valley. The opening celebrations, on 2 August 1879, were certainly impressive. The participants represented a cross-section of Heywood society probably at the height of its prosperity. About 10,000 people took part in the procession, led by six companies of the 8th Lancashire Rifle Volunteers and their band, followed by local Sunday schools, with flags, banners and more bands. There were 4,000 marchers in the 'Nonconformist' section alone and large contingents from other schools. Behind the children were dignitaries in carriages, including the High Sheriff and Colonel

Thomas E. Taylor, MP and 'Chancellor of Her Majesty's Duchy and County Palatine', accompanied by a troop of the Duke of Lancaster's Yeomanry. As the representative of the Queen, Taylor was responsible for handing over the keys of the park to the Local Board. Serving and former members of the Heywood Local Board were next in the parade, in private carriages, followed by the 'friendly and trade societies'. The Heywood Handbell Ringers 'rang out a merry tune as they went along' and the Waterworks Department followed with their float drawn by six horses. Behind them were several horses carrying specimens of coal from various local collieries. There followed floats displaying industrial machinery of local manufacturers, including steam boilers, carding engines and woollen looms. There were also wagonloads of flour, limestone, 'bleached waste', brushes, freshly-butchered pigs, and tinplate. At the rear was a 'mounted masquerade, representing Henry VIII, Charles II, a courtier, a jester, a brigand, and a Russian bear.[4]

The streets were lined with thousands of spectators and the parade took one and a half hours to pass by. When they reached the main gates by the park-keeper's lodge, Colonel Taylor and the Heywood Local Board members entered the park and 7-year-old Bessie Hill Booth presented the gate key to Mr Taylor, who then formally handed the park over to William Bell, chairman of the Local Board, 'in the name of the Queen'.

The Heywood Advertiser was in exultant mood and told its readers that, "Never did the sun's brightest beams illuminate a fairer, a gayer, or a more brilliant scene in Heywood than was witnessed on Saturday morning. Never before was the town such a centre of attraction and interest to its numerous neighbours."[5]

The park proved popular with the people of Heywood. The town attained 'borough' status and maintained and further developed the park. During the 1920s a boating lake was added, as well as,

> a large array of newly-laid lawns and up to 25,000 shrubs, flowers, and enduring trees such as beech, horse chestnut, sycamore, and elm … there was an ornamental iron bandstand with 'dancing lawn', a bowling green and pavilion, a refreshment room, and a Tudor-style Lodge House built of stone and timber, with a red Staffordshire tiled roof.[6]

There was also a grand three-basin ornamental fountain, elaborately decorated with dolphins and swans, which remains.

The role of Park Superintendent—like that of Chief Librarian—was a responsible one and the 'Super' had to report to the Parks and Cemeteries Committee, members of which could be a tetchy bunch. They had high expectations of their parks, seeing them as examples of beauty in urban life.

Manchester's people's parks

Heywood was very much the junior partner compared with its Manchester neighbour, though I think it punched way above its weight with Queens Park. It would have been inspired by the spectacular progress Manchester had made since 1846.

The morning of 22 August 1846 was marked by great celebrations in Manchester and Salford, marking the opening of no less than three municipal parks—Queens Park and Philips Park in Manchester and Peel Park in Salford. A large procession "comprising vast bodies of working men and clerks" set off from Manchester Town Hall towards Salford, accompanied by several brass bands. When the assemblage got to Peel Park the Mayor of Salford declared it "open, forever … and free to the public". The announcement was greeted by cheers, trumpet blasts and cannon fire![7]

Several more parks followed. One of the city's largest, Alexandra Park, opened in 1868, though by far the biggest was Heaton Park, covering 650 acres, which opened in 1902. The final phase of park-building was in the 1920s with the construction of parks at Broadhurst, Chorlton, Fog Lane and Wythenshawe.

The motivation behind this remarkable park-building programme varied. The early 1840s had seen major social unrest and the Chartist General Strike of 1842; Manchester was a major centre of radical sentiment. Some sections of the local establishment saw parks as a way of diverting people's attention away from political issues and encouraging 'social mixing'. However, in many cases, the philanthropists who donated land to the corporation did so out of a desire 'to do the right thing'. Above all, the push for municipal parks was about civic pride. Most pressure for public parks in the city came from 'prominent citizens' who presented a petition to the mayor in 1844. A 'Parks Fund' was established but the corporation gave no support in building the parks, which came from private subscription. However, once established, the city authorities took on their maintenance.[8]

The Battle of Boggart Hole Clough

There were occasions when municipal parks became centres of controversy. Manchester Corporation created a new park at 'Boggart Hole Clough' in 1894. The name is redolent of Lancashire folklore, 'boggarts' being old Lancashire hobgoblins with a reputation for mischief. They certainly put their talents to use during 1896 when the park became a focus of national attention.

Socialist meetings had been held at the Clough, part of a private estate, as early 1892 by the North Manchester Fabian Society and later the Independent Labour Party (ILP). In 1895 the Corporation of Manchester purchased the property for £8,000 bringing the park under the jurisdiction of the council's Parks and Cemeteries Committee.

Following the change in ownership, the ILP continued to hold their meetings. However, in the following year the Parks and Cemeteries Committee, under the chairmanship of Councillor George Needham, decided to put an end to the meetings of a 'certain party', i.e. the local socialists of the ILP. The park constable warned the chairman of the ILP that should a meeting scheduled for the following week take place, promoters of the meeting would be summonsed.

The meeting went ahead, chaired by John Harker, vice president of the Manchester and Salford ILP. The threat of the summonses had the effect of substantially increasing the numbers attending, to about 1,500. John Harker, along with five others, received a fine of 10 shillings.

A further twenty summonses were issued for meetings held on subsequent Sundays. Despite the plea that meetings were orderly, the magistrates imposed heavier fines of £5 to £10 plus 40 shillings costs. The action by the council served only to further increase the numbers attending the meetings. Two thousand people heard Leonard Hall and Emmeline Pankhurst speak on 7 June. More summonses were heard and the meetings continued, growing in size.

Several of the ILP activists who received fines refused to pay. Leonard Hall and Fred Brocklehurst were both fined £5. After refusing to pay they were imprisoned for a month in Strangeways.

On 20 June, Emmeline Pankhurst addressed a gathering of 20,000, her daughters, Christabel and Sylvia, standing alongside her. Unlike previous meetings, the Park Committee decided, no doubt wisely, not to issue summons on Mrs Pankhurst. By then they had probably realised they were digging a very big hole for themselves, as deep as any boggart could make.

A few weeks later the Pankhurst family and Keir Hardie were billed as the main speakers at a rally in the Clough. They arrived in an open barouche; travelling along Piccadilly and Rochdale Road they were cheered by crowds of bystanders. As usual, summonses were served but this time included Keir Hardie and Emmeline Pankhurst. The hearing took place the following week but was adjourned.

The Parks and Cemeteries Committee held a special meeting to consider a new bye-law to ban meetings in parks across Manchester. It was not passed due to twenty-six councillors walking out in protest, but was eventually passed a few weeks later but not ratified until January 1897 as the Home Secretary insisted on watering down the provisions. The new bye-law allowed meetings 'at the discretion of the Parks and Cemeteries Committee' but the committee had to accept 'any reasonable demand'. The summonses against Hardie and Pankhurst were dropped.

In May 1897, the Manchester ILP opened its summer propaganda campaign at Boggart Hole Clough with an audience of 2,000 people. Meetings continued at the Clough and were generally free of interference. The national publicity boosted the fortunes of the ILP whose votes in several local elections increased the following year. In September 1913, Hardie returned to the Clough to celebrate the ILP's victory for free speech.[9]

Lancashire's love of flowers: the horticultural tradition

Lancashire has a long horticultural tradition which encompasses some of the great formal gardens of the aristocracy at places such as Knowsley Hall of the Stanleys (Earls of Derby), Levens Hall, Holker Hall, belonging to the Cavendish family, and Towneley Hall near

Burnley. Most are now open to the public, and some (e.g. Towneley Hall) are owned by the local authority.

The job of Head Gardener was a prestigious role and he (and it always was a 'he') would be responsible for a large team of gardeners whose job was both decorative but also supported large kitchen gardens.

The Lancashire Cotton Famine had a major impact on Lancashire working-class horticultural habits. One of the most memorable poems from the 'famine' was Samuel Laycock's 'I've Turned Mi Bit o' Garden O'er'. The poet's garden remains one of his few pleasures:

> Aw've daisies, pinks, carnations too,
> An' pollyants an' o.
> Yo' couldn't think heaw preawd aw feel,
> O' every plant an' flower.[10]

Yet Laycock's pleasure in his garden was not shared by fellow dialect poet Joseph Ramsbottom, who, in 'Philip Clough's Tale', says "Aw've gan me little garden up / Wi' mony a pratty fleawr an'roo", as well as being forced to sell family heirlooms such as "mi gronny's silver cup".[11]

The development of municipal parks (see above) from the middle of the nineteenth century encouraged more civic gardening—often lavish statements of local civic pride. Farnworth's municipal park had been opened by Gladstone in 1864 (see above) and prided itself on its floral displays. William Cryer (see biography below) joined the gardening staff at Farnworth Park in 1868 and became Head Gardener. He was a well-known poet and had work published in the local press. His first collection, published in 1879, was called *Spring Blossoms*. A further collection appeared in 1902 titled *Lays After Labour* which included several poems with floral themes, including 'Lancashire's Love of Flowers', 'The Daisy', 'Wallflowers! Sweet Wallflowers' and 'Lily of the Valley'.

* * *

Lancastrians: William Cryer 1845–1917

William Cryer was born near Castleton, Rochdale on 22 September 1845. His family were small farmers and he grew up 'on the soil'. One of his earliest poems was 'A Snowdrop in a Moorland Glen'. Jessie Anderson wrote that "the only schooling which he ever had was obtained at evening classes"[12] and at the age of seventeen, at the height of the Lancashire Cotton Famine in 1862, he walked from Rochdale to London to seek work. He found a job as an assistant gardener in Hornsey Rise and was able to develop his horticultural skills.

He moved on to another gardening job in North Wales before returning to Lancashire, as gardener for the relatively new Farnworth Park, in 1868 where he married local girl Frances Horrocks. He wrote poetry in both dialect and standard English and was a regular contributor to the Manchester Weekly Times. Lays After Labour, *published in 1902, is the most complete collection of his writing and was re-published in 1913 with additional material. His son Joseph was also a talented writer and after his father's death, James produced* Poems by Father and Son, *published by Tillotson's of Bolton in 1919. In politics he was staunchly Liberal and celebrated Gladstone in one of his poems.*

* * *

The park gardeners in the nineteenth century worked long hours, in all weather. In Manchester's parks a Head Gardener worked 55½ hours in summer and 48 in winter for 32 shillings a week, with a house rent-free. They had considerable autonomy and several introduced their own species or re-designed some of their territory.[13]

The growth of individual gardens for working-class families was an important feature of Lancashire life in the Victorian era. In urban areas most terraced streets had no garden and a very small 'back yard'. Very often these were transformed into delightful displays of horticultural brilliance. In other cases, when even back-yard space was not available, people used window-boxes to get maximum advantage of what little sunlight may have got through. Abraham Stansfield, the Todmorden-born antiquarian, wrote extensively on urban gardening including a paper on 'Sweetness and Light for the Manchester Slums', featuring window-gardening in Ancoats and Hulme, as well as 'Town Gardening and Climate'.[14]

Stansfield describes a walk through Hulme, a densely-populated, poor, working-class area of Manchester, after returning from a walk from Cheshire, "where the whole beautiful Spring was bursting and unfolding with a fullness and a splendour most unwonted for so early a period of the season, and the contrast between town and country was at once striking and pitiful". However, he continues:

> But there are compensations even for the Hulmeans. As we paced the endless streets, we glanced in passing at each window. 'What!' says the reader, 'staring in at the window?' But how could we do otherwise, when we found in the front window of almost every other dwelling the imperative notice: 'Look here!'. The notice, though of uniform import, was in a hundred forms. It was sometimes a window plant—an Aspidistra ... or a shining leaved Aralia ... sometimes a simple pot of musk, sometimes a small fernery in the form of hanging basket ... Besides a most amiable vanity, what did we see in all this? We saw—and most clearly declared—a great love and longing for the country and things rural, and a desire to satisfy that longing.[15]

Stansfield was invited into the home of "a most ancient tailor and his loving spouse" who was Cheshire-born. Most of the horticultural displays—the window-plants—had been the handiwork of the tailor's wife who specialised in French water elders. Stansfield regrets the absence of 'Irish ivy' (*Hedera canariensis*) plants, described by Stansfield as "always beautiful, very easy to procure, very easy to cultivate, and particularly patient of the smoke and dust of towns", and declares that he would love to be able to distribute a thousand Irish ivy plants "and distribute them through the slums of the city ... by this means, and at this small cost, we should be able to brighten and enliven one thousand dingy rooms and cheer and sweeten the lives of five thousand poor people".[16]

Stansfield prefigured the ideas of Mary Higgs in Oldham, whose work with the 'Beautiful Oldham Society' encouraged slum-dwellers to beautify their houses and streets.[17]

* * *

If most working-class homes in industrial Lancashire had little if any space for gardens, allotments became a popular alternative. Plots of land had been provided 'for the labouring poor' by well-intentioned philanthropists since the eighteenth century, but the issue became a national political issue in the late nineteenth century, partly as a result of increasing urbanisation and loss of open space as well as rural poverty. It became a major rallying cry of the Liberal Party and their efforts were finally crowned with success in 1908 by the passing of the Small Holdings and Allotments Act.[18] The act meant that any applicant from 'the labouring population' could require their local council to provide an acre of land, with a maximum of five acres permitted.

Afield with the naturalists

Perhaps it's unfair on Lancashire's naturalists to put them in the 'play' chapter. It's a pursuit that incorporates science and health, or what we'd today call 'well-being'. But it gave thousands of working men, and some women, a lot of pleasure as a means of getting out into the country. There was a spin-off into other areas, including literature and antiquarianism. Their main focus was to explore the surrounding countryside, identify wild flowers and in some cases collect specimens. There was a direct link to medical herbalism, with some of the collected specimens being used for medical purposes.

The Accrington Naturalist and Antiquarian Society was formed in 1855 and has a distinguished history, stretching into the second half of the twentieth century. It grew out of the Accrington Botanical Society, formed in 1847. It wasn't exceptional—many of the developing industrial towns of Lancashire were seeing similar groups emerging. So Accrington is of interest because of its 'typicality'. Its first members were 'respectable working men': cotton spinners, engineers, perhaps a few of the declining group of highly skilled handloom weavers. They met in a cottage on Wellington Street belonging to an elderly widow, Betty Lomas.

The coming of the railway opened up opportunities for more long-distance trips and also the chance to meet with like-minded groups. On one occasion they met similar groups from Manchester, Middleton and Bury at Accrington station and walked en masse to Cock Bridge where the party split into three, exploring different parts of the local countryside. The meetings seem to have been lively affairs. Its chronicler, writing in 1905, said, "Lancashire dialect was blurted out in profusion … the gatherings were of a lively and exciting character, mixed with humour and occasional song."[19]

There were limits to the jollity amongst some members. The main controversy in the group's history was whether to meet on licensed premises or assemble in more sedate surroundings. In the end, 'The Brown Ale Gang' lost out to the majority who opted for a drink-free mechanics' institute.[20]

Wakes week and the 'cheap trip'—holiday time

Lancastrians of a certain age will remember fondly the 'day trip' to Blackpool, by train. It has a history stretching back to the middle of the nineteenth century and was known for generations as 'th' chep [cheap] trip'. Allen Clarke, in his novels, poetry and dialect sketches wrote lovingly and realistically about it—an important part of life in all of the Lancashire cotton towns.

The railway linking Manchester with Blackpool—the main rail corridor for access to the coast from the mill towns—opened in sections. You could reach Preston by 1838 but Blackpool only got its railway in 1846, after Fleetwood had been connected seven years earlier. Blackpool was starting to grow as a resort and after the Fleetwood line opened enterprising hoteliers arranged horse-drawn 'traps' to collect guests from the train at Poulton-le-Fylde. The Lancashire and Yorkshire Railway began running excursions to Blackpool from the late 1840s but it took some years for the business to really take off.

The days out to the seaside—Blackpool mainly but also Southport and to a lesser extent Morecambe—were only possible as working hours were reduced, giving the chance of a day out on a Saturday afternoon. Mills and factories began to close at one in the afternoon following conclusion of a long dispute between the unions and mill owners.

Lancastrians kept Whit Friday special, when the spinning mules and looms stopped for the day. Later in the nineteenth century most of the large cotton towns had their own 'Operatives' Holiday' when a similar exodus to the seaside took place.

John Walton mentions Burnley in the late 1890s, when,

perhaps three-quarters of the population left town for at least a day at the annual fair holidays, and it was in this area of relatively high and reliable family incomes that by the turn of the century only the poorest and most disadvantaged by low wages, illness or the poverty cycle were unable to take some sort of holiday. It was here, too, that the popularity of Blackpool itself became over-whelmingly dominant.[21]

In 1891, Bolton Co-operative Society, through its monthly maga-zine, advertised 'specials' to Llandudno, Liverpool and two trains each to Morecambe and Southport with no less than three to Blackpool. All of the Blackpool trains were advertised leaving from Bullfield Siding with a day return fare of 2s 3d and an 'extension ticket' costing 3s 6d. This allowed families and couples to stay over for the weekend, using the hundreds of lodging houses which had developed in Blackpool in the second half of the century. There were also day trips to Belle Vue, in Manchester.

Allen Clarke remembered the facilities on the trains being basic:

> The 'chep trip' of those days started very early in the morning, and the day fare was half-a-crown. The train accommodation was crude, primitive. Hard cushionless carriages. Indeed, sometimes cattle trucks were cleaned and fitted up with a few seats for cheap excursions.[22]

Despite the hard wooden seats and lack of toilet facilities, the trips were a joyous adventure. *The Knobstick*, set in Bolton in 1887 during the 'Great Engineers' Strike' describes a trip to Blackpool by the novel's hero Harry Belton and the Banks family, prefacing it with this description of the Whitsun Holidays, when,

> dozens of railway trains rush seawards with thousands of noisy, merry operatives of all sorts and conditions. Ere the sun has risen cheap trips are cleaving through the dawn; and long after the sun has set at night the heavy-laden trains are returning home one by one.[23]

Clarke enjoyed his train journeys. As late as August 1935 he was corresponding with his Bolton friend and radio broadcaster Jim Fleetwood, suggesting they meet up to discuss the impending broadcast of some of the 'Tum Fowt' sketches on BBC radio. He recommends Jim takes the long-lived '2.00 trip train' if he fancied coming over to Blackpool to visit. The train was still running, and still offered 'cheap rates'!

By the end of the nineteenth century, cotton was a highly organised industry, with the owners combined in powerful trade associations; their counterpart were the cotton unions, equally well organised and influential.[24] The employers decided between themselves which town would have its week's holiday, in turn. Oldham and Rochdale went first, followed by Bolton the week after at the end of June. Burnley, Bury and Wigan had their holidays in early July followed by Blackburn and the north-east Lancashire towns at the end of the month. The week's shutdown, only lengthened to a fortnight after the Second World War, enabled the mill engines and machinery to be overhauled and given a thorough clean. Paid holidays didn't come until 1941, so it was only after the war that the holiday 'boom' really took off. A further week's holiday was added in September.

The 'staggered' holidays were helpful for the railway companies and coach firms who would have been overwhelmed if every town had its 'wakes week' around the same time. As it was, the railways struggled to cope with the huge demand for 'specials' taking families to Blackpool, Southport, Morecambe and further afield including North Wales and the West Country.

Wakes Week

For thousands of Lancashire children it was the most exciting time of the year, at least next to Christmas. The annual holidays—or 'Wakes Week'—was when towns like Rochdale, Oldham, Bury and Bolton emptied, with thousands of families heading for the Lancashire seaside resorts, mostly Blackpool, or further afield. It was common for families to return to the same resort, and same boarding house, year in, year out.

Carol Walsh recalls: "I remember Wakes Weeks, my grandma used to take me and my brother on the train to Blackpool, the same boarding house in York St. every year. Great memories."

Arthur Singleton rememebers the 1950s:

We always went for a week's holiday in Bolton's Wakes Week. Always went to Fleetwood. Did this for a decade; lunch at the same fish and chip shop near the North Euston Hotel. We always stayed with Mrs. Hawkins' B&B at 16 Windsor Terrace just opposite the pier. I was fascinated by a fortune teller on the sea front, the Marionette Man near the bowling greens and remember glorious long days in the open air swimming pool—it was too dangerous to go in the sea because of the river. We always took the steam train from Bolton and when we got there we went to Knott End by the ferry. For years my Dad convinced me we had been to the Isle of Man. What made me laugh was all the Bolton workmen sat in deck chairs sleeping the lunchtime boozing off—with suntanned faces and arms and white bodies that looked as though they had never seen the sun.[25]

Christine Salt worked in the Ribble travel office at Bolton's Moor Lane bus station for many years:

Bolton holidays were mad busy, dozens of coaches going to places such as Rhyl, Llandudno, Newquay, Bournemouth etc., and every day hundreds of customers taking day trips to Blackpool, various zoos, Betws-y-Coed in Wales, and many more. Some days we didn't even manage a cup of tea! Even when Continental holidays really took off, we still did lots of day and weekly excursions, as well as cruise bookings and many package holidays. Obviously none of us were able to go away for Bolton Holidays.[26]

Probably the high point of Lancashire mill town holidays was the late 1950s and early 1960s. Successive weeks would see dozens of special trains leaving the cotton towns for a wide range of destinations. Overnight trains left on the Friday evening for Devon and Cornwall resorts, Heysham (for the boat to Northern Ireland), Bournemouth, London and East Anglia. On the Saturday, dozens of special trains would leave for the Lancashire coast, North Wales and the Yorkshire coast. The more adventurous could get a special train to Liverpool for Douglas, Isle of Man.

During the inter-war years families would save up all year for their week's holiday. Thousands were members of savings clubs, known locally as 'Diddle 'em clubs' because of the frequency of the collectors running off with the takings! The safest option was to save with the Co-op, which also organised holidays, including transport by train or 'charabanc'. Some companies ran their own 'holiday fund' which employees paid into each week.

In those days it was normal for families to take their own food in tin containers—the landlady would cook the food for them, though there was the more expensive option of having meals made for you. In many guest houses families would invite neighbours or other members of the extended family to join them for their tea!

So for one week in every year, popular destinations such as Blackpool and Rhyl became 'Bolton/Rochdale/Oldham by the sea'. The local paper—*Rochdale Observer*, *Oldham Chronicle*, *The Bolton Evening News* and *The Bury Times*—was on sale along the seafront depending on whose 'week' it was. The newspapers sent staff photographers to snap happy holiday-makers. Pete Sharples remembers being at Fleetwood in 1976: "While enjoying messing about on the shore, we heard a bloke shouting, 'Anyone from Bolton?' Repeatedly. It was a photographer from the B.E.N."

Life in the cotton towns, especially in the first week, was completely different from usual. They became ghost towns. The factory chimneys stopped smoking and you could see the Welsh mountains or Derbyshire hills. Most shops closed, including newsagents. Children set up makeshift paper shops on the pavements, sometimes earning a bit of extra pocket money, but not always.

The decline happened almost imperceptibly. As the mills and engineering factories went into decline there wasn't the same co-ordinated 'shutdown' at the end of June; the mills had shut for good. If there can be said to have been an 'end' it was in 1992, when schools went over to a standardised national pattern of summer holidays. By then, Lancashire had changed dramatically and people's leisure habits had too. Cheap foreign holidays by air became normal, though some people maintained the old traditions of Blackpool or the North Wales Coast.

Christmas and New Year in Lancashire

Christmas in Lancashire, a century and more ago, had some recognisable similarities to how we celebrate it today—but some differences too. We lived very different lives. Most south-east Lancashire families were dependent on the cotton industry for their livelihoods, with the men, women and children employed in the spinning mills or weaving sheds. Christmas for a mill worker's family wasn't the sort of extended affair lasting until after New Year that it has become. The mills closed for Christmas Day and they'd be back at full power on Boxing Day. It was New Year when Bolton people really let their hair down, with its famed New Year's Fair.

The everyday lives of ordinary people have often been ignored. However, in the novels of Allen Clarke, we get some accurate and unsentimental descriptions of people's day-to-day lives—including how Christmas was celebrated. *Lancashire Lasses and Lads* was written in the 1890s and published in 1906. It's a contemporary story mixing melodrama with the day-to-day, set in a typical large cotton town—'Spindleton'. He describes a Christmas in the 1890s:

> With frost and chilly rain, and then snow, the days went by and Christmas Eve came, when the factories closed for a day's Christmas holiday, and church and chapel choirs went about the darkness singing carols, and brass bands made the night more or less musical, and the working class cottages in Spindleton were decorated with sprigs of holly and mistletoe with a 'kissing bush' hung near the doorway…[27]

Goose was at the heart of the Christmas dinner, served early afternoon and often shared with neighbours or close family. In Clarke's novel the bird has been purchased on Bolton Market by Mrs Hamer, the matriarch of the household. The ceremonial honour of carving the bird was given to her husband, who entertained the family party with dialect stories.

Lancashire mill workers—the people whom Clarke was writing for—were not affluent but neither were they desperately poor. Christmas was a time for gifts and hospitality. The exception was when mills went on 'short-time' and wages plummeted, or if there was a strike. Normally, children got presents, left in stockings for Santa to fill. Some would have been taken to see a pantomime, such as *Babes in the Wood*. Yet most of the children enjoying the delights of Christmas dinner would be back at work in the mill on Boxing Day.

Bolton's 'New Year Fair' spread over three days, starting on New Year's Eve, and was known as the greatest fair in the North of England. It was a remarkable occasion. Allen Clarke described it as "a vast and interesting sight, and tens of thousands of men, women and children—youth predominating—sample the various diver-sions". He stressed that this was very much about having a good time, unlike some of the more 'agricultural' fairs that took place around Lancashire.

The Fair features in at least two of Clarke's novels—*The Knobstick* (above) set at the time of the Great Engineers' Strike of 1887, and *Lancashire Lasses and Lads* published a few years later. *The Knobstick* includes some dramatic events but Clarke gives the reader a bit of seasonal holiday relief as well. The secretary of the engineers' union, Peter Banks, takes his guest, Harry, to visit the fair, explain-ing: "This is the big annual holiday here, and I assure you the work-ing folks make the most of it. For the once, spindle and shuttle are forgotten; the mills are left to themselves and are silent and deserted; and none but asses think about the spinning mules."[28]

Harry is astonished by the scene of 'noise and bustle' that greets the two friends:

> The firing oil-lamps in front of the shows shot out curling tongues of fire into the air and gaudy gilt-work glittered brilliantly in the yellow light. Hobby horses were whirling round; blood-curdling whistles were shrieking merrily; girls in tights and clowns in motley paraded the little platforms in front of the booths; Drums were droning, trumpets snorting, and fifty various musical instruments were all playing at once.

In *Lancashire Lasses and Lads* there's a good description of 'letting the New Year in' on the town hall square. A brass band had been playing on the steps and stops just as the clock started to strike midnight:

> Then came the first deep boom, with eleven others following it; sounding very solemn in the night. As soon as the twelfth stroke touched the ear, all units in the vast crowd started shaking each other by the hand, and wishing 'A Happy New Year'; but amongst the younger part of the throng, where there were male and female, it seemed that the handshake was not sufficiently expressive of the heart's high glory, so lips were set to lips in sweet goodwill.[29]

The band re-commences, beating out 'Hail Smiling Morn'; church bells peal and people sing. The characters in the novel—a group of six young 'lasses and lads'—then head off to the fair for more fun.

They each have a cup of hot peas and then ride on the hobby-horses, followed by a visit to a ghost show. Then it's time to go home, and 'let the New Year in'.

On two wheels to the countryside

The Lancashire cotton towns were at the forefront of the 'cycling craze' before the First World War. Each Sunday, hundreds of men and women who toiled in the mills and weaving sheds from Monday to Saturday, would head out on their bikes to Blackpool, Southport, or as far afield as the Yorkshire Dales and the Lake District. Many were members of local or national cycling groups such as 'The Clarion' which survives to this day.

The first bicycle in common use was 'the Penny Farthing'—a daunting machine with a huge driving wheel balanced by a small rear wheel. It was invented in 1871 and was called 'the ordinary', though it looks anything but. What became the standard design—initially named 'the safety bicycle'—emerged in the mid-1880s. At first, it was only affordable to people on a good income, and the early cycling clubs tended to be middle class—only admitting 'gentlemen'. Change came rapidly as the cost of the 'safety bicycle' came down and was affordable to better-off workers in the Lancashire industrial towns.

Allen Clarke was an early champion of cycling. Writing as 'Teddy Ashton', he extolled the virtues of this new mode of transport in his satirical paper *The Trotter*. In the issue of 25 November 1892 the main story is 'Bill Spriggs Gets a Bicycle'. Clarke established *Teddy Ashton's Northern Weekly* in the late 1890s and helped to promote cycling through its columns. The paper's publishing base at 54 Higher Bridge Street became an outlet for bicycle sales, with Clarke acting as agent for 'Tam o'Shanter' cycles in Liverpool.

One of his serialised novels, *A Man's Sake*, features a young man and woman who become lovers through meeting on cycle rides around a fictionalised Bolton. The heroine, Babs, thinks nothing of cycling a hundred miles in a day and represents the 'new' liberated working woman. In the novel she reflects on her mother's disapproval of women riding a bike ('indecent'!) but sees changes coming about: "Such unreasonable dogmatisms were all dying out with the old generation. The new generation was making men and women—husbands and wives—into chums, who rode bicycles together. As indeed they ought to!"[30]

A typical example of the 'new woman' was Alice Foley, brought up in a typical working-class Bolton family, who started work in a weaving shed at the age of 13.[31] Writing of the late 1890s, she recollected that,

> scrupulously hoarding my scanty pocket-money I bought a second-hand bicycle for twenty-five shillings. Then followed a determined struggle to ride the thing. We were on short time at the mill, so each Monday, after helping mother with the washing, I trundled the machine over cobbled streets to a stretch of macadam road...

After numerous attempts she gets the hang of it and returns home in triumph, to be greeted by her mother saying, "Well, tha'art a seet, thee an' that crazy thing."[32]

Alice joined the increasingly popular Clarion Cycling Club, a spin-off from Robert Blatchford's socialist newspaper, *The Clarion*. The cycling club and the associated sporting and cultural bodies spawned by *The Clarion* attracted women as well as men. She wrote that "I joined the Clarion Cycling Club and a new era of fun and comradeship opened out. In merry company we slogged up hills and freewheeled joyously down them thrilling to the beauty and excitement of a countryside as yet unspoiled by the advent of motor transport.[33]

Other local groups were formed. My grandfather, Tom Molyneaux, was captain of Moses Gate Cycling Club at about the time Alice was learning to ride her new bike. A photograph of the club, about to set off on a 'club run', used to adorn the old Co-operative Society store in Farnworth. The Cyclists' Touring Club was formed as early as 1878 and most Lancashire towns had their own sections.

A feature of the Clarion Cycling Club was the network of 'club houses' established across the North of England. Members of Bolton Clarion, and other local clubs, would cycle to Ribchester, Whalley, Bucklow Hill (Cheshire) and other places where they could have lunch or, in some cases, stay overnight. Some of the club houses featured tennis courts, reading rooms and other facilities normally out of reach to working-class pockets. Remarkably, one still survives—Clarion House at Roughlee, near Burnley. It was established in 1912 and opens every Sunday.[34]

I'm a rambler, from Manchester way …

Alongside cycling, the early socialist movement encouraged walking groups and 'field naturalists'. A network of Clarion, ILP and Labour Church rambling groups developed in the 1890s. There was a political edge to this activity. The ethical socialism of the 1890s, strongly influenced by Whitman, had a deep attachment to the open air and countryside. This chimed with an inherited attachment to the countryside, which was far from having been eradicated by industrialisation. Many thousands of rural working-class families had been forced into overcrowded towns and cities at the beginning of the nineteenth century. But if they were lucky enough to live in towns like Oldham, Bolton, Rochdale, Burnley, Huddersfield and Halifax they were within a walk—or a tram ride—of open countryside. Rights of way over the moors were jealously guarded, and encroachments on these rights were firmly resisted.

The popular narrative runs that 'Kinder Scout' in 1932 was the first major rights-of-way battle. That's not so. Kinder Scout was certainly important, but major rights-of-way campaigns had been fought as far back as the 1820s, notably in Flixton, now a Manchester suburb, where attempts to close a right of way enjoyed by generations of local people resulted in pitched battles. Throughout the nineteenth century working-class people contested attempts to close public rights of way. One of the most well-documented fights was over access to Darwen Moors, which was won in 1896. The victory was celebrated by the erection of the 'Jubilee Tower' to celebrate Victoria's Golden Jubilee the following year. It looks like a rocket about to take off.

The biggest rights of way struggle in the nineteenth century was over Winter Hill, a tract of moorland north of Bolton. Allen Clarke wrote that "on Sunday September 6th 1896, ten thousand Boltonians marched up Brian Hey to pull down a gate and protest against a footpath to Winter Hill being claimed and closed by the landlord".[35]

On three successive weekends in September 1896 thousands of Bolton workers attempted to reclaim a right of way which had been blocked by the local Tory landowner. It was a highly political—and personal—dispute. The squire, Richard Ainsworth, was widely disliked, and his opponents were a mixture of local socialists and radical liberals. Joseph Shufflebotham, secretary of the Bolton branch of the Social Democratic Federation (SDF), was the key figure from the socialist side, supported by Solomon Partington, radical Liberal, journalist and future councillor.

* * *

Lancastrians: Solomon Partington 1844–1927

Allen Clarke called him "as great a champion of liberty and justice as ever used a pen on behalf of the robbed and oppressed".[36] Solomon Partington was one of the key figures in the Winter Hill 'Trespass' of 1896 but there's a lot more to this extraordinary man than that single event, important though it was. His campaign for children's play facilities in Leigh, and his 'March of the Thousand Lads' is a remarkable episode in the history of children's rights.

He was born in Middleton in 1844, an expanding cotton town, famous for being the home of the hero of Peterloo, Samuel Bamford. Silk handloom weaving was still a common occupation and it is thought that Partington's father was a handloom weaver himself, part of a highly cultured and well-read industrial community which was, by then, beginning to disappear. The young Solomon got a job on the local newspaper, The Middleton Guardian, *and in 1874 was appointed editor of* The Leigh Journal, *part of the Tillotson group of newspaper publishers whose titles included the Bolton Evening News and Bolton Journal and Guardian.*

Partington became involved in local politics as a member of the Liberal Party. He had already been active in the co-operative movement in Middleton, and subsequently wrote its history, published in 1900.

During his time in Leigh, Partington was involved in campaigns for better children's facilities. On 27 February 1885 he reported in The Leigh Journal *on a meeting held at the Co-op Reading Room with influential businessmen and community leaders, to discuss their concerns about Leigh's children having nowhere to play. The issue was taken up by the local council of the day, Leigh Local Board. They met to discuss the issue in August that year and Partington decided to exert some public pressure. Whilst the councillors deliberated in the town hall, Solomon Partington led a 'Thousand*

Lads of Leigh' march past the building, with hundreds of boys carrying bats and balls shouting, 'We want a playground.' One of the participants was young cotton piecer Joseph Ashworth who became mayor of Leigh and finally saw his dream of better children's play facilities realised.[37]

The 'March of the Thousand Lads of Leigh' was an important and largely forgotten event: a rare example of children becoming involved in a local campaign. As a result of Partington's efforts he became celebrated as 'The Children's Friend' and was presented with a testimonial when he left Leigh in 1887 to work for The Bolton Evening News. He wrote for several Tillotson publications and developed a speciality in local history, using the by-line of 'Historicus'.

He was one of the leaders of the 1896 Winter Hill Mass Trespass of 1896 and despite losing the legal case he continued his fight for public rights of way. Between 1899 and 1901 he produced a series of six 'Truth' pamphlets arguing the case for public rights of way, using ancient records. In 1904 he was elected onto Bolton Council, running on an independent 'public rights' platform supported by Clarke and his Northern Weekly. It seems he became frustrated with the lack of support for his campaigns within the local Liberal Party and became more aligned to the local Labour Party. His election agent was Allen Clarke who used the pages of his Teddy Ashton's Northern Weekly to win support for Partington.

He served the people of West Ward (Halliwell and Smithills) until 1911, with a year's break in 1907. He was a key figure in the Bolton Municipal Reform League, together with his socialist friend Sarah Reddish, with whom he shared a common passion for the principles and practice of co-operation. His history of Middleton and Tonge Co-operative Society was published in 1920. Partington remained in touch with public-rights-of-way campaigners in Bolton and wrote an extended letter to Bolton Housing and Town Planning Committee in 1915, highlighting unresolved footpath issues.

Partington shared Allen Clarke's love of the Lancashire dialect and was a member of the Lancashire Authors' Association which Clarke set up in 1909. After his move to Silverdale, and then Grange-over-Sands, Partington devoted himself to historical research though he never completed his intended 'magnum opus'—a history of Lancashire dialect writing. His two books on the dialect, The Future of Old English Words and Romance of the Dialect, show what might have been achieved.

He died in August 1927 and his obituary in The Bolton Evening News paid tribute to "a trenchant and fearless writer who used the Press *in full measure, though never unfairly, for the advance of schemes for the public good".*

* * *

Ainsworth closed the main path over Winter Hill—Coal Pit Lane— to allow his grouse-shooting to go unimpeded, and positioned gamekeepers across his land to turn people away. In response, Bolton SDF appealed to local people to join them 'for a walk' to reclaim their right of way, on Sunday 5 September 1896. They assembled on the outskirts of the town centre, mustering a respectable crowd of a few hundred. As the demonstrators marched up Halliwell Road, through a densely populated working-class area of town, many more joined in. By the time they reached the outskirts of town, around 10,000 people were on the march.

A further walk was organised for the following Sunday, and the SDF and their supporters held nightly demonstrations on the town hall steps to raise support. The second march attracted even more support than the first, estimated at around 12,000 people, nearly all of whom were local. The final march took place on the following Saturday, with a turnout numbering around 6,000.

Eventually, a group of the 'ring leaders' including Shufflebotham and Partington, were taken to court. There they were defended by Richard Pankhurst—husband of Emmeline, the women's suffrage leader, and a leading figure in the Manchester ILP in his own right, who had recently defended the Boggart Hole Clough campaigners (above). Despite a strong defence, the case went in favour of Ainsworth. Although the defendants were not sent to prison— unlike the later Kinder Scout campaigners—they were heavily fined. The case caused shockwaves across Lancashire, and may have influenced people in Darwen to take similar action to claim a right of way over the Darwen Moors—which proved more successful. The Winter Hill campaign helped strengthen Bolton's SDF branch, and even led to the composition of a song by Allen Clarke, which was sold as a broadsheet to raise money to help pay the fines.[38]

Despite the public support, Partington and his colleague William Hutchinson had to find nearly £600 from their own pockets. William Hesketh Lever was the most generous supporter, donating £100 towards Partington's costs.[39]

The memory of the struggle, and the treatment meted out to the leaders of the campaign, rankled with Bolton people and helped Partington ensure a stunning victory when he stood for election on a radical platform in Bolton's 1904 local elections. His election agent was Allen Clarke who used the pages of his *Northern Weekly* to win support for Partington. After his victory, Clarke wrote:

> We addressed outdoor meetings at the gates of the big iron works, and other places; also on the town hall square. Dozens of *Northern Weekly* readers also worked quietly for us, in their own streets— and all of these, known or unknown to us, have a share in the great victory.[40]

The events of 1896 were celebrated eighty-six years later with a march over Winter Hill, led by Benny Rothman who took part in the 1932 Kinder Scout Mass Trespass. It was led up Halliwell Road by Eagley Band and the Horwich Morris troupe. An 8-year-old Maxine Peake took part in the procession. A further event took place in 1996 when the road was finally declared a public right of way. A memorial was erected at the gate recalling the events of 1896. A group of Bolton people got together to organise a celebration in 2021 to mark the 125th anniversary, with over 500 attending.[41]

Picnics and garden parties

The ILP and its sister group the Labour Church often combined countryside walks with picnics. Allen Clarke recalls Labour Church outings to the local moors when they had 'gypsy teas' and sang 'England Arise!' It was normal for the cycle of winter evening meetings to be replaced by weekend outdoor activities during the summer months, and these invariably included socialist songs and, often, a short homily from a local speaker. A love of botany was often a feature of the ILP outdoor enthusiasts, and Clarke mentions Fletcher, 'the clever collier botanist' from Westhoughton, in his *Moorlands and Memories*, who often accompanied Labour Church and ILP walks. James Sims, who was one of the central figures of the Labour Church movement and president of the Bolton branch, was a skilled botanist, with a particular knowledge of ferns and mosses. In his later years he lived on the Fylde from where he pursued his interest in mosses and ferns.[42]

Allen Clarke perhaps did more than anyone to develop the socialist picnic, based on his *Northern Weekly* readership. The first 'Teddy Ashton Picnic' was held at the local beauty spot of Barrow Bridge, on the outskirts of Bolton, in May 1901. It attracted a massive crowd totalling around 10,000 and helped raise money for the locked-out Bethesda quarry workers. The picnics became annual events, attracting large crowds, often entertained by Clarion choirs.

9

SPORTING LANCASHIRE

Sport is a big part of Lancashire identity. We can lay claim to being the home ground of many if not most British spectator sports; and it was very much a 'bottom-up' thing. John Walton has suggested that 'cotton' Lancashire was well ahead in many games,

> as in the case of the Rochdale-style Co-operative movement or the working-class seaside holiday, this part of the county of Lancashire was identified with innovations in popular culture and consumerism which were every bit as important globally as the inventions and innovations in industry and trade which enabled the rise of the factory system. With few exceptions, these developments arose spontaneously from the grass-roots rather than being imposed from above or promoted from without: they are a tribute to the power of the region's social networks, based in and beyond the manufacturing communities, factories, churches, chapels and neighbourhoods, and to the combination of local rivalries and networks of social solidarity, which characterised the 'cotton towns' to a remarkable and perhaps a unique extent.[1]

Perhaps Rugby League is our most 'Lancastrian' of sports, shared with our Yorkshire neighbours. But let's celebrate Lancashire's cricketing heritage, Lancashire CCC still firmly based in Old Trafford, giving two fingers to 'Greater Manchester' upstarts.

The Holcombe Hunt is one of Lancashire's oldest organised sporting activities, love it or hate it. I can see the excitement of being out on horseback on a chill, misty autumn morning, riding across the moors, to hounds. It's a Lancashire thing, celebrated in the wonderful hunting songs of the improbably named Cicely Fox-Smith. The

Saddleworth poet Ammon Wrigley, with impeccable working-class credentials, wrote some fine hunting songs, such as 'The Hounds Are Out at Lingards'.[2] But what true Lancashire patriot's heart could not stir at this, sung with a pint of good ale in hand:

> I wish't I was in Lancashire a huntin' o' the hare
> All across the wide moorlands an' the hollows bleak an' bare,
> Hearkenin' to the good hounds' cry, hearkenin' to the horn,
> Far away in Lancashire on a windy morn.

> I wish't I was in Lancashire among o' folks I know,
> Rangin' o'er the countryside in all the winds that blow
> As they blew when I was yet a lad, in the place where I was born,
> Far away in Lancashire on a good huntin' morn.

> There's gradely hounds in Lancashire, as such there always were:
> There's gradely hills in Lancashire as how they're bleak an' bare:
> There's jannock lads in Lancashire, and that I tell you true,
> An' I wish't I was in Lancashire all the day through![3]

Maybe I'm just an old-fashioned chap that's out of step with 'modern times', but it's a great song.

* * *

The Northern sporting and cultural historian Dave Russell makes some telling observations about the importance of sport in bolstering a Northern identity, identifying three key cultural functions. He suggests that "it has provided a powerful means of expressing a body of supposed northern values; acted as a site for the definition and symbolic resolution of differences between North and South; and facilitated the expression and construction of a range of personal and collective northern identities".[4] He is right, but you can possibly substitute 'Lancashire' (and Yorkshire) for the North of England with as much, if not more, force. As with many aspects of 'Northern' and county identity, the two don't often conflict, though they can do on the cricket pitch and between some of the big Northern football and rugby teams where it can be as much about inter-county rivalry as between cities such as Manchester and Liverpool against Leeds or Sheffield, or (in the case of Rugby

League particularly) between Lancashire and Yorkshire towns such as Wigan, St Helens, Castleford and Wakefield. Dave Russell pretty much admits that, quoting a Blackburn Rovers fan (historic rivals of Burnley FC) saying, "When Blackpool played Newcastle in the Cup Final (1951) we wanted Blackpool to win because they were from Lancashire."[5]

Rugby League: quintessentially northern

Lancashire—and parts of Yorkshire—is the bastion of Rugby League. Richard Holt commented that,

> Rugby League ... is Northern in a way no other team sport could claim to be, it was played only in the North. Northern Union, as it was known at first, was concentrated in the woollen textile towns of the West Riding and in South Lancashire beyond Manchester, in a pattern *The Times* called perverse and curious.[6]

Rugby League, as it became known, was the result of a row within the rugby union which had many facets, not least around class identities. Many rugby clubs, particularly in the South, were gentlemen's bodies and operated on a strictly amateur basis. In the North, it became more of a working-class game but the players could not afford the luxury of amateur status as the game became increasingly popular. Playing professional was a way of escape from mine and mill.

In the twentieth century Rugby League became a mass sport in many Lancashire towns—mainly the coal belt but by no means exclusively. For decades, the names of Wigan, Leigh and St Helens figure amongst the top clubs, along with Warrington and Widnes. However, Rochdale Hornets, Salford, Oldham and Swinton eclipsed the popularity of local football. It had a much smaller following in the east Lancashire cotton towns and was almost invisible in Manchester and Liverpool.

A highly entertaining and informative account of Rugby League is given in Dave Hadfield's *Up and Over*, describing a 200-mile trek from Hull to Widnes, visiting as many Rugby League towns on the way that he and his mates could manage and when he got to Widnes carried on to Barrow and Workington. He pays homage to Lancashire stars such as Wigan's Billy Boston saying, "Billy's 478 tries for Wigan, combined with his charismatic personality, have made him the most enduringly famous figure in the game."[7]

* * *

Lancastrians: Billy Boston 1934—

Billy Boston is one of the greatest of Rugby League players since the game began in the 1880s. He was born in Cardiff's Butetown, the sixth of eleven children born to John Boston, a merchant seaman from Sierra Leone, and Nellie who came from Cardiff's Irish community. He began his rugby career playing rugby union with Cardiff Internationals Athletic Club which represented Grangetown, Cardiff Bay, Butetown and the docks areas of the city. The team's makeup reflected the multinational nature of those communities.

In the early 1950s his talent had become well known and he was scouted by a number of Rugby League clubs. On 13 March 1953 officials from Wigan met Boston in Cardiff and after some hard bargaining by his mother, he signed for the club.

Boston made his 'A' team debut before a crowd of 8,000 assembled inside Central Park, Wigan. He made his first-team debut against Barrow in November 1953 scoring a try. For the next fifteen seasons he became a living legend and played his final game in 1968. He played 31 games for Great Britain, and was the first player to score four tries in a game against New Zealand. He was the first non-white player to be selected to tour Australia and New Zealand in 1954, on which he set a new record of 36 tries in 18 games. Boston also played in the 1962 tour, scoring a further 22 tries.

Towards the end of his career he played for Blackpool Borough, making his final appearance in 1970. He scored a total of 571 tries in professional rugby, making him the second highest all-time try scorer in the history of the game after Brian Bevan. After finishing his playing career, he took over the running of the Griffin Hotel near Central Park. In 1986, he was awarded an MBE for his services to Rugby League, and the Billy Boston Stand at Central Park was named in his honour. In December he was named as one of three Welsh Rugby League players to be honoured with a new statue in Cardiff Bay, the other two being Gus Risman and Clive Sullivan. He is commemorated by a fine statue in Wigan's town centre.

* * *

Cricket—the county game

Lancashire county cricket goes back to the 1860s though the game was played well before that. The first Lancashire 'county' game was in 1865 when Lancashire played Middlesex at Old Trafford (Lancashire won by 62 runs). It was initially very much a game for 'gentlemen'. The leading figure in Lancashire cricket for fifty years was the Harrow-educated A.N. 'Monkey' Hornby. However, county cricket grew in popularity and a game at Accrington against Enfield had a crowd of over 6,000. A large number of young people 'tripped the light fantastic to the strains of Enfield Old Original Brass Band'.[8]

A feature of Lancashire county cricket, which sheds much light on the county's relationship with its neighbour, is the friendly rivalry between Yorkshire and Lancashire. The first county match was actually played in 1849, before country cricket was formalised in 1865. Yorkshire celebrated the centenary of the first match against Lancashire with a celebration dinner and the unfurling of a flag with entwined roses. The centenary history of Lancashire Cricket Club observed that,

> This memorable occasion and gesture represented the heart of the two counties' cricketing attitude towards each other. They bind themselves together by resolute opposition on the field, agreeable and appreciative behaviour when stumps are drawn and high mutual respect for ability and endeavour. They have the family affection that embraces occasional quarrels, restrained expression, praise and a pervading sympathy of outlook.[9]

Some of the most interesting aspects of Lancashire cricket lie in the growth of small, local teams that were very much part of the local community. The 'VIMTO Bolton and District Cricket Association' was formed in 1888 which brought under its wing dozens of local clubs. By the time of it centenary, no less than 300 clubs had played under the association's banner.[10] The association was formed on 9 November 1888 at a meeting held in Bolton's Coffee Tavern, on Bradshawgate, a popular venue for a wide range of local groups. A large number of 'vice-presidents' were elected which constituted a roll-call of Bolton's establishment figures. However, political rivalries were put aside and both Conservative and Liberal politicians were nominated. Several, including J.P. Thomasson and Edward Cross were prominent textile manufacturers in the town. Ten senior clubs and thirty junior teams were represented, from surrounding communities and villages.

Employer sponsorship of football, and indeed cricket, came later than you would perhaps expect. In 1900 towns such as Bolton and Oldham had very few football or cricket teams sponsored by an employer, whereas by 1930 there were several. Burnley had just three employer-sponsored cricket teams out of a total of eighty-one, whereas by 1930 the number had grown to twenty, out of 145 clubs in all.[11]

The new railway works at Horwich had its own club—'Horwich L&Y'. The Lancashire and Yorkshire Railway Company provided land for the cricket ground and the first match was played against Little Lever to a crowd of over 700 people. At the interval, the L&Y Band, comprising employees of the loco works, played a programme of popular music.

Other sponsors of local teams included Atherton Collieries (Fletcher, Burrows) and Abram Colliery. Later, the Bolton tannery company Walker's sponsored a team and provided land for the club pitch. Other teams in the association were based on local churches, including Congregationalists and Primitive Methodists.

The 1926 General Strike—and the much-longer Miners' Strike of the same year—saw striking miners help build the ground at Chapelfield for Walkden Moor Methodists.[12] The connection with VIMTO goes back to 1937 when the company was asked to sponsor the Bolton area association. It had the benefit of being non-alcoholic, so the sensibilities of several clubs linked to the local Methodists would not be offended.[13]

The participation of some outstanding black cricketers in east Lancashire cricket has been well documented. Learie Constantine ('Connie') was signed by the small Nelson Cricket Club in 1928.

* * *

Lancastrians: Learie Constantine 1901–1971

Learie Constantine was one of the outstanding figures in world cricket and was also a powerful advocate of black people's rights. He was from Trinidad and was already making his name as an outstanding all-rounder. Connie's time at Nelson is an amazing story. He played for the club with distinction between 1929 and 1938, while continuing as a member of the West Indies Test team in tours of England and Australia. He transformed the fortunes of the ailing club at a time when north-east Lancashire was struggling with the collapse of the cotton industry during the depression. He stayed with the club for ten years but continued to play for the West Indies. After his move to Rochdale Cricket Club he continued to live in Nelson and became a naturalised Nelsonian, loved by everyone. Constantine's appearances boosted attendances and gate receipts for all Nelson's matches, and was of great financial benefit to both the club and the league as a whole. In Constantine's nine seasons at the club, Nelson never finished lower than second, won the league competition seven times and the knockout cup twice. In nine years at the club he scored 6,363 runs at an average of 37.65 and took 776 wickets.

In the mid-1930s, Lancashire County Cricket Club twice approached Constantine with a view to him joining the club—his time in Nelson meant that he qualified to play for Lancashire, having lived in the county for the required time. However, nothing happened, as members of the Lancashire Board and, later, players in the team opposed the idea of a black man playing for the county.

For the 1938 season, Constantine played for Rochdale in the Central Lancashire Cricket League, although he continued to live in Nelson, which he had come to regard as 'home'. He performed well but did not enjoy his time at Rochdale. There was some resentment of his high earnings amongst other players and there was also an incident of racial abuse which Constantine believed the Central Lancashire League committee effectively covered up. During the war he returned to play for Nelson as an amateur.

During the Second World War, Constantine worked for the Ministry of Labour and National Service as a Welfare Officer responsible for West Indians employed in English factories. In 1943, the manager of a London hotel refused to accommodate Constantine and his family on the grounds of their race in an instance of the UK colour bar; Constantine successfully sued the hotel company. The case was a milestone in British racial equality. He qualified as a barrister in 1954, while also establishing himself as a journalist and broadcaster. He returned to Trinidad and Tobago in 1954, entered politics and became a founding member of the People's National Movement, subsequently entering the government as Minister of

Communications. From 1961 to 1964, he served as High Commissioner to the United Kingdom and, controversially, became involved in issues relating to racial discrimination, including the Bristol Bus Boycott. In his final years, he served on the Race Relations Board, the Sports Council and the Board of Governors of the BBC.[14]

* * *

His employment by Nelson was not the only example of small Lancashire clubs 'buying' West Indian cricketers. Nearby Haslingden had George Headley playing for them in the Lancashire League. Other great names followed including Wes Hall, Charlie Griffith and Viv Richards who described himself as 'an honorary Lancastrian'.[15]

The BBC made a documentary about black cricketers in Lancashire in which some players commented on the racism they faced initially. Gladstone Afflick moved to Preston in 1960, but said he was only welcome in one of the town's 365 pubs. "Preston was a horrible place because of people coming from out of town, not Prestonians. You couldn't go into town because they would all be on your back," Afflick told the BBC.[16]

Although West Indian players became 'accepted' in the Lancashire cricketing world, the same was not the case for Asian cricketers. Ibrar Ali played against Viv Richards for Todmorden, becoming one of the league's first Asian amateurs. Historian Jeff Hill told the BBC, "I think the clubs were a bit slow on the uptake to be honest. There were plenty of examples where cricket was still segregated."[17]

In 2017, Nelson player Khurram Nazir said the town still had a 'problem' with segregation—it still had a British National Party councillor—but the club was helping communities to mix: "I am sure we can be used as an example to show how we've helped integrate our society and our communities together just through one sport".[18]

Lancashire and England player Andrew 'Freddie' Flintoff has been working with mixed groups of deprived young people in Preston to instil a love of cricket and help social cohesion in the city, as well as in the game itself. A traumatised 16-year-old Afghan refugee, Adnan, has been one of the lads to be coached by Flintoff. Flintoff's work with the youngsters was made into a TV series, *Freddie Flintoff's Field of Dreams.*

Football—Lancashire to the fore

Lancashire was the birthplace of football as a mass spectator sport. John Walton points out that "no fewer than 25 of the hundred clubs that went into the draw for the second round of the FA Cup in April 1883 were from the cotton district, including at least three teams from Darwen, two from Blackburn, three from Bolton and an amazing array of village sides, including factory settlements like Low Moor near Clitheroe, Eagley and Turton".[19] Turton, a small moorland settlement north of Bolton, lays claim to being the very first football team in Britain using 'modern' rules. It was formed in 1870 though football was being played in the village as early as 1830.

The Football League was formed in 1888 and Lancashire clubs dominated. Six of the twelve clubs in the league were Lancashire teams. The introduction of half-day Saturday working in mills and factories enabled supporters to attend afternoon matches and the sport grew rapidly in popularity.

There were similar tensions within football between a desire for the sport to remain completely 'amateur' (and by implication, the preserve of middle-class gentlemen) and its becoming more professionalised. The conflict was played out between the rival clubs of Darwen and Blackburn in the 1890s.

The main sponsors of football and cricket teams were local churches (see above re Bolton Cricket Association and its members). Whilst this seems to have stretched across the divide of Anglican, Nonconformist and Catholic, there were some exclusively Catholic football leagues in some of the bigger Lancashire towns, such as Bolton, Oldham and St Helens.[20]

* * *

Lancastrians: Tom Finney 1922–2014

Tom Finney was born on 5 April 1922 in Preston, not far from Deepdale stadium, the home of Preston North End (PNE) FC. Like most Lancashire boys, he was a keen football fan. His ambition to become a professional footballer grew, though his health was poor and he was also quite short for an aspiring footballer. He left school in 1936 at the age of fourteen and became an apprentice for a local plumbing company.

The following year, he joined 'the juniors' at Preston North End in the local newspaper for junior players aged 14 to 18. He was offered a contract at the wage of £2 10s a week. His early footballing years were inspired by Bill Shankly, who was a first team regular at North End. In January 1940 he signed on with PNE as a professional on wartime terms of 10s a match. He was called up in April 1942 and joined the Royal Armoured Corps, serving in Egypt with Montgomery's Eighth Army; he took part in the Battle of the Argenta Gap as a tank driver.

Football resumed in 1946. Preston were in the First Division and began the new season with a home match against Leeds United. Finney made his debut in a team that included Bill Shankly and Andy Beattie. In front of a crowd of over 25,000, Preston won 3–2 with Finney scoring one of the goals.

Finney went on to play for Preston in fourteen English league seasons from 1946–7 to 1959–60, including twelve in the First Division. In what seems incredible today, Finney continued as a plumber, needing the extra cash to supplement the £14 he received from Preston North End. Despite a lucrative offer to play for Palermo, Finney stayed loyal to Preston for his entire football career.

He won 76 caps and scored 30 goals in an England career that spanned twelve years. He scored his 29th international goal in June 1958 against the Soviet Union to become joint England all-time top-scorer, sharing the record with Vivian Woodward and Bolton's Nat Lofthouse. He was voted Footballer of the Year in 1953–4. He won the award again in 1956–7, becoming the first player to win it a second time. He had a great reputation as a thoroughly decent and unassuming player; he was never booked or sent off in his career.

Finney continued to run his plumbing business in Preston and he also worked for local charities and hospitals. On 31 July 2004, Finney unveiled the water feature sculpture The Splash, by sculptor Peter Hodgkinson, outside Deepdale stadium which at that time housed the National Football Museum.

He maintained his links with Preston North End as the club's president and was awarded an OBE and then a CBE, in 1992. He was knighted in the 1998 New Year Honours. He died in Preston on 14 February 2014. His former teammate Bill Shankly described him as "the greatest player I ever saw, bar none". The Football Association said he was "one of England's all-time greatest players" and Bobby Charlton said Finney's contributions to football were "immeasurable". In April 2014, Northern Premier League club

Bamber Bridge announced their Irongate Ground would be renamed the Sir Tom Finney Stadium.

* * *

Lancashire lionesses

The spectacular success of the 'Lionesses' in the 2022 Women's European Championship is a reminder that women's football in England is nothing new. Its roots go back to the 1890s. The most famous team was sponsored by the Preston engineering firm of Dick, Kerr and Co., formed in 1917 as Dick, Kerr Ladies FC.

The team played 'Bolton Ladies' at a well-attended match at Burnden Park in 1921. A report in *The Farnworth Weekly Journal* commented that the match "seems to have stirred girls of this district to emulation", observing that young women employed at two local mills had formed their own teams. These were at T. Barnes's Mills at Farnworth and Burgess and Ledward's at Walkden.

The girls would mostly have worked in the card room or weaving shed which required fitness and agility. Barnes's Mill was quite a progressive concern having its own welfare centre with a social and athletic club which supported the team, with a Miss Hulme acting as trainer. Two matches were held, the first at Linnyshaw close to the Walkden Mill, with Barnes's team beating their rivals 2–0. A return match was played the following week on Farnworth cricket ground in front of a large crowd of employees of both mills. Barnes's team won again. Stars of the matches were Sarah Ellison of Barnes's and Martha Coucill of Burgess's, both of whom played for Bolton Ladies.

Despite, or perhaps because of, the growing popularity of women's football, the FA banned women from playing on Football League grounds later that year. They pompously stated that "the game of football is quite unsuitable for females and ought not to be encouraged". Despite the FA's ban, the Dick, Kerr Ladies continued playing until 1965. What became of the two mill teams we don't know. More research required!

Mill girls' tennis

Rounders in Lancashire has a long history going back around 120 years to when it began as 'mill girls' tennis'. Teams from Bolton cotton mills and Sunday schools played each other as the Bolton game evolved with its own distinctive flat bat as opposed to the rounder, baseball-type bat used elsewhere in the country, and with some distinct rules. Players competed at first in ordinary, long-layered day clothes—including large hats. It was only in the 1930s that a rule banning the use of hat pins came in.

This 'uniform' soon evolved into long gym slips, stockings and plimsolls to allow the young women more movement. The Bolton Sunday Schools' Rounders League was founded in 1921 and this later became the Bolton Ladies' Rounders League, which is the title it still holds today. The sport has always been popular, with decent numbers always turning up at matches. During the last century, however, huge crowds would gather for the highlight of the rounders year: the Chadwick Cup final. The sport is still thriving in and around Bolton—with a smaller, although still highly competitive, league running in Bury.[21]

Equestrian sports

Lancashire has a love of horses, which has endured over centuries. The racing tradition is still strong and Aintree still hosts the Grand National each April. Other racecourses such as Cartmel and Haydock have survived, though some, such as Agecroft, have not.

Lancashire has a strong hunting tradition and it formed an important part of the pre-industrial Lancashire social structure. The Holcombe Hunt was probably the first formal hunting body in the country. It was in existence well before the King's visit to Hoghton Tower in 1617 when it was formally recognised, with the King permitting the hunt to wear royal scarlet. Prominent in the Holcombe Hunt were many of the major figures in the Lancashire cotton industry, including the Quaker triumvirate Henry Ashworth, Richard Cobden and John Bright. An Ashworth was often Master of Harriers, "thus enduring the criticism of the Society of Friends for hunting and shooting".[22]

One of the Hunt's most interesting ventures came after the First World War, with the start of the Holcombe 'Point to Point' race in 1921. It was the brainchild of Myles Kenyon, Master of the Holcombe Hunt. The event was free—the only money that exchanged hands was for the race card, priced at 2/6d.

The annual meeting attracted tens of thousands of visitors between the 1920s and 1960s. It used an informal 'racecourse' of farmed fields around Harwood and Ainsworth starting at Nab Gate. The races quickly became known as 'The Millworkers' Grand National'. Mills shut down for the afternoon to allow workers— and managers—to visit the races, drawing thousands from Bolton, Bury and Ramsbottom.

Former *Bury Times* editor Harold Heys recalled the "big strapping horses, one-day-a-year jockeys from schoolboys to beefy, middle-aged farmers; the landed gentry and the wags and the chancers".[23] The first event, in April 1921, attracted about 40,000 people. *The Bury Times* said "the event was like a great picnic party—all classes were represented and all mingled together in joyous sport".[24] It was a 3-mile course, with riders performing three circuits, jumping nine brushwood fences. Casualties, both riders and horses, were frequent.

The event kept on growing. The official history of the Holcombe Hunt said that, by the late 1920s, "we would not be surprised if the attendance numbered 100,000 ... not only was there a great assembly of people at the starting and finishing points, but practically at every point of vantage round the course".[25]

People got there on foot, bicycle, charabanc and more than a few on horseback, pony-and-trap or car. As well as the mills shutting for the day, the kick-off at Bury's Gigg Lane ground was postponed for a couple of hours to avoid a clash with the races. For the first event, a large number of coal miners from Radcliffe marched in procession to the course. The great Lancashire artist L.S. Lowry did a painting of the races in 1953.

The races began at Nab Gate, Ainsworth, and took in a course around Ainsworth and Affetside (some locals called it 'The Cockey Moor Races', the old name for Ainsworth). Six races took place including a 'Ladies' Race'. It was in fact a lady, the redoubtable 'Babs' Cort who managed the event for many years.

Harold Heys called it "English eccentricity at its daftest". Anything could happen and sometimes did. At one race a police horse watched the thundering field of horses as they passed and decided it wanted to join in. The horse bolted—with the constable on his back—and entered the race. They made it over four fences before the officer persuaded his steed to stop.

The races were increasingly dogged by wet weather, with several events having to be cancelled owing to heavy rain making the course impassable. An additional threat on the horizon was a proposal to build housing on part of the course. A reluctant decision was taken in the late 1960s to move the event to a course at Whittington, near Kirkby Lonsdale though many people lived in hope that it would return to the Bolton area. In the early 2000s plans were well advanced to transfer the event to the Hulton Park estate but the deal fell through.

Although the 'Point to Point' no longer takes place, the Holcombe Hunt has survived. The ban on hunting with hounds in 2005 has not diminished the hunt's popularity, with large crowds turning out for the Boxing Day and New Year meets. The Holcombe Hunt is committed to continuing the Lancashire hunting tradition within the law, using 'drag hunts' instead of animals.

A 'Greater Lancashire' sport: crown green bowling

Crown green bowling was once a popular Lancashire sport, and is still played around the county—though far too many bowling greens have been destroyed to create pub car parks and the like. John Vose (the biographer of Lancashire opera singer Tom Burke) has written an affectionate account of the sport, placing it very much within the 'North of England' but extending out to North and West Wales and south to Chesterfield. It is distinguished from 'flat green' bowling which is very much a southern pastime.

There is an Irish section, based in the historic city of Armagh. The all-Ireland 'Bol Chuman Ard Comhairle' was formed in 1968 to provide an umbrella body. In 1929 the counties of Lancashire, Derbyshire and Cheshire formed the 'National Crown Green Bowling Association' though it didn't survive.[26] Crown green bowling seems to have been particularly popular in the Chorley area, with the best bowlers reckoned to live "somewhere inside ten miles fra' Chorley".[27] Some of the names of bowling clubs say much of a Lancashire that has gone; and many of the clubs with it: Sutton Manor Colliery Institute, A.E.I. (Stretford), Nelson Band Club, Oldham Batteries and I.C.I. Hyde. Conservative clubs featured strongly in the sport, Labour clubs less so. Municipal parks had their own leagues for Lancashire, Yorkshire, Staffordshire, Warwickshire and Cheshire and formed 'The British Parks and Recreation Amateur Bowling Association'.

I'd like to think that there's a future for crown green bowling, keeping within its self-imposed Northern and Irish boundaries. Might even give it a try myself (and I live within ten miles of Chorley).

10

LANCASTRIANS AT WAR

Britain has been fortunate in having had no all-out conflicts within its shores since the English Civil War (1642–51) when Lancashire figured significantly in the conflict between King and Parliament and experienced the worst atrocity of the war. Some parts of Lancashire saw little of the civil war, but other towns were less fortunate. Manchester, a centre of Parliamentary support, managed to avoid the attentions of the rampaging Royalist forces who instead headed north to Bolton, where the worst atrocity of the war took place. Royalist forces under Prince Rupert and the Earl of Derby laid siege to the town in May 1644, and succeeded in over-running the town's defences. A large number of civilians, men, women and children, were massacred. An accurate figure (see below) has never been determined but it was generally accepted that deaths ran into four figures. The Earl of Derby paid for his part in the carnage by being executed in Bolton's market square in 1651.

The impact of 'The Bolton Massacre' has been felt down the centuries. Allen Clarke's first novel was *The Lass at The Man and Scythe*—subtitled *a story of the siege of Bolton*.[1] It was published in 1891 and represents a view of the conflict through the lives of local people, particularly the denizens of the ancient pub, The Man and Scythe, where the earl had his last drink before being beheaded.

The immediate aftermath of the civil war saw little change to the lives of most Lancastrians. The Derbys lost some of their land as did some of their landed allies. Catholicism as a faith continued, despite restrictions. The early years of the eighteenth century saw a county that remained poor but with a growing independent sub-culture of radical Protestantism in the textile districts. Some histories make much of the Jacobite rebellions of 1715 and 1745, though neither event had long-lasting impact on Lancashire; perhaps it could be said that their defeats marked the definitive end of 'old Lancashire'. The Young Pretender's attempts to enlist potential supporters in Lancashire in the 1745 rebellion largely fell on deaf ears.

That said, the 1715 rebellion had disastrous consequences for many of the followers of 'The Old Pretender' Prince James Edward. The Jacobite forces arrived in Lancashire in November 1715 and received some measure of support—there had already been riots in Warrington and Manchester in support of the Jacobite cause. James III was proclaimed king when he arrived at Preston on 9 November, but government forces attacked the town a few days later and a major battle ensued. The rebels surrendered, leaving a death toll of some 350 people. Retributions followed with summary executions of the rebels, in centres of Jacobite support including Preston itself, Manchester and Garstang.[2] Many supporters, who had the means to do so, fled abroad. The scenario was repeated thirty years later when 'Bonny Prince Charlie' attempted to win support in the North of England. Fewer people rallied to his cause than in the earlier uprising and only a small number joined his army, which reached Derby before being defeated. Charles's main supporter in Lancashire, Francis Towneley of Burnley, was executed for treason.

* * *

Lancastrians: The 7th Earl of Derby 1607–51

James Stanley, the 7th Earl of Derby, was a staunch Royalist, as were most of the Lancashire Catholic gentry. He was executed in Bolton for his part in the 'Bolton massacre' of 1644. A plaque stands in Churchgate marking the spot outside The Man and Scythe pub where he was beheaded.

James Stanley was born into a life of privilege, status and a family with great power and influence in Lancashire. He held the title of Lord Strange until he inherited the Earldom of Derby in 1642. At the age of 18 he was elected Member of Parliament for Liverpool and by the time Civil War broke out in 1642 he had become the Lord Lieutenant of Lancashire and Cheshire.

The Earl and his cousin, the King's nephew Prince Rupert, laid siege to Bolton with a force of 12,000 horse and foot soldiers. Bolton was defended by less than a fifth of that number. The first assault was beaten off, but a second was successful. As many as 1,500 Bolton people were massacred and much of the town destroyed.

Parliament condemned the taking of Bolton as a crime and Oliver Cromwell himself demanded the death penalty for the Earl—who had fled to the Isle of Man. He returned to England in 1651 in a bid to help the Prince of Wales regain the throne but was captured after a battle in Worcester. He was court-martialled on grounds of high treason and executed on 15 October 1651. His body was buried in Ormskirk.

Allen Clarke was both fascinated and repelled by the story of the 'Bolton Massacre'. His first novel, The Lass at The Man and Scythe, *was sympathetic to the Parliamentary cause but the book deals even-handedly with the earl, whom Clarke described as "a cultured and kindly sort of man ... the big fault with him was that he was on the wrong side in the Civil War. He was on the side of royal tyranny and aristocratic arrogance opposed to the government and the people..."[3]*

* * *

Two world wars

It was common for working-class boys to 'sign up' to the British Army, which offered hard but secure employment. Lancashire had several regiments which served to bolster a sense of identity and 'belonging'—the Manchester Regiment, the Lancashire Fusiliers, and the York and Lancaster Regiment.

On one level, the history of the First World War (1914–18) is well documented. Yet we know little about the lives of many of the working-class men who fought in the trenches. Larysa Bolton has documented the lives of several who volunteered with the Manchester Regiment.[4]

A feature of the First World War was the creation of 'pals' battalions', formed of men from the same town. The most well known were the 'Accrington Pals' of the East Lancashire Regiment, who were virtually wiped out in the Battle of the Somme. There is a memorial, built of Accrington red brick, at Sheffield Memorial Park at Serre, on the former Somme battlefield. Peter Whelan's play *The Accrington Pals* (1981) is a moving tribute to a brave group of men, and the women who were left behind. Manchester had its own 'Pals' together with Oldham and other large towns.

* * *

Many parts of Lancashire were given over to armament and munitions production. The major railway engineering works, such as Horwich and Gorton, adapted well to war production, with both shells and guns being manufactured, often with a mainly female workforce. Other factories across the region did likewise, though it came at a cost. On 13 June 1917 a munitions factory in Ashton-under-Lyne exploded, prompting the publication of a poem, written by Arthur Grimshaw of Duke Street, Ashton, sold 'in aid of the crippled and injured':

> 'Twas a terrible blow to the people,
> In history this will remain,
> For Ashton has done its duty,
> In which it has taken great pain'[5]

Many casualties were 'hushed up'. A munitions factory on the remote Belmont moors was known to have experienced numerous deaths and serious injuries but no records were kept. One disaster was so big that it was impossible to keep secret—the explosion at White Lund, near Morecambe. However, it would be over two years before the full story, and the scale of the casualties, were made public.[6] At about 10.30 p.m. on the evening of 1 October 1917, there was a massive explosion in part of the complex that formed National Filling Factory 13. Further explosions continued throughout the night until the following day, with the biggest explosion in the middle of the night. The enormous explosion destroyed every piece of plate glass or window for miles around. Fires spread from building to building, setting off loaded shells where it found them. At the time of the fire 22,000 filled shells were waiting to be sent to France. Some explosions could be heard as far away as Burnley and Rossendale and the glare in the sky from the fires was reported to be seen from the outskirts of Liverpool. The factory fire brigade was unable to contain the fires and fire crews from all over the region were called in. The last fires were not put out until the early morning of 4 October.

When the alarm was raised most of the workers were in the canteen on their supper break. This probably saved many lives. It is remarkable that only ten men were killed in the disaster. Most of them died while actually fighting the fires: five of them were fire-fighters and five were munitions workers. Several bodies were not discovered until all the fires were out. There were many injuries, some serious, caused by falling debris, shrapnel, burns, crowd panic and confusion. In the neighbourhood, injury was caused to local residents by falling masonry, shattered glass, shrapnel, accidents in the streets and inadequate clothing and exposure on a cold night.

Further incidents occurred. The parish council records:

Most Factory workers were soon paid off or transferred to another part of the country. Some months after, two more men were killed when a shell exploded during the clearing of debris. Yet such was the perceived war-time need that National Filling Factory 13 was soon rebuilt with the use of more brick in construction. From the summer of 1918 the re-opened Factory was engaged in meeting the increase in demand for HS (mustard gas) shells. After the Armistice in November 1918, shell production ceased and the Factory went into reverse gear—part of it was used for emptying unused shells. This led to another disastrous, although more contained, explosion on 14 January 1920 when nine men in one building were killed. National Filling Factory 13 closed soon after and the site slowly evolved into the Industrial Estate which thrives today.[7]

A memorial to the dead was unveiled by the parish council in October 2017.

The Second World War

Lancashire men served bravely during the Second World War and there are many accounts of their heroism. An unusual, and very moving, personal account appeared in the Lancashire Authors' Association *Record*, from the son of the association's president Major Brierley. Captain J.R. Brierley was serving in the Sherwood Foresters and he was writing after the fall of Tunis to the Allies:

You ask what have I been doing? Well! I have danced with Arabs, French and Palestinians. Have attended super concerts in the cities of Egypt and home-made affairs in the desert wastes and the orchards. Have got gloriously 'lit-up' at Shepheard's in Cairo, and at Tel Aviv in Palestine. I've seen dirt and flies and SAND (miles and miles of it). Have seen men marching, and listened to the tramp of their feet behind me. Have seen bombs leave Stukas as they attacked, and the dust rise in clouds as they landed amongst us ... I have seen trucks blazing furiously after a German fighter strafed us. Have heard the whine of Jerry shells and felt the peculiar 'crunch' they make when they arrive—and the lumps of shrapnel singing past your ears as you crouch down. Have shrunk behind the truck wheels as machine-gun bullets spit in the sand around you. I have watched the dawn break gloriously in the Western Desert—seen the moon shining bright as day and glistening on the wet stones as I lay in my greatcoat and thought of you all. Have sweated and fought through Sollum Pass—a deathly, unnatural God-forsaken spot, lettered with the debris of war ... We have marched through the ruins of Tobruk and Benghazi. Have seen death in some of its worst forms, and wooden crosses in the lonely desert surmounted by a German, Italian or British helmet. Have smelled the fragrance of the flowers in Tripolitania for days on end, and stood amongst the poppy fields of Tunis ... And now it's all finished it seems queer—as though you were no longer required, and we ask ourselves—what next?[8]

Many Lancashire soldiers, and medical personnel, were among those who liberated the concentration camps towards the end of the War. Their stories would make anyone weep. *The Lancashire Post* carried the story of Ken Allen and nurse Emily Harding, seventy-five years after the war's end.

Bergen-Belsen concentration camp, in northern Germany, was packed with 40,000 people of all nationalities from across the Continent. It was liberated by the British on 15 April 1945 and for the first time photographs and newsreel films showed the world the shocking capabilities of man's cruelty and inhumanity. Ken Allen, of Penwortham, Preston, was a 27-year-old sergeant gunnery instructor with the 58th Light Anti Aircraft Regiment, and one of a 112-man detachment which liberated Bergen-Belsen. He saw things that remained with him to the end of his life:

Before we even got in sight of the camp, we could smell the awful stench of the place, it was terrible—but that was nothing to what we saw when we arrived. It was unbelievable ... a nightmare. There

were piles of bodies scattered all over the desolate camp—an estimated 10,000, rotting, unburied bodies. There were 40,000 starving inmates, dressed in rags, who were nothing but walking skele-
tons and they were dying at the rate of 500 a day. In control were
400 German guards, half of these were SS troops, and about 4,000
Hungarian soldiers. What struck us was the arrogance of the SS and
their complete disregard of the suffering going on around them. We
immediately ordered all of the guards, including the officers, to use
picks and shovels to dig huge communal graves to bury the dead.[9]

In January 1945, with Allied troops advancing on Germany from
the west and the Russians advancing from the east, thousands of
prisoners from other concentration camps across Nazi-held territory
were moved to Bergen-Belsen, which led to sanitation, water and
food supplies breaking down. When British and Canadian troops
entered in April they found more than 13,000 unburied bodies and
60,000 inmates, most acutely sick and starving. The prisoners had
been without food or water for days before the Allied arrival and
typhus was rife.

Sister Emily Harding, also of Preston, saw at first hand the sufferings of the death camp inmates. Two weeks after Allied troops
moved in, she was posted to a camp in Belsen to care for some of
the victims of the Nazis. Journalist Mike Hill wrote that "her harrowing experiences are recorded in letters and newspaper articles
which were passed down to her niece Emily Watkinson and shared
with the *Post* in 2001". In one particularly harrowing interview
Sister Harding talks about the camp in Belsen. She said:

> It would be impossible for anyone who had not witnessed it to imag-
> ine anything so terrible. The lowest types of barbarism seemed to
> have been reached. Moving down the corridors one saw it was a
> place of death, it looked out of every face and was emphasised by
> the awful stench. Patients that we attended bore traces of brutality.
> There were bruises from whips, sores from different diseases which
> had not healed and they were covered with lice.[10]

The Blitz in Lancashire

Manchester and Liverpool suffered heavily during the Second World
War. There was a foretaste in 1916 of what was to come, when a

German Zeppelin bombed Bolton. Kirk Street suffered a direct hit and thirteen people were killed.

By the mid-1930s the likelihood of war was becoming increasingly apparent. Air Raid Precaution (ARP) measures were set up in Manchester during 1935 following a government directive. A detailed plan for Manchester's defences in the event of an attack were submitted to the Home Office in August 1938. It was prescient—the plan was published weeks before Hitler invaded Czechoslovakia. Air raid wardens were enlisted and air raid shelters were constructed. The famous 'Anderson Shelters', capable of being constructed in small gardens, became familiar sights in all Lancashire towns and cities. Gas masks were distributed, with Manchester alone requiring 800,000. By the end of September 1938 some 699,000 had been made available.[11]

Although war was declared on 3 September 1939 it was over a year before the full horror of war was felt on the streets of Manchester and Liverpool. In the meantime, some 180,000 children had been evacuated from Manchester alone. On the first day of the evacuation, 1 September 1939, 109 special trains were run taking 46,000 children plus 6,000 teachers and helpers to their 'billets' across Lancashire, Cheshire, Shropshire and Derbyshire.[12]

A few bombs were dropped on Manchester and Salford during 1940 but the worst was yet to come. The first major attacks took place on 22 December 1940, followed by further large-scale raids the following night. On the first night, sirens sounded at 6.38 p.m. and the raids continued for over five hours with 233 high explosive bombs being dropped on Manchester, Salford and Trafford Park. Thousands of incendiary bombs were also dropped creating a firestorm which destroyed hundreds of homes and factories as well as public buildings. The Manchester Fire Brigade, supported by the Auxiliary Fire Service, performed an heroic role in controlling a situation that could have got out of control. As it was, over 9 acres of central Manchester were devastated by the bombing.[13]

Liverpool had an even harder time. It was the most heavily bombed city outside of London and the death toll was heavy. The first major air raid on Liverpool took place in August 1940, when 160 bombers attacked the city on the night of 28 August. On 28 November an air raid shelter was hit, causing 166 deaths; several other air raid shelters suffered direct hits with dozens of casualties. A series of heavy raids took place in December 1940, referred to as the Christmas Blitz, when 365 people were killed. May 1941 was possibly the worst time of a terrifying year. Over 2,300 high explosive bombs and 119 other explosives were dropped on the city, devastating the dock area and causing 2,895 casualties. Liverpool Cathedral was hit by a high-explosive bomb which pierced the roof of the south-east transept before being deflected by an inner brick wall and exploding mid-air, damaging many stained-glass windows. The seven-night bombardment resulted in over 6,500 homes being completely destroyed and nearly 200,000 damaged.

The horrific sight, and sound, of the Liverpool Blitz has been described by people living as far away as North Yorkshire. The fires could be seen from the top of Blackstone Edge, on the Yorkshire border. Other major industrial towns were fortunate in escaping serious bombardment. Preston, despite being a major railway junction, port and engineering centre escaped lightly.

Further north, Barrow-in-Furness wasn't so lucky. The town was less well prepared than Manchester or Liverpool and although total casualties were less than in either, the actual percentage of homes destroyed and people killed or seriously injured was higher. What made things worse was that the Luftwaffe missed their main targets— the shipyards—and most of the bombs fell on residential areas.

The first attack on the shipyard town was on the night of 12–13 September 1940. Over 300 incendiaries were dropped on Salthouse and a 5-year-old boy was killed. The bombings led to the evacuation of hundreds of children in the town to rural locations across Westmorland and Cumberland. A much heavier attack came on the nights of 14 and 16 April 1941. This was followed by further raids in early May which resulted in 600 homes being destroyed and over 1,400 severely damaged; 83 people died and 330 were injured.[14]

Children in the main towns and cities, particularly Manchester and Liverpool, were evacuated. Some parts of Lancashire were 'neutral', where children would 'stay put' but would not receive evacuees. 'Reception areas' were those that could accommodate refugee children. In June 1940 Burnley received 800 adult and child refugees from the Channel Islands, though some were later dispersed to Tottington. Michael Townend wrote that "Coming to

Burnley was a wrench for some families but this was partly eased by their reception in the town. Short tours of the district, teas and concerts were organised by the women's section of the British Legion and a Channel Islanders' Society was formed."[15]

Some of the children evacuated from Liverpool and Manchester were from slum areas and were often in poor health and suffering psychological problems. A local voluntary worker said that some "brought with them a variety of ailments—head lice, impetigo, scabies and not least a large proportion of bed-wetters".[16]

Some were evacuated quite locally: in 1940 a trainload of children arrived at Littleborough from Manchester. Keith Parry tells the story:

> The women of the town had heard of the impending arrival and were at the station when the train pulled in. The children, all correctly labelled, ready for a walk to the dispersal centre. The local people did not wait for that—they plucked children out of the crowd and, ignoring the protesting officials, simply took them home! The local 'grape-vine' eventually informed the harassed officials where the children were.[17]

A similar story was told of children arriving at Accrington from Salford, with many simply 'grabbed' and taken away by over-enthusiastic adopters. The confusion was solved by the simple expedient of issuing named ration cards by the town clerk.[18]

* * *

Whilst safety precautions in Munitions Factories during the Second World War were generally much better than in the First World War, a major explosion took place at the Royal Ordnance Factory in Kirkby in February 1944. In one building nineteen workers, mainly women, were filling trays of anti-tank mine fuses when one of the fuses exploded, setting off the rest of the fuses in the tray:

> The girl working on that tray was killed outright and her body disintegrated; two girls standing behind her were partly shielded from the blast by her body, but both were seriously injured, one fatally. The factory was badly damaged: the roof was blown off, electric

fittings were dangling precariously; and one of the walls was sway-
ing in the breeze.[19]

Some munitions workers handled toxic chemicals every day. Those
who handled sulphur were nicknamed 'Canary Girls', because their
skin and hair turned yellow from contact with the chemical. Former
munitions worker, Gwen Thomas from Liverpool remembered her
work vividly:

> [T]here was no training. You were put into what they called small
> shops where they made different sizes of shells and landmines and
> different things like that … you were just told what you had to do,
> filling them with TNT. And there was a lot involved in doing them,
> and they had to be filled to a certain level and then you had to put
> a tube in which was going to contain the detonator. Then it had to
> be all cleaned and scraped until it was exactly the right height inside
> the shells or the mines. I slipped on the floor with one of these big
> cans and I was covered in TNT. My eyes were concealed and
> everything, up my nose, it was everywhere. Some of the chaps that
> were working there got hold of me and put me onto a trolley and
> took me down to the medical place and obviously I had to wait for
> it to set on my face. I had quite a job getting it off my eyelashes,
> you know, and that sort of thing. And of course my face then was
> red and scarred with the hot TNT, you know. They put me on the
> bed for an hour or something, and then it was straight back to work
> after that.[20]

The Battle of Bamber Bridge

The 'Battle of Bamber Bridge' (see below) has only recently become
public knowledge to people outside of this small mill town east of
Preston.[21] The remarkable, and tragic, incident took place during
1944 when a large number of American service personnel were
based in Lancashire in preparation for the D-Day Landings. The
1511 Quartermaster Truck Regiment, a logistics unit for the US
Eighth Air Force, was based in Bamber Bridge where they supplied
other US regiments across the county. They were camped near to
the 234th US Military Police Company who had quarters on the
north side of the town. Following race riots in Detroit, the military

police called for a 'colour ban' in Bamber Bridge, hoping that this would stop any of the black soldiers from replicating the riot in Lancashire. The three Bamber Bridge pubs reacted by putting up signs that read: 'Black Troops Only'.

On the night of 24 June 1944, several American troops of the 1511th were drinking with the locals at Ye Olde Hob Inn. Two passing MPs were alerted after soldiers inside the pub attempted to buy beer after last orders had been called. They attempted to arrest Private Eugene Nunn for a minor uniform offence and an argument broke out with the military police on one side and the African American troops, with the locals, on the other. One black soldier, Private Lynn M. Adams brandished a bottle at the MPs causing one of them to draw his gun. A staff sergeant was able to defuse the situation but as the MPs drove away, Adams hurled a bottle at their jeep.

Further trouble ensued when some of the military police intercepted a group of black soldiers making their way back to base. A fight broke out and a shot was fired, hitting Adams in the neck. By midnight several jeep loads of MPs had arrived with an armoured car, fitted with a machine gun. British officers claimed that the MPs then ambushed the soldiers and a fire fight began. Troops warned locals to stay indoors as they exchanged gun fire; fortunately the darkness ensured that casualties were fewer than might otherwise have been the case. By 4 a.m. the 'battle' was over, leaving one man dead, Private William Crossland, and seven others were wounded.

Thirty-two soldiers were found guilty of a number of crimes including mutiny, seizing arms, and firing upon officers, at a court martial in Paignton in October 1943. Their sentences were reduced following an appeal.

Lancastrians in Spain

Many Lancashire men fought in Spain, the vast majority for the Republican side, against Franco's fascist coup in 1936. It became a rallying call for socialists and communists, as well as a great many others (the future Tory Prime Minister Edward Heath volunteered to fight on the Republican side). Every town in the North had an 'Aid Spain' campaign. But many men, and some women, decided that standing on the sidelines wasn't enough, and volunteered for the International Brigades.

In the 1930s, Lancashire was the scene of pitched battles between communists and the ILP against Mosley's British Union of Fascists. Many of the young men in Manchester's Jewish communities joined forces with them to oppose fascists and it was inevitable that many of the anti-fascists eagerly volunteered to go to Spain. Maurice Levine, from a Lithuanian Jewish background, was brought up in Cheetham Hill and joined the Communist Party as a young man. He volunteered to join the International Brigades in 1937, with his friend Bill Benson from Eccles. His story is told in *Cheetham to Cordova* and is a good account of the realities of life during the civil war for a young working-class man.

One of the first men to volunteer for Spain was Clem Beckett, known as 'Daredevil Beckett' on account of his racing exploits as a dirt track rider. Other volunteers included George Brown, a Communist Party official from Manchester, who was killed in action.[22]

Many women volunteered to go to Spain as nurses and doctors, including Mary Slater (see biography below).

* * *

Lancastrians: Mary Slater 1903–83

Mary Slater, born in Preston in 1903, started her working life as a weaver at the age of 14. She became active in her trade union and the Labour Party League of Youth. She was part of a youth delegation to the USSR in 1926 and was introduced to Stalin and Trotsky.

1931 saw a career change for Mary and she became a nurse. The 1930s saw the rise of fascism in Europe and when the Spanish Civil War broke out she immediately offered her services to the Republican government via the Spanish Medical Aid Committee.

Mary arrived in Spain on 29 September 1936 and was deployed to the Aragon Front. Her duties were varied, and included training Spanish women on nursing techniques, running clinics for local peasants and nursing wounded soldiers.

She was well travelled, being stationed in Granada and Benicasim, one of the main convalescent bases/hospitals for members of the International

Brigades. Mary served from September 1936 to August 1938 and during that period she had only one period of home leave—which she devoted to raising money for Spanish Medical Aid.

After the International Brigades' demobilisation in 1938 she was included in a group of Brigaders touring the UK to raise money for Spanish Medical Aid. Following this UK tour she applied for her post back and was promptly charged £5 for leaving her post without serving a period of notice. She carried on nursing throughout the London Blitz, returning to Preston as a senior nurse/matron at one of the care centres. Her life is commemorated by a plaque in Preston, which was unveiled in June 2018 in the city's Peace Garden.[23]

* * *

Several men from east Lancashire joined the International Brigades, including Burnley weaver Freeman Drinkwater who joined up at the age of 23 with Samuel Martin, of nearby Tiber Street. Both were Communist Party members. They entered Spain in secret over the Pyrenees to serve with the Major Attlee Battalion. They fought at Jarama River, to repel efforts to encircle Madrid, and were involved in an offensive at Brunete; Drinkwater was killed by a sniper just yards from his friend Samuel Martin during the battle. Nineteen-year-old George Buck, from Nelson, also travelled to Spain with Drinkwater and Martin, and was wounded. Another weaver, John Jolly, of Ann Street, Burnley, was the British Battalion's quartermaster in Madrigueras and was wounded in service. James Bridge, also of Nelson, took part in the Battle of Jarama.[24]

Bolton International Brigader James Alwyn was killed at Jarama and is honoured by a plaque outside Bolton Socialist Club, at 16 Wood Street. Other Bolton men who went to Spain included Joseph William Moran, Philip Harker,[25] John Kremer, and Henry Saunders-Bury, a doctor who was in charge of the hospital train repatriating the British wounded.

The impact of the Spanish Civil War on Lancashire had another aspect, caring for some of the 4,000 Basque children who were dispersed around the UK in 1937. About 250 children came to Manchester. On leaving their parents the children were told they would be away from their families 'solo por tres mesas' (only for three months) though some never returned. Some of the children were accommodated at Roman Catholic centres including the Brothers of Charity at Buckley Hall in Rochdale, Holly Mount Convent in Tottington and Our Lady of Lourdes Home in East Didsbury. The Basque Children's Committee, mostly comprising Quakers and socialists, arranged accommodation for fifty-six Basque children at Watermillock House, Bolton.[26]

Remembering brave Lancastrians

Lancashire has several museums dedicated to its military past—the Lancashire Infantry Museum at Fulwood, Preston, the Museum of the Lancashire Fusiliers in Bury and the Museum of the Manchesters in Ashton.

One of the most poignant memorials to war is the sculpture outside Manchester's Piccadilly station depicting a group of blinded soldiers. *Victory Over Blindness* is a bronze sculpture by Johanna Domke-Guyot. It depicts seven blind figures guiding each other and walking together; their likenesses are based upon real veterans who all suffered blindness as a result of action on the frontline. It was commissioned by Blind Veterans UK and was unveiled in October 2018. It is believed to be the only memorial to depict those wounded in the First World War. The sculpture was officially unveiled on 16 October 2018 by the Countess of Wessex. She said that, "As we approach the anniversary of the end of the First World War and, quite rightly, remember all of those who never returned, it is also important to remember those who did, changed by their experiences."

'Changed' was putting it mildly. The physical but also mental scars following any war are immense, but perhaps the First World War, not only for its sheer scale but also the unimaginable horror of the trenches, make it stand out above all conflicts. That's in no way to minimise the after-effects of the Second World War. The British men and women who liberated the concentration camps— the Ken Allens and Emily Hardings—had to live with the trauma for the rest of their lives and we can only salute their bravery.

11

CO-OPERATIVE LANCASHIRE

The co-operative movement was so influential in Lancashire that it deserves a chapter to itself. It literally supported Lancastrians 'from the cradle to the grave'. It didn't just feed and clothe you, it provided educational facilities, libraries, holidays, insurance and in some cases housing.

The 'Rochdale Pioneers', formed in 1844, were far from being the first co-operative society, but they were the most significant. They 'pioneered' a particular model of co-operation which met the immediate needs of hundreds of thousands of working-class people for good quality, unadulterated and affordable food, but they were more than just a shop.

The movement grew dramatically and Lancashire became the bastion of co-operation; Manchester remains the world headquarters of modern co-operation. The statue of Robert Owen, dubbed 'the father of co-operation', is a familiar sight to commuters arriving at Manchester's Victoria station. The statue, with Owen comforting a child, stands outside the Co-op's headquarters building.[1]

Yet the 'Owenite' myth isn't that helpful in understanding co-operation. Owen was a well-meaning philanthropist but his approach to co-operation was very much a 'top down' one, though he did inspire a rich crop of societies and unions bearing allegiance to Owenite principles. By the 1830s, co-operation was an established movement in Britain, especially the North, with strong organisation which included annual congresses, the first of which was held in Manchester in 1831.

The working men and women of Rochdale represent an enduring model of co-operation, even if it was less concerned with socialist utopias than feeding hungry families. T.W. Mercer in his celebra-tory *Towards the Co-operative Commonwealth*, published in 1936, said:

> If ever workers at the bottom of society resolved to make a gallant attempt to rise together to a much higher level of security and com-fort the weavers who pioneered a new co-operative venture in Rochdale were the men! The co-operators had loftier objectives than just selling bread, fresh vegetables and clothing. They aspired to a fully co-operative society and that as soon as practicable the "society would range the powers of production, distribution, educa-tion, and government, or in other words to establish a self-support-ing home colony of united interests".[2]

The Rochdale model was a break from previous co-operative societ-ies which had a restricted membership; it provided a very successful template for the rapid take-off of the co-operative movement. Before long, the Lancashire and Yorkshire textile towns had dozens of local shops, usually with one major store dominating the town centre but with many branches springing up in the outlying com-munities. Some remain to this day, some still doing good business, though many have vanished or been converted to other uses.

By the 1870s 'the Co-op' was a mature business, controlled by its mainly working-class membership. The directors of the local co-operative societies were largely working-class men. They were certainly not revolutionaries; they tended to be drawn from 'the respectable working class'—the spinners, engineers and other highly-unionised sectors of industry. Many would be active in their local chapel. They were cautious with their members' money and suspicious of utopian schemes for 'home colonies'.[3]

However, the co-operative societies did play an important role during major industrial disputes when they would provide credit to strikers' families. Without this support many strikes would have collapsed with workers driven back by sheer starvation.

Part of the 'respectable' working-class ethos was education, and many societies—Rochdale was one of the first—created well-stocked libraries years before Carnegie and the advent of municipal libraries.[4] Suitably uplifting works by Carlyle, Smiles, Ruskin and other Victorian icons were available to the studious working man—and woman. It encouraged arts groups, dramatic societies, choirs and orchestras. These all came together at the Co-operative Festival, held each year at the Crystal Palace between 1888 and 1905.

The Co-op became part of most aspects of working-class life in the North. Increasingly, towards the end of the nineteenth century, it had become a major employer. Within the complex of Co-op buildings in Manchester was a tobacco factory along with offices employing hundreds of staff. It had its own farms, dairies, bakeries and even coal mines. It owned a couple of coastal steamers. The Co-operative Society's *Pioneer* brought the first seaborne cargo into Manchester through the Ship Canal in 1896. The Co-op became involved in actual community building, with the creation of homes and in some cases factories.

Women as well as men had equal voting rights. Allen Clarke's novel of co-operation *The Men Who Fought for Us* highlights the importance of Ann Tweedale—"solitary and glorious" as one of the twenty-eight Rochdalians who formed the Pioneers' co-operative society in 1846. She had already been involved in earlier attempts at co-operation and was a supporter of the Chartists. Women inched their way into the co-operative movement, though photographs of committees of Northern societies, well into the 1890s and early 1900s, suggest that most active members were male.[5] The Co-operative Women's Guild was formed in 1883 and became a formidable force in promoting co-operation as well as supporting women's suffrage in the early 1900s.

* * *

Lancastrians: Sarah Reddish: Feminist, Co-operator 1849–1928

Sarah Reddish was born in Leigh in 1849 and left school at the age of 11 to work at home with her mother, a silk weaver. Her father, Thomas, was active in the co-operative movement and the family moved to Bolton where he became librarian and secretary to the Bolton Co-operative Education Committee. His co-operative principles rubbed off on his daughter. Sarah went on to work as a winder and reeler in the local mills and eventually became a forewoman in a hosiery mill.

Most of her busy life was devoted to the co-operative movement, but she was also prominent in the women's suffrage campaign and the Independent Labour Party (ILP). She was a popular public speaker and she travelled around the country with the first women's 'Clarion Van' tour of 1896, inspired by Robert Blatchford's popular Clarion *newspaper. From the back of the horse-drawn van, Sarah and her sisters propounded the new gospel of socialism, to audiences which varied from bemused and hostile to enthusiastic. In 1899 she was appointed part-time organiser of the Women's Trade Union League.*

She founded the Bolton branch of the Co-operative Women's Guild and was the national president for many years. The official history of the Guild noted that her "clear, logical and convincing speech came as a revelation of women's power". She played a key role in the women's suffrage movement in Lancashire. In 1903 she helped form the Lancashire and Cheshire Women's Textile Workers Representation Committee. Two years later she was involved in a major demonstration of Lancashire women cotton workers in London. Closer to home, she organised a demonstration on the steps of Bolton Town Hall to protest against the money being spent on the coronation of Edward VII, suggesting the money would have been better spent on feeding the poor.

She was the first woman on the Bolton Education Board 1899 and later was elected to the Poor Law Guardians. She was the first woman to stand for Bolton Council, representing women's organisations in the town, in 1907. She polled a respectable 737 votes but was not elected. She was a member of the Independent Labour Party and worked tirelessly to bring together different parts of the local Labour movement, culminating in the creation of the Bolton Socialist Party.

One of her most outstanding contributions to Bolton was her work for better childcare facilities. In 1906 she travelled to Ghent and Brussels to study childcare initiatives being launched by co-operative societies. On her return she established a 'School for Mothers' in Bolton to provide support for working-class mothers, naming it 'Babies Welcome' to avoid appearing to be condescending to the women who used it. It proved to be very successful and eventually eight centres were opened, leading to a dramatic reduction in child mortality in Bolton.

She was opposed to the First World War and played an active part in the anti-war movement in Lancashire. She died, at the age of 78, on 19 February 1928, and is buried at Heaton Cemetery. She was an active member of the Bolton Socialist Club which survives to this day; its members are keen to do more to celebrate her contribution. Moves are afoot to establish a permanent memorial to Sarah.

* * *

Another Allen Clarke novel which featured the Co-op was *The Knobstick*. He puts his finger on why the Co-op was so popular amongst hundreds of thousands of working-class Lancastrians:

> Nearly every working man in Spindleton was a member of the Co-operative Society, which had two dozen branch shops scattered over the district, and was in a most flourishing condition. The dividend, or 'divi', as it was briefly and fondly designated, was regarded with the most affection in Spindleton, and no wonder, for it was always close upon three shillings in the pound, and sometimes over. It was a means of saving money of which thrifty operatives availed themselves readily.[6]

Allen Clarke was writing about Lancashire in the mid-1880s. I asked a Bolton friend recently what they remembered as the main attraction of the Co-op to her family when she was growing up in the 1960s. The reply was instant: "The Divi!"

The Co-op was deeply rooted in Lancashire society and culture. Its local magazines promoted local writers and it provided a concert platform for entertainers such as Edwin Waugh, the great Lancashire dialect poet. Its libraries stocked work by local writers who themselves would have been members of the Co-op, and it was normal for co-operative societies to feature among the list of subscribers for local historical and literary publications.

The co-operative movement made much of its local roots and during the 1920s placed adverts in several Lancashire publications extolling the values of co-operation—in broad Lancashire Dialect![7]

The Co-operative Press

All of the larger (and many smaller) Lancashire industrial towns had substantial co-operative societies, mostly established from the 1850s onwards. Many of these societies produced their own monthly magazine, though they were mostly started some decades after the societies themselves had been established. The great majority of the magazines were printed at the Co-operative Wholesale Society's print works at Longsight, Manchester, keeping the production within the Co-op 'family'. *The Bolton Co-operative Record* started in

1889 and circulation quickly rose to 10,000 copies each month, reaching 15,000 in 1905.[8]

* * *

Lancastrians: John Thomas Taylor 1851–1926

J.T. Taylor was active in the Oldham co-operative movement, serving as secretary and chairman before becoming editor of the Oldham Co-operative Record in 1894. He also wrote the 'Jubilee History' of the Oldham Society, in 1900. He contributed numerous stories and poems to the local press which were published in book form in 1928. He worked for most of his life as an engineer at Platt Bros. of Oldham. In religion he was Unitarian and in politics Liberal.[9]

He was born in what was then a semi-rural community at Busk, near Chadderton. His parents were handloom silk weavers and John worked 'at a very early age' helping to wind the silk bobbins. His father's poor health and the decline of handloom weaving forced John to get work as a half-timer in a nearby mill. He later got a job at Platt Brothers.

As a young man he used the Co-operative Society reading and reference rooms in Oldham, where "he became a great reader and a clear thinker, and by persevering in self-education he laid the foundations of a literary and political knowledge which gave him confidence in himself".[10]

He became active in the Liberal Party as well as Oldham Industrial Co-operative Society, for which he served as both secretary and chairman. He became a writer in both standard English and dialect. In his professional career at Platt's he visited the United States and became a highly skilled engineer.

* * *

The Oldham Co-operative Record began in 1894 as a monthly magazine edited by J.T. Taylor (see above). By the early 1890s it had a circulation of 9,000.[11] Tiny Greenfield, just a mile over the border into the West Riding, had a very active society that was part of the Oldham district organisation. David Lawton (nom-de-plume 'Th'Owd Weighver') edited *The Greenfield Co-operative Messenger* and was secretary of the Greenfield society for many years.[12]

Leigh was somewhere in between the mighty Bolton and Oldham societies and the small community of Greenfield. It published *The Leigh Co-operative Record* for many years and provided an outlet for working-class writers such as Mary Thomason (see below).

Co-operative communities

The Rochdale Pioneers aspired not only to provide affordable, good quality food and clothing to its members, but to create an alternative society, based on 'home colonies'—or self-governing communities. In reality, the Pioneers quietly shelved this objective and got on with the day job, but there remained—over many decades—a tiny but enthusiastic minority who wanted to establish 'heaven on earth' through such co-operative colonies. They are of more than purely historical interest to socialists today. The desire to create alternative communities remains, and perhaps reached its most developed form in Israel's kibbutz movement. In a diluted form, the garden cities and villages were based on similar attempts to create new, democratic communities.

One of the earliest attempts to create a co-operative community in Lancashire was at Birkacre, near Chorley, in the early 1830s. The co-operative movement was already well established across England by the time of the first Co-operative Congress, held in Manchester on 26 and 27 May 1831. An address to the congress stated that "co-operation seeks to put the Working Classes in that situation where they shall enjoy the whole produce of their labour, instead of the small part called 'wages'. This can be done only by the establishment of Communities."[13]

The Chorley co-operators took up the challenge and established the 'Co-operative Society of Silk and Calico Printers, Birkacre, Lancashire' and took on the lease of a large mill in September 1831. It was an ambitious project. In addition to the mill there were thirty cottages and the former mill owner's house which was converted into apartments. The co-operative employed about forty workers, mostly 'journeymen calico printers'. A library, reading room and school were provided. The first two years of trading seem to have been successful, yet by 1834 the company went bankrupt. John Harrison suggests several reasons for the failure, including differing objectives for the project: was it an exercise in community building or was its prime purpose to provide well-paid jobs to calico printers? In all probability, like many other producers' co-operatives, it was under-capitalised from the start and they had simply taken on too much.[14] However, it was a brave and pioneering attempt to create an alternative society.

Co-operation struck deep roots across the North, nowhere more so than Lancashire. The societies which grew so rapidly were proud of their independence but knew when it was right to co-operate between themselves. The Co-operative Wholesale Society (CWS) was formed in Liverpool in 1853 out of some earlier initiatives (see page 258) but quickly moved to Manchester to be nearer the growing number of societies in the 'cotton belt'. The CWS expanded rapidly and commissioned its own ship to carry goods from the Mersey (Garston Docks) to Rouen. Perhaps the CWS's finest hour was in 1913 during the Dublin Dock Strike. Thousands of families were on the brink of starvation and the CWS, with the assistance of Liverpool and Dublin dockers, shipped 50,000 parcels of food to Dublin. The shipments continued for four successive months with a weekly cargo of 500 tons.

Co-ops and local histories

Any history of the co-operative movement must recognise local distinctiveness and independence. The societies which developed in the second half of the nineteenth century were locally owned and managed, though it was very much in their DNA to 'co-operate' with other societies and share resources when appropriate. There was a stream of local co-operative society histories between 1900 and the First World War when many Lancashire societies celebrated their golden jubilees.

* * *

Lancastrians: Mary Thomason 1863–1937

Mary Thomason was an example of an 'organic working-class intellectual', very much a part of Leigh's co-operative movement in the years between the

1870s and 1930s. She worked for most of her life as a weaver and wrote poetry, short stories and non-fiction. Many of her poems were published in The Leigh Co-operative Record. *She was a member of the society's management committee and active in the Women's Co-operative Guild.*[15]

Mary Thomason née Pemberton was born on 3 March 1863 at Barlows Factory, Westleigh. She was the daughter of Thurston Pemberton and wife Alice. Thurston was a silk weaver, then a coalminer and finally a colliery checkweighman.

She married Joseph Peter Thomason in 1888 at the Wesleyan Chapel in Pennington, near Leigh. They had three children, though only one survived childhood.

At the age of 13, in 1876, Mary became a pupil-teacher at Leigh British School and on the 1881 census she was living in Victoria Street. By 1901 she was living in Catherine Street and had become an assistant schoolmistress. Mary was a schoolteacher for 34 years and taught at Westleigh Wesleyan Schools, but during her time as a supply teacher, taught at most schools in Leigh.

Mary took a deep interest in the educational and religious life of Leigh and at one time was a representative on the Lancashire and Cheshire Institutes, the first woman from Leigh to enjoy that distinction. She also served for many years on the Educational Board of Leigh Friendly Co-operative Society. She was a member of Leigh Literary Society, and became a talented poet, with many of her poems covering local themes; she was fiercely proud of her home town.

Mary's daughter, Alice Maud Prescott, privately published Mary's book Warp and Weft: Cuts from a Lancashire Loom *in 1938. This book contains articles and poems, many of which had appeared in the* Leigh Chronicle, *the* Leigh Journal *and the* Leigh Co-operative Record. *In the preface, Alice writes that she decided to publish the book "to place on record in permanent form a cameo of Leigh and its people of fifty or sixty years ago".*

Leigh Local History Library and Museum has some of Mary's poetry displayed and a recording of her reciting a dialect sketch.

* * *

Very often, part of the celebration included a well-produced, often quite detailed, history of the society. They were invariably printed

by the Co-operative Newspaper Society in Manchester. They sometimes crop up in second-hand bookshops and offer fascinating
insights into nineteenth-century co-operation at a very local level.
I've selected Accrington, Liverpool and Littleborough to illustrate
three very different examples of successful local co-operation.

Accrington: what they can do in Rochdale …

The Accrington and Church Industrial Co-operative Society celebrated its jubilee in 1910. The society commissioned professional
journalist James Haslam (who crops up elsewhere in these pages)[16]
to write its history.[17] He not only trawled the society's records but
was able to interview some of the early pioneers who were still
living. He clearly enjoyed his task. He wrote that "The writer of
these pages has felt more pride and realised more joy in wandering
about the streets of Accrington with one of your pioneers—
Mr. James Parkinson—than he would have done with any of the
more distinguished citizens."[18]

The beginnings of co-operation in Accrington go back to the late
1850s and were directly inspired by the success of the Rochdale
'Pioneers'. Haslam quotes his companion James Parkinson saying,
"We said among eawrsels, 'what they can do in Rochdale, we can
do in Accrington.' An' we had a try."[19]

Most of the early co-operators were weavers, as well as some
print workers. They met in the room of the Accrington Weavers'
Society in Briggs' Entry, a modest place down a back entry. The
co-operative developed slowly during the 1850s and was registered
in 1860. There was a close link between the society and the emerging trade union movement in the town. Their ranks were swelled
by several weavers from Settle who had been victimised in a strike.

Their first venture was the bulk purchase of tea, which was divided
out between members in the weavers' room. The society adopted the
'Rochdale' model rules and had as their objects 'the supplying of all
kinds of weaving and eating', suggesting they had aspirations to
become a producers' co-operative at some stage, as well as supplying
basic foodstuffs. As Haslam commented, "that was the new political
economy summed up with remarkable pithiness".[20]

The first shop was opened on Birch Street in August 1860; the
accommodation was basic but it was a start. They sold a range of

foodstuffs including potatoes, meats, preserves—and of course, tea. When the society was formed it had 81 members. By the year end, December 1860, it had grown to 263. By the end of 1862 membership stood at 713 and rose again to 1,143 the following year with a share capital of £5,475. This was particularly remarkable as Accrington suffered as much as any town during the Cotton Famine from 1861 to 1864. At the depth of the crisis in December 1862 the society was able to provide financial relief to members as well as supporting local charities.

The society built up a strong financial base and was able to invest in many local businesses as well as other co-operative enterprises, including the Co-operative Landowning Company. It invested £5,000 in a Mill Building Company in 1905, using the common east Lancashire 'room and power' model. A company would own the infrastructure—the actual building, looms and engine, renting the space to small manufacturers. Interestingly, the local Weavers' Association also invested £1,000 in the project. It had an even more ambitious plan to purchase nearly a thousand acres of land on the Stanhill estate and build a complete 'co-operative community', but this seems to have fallen foul of the First World War.

The society quickly developed a 'social' side. Its third soiree, in 1862, was attended by 600 people; the 1871 event, at the Peel Institute, had over a thousand. It was agreed that 1.5% of the society's profits should be used for educational purposes, and a lecture hall, reading room and library was provided, 'stocked with newspapers and books suitable for working men'. The educational work included classes in a varied range of subjects. In 1871 there was a total of sixty-four students attending classes in arithmetic, reading, writing, dictation, geography, history and composition. Further classes were added in chemistry, physiology and mathematics. As the society expanded, more libraries and reading rooms were opened across the town. A branch of the Women's Co-operative Guild was formed in 1891 at a meeting addressed by Sarah Reddish of Bolton.[21] The society's choir developed a strong reputation and won first prize at the Lytham Musical Festival in 1906.

The society became an important player in the local housing market. In its first fifty years it built 179 houses, of which it sold ninety-six and rented the remainder. It had a policy of 'affordable rents and quality homes', within the reach of working-class people. By 1910 it had fifty-nine 'places of business'—mostly grocery and butchers' shops, but also seven cloggers, a furniture department, drapery and millinery stores and three bakers' shops.

The society had much to be proud of when it celebrated its jubilee in 1910. It did so with panache—a series of events culminating in a conference, procession and concert. The children's gala and demonstration was held on a sunny July day and attracted over 10,000 participants.

Liverpool: say not the struggle nought availeth[22]

The story of the Liverpool Co-operative Society stretches back to 1829. A centenary history was written by W.H. Brown and published by the Liverpool Co-operative Society in 1929. Temperance reformer John Finch initiated what became the First Liverpool Co-operative Society, with a membership of a dozen 'working men' who met in school rooms on Stanhope Street. In similar fashion to the Accrington pioneers, they made collective purchases of basic necessities to help bring costs down. The following year, 1830, women were admitted as full members and, as Brown records, "the idea caught on". By the summer of 1830 there were "seven or eight co-operative societies in Liverpool, all doing well".[23]

The First Liverpool Co-operative Society developed a novel idea that had massive ramifications. It used its resources to become a wholesaler to other co-operative societies and formed the basis of what became the Co-operative Wholesale Society. By 1830 societies as far afield as Birmingham, Kendal, Coventry, Bradford and others were trading with the Liverpool society. At the Manchester Co-operative Congress, held in May 1831, Robert Owen proposed that "The North-west of England United Co-operative Company should be established at Liverpool." It was unanimously adopted and was able to build on the existing activities of the Liverpool society. The Co-operative Wholesale Society emerged from Owen's proposals and registered its office at 15 Camden Street, Liverpool in 1863. It subsequently transferred to Manchester two years later.

In the early 1830s Liverpool was emerging as the main centre of co-operation in England; in October 1832 the fourth Co-operative

Congress was held in the city. There were thirty delegates from thirty-eight societies and the meeting lasted nearly a week. A feature of the congress was an exhibition held in the Assembly Room on Castle Street. The Earl of Derby was invited to support the event but declined because of his concern that "co-operative societies were combinations of men to oppose their employers and raise wages". His lordship subsequently modified his stance and one of his successors presided at the Co-operative Congress in 1881. However, if the Stanleys were at first wary, Lady Noel Byron, wife of the poet, sent £5 towards the cost of the exhibition and expressed interest in setting up a co-operative society on her land at Gateacre, on the city's outskirts.[24]

The Liverpool Co-operative Provident Association was formed by a small group of men in May 1851 to sell groceries, soap and candles. Some of the first members were veterans of earlier co-operative ventures in the 1820s and 1830s. By January 1854 a gathering of over 500 members and friends celebrated its third annual festival with a tea party, music, songs and sketches. During the 1860s further societies were formed and a festival was held in the city's grand St George's Hall to celebrate the Provident Society's new premises. Three thousand tickets were sold and the audience was entertained by the 4th Lancashire Artillery Volunteers band. Speeches were made by William Rathbone, Abel Heywood and other luminaries. Reversing his previous opposition, Lord Stanley (Earl of Derby) welcomed the society's work and hoped that, "if speculative transactions are avoided, they will extend their operations into every branch of business and very materially alter the position of the working man". Gladstone also sent a message of support.

By 1863 co-operation had taken root across the Northern region. The five biggest societies in Britain were all in the North, "proof of the fidelity of Lancashire and Yorkshire to the co-operative principle, which had been woven into the texture of the North".[25] The 'big five' were Halifax with 4,300 members, Rochdale Pioneers (4,013), Hull Corn Mill (3,818), Leeds Holbeck (3,555) and Liverpool Provident (3,154).

Despite its early success, the Liverpool Provident fell on hard times and was wound up in the late 1860s. Its large building was rented out for entertainment purposes and in 1872 became 'The

Royal Temple of Magic'. W.H. Brown makes the perceptive comment that co-operation in Liverpool faced specific challenges, different to those of the south-east Lancashire cotton towns:

> Since 1829 Liverpool was bestrewn with memories of seemingly futile endeavours to organise the consumers for their mutual protection. Men kept on getting together for another try. Their problem was of a different order to that of the workers in the textile areas where the people clustered around the mills and marched in battalions to their own stores. Merseyside was inhabited by folks of a migratory habit. Many were seafarers whose wives accumulated debts ready for clearance when the ships came home ... The cosmopolitan make-up of the population militated against the mutuality of the daily interests that gave permanence to co-operative societies in other Lancashire towns.[26]

People were prepared to have another go; new local co-operative societies were formed around the city—at Garston, in 1884, Edge Hill and Wavertree in 1890, Toxteth, Bootle and Seaforth the following year. The City of Liverpool Equitable Society was formed in 1885 and covered a bigger area.

This time it worked. There was a series of amalgamations with the Bootle and Seaforth society merging with the City of Liverpool; Toxteth followed suit in 1915. The enormous 'Unity House' opened in 1920 as the City of Liverpool's showpiece store. Four years later the society took over the management of the co-operative society at Douglas with a view to the development of co-operation across the Isle of Man. By the time Liverpool co-operation celebrated its centenary in 1929, the Liverpool Co-operative Society closed the year with a membership of 120,000, sales of over £3 million and capital of £1.5 million.

Some branches, including the previously independent Toxteth, were particularly active in their communities, with choirs, lectures, children's events and many other activities. Branches of the Co-operative Women's Guild were formed in the early 1900s and a 'country retreat' was set up near Cronton in 1907, "so that tired mothers and their babies could have a change of air".[27]

Littleborough: mind your own business

Very different to Liverpool, or Accrington—Littleborough is a small former mill town on the edge of the Pennines, a few miles east of the 'Mecca' of co-operation, Rochdale. The local co-op celebrated its centenary in 1950. Its programme of celebrations contained a full history of the society. Whilst not as spectacular as Liverpool's, or Accrington's, it showed steady progress across a century. The fore-word to the *Programme of Celebrations* is suitably triumphal:

> We are the premier trading concern in town and district with a membership of over 2,900 and share capital exceeding £84,941. During the past 100 years we have paid to our members £488,660 in dividend alone. Our Society is open to all and offers security with satisfaction. By trading at your own stores you can *Mind Your Own Business.*[28]

Few of the society's early records have survived and what we do know was pieced together by N.H. Gregory in his historical notes to the 1950 souvenir programme. One of the founders, Thomas Dawson, was still living (in Bury) in 1910 and some of his memories of early co-operation in Littleborough were recorded.

A group of 'working men' met at a cottage at 84 Church Street, where a small shop was opened in November 1850. There were thirty-one original members, most of whom worked at the Sladen Mill. They subscribed £96, not an inconsiderable amount for the time. Gregory notes that there was an earlier example of 'informal co-operation' during the construction of the Manchester and Leeds Railway, which ran through Littleborough. Thomas Schofield, of Smithy Nook, recalled that several of the workers rented a house at Stoneyroyd, in the late 1830s, bought goods wholesale and sold them on to members. It seems to have closed when construction of the railway was completed.

Gregory estimates that in its first year of business the shop brought in less than £50 a week, but sales were growing. In its first six years, total sales reached £2,538 a week and the society decided to move to larger premises on Church Street. Membership had grown to 161 by 1856. A second shop was opened in 1861 and membership then stood at 440. In 1869 the society acquired land to build forty-eight cottages on the Bare Hill Estate and also built Wellington Terrace. It opened its new 'central' store in Hare Hill Road in 1883; by then it had six branches and a drapery department. The central store included a library—the only such facility in town at the time. When a new municipal library was opened in Littleborough the society closed its own book service and transferred its stock to the new municipal facility.

It wasn't all plain sailing and in 1887 the society ran into trouble through the failure of the Frankfort Cotton Mill. Although not owned by the society, many of its members worked there and it invested £28,000 in what was known locally as 'Co-op Mill'. The company failed in 1881 and the society lost £22,000, reducing its share price significantly. To add to the society's woes, in 1897 the society secretary was found guilty of embezzlement, further affecting its financial standing.

Things got better. In 1900 the Co-op celebrated its 50th anniversary and was able to record healthy sales and consequent profits. In 1903 the society presented an ornamental drinking foundation to Littleborough District Council, which was erected at Hare Hill Park. It had two cloggers' shops and a seventh branch opened in 1905. Two years later a Bakery and Co-operative Hall opened on Bare Hill, capable of accommodating 400 people. It was used for a range of larger social events and the Co-operative Society held an annual tea party and concert. A confectionery department and cafe were opened in 1916, followed by a fish and game department two years later. Clearly, the war did not have an adverse effect on sales. However, economic depression in the 1920s and 1930s did have a negative impact on the society's activities and sales plummeted. Further difficult trading conditions ensued after the Second World War, though things recovered in time for the centenary celebrations.

By 1950, the society's membership stood at nearly 3,000, with more than 80% of the town's householders in membership. The centenary history noted that more than half its members were women but there "has never yet been a woman on the Committee of the Society".[29]

The society maintained a range of member benefits including a 'Wakes Holiday Club', introduced in 1918 to fund members' holidays, and a Sick Club which provided help with stays at Co-operative Convalescent Homes.

The centenary celebrations included a 'Grand Opening Concert' in the Co-operative Hall, a Pageant of Fashion, a Centenary Ball, Children's Night, Grand Whist Drive, Aged Folks' Night and a Grand Closing Concert, addressed by the general secretary of the Co-operative Union, R. Southern.

The 1960s saw changes to the Co-op with the commencement of store closures including Summit and Caldermoor. Discussions with Rochdale Equitable Pioneers Society Ltd led to the transfer of the Littleborough Co-op's assets to the Rochdale Equitable Pioneers Society Ltd in 1967. Most of the branch buildings remain in other uses though some have disappeared. The Co-op retains a presence in the town, with a large modern store on Railway Street.

Lancashire co-operation today

Manchester remains 'the world capital' of co-operation and the museum at Rochdale's Toad Lane does much to keep the history of co-operation alive. The days of the small, locally owned and managed co-operative society have all but gone, though there are still some surviving local independent co-operative stores such as Coniston.

However, it is in the broader field of small co-operatives where the real growth has been. Co-operatives UK is the umbrella body for Britain's thousands of independent co-operatives—of which there are currently 746 in the North-West who are members of Co-operatives UK. They comprise a huge array of businesses ranging from pubs and breweries to bike shops, energy co-operatives, credit unions, football clubs (including the famous Accrington Stanley), bands and allotment societies.

If co-operation is not the same as it once was in the pioneering days its basic principles are very much alive and well.

12

LANCASTRIAN ART AND LITERATURE

Lancashire has a strong literary and artistic tradition; it has excelled in the visual arts, though too often people's awareness of Lancashire art doesn't go beyond Lowry's 'matchstick men'. Lancashire was a much-written-about county in the nineteenth century but few novelists were 'of Lancashire'. A remarkable exception is Elizabeth Gaskell who wrote powerful fiction about life in industrial Lancashire. John Ruskin was a major influence and spent the last thirty years of his life in Coniston, Lancashire. He loved the Lakes but despised industrialism. However, his influence was considerable, not only in art and literature but also in politics and—perhaps less obviously—today's environmental movement. Dickens wrote *about* Lancashire but was not *of* it—*Hard Times* remains an important literary description of life in industrial Lancashire, but the work of an outsider.

One of the most significant social groups in the development of a distinctive regional culture—in literature, but also music, botany and mathematics—were the handloom weavers, whose 'golden age' was quite short—from the middle of the eighteenth century to the 1830s. As E.P. Thompson said, "a unique blend of social conservatism, local pride and cultural attainment made up the way of life of the ... Lancashire weaving community ... there was certainly a leaven amongst the northern weavers of self-educated and articulate men of considerable attainments".[1]

Samuel Bamford would have taken offence at the well-meaning academic's words. "Leaven? Mooar nor that..." Referring to the handloom weavers, he wrote in his 1844 *Walks in South Lancashire*:

And what shall I say of the working class? That they are the most intelligent of any island—in the world. The Scotch workers are the only ones who approach them in intelligence; they are the greatest readers; can shew the greatest number of good writers; the greatest number of sensible and considerate speakers. They can shew a greater number of botanists; a greater number of horticulturalists; a greater number who are acquainted with the abstruse sciences, the great number of poets and a greater number of good musicians, whether choral or instrumental.[2]

He added, almost as an afterthought, that they were pretty good weavers too.

They were politically radical. Tom Paine's *The Rights of Man* was widely read and contemporary accounts record well-read copies in many a weaver's cottage. A highly articulate and self-educated radicalism combined with a few decades of prosperity as the spinning industry became automated in the 1780s and created a huge demand for weaving.

* * *

Bamford was an early example of a working-class writer who used both standard English and dialect. Dialect literature was a distinct form of literature—'an invented tradition' from the mid-nineteenth century. It is separate, but closely related, to dialect speech which is looked at in Chapter 3.

Lancashire had its own subversive caricaturists such as 'Tim Bobbin', or John Collier, known as 'The Lancashire Hogarth'. Collier was 'the father of Lancashire dialect literature'[3] and used his literary and artistic skills to poke fun at local dignitaries.

In theatre, talented writers such as Shelagh Delaney pioneered what was derisively called 'kitchen-sink drama' but reflected real life in Northern working-class communities. The hugely popular TV series *Coronation Street* reflects the changing cultural mores of Lancashire over seventy years. Twentieth-century Lancashire writers included Walter Greenwood, Harold Brighouse, Bill Naughton and William Holt. Contemporary writers include Jeanette Winterson (exiled in London) and Salford poet John Cooper-Clarke—a modern-day Edwin Waugh?

Lancashire's fine artistic tradition is sometimes obscured by its description as 'The Northern School' of artists; it's really a 'Lancashire' school and described as such in the subtitle of Peter Davies's great book on Northern art.[4] Of course Lowry figures strongly but his influence has been controversial for its depiction of a romanticised industrial Lancashire—and in particular for his subsequent influence on younger artists encouraged to ape his distinctive style. The contributions of Geoff Key, Theodore Major, Harold Riley and many others need emphasising.

It is more difficult to argue for a specifically 'Lancashire' film industry. However, Lancashire was the setting for some well-known films in the 1960s, such as *Spring and Port Wine* and *The Family Way*. Today there are some outstanding Northern film-makers and a growing number of small film studios and companies. International film festivals have developed over the last few years in Bolton and Manchester.

A Lancashire press

Lancastrians have always had a thirst for 'news'. The history of the press in Lancashire is fascinating and multi-faceted. Without doubt, a healthy, locally-based press helped to develop and bolster a distinct regional identity. In this chapter I want to look at the emergence of a strong local newspaper culture in the eighteenth and nineteenth centuries, but also specifically regional publications which catered for a more specific readership, such as *The Cotton Factory Times* and, much earlier, the Chartist *Northern Star*. Some newspapers, such as Robert Blatchford's *Clarion* catered for a mainly (but not exclusively) North of England readership and was, in its early years, published in Manchester.

Stanley Harrison, in *Poor Men's Guardians*, made the point that 'news' was potentially seditious, suggesting that "every presumption to circulate *news* touched sovereignty—monarchical or republican, State or Church, Anglican or Presbyterian. For news interprets, and serves views and causes."[5]

The beginnings of a popular press go back to the seventeenth century. Harrison points out that the Civil War "tore a wide breach in the whole conception of publishing as a closed preserve of authority",[6] though attempts were made to restore the breach following the

Restoration of 1660. However, the genie was out of the bottle and the House of Commons allowed newspaper licensing laws to lapse in 1695. By the beginning of the seventeenth century several newspapers appeared, mostly London-based such as *The Daily Courant*.

The *Lancashire Journal* appeared in 1738. It was sold in Warrington, Liverpool, Manchester, Preston, Rochdale and also through a number of outlets in Cheshire and Yorkshire. It ran to over a hundred editions. It included a history of the Bible and what amounted to local tittle-tattle to amuse readers. It was a sort of early version of the modern-day popular press. The publisher kept himself busy with many other activities. As William Axon commented:

> The early Lancashire journalist was a man of many parts. Thus the *Lancashire Journal* of December 1740 is said to be "printed by John Berry, Watchmaker and Printer, at the Dial near the Cross, who makes and mends all sorts of Pocket watches, also makes and mends all sorts of Wedding, Mourning and other Gold Rings, and Earrings Etc...."[7]

The list went on ... and on. Mr Berry's other activities included the sale of musical instruments, bird cages, various elixirs, 'sick pills' and other remedies. Axon laconically observes that,

> we cannot estimate the feelings of our great-grandfathers as they turned over the leaves of their small paper; but the antiquary of the present day would gladly dispense with a good deal about bashaws and conventions for a little bit more about those who lived and moved and had their being in the county.[8]

Restrictions on the press did, however, continue. The Stamp Acts, brought in during 1750, imposed a tax on newspapers which made the economics of publishing more difficult. That said, it did not prevent a major growth in newspapers across the country.

It's more difficult to pin down the appearance of the first newspaper in Lancashire. In neighbouring Yorkshire *The Leeds Mercury* began in 1718 and became part of *The Yorkshire Post*, which is still going strong.[9]

The Manchester Guardian appeared in 1821, reflecting the need for a radical newspaper for the wider Lancashire region, two years after the Peterloo Massacre. Other local newspapers followed. *The*

Southport Visiter (sic) started publishing in 1844 followed by the nearby *Ormskirk Advertiser* in 1853, just two years before all taxes on newspaper publishing were abolished.

* * *

Lancastrians: James Taylor Staton 1817–75

Staton was a most unusual character, described as "one of the most versatile Lancashire authors of the last century".[10] Perhaps his main claim to fame in terms of dialect literature was that he pioneered the production of sketches adapted for public recital, as 'penny readings'. Whilst important as part of the canon of Lancashire dialect literature, he was an important figure in local journalism. He was born in Bolton in 1817 but was orphaned at an early age. He obtained a place at Chetham's School (The Blue Coat School) in Manchester and was later apprenticed to a Bolton printer. His first piece of writing was The Bowtun Loominary, *first published on 10 April 1852, which ran for ten years, being killed off by the Lancashire Cotton Famine (1861–4).*

The Manchester publisher John Heywood recruited him to edit a new paper, mostly in dialect, called The Lancashire Loominary. *It lasted a few years before he was persuaded to return to Bolton by John Tillotson to work on* The Bolton Evening News, *where he became a sub-editor. He became Editor in Chief of* The Farnworth Observer, *another Tillotson publication. Staton was radical in his political views and used his publications to attack corruption and injustice. He was appointed a Guardian for Great Bolton in the 1860s. His publications included* A Guide to Rivington Pike, The Purpose and Design of the Ragged Schools *and* What Must We Do to Be Saved?[11]

* * *

The abolition of taxes on newspapers led to a dramatic reduction in prices which fuelled the growth of a local press. The typical cost of a local newspaper in the pre-1850s period was around 4d—quite a big chunk out of many people's weekly incomes. *The Bolton Free Press* in 1840 would have cost you 4½d, although Soulby's *Ulverston Advertiser and General Intelligencer* was a slightly more affordable 3½d by 1850, just before taxes were abolished.[12] By 1870 *The Bacup Times and Rossendale Advertiser* was available for just a penny.

The local press of the second half of the nineteenth century was well established across Lancashire and the typical local paper was far from the 'picture-heavy, content-light' rag that tends to pass for local journalism today. Important local meetings would be covered in depth, often with verbatim reports of speeches. Many larger towns had at least two newspapers, typically representing opposing political views, Tory or Liberal. In Blackburn, the *Standard* was staunchly Tory (and anti-Catholic) whilst the *Times* was Liberal.

Manchester developed as a major regional and national publishing centre. *The Manchester Guardian* stands out but it had some strong local competitors. C.E. Harford described the *Guardian* as "a great political organ" and praised "the momentous services which, especially during the last half century, it has rendered to the intellectual and social life of Manchester". He went on to record that four years after the *Guardian*'s establishment,

> a rival organ, the *Manchester Courier*, was founded with Alaric Watts, a brilliant young journalist, as its first editor. A second Liberal paper, *The Examiner and Times*, was conducted during the third quarter of the century with distinguished ability. Its last editor, Henry Dunckley ('Verax') stood in the highest rank of living journalists.[13]

Regardless of their politics, the local press would promote a strong sense of pride in local identity. A regular feature in many Lancashire newspapers was the work of local poets, often in dialect.

The use of the vernacular reinforced this strong sense of local identity. John T. Baron ('Jack o'Ann's) was a regular contributor to *The Blackburn Times* over a period of 33 years, from the mid-1880s. He combined a weekly 'Rhymes in the Dialect' column with a demanding job as a skilled engineer and union official.[14] J.T. Taylor, whose day job was a textile machinist for Platt's of Oldham, wrote dialect poetry and prose for the *Oldham Chronicle* from 1873, using noms-de-plume such as 'Jammy o'Jim's' and 'Mally o'Tum's'. He edited *The Oldham Co-operative Record* from 1894 which was another outlet for his dialect writing.[15]

* * *

Lancastrians: James Haslam 1858–1937

James Haslam was one of the most interesting figures in Lancashire writing in the inter-war years. He was proud of having been brought up in a hand-loom-weaving family in Bolton in the 1850s. He started work in the mill as a half-timer and quickly showed a talent for writing.

As a young cotton worker he knocked on the door of Allen Clarke who was then editing his Teddy Ashton's Northern Weekly, *asking if he'd employ him. Perhaps mindful of his own rejections as an aspiring young writer, Clarke agreed to give him a chance. He became a permanent part of Clarke's team. He worked for the* Blackpool Gazette *and later the* Liverpool Courier. *He was appointed 'special commissioner' for the* Co-operative News *which led him to become editor of the magazine itself. He became chief of the Co-operative Wholesale Society's publicity department, a role he held for 17 years before retirement in 1934. He wrote several histories of local co-operative societies, including Accrington and Eccles.*

He published a novel set in early nineteenth-century Lancashire, The Handloom Weaver's Daughter, *first serialised as 'The Mill on the Moor' in* Northern Weekly. *Haslam went on to work for mainstream titles and became president of the National Union of Journalists.*

He became editor of The Cotton Factory Times *in 1932 and remained in the job until the paper ceased publication in 1937. He was a member of the Lancashire Authors' Association but was ambivalent about using dialect, which he saw as a hindrance to bright working-class children.*[16]

* * *

The Cotton Factory Times ran from 1885 to 1937 and was widely read amongst Lancashire cotton workers. It had a sister paper, *Yorkshire Factory Times*, also published by Andrews of Ashton-under-Lyne and which shared some content. As well as having extensive news coverage on cotton industry issues from a trades union perspective, it carried short stories, poetry and serialised novels.[17]

* * *

Lancastrians: W.H. Jenkins ('Harry o'Tum's') 1859–1926

Jenkins was born in Portsmouth but came to Oldham with his family when he was seven. The following year he started work as a half-timer in an

Oldham mill. He worked in the mill all his life but found time to be a public singer, a composer, band conductor and instrumentalist. He wrote in both standard English and dialect and his work was published by Allen Clarke in Teddy Ashton's Northern Weekly *in the early 1900s. In his later years he became a devoted Spiritualist. This spilled over into his literary work, developing 'automatic writing' techniques, in which he claimed 'the spirits' guided his hand. He was probably the only Lancashire dialect writer to claim this skill.*

Allen Clarke (as 'Teddy Ashton') wrote a tribute to him in The Cotton Factory Times *noting that, "at eight year owd he were warkin' as hauve-timer in an Owdham factory ... in his latter years he geet vastly interested in spiritualism, an' did a lot o'drawin's an' writin' that he said were th'wark o'spirits usin' his hond. Some ancient Egyptians, a theausand years deead, possessed him an' made revelations through him, he claimed ... Be that as it may, I durnt think they helped him mich, an' happen he only fancied it aw. But spirits or no spirits, Jenkins had a faith as firm as Walt Whitman's in immortality an' he passed on to th'next world in November 1926."*[18]

He was also a "public singer, a music composer of much ability, a band conductor and instrumentalist, a writer of numerous hymns and songs, dialect sketches and verses, stories and essays, a local preacher and lecturer".[19]

A tribute to him from the Lancashire Authors' Association, of which he was an active member and for many years secretary-treasurer, mentioned his "robust personality ... he could hold and sway assemblies by his powerful voice and hearty manner".[20]

* * *

Contributing to the local press was often the first 'leg up' the publishing ladder for working-class women writers. Elizabeth Eckersall ('Busy Bee') started her working life at the age of 8 as a half-timer in a Heywood mill. She contributed poetry in both dialect and standard English to *The Bury Times* and *Bury Guardian* from the late 1880s.[21]

Sarah Robinson of Padiham also started life as a half-timer and went full-time as a weaver in her early teens. She contributed hundreds of poems to the local press, notably *The Burnley Express*. Leah Smith, writing as 'Owd Linthrin Bant', contributed a regular column on 'Bits of Local History' to *The Radcliffe Times*, between 1880 and 1902. She was the daughter of a handloom weaver; two of her sons became professional journalists, writing for Lancashire newspapers. Two of her sons set up *The Radcliffe Express* whilst a third became the assistant editor of *The Manchester Weekly News*.[22]

Whilst the newspapers of the Lancashire cotton towns provided the main outlets for aspiring working-class writers, particularly those writing in dialect, *The Manchester Weekly Times* encouraged the vernacular as well as standard English. Farnworth poet William Cryer began writing for the paper in 1886 and many of his contributions were subsequently published in book form as *Lays After Labour*.[23]

All of the larger (and many smaller) Lancashire industrial towns had substantial co-operative societies, mostly established from the 1850s onwards and many of these societies produced their own monthly magazine, which encouraged members' writing.[24]

* * *

A key factor in the emergence of a strong Lancashire press—in both standard English and dialect—was the existence of independent local publishers. Manchester supported several—notably John Heywood and his brother Abel Heywood, who ran two separate businesses. Stalybridge had Whittaker and Sons while Blackburn's long-standing printer and publisher was J. and G. Toulmin who published *The Blackburn Times*. Pendlebury's of Bolton supported many local writers, including Allen Clarke. As well as having its own printing press, the Co-operative Wholesale Society, with its headquarters in Manchester, published several books and pamphlets, mostly related to co-operative topics. Rochdale's main local publisher was James Clegg ('The Aldine Press') whilst Oldham had H.C. Lee.

Some London-based publishers had partnerships with local publishers. Simpkin and Marshall published several Lancashire titles in conjunction with local firms. For example, Thomas Newbigging's *History of the Forest of Rossendale* was published by Simpkin and Marshall of London and T. Brown of Bacup in 1868. The same firm collaborated with Tubbs, Brook and Chrystal of Manchester to publish Axon's *Lancashire Gleanings* in 1883. George Routledge of London published Harland and Wilkinson's *Lancashire Legends* in conjunction with L.C. Gent of Manchester in 1873.

A Lancashire Newspaper Society was formed in the early 1900s to act as a network of local newspapers. R.S. Crossley, founder and editor of *The Accrington Observer and Times* and an active member of the Lancashire Authors' Association, was president of the society during the First World War.[25]

Brave attempts were made during the twentieth century to develop a distinctly Lancashire, or at least 'Northern' paper, though it could be argued that *The Manchester Guardian* occupied that role, perhaps reluctantly. There was the well-established *Yorkshire Post*, dating back to the eighteenth century, and publishers, perhaps not unreasonably, thought there might be a similar market in the North-West. Titles included *The Northern Daily Telegraph* and *The Daily Dispatch*. The *Dispatch* was published in Manchester and aimed at a specifically 'Lancashire' readership. During the 1930s it sponsored the 'Cotton Queen' competition, using the popular song 'She's a Lassie from Lancashire' as the contest's theme![26]

The Liverpool Weekly Post (1878–1940) also competed for a wider 'Lancashire' market than its immediate Merseyside area and carried regular features on Lancashire history together with dialect sketches by writers such as Allen Clarke.

Clarke himself edited, wrote and published *Teddy Ashton's Northern Weekly* between 1896 and 1908. It contained a chaotic but highly creative mix of comment, dialect sketches, short stories and serialised novels and political as well as philosophical debate. It circulated in the south-east Lancashire 'cotton belt' but also had some sales in the West Riding woollen districts.[27]

The removal of the *Guardian* from Manchester to London was more than a geographical change of location. It was about a fundamental shift in focus. Today, the paper is possibly one of the most London-centric of all the nationals with only a token presence in the North.

Attempts to fill the gap left by the *Guardian*'s removal have failed. The *North-West Times* was launched in 2012 and aimed at a 'quality' regional market but had an all-too-brief existence. The advent of digital media has made relatively low-cost local and regional publishing more possible and *North-West By-Lines* and the Manchester-based *Mill* are proving to be useful additions to regional media, with quality news, features and comment.

A Lancashire school of artists

As noted above, 'Lancashire' and 'art' usually inspire the standard response: L.S. Lowry (and perhaps Helen Bradley). There's no doubt that Lowry was a great artist and deserves the recognition he's had. But there is a lot more to Lancashire art than that. Several municipal galleries around Lancashire have great regional art collections, though perhaps Salford's at Peel Park stands out (see page 280). Most of the Lowry collection has migrated to the Lowry at Salford Quays but the original gallery is a treasure trove of outstanding twentieth-century Lancashire artists. The work of Peter Davies's excellent overview *A Northern School: Lancashire Artists of the Twentieth Century* has been complemented by his later *A Northern School Revisited* and Martin Regan's *The Northern School: A Reappraisal*.[28]

Taken together, they provide a comprehensive overview of outstanding Lancashire painters of the last century, including Theodore Major (Wigan), Roger Hampson (Tyldesley), Harold Riley (Salford), William Turner (Salford and Stockport), Harry Rutherford (Denton), Brian Shields 'Braaq' (Liverpool), Geoff Key (Manchester) and Alan Lowndes (Stockport). I would add the remarkable Leonora Carrington (Chorley, then Mexico).

The above artists were born in Lancashire though not all stayed there. Some of the outstanding artists who adopted Lancashire as their home include Adolphe Valette, whose street scenes of Manchester and Salford are well known.

There are difficulties in talking about a 'Northern School', which both Peter Davies and Martin Regan acknowledge. Davies was closer to the mark when he subtitled his first book 'Lancashire Artists of the Twentieth Century' because that's what they were and to me, as a non-specialist, it seems that they shared a common regional identity and not much else. Yet the 'brand' has stuck and Martin Regan observed that, "the Northern School has been one of the most commercially successful regional art movements in the country", adding, "but few—even its most successful dealers and collectors—can define it with precision".[29]

Many, such as Roger Hampson, Theodore Major, Charles Holmes, Brian Bradshaw and Julian Trevelyan had classic Lancashire industrial scenes for some of their subject matter, but they treated the subject in very different ways. A 'school' does suggest a community of artists sharing a similar approach and style and having some degree of social interaction. That was not the case of the so-called 'Northern School', though some of its members knew each other and socialised together.

The 'Manchester Academy' was closer to being a 'school'. In the post-war years it included artists who moved away from perhaps more traditional subjects and depicted life around them. Peter Davies said the work of younger artists moved towards a more socially committed art. "The Academy, while continuing to represent a hybrid collection of styles, started to accommodate a new generation—Harold Hemingway, Alan Lowndes, Roger Hampson, Theodore Major, Brian Bradshaw among them—who seemed to represent an authentic Lancashire voice contributing towards post-war realism."[30]

There were some interesting outliers amongst Lancashire artists, not least Frederick W. Jackson (1859–1918) who was described by Susan Thomson as "fiercely proud of his Lancashire roots".[31] He was a talented landscape painter as well as a designer and illustrator. He produced a number of drawings for Manchester dialect writer Ben Brierley's *Ab'o'th'Yate* sketches. His painting *The Hand-loom Weaver* illustrated volume 3 and is part of Manchester City Art Gallery's collection.[32]

Liverpool had the Sandon School, formed in 1905 by a group of local artists, mostly former students of Liverpool University School of Architecture and Applied Art. Martin Regan notes that, "the Society was in no way provincial as in 1911 it displayed a selection of works from Roger Fry's first Post-Impressionist exhibition and in 1931 it showed sculptor Jacob Epstein's controversial 'Genesis', attracting nearly 50,000 visitors in a month".[33]

Lancashire nurtured some fine artists in the post-war period which included the muralist Walter Kershaw (Littleborough). Kershaw also painted the mills around Rochdale including *Mutual Mills, Heywood*. A major touring exhibition titled *Lancashire South of the Sands* included work by Lesley Young (Manchester) and Ray Haslam (Bolton).[34]

Martin Regan pulls no punches when he compares the pre-war 'Northern School' with what he terms the 'New Lowry School':

At its artistic height, the Northern School depicted Lancashire in the terrible beauty of its decline. From the drawings of Valette to the etchings of Norman Jacques (1926–2014) and the linocuts of Roger Hampson, it did so with consummate technical skill. The New Lowry School merely attempts to offer a nostalgic pastiche of a past in which none of the artists actually lived. It is art drawn from the imagination of the imaginative and usually delivered with appalling technique.[35]

First in Regan's sights was Helen Bradley who "took what she imagined was Lowry's appeal and transported it back fifty years, painting cloyingly poor pictures", and made a lot of money in the process. Arthur Delaney and Brian Shields earned further opprobrium, but had similar commercial success.[36]

It's hard to disagree with his assessment. The work of the 'New Lowry School' has become immensely popular and plays to people's nostalgia for a world that has gone, but that they remember as children. It's on a par with older East Germans' nostalgia for the GDR, so hilariously portrayed in the film *Goodbye Lenin*. In a Lancashire context, it sadly has parallels with some contemporary Lancashire dialect writing which finds it impossible to avoid references to clogs, cobbled streets and mill chimneys.

One of the most interesting figures in Lancashire post-war art is Shaun Greenhalgh, or 'The Bolton Forger'. Greenhalgh was following in a long Bolton tradition of 'trotting', the practice of taking someone, often a person or institution of high standing, for a ride. Greenhalgh succeeded in convincing the Victoria and Albert—and many other bodies—that his forgeries were in fact the genuine item. Over a 17-year period, between 1989 and 2006, he produced a large number of forgeries with the assistance of his brother and elderly parents. He sold his fakes to museums, auction houses and private buyers across the world, making over £1 million. The family was described by Scotland Yard as "possibly the most diverse forgery team in the world, ever", which is certainly one way of describing them. They were finally discovered when, attempting to sell three Assyrian reliefs using the same provenance as they had previously, suspicions were finally raised.[37]

In 2007 he was sentenced by Bolton Crown Court to four years and eight months in prison, a sentence which many thought was disproportionate to the crime. In his autobiography Shaun says that his sentence "was longer than any comparable one for faking art-work in recent times", but with characteristic Lancashire sang-froid, added, "Personally, I have never considered my sentence excessive. The law's the law and where would we be without it?"[38] Today, Shaun Greenhalgh has his own studio in a former cotton mill in Bolton, revered as a local hero who fooled 'the toffs' of the art world.

Most of the larger Lancashire towns had artistic communities, often supported by the local municipal art gallery. Oldham is one example. Trevor Coombs commented that "since its opening in 1883 Oldham Art Gallery has consistently collected the work of artists born in Oldham or connected in some way with the town".[39] Artists in Salford, Bolton, Rochdale, Blackburn and Burnley enjoyed similar support, as well, of course, as the two cities, Manchester and Liverpool.

Design in Lancashire

Lancashire has a strong tradition of design. To an extent this grew out of the importance of good design in the weaving process, going back to handloom-weaving days. Textile design was taught in all of the major technical schools in Lancashire. Solomon Partington, best known for his role in the Winter Hill Mass Trespass of 1896, researched the history of the Middleton silk weavers in the early nineteenth century as part of his history of co-operation in Middleton. He noted that they "were among the earliest to realise the importance of technical education" and established a design school "the avowed intention being to get abreast with their Lyons rivals in the trade. Tom Brierley, the dialect writer, was one of the school."[40]

James Holmes was master of the textile department at Burnley Municipal College and became a figure of international importance. His *Manuscript Notes on Weaving* is a fascinating handwritten descrip-tion of the weaving process and aspects of design which included cloth samples.[41]

Textile design separates into woven and printed fabrics and Lancashire's textile industry played a dominant role in both, though it was sometimes suggested that more 'artistic' approaches developed outside of Lancashire. However, the role of Walter Crane in promoting design excellence, during his time as director of design at Manchester Municipal School of Art, from 1893, marked a sea-change.[42] Bolton-based Tootal Broadhurst Lee Co. Ltd exhibited at the 1925 Paris international design exhibition and promoted artist-designed fabrics to a world market.

The Red Rose Guild and the Manchester branch of the Design and Industries Association (DIA) were the two premier organisations promoting good design in Lancashire in the inter-war years. Despite their different objectives, with the former focusing on hand-made work and the latter on machine-made objects, the two organisations co-existed comfortably. Margaret Pilkington was a founding member of the DIA and a strong supporter of Manchester City Art Gallery in developing its Industrial Art Collection. Charles Sixsmith[43] was a founder member of the DIA's Manchester branch and also a member of the planning committee that met in late 1920 leading up to the formal inauguration of the Red Rose Guild in January 1921. Whilst he had less presence in the DIA from the mid-1920s his involvement in the Red Rose Guild increased. He followed Hugh Wallis as chair of the guild, holding the post for most of the 1930s.

Manchester Art Gallery was a very good friend to the DIA and an active supporter of the Red Rose Guild. Councillor A.P. Simon and Lawrence Haward were early joiners, the latter serving on the committee. Cllr Simon was occasionally chosen to open the annual Red Rose Guild exhibition, from which "sporadic craft acquisitions were made" for the gallery. In 1940 the Art Gallery hosted the joint exhibition *British Handicrafts* by the Arts and Crafts Exhibition Society and the Red Rose Guild.[44]

Galleries, museums and theatres

Lancashire has a rich collection of art galleries, museums and the-atres. The gallery and museum collections make for an interesting book in its own right. Whilst Manchester and Liverpool each have several outstanding art galleries, including Manchester's Whitworth and the City Art Gallery and Liverpool's Walker and Tate, some of the surrounding towns have galleries which are outstanding.

Southport's Atkinson, Rochdale's Touchstones, and municipal galleries at Salford, Bolton, Oldham and Preston each have European-class galleries.

In his introduction to *Creative Tension: British Art 1900–1950*, Stephen Whittle, of Oldham Art Gallery, observed that:

> At one time Lancashire's prosperous textile-producing towns were among the most important patrons of modern art, benefiting from individual benefactors, large endowment funds and generous purchasing budgets. Slow to react to change, regional galleries amassed large and very broad-ranging collections of contemporary art.[45]

Creative Tension was a touring exhibition using the collections of Oldham, Preston, Bolton and Rochdale though work from the municipal galleries of Blackburn, Bury, Southport and Blackpool were also used. Interestingly, only quite a small number of the exhibits were by Lancashire artists, reflecting the broad purchasing policy of many of Lancashire's municipal galleries in their heyday, when funding was not a problem and talented curators were often encouraged by the elected members of the relevant authority.

The stereotype that only very conservative, traditional artwork was of interest to Lancashire's galleries is belied by the work in *Creative Tension*. Oldham, for example, has a rich collection of work by Lucien Freud, Mark Gertler, Roger Fry and Paul Nash while Bolton is home to a collection of work by British post-Impressionists and some outstanding surrealist art. Some of Julian Trevelyan's work depicts scenes of Lancashire milltowns but not in the traditional styles of Lowry or Helen Bradley.[46] Salford Art Gallery, opened in 1850 in Peel Park, has a magnificent collection of work by Lancashire artists including Lowry, Harold Riley, Geoff Key and Fred Cuming. It is also home to a superb display of ceramics from former Clifton Junction-based Pilkington's Lancastrian Pottery (later 'Royal Lancastrian Pottery').[47] Much of Salford's Lowry collection is now housed in the new Lowry Gallery at Salford Quays.

In addition to larger galleries there are several outstanding smaller municipal galleries such as the Astley Cheetham Gallery in Stalybridge, the Whittaker in Rawtenstall and Warrington with its fascinating collection of works by Eric Tucker, whose work had lain forgotten for many years until recently. His work depicts life in

Warrington in the early post-war years.[48] There's a plethora of private galleries but special mention should be made of ClarkArt in Hale which has done much to promote 'Northern Art', most of which is actually 'Lancashire'. The gallery specialises in work by Lowry and 'The Northern School' of artists (see above).[49]

Lancashire municipal authorities in the late Victorian period invested heavily in museums, as well as art galleries. Despite cuts in local government spending, most have survived. Lancashire County Council's Helmshore Mill has had a troubled time in recent years, though Burnley's Queen Street Mill, with its remarkable collection of over 300 Lancashire looms, has survived. Some that have run into trouble tend to be more recent museums such as that at Park Bridge, between Oldham and Ashton. However, there are exciting plans to re-instate the former railway viaduct which once crossed the Medlock as part of a cycle route. A visitor centre has re-opened and this remarkable example of a former industrial community is getting the attention it deserves.

The Dock Museum at Barrow-in-Furness is a completely new, purpose-built museum celebrating the town's social and industrial heritage. It opened in 1994 and ought to rank as one of the North-West's finest museums and includes a stunning collection of model ships designed and built by apprentices in the shipyards. It tells the story, from local people's testimonies, of 'the Barrow Blitz'.

Manchester's Museum of Science and Technology at Castlefield highlights the city's—Lancashire's—development as a hub of scientific and technological innovation and doesn't neglect the human story. A darker side of Lancashire history is shown in Liverpool's International Slavery Museum. Working in partnership with other museums with a focus on freedom and enslavement, the museum provides opportunities for greater awareness and understanding of the legacy of slavery today.

Lancashire has a growing number of volunteer-run museums which celebrate important aspects of the county's heritage. The Lancashire Mining Museum at Astley Green Colliery, near Leigh, is developing as a major attraction and has huge potential to be both a museum of mining machinery—the impressive head gear for one of the shafts has survived together with the engine—and also to tell the story of mining communities in Lancashire. The Fleetwood Museum is now run as a community venture and highlights the history of the town's fishing industry.

The renaissance of the Lancashire theatre is evident in the new 'Shakespeare North Playhouse' theatre at Prescot and the major refurbishment of Bolton's Octagon Theatre during the Covid lockdown. 'Shakespeare North' opened in July 2022 and celebrates the area's historic links with the great bard, who may have spent time at Knowsley Hall in the 1580s; certainly his work was performed in Prescot.[50] The new theatre is a huge act of faith by Knowsley Council, with support from other funding agencies. The theatre is managed by the Shakespeare North Trust. Let it speak for itself:

> At its heart is a traditional 470-seat timber-framed Shakespearean theatre that will host a mix of vibrant new performances. Theatre, music, comedy, workshops, events and activities will spill out into the exhibition gallery, Studio and Sir Ken Dodd Performance Garden, creating an accessible space full of joy and creativity, where everyone is welcome. Inspired by Prescot's historic connections to William Shakespeare and a real love of storytelling, Shakespeare North Playhouse will play a key role in the ongoing regeneration of Knowsley; a place full of brilliant people with a story to tell. Working together with audiences, artists and its local communities, the creative programme, learning opportunities and social spaces will help to open doors, invite debate and inspire a love of learning that will reach far beyond the walls of Shakespeare North Playhouse.[51]

The Playhouse deserves to go from strength to strength and become a major centre for theatre in the North of England.

* * *

Lancashire was home to several dramatists in the twentieth century who had strong affinities with the county. Stanley Houghton, Allan Monkhouse and Harold Brighouse formed a 'Manchester school' of dramatists in the first half of the century. Houghton's most well-known work is *Hindle Wakes*, written in 1911 and performed by Annie Horniman's company at the Aldwych Theatre in London in June 1912. He worked for most of his life as a greycloth salesman in the cotton industry, only going professional as a dramatist in 1912; he died a year later. As L.M. Angus-Butterworth commented: "For most of his adult life he was connected with the cotton trade of the city, his Lancashire shrewdness causing him to keep an occupation that yielded a steady income while he was developing his dramatic art."[52]

Comic Lancashire

Lancashire may not be able to rival London when it comes to composers, novelists and painters, but I'd put money on Lancashire beating anywhere for the number and quality of its comedians. A list could start with Stan Laurel, Tommy Handley, Arthur Askey, Hilda Baker, Les Dawson, Caroline Ahern, Victoria Wood, Steve Coogan and Peter Kay—and that's just a beginning.

There was a genre of Lancashire comedian who worked in dialect, performing 'comic sketches' to often huge audiences. J.T. Staton may have started the genre Edwin Waugh performed a mix of comic and 'serious' readings, followed by Ben Brierley and Allen Clarke, using his pseudonym 'Teddy Ashton'. Clarke himself claimed that Lancashire has,

> the richest and raciest humour in the British Isles, ay—in the world.
> It combines the wit of the Irish, the subtle pawkiness of the Scots,
> and the sprightliness of the Welsh, with a local special quality which
> I can only describe with the word 'gradely' … in humour, especially with a lively element of farce in it, the Lancashire dialect is
> unrivalled.[53]

Lancashire's dominant industry, cotton, spawned its own extensive genre of comedy. A particular butt of hundreds of jokes was 'the tackler'. Penny pamphlets of 'Tacklers' Tales' were sold in their thousands in the early years of the twentieth century. I've a much-thumbed copy of *Tacklers' Yarns: Fun from the Weaving Shed* which indicates it being 'third edition—thirtieth thousand'.[54] Papers such as *The Cotton Factory Times* published many of them. It carried a regular feature, 'Mirth in the Mill', with stories submitted by readers and illustrated by dialect writer and cartoonist Sam Fitton. They often had a Labour or trade union message, or satirised poor working conditions. Many of them have been brought together in Alan Fowler and Terry Wykes' *Mirth in the Mill: The Gradely World of Sam Fitton*.[55]

Les Dawson was the Lancashire comedian par excellence, at least in living memory. He was a true Lancashire 'patriot' and his book *Les Dawson's Lancashire* is a knockabout celebration of all things 'Lanky'. As he boasted:

> I have travelled far and wide in the world but I always return to my beloved Lancashire. I have to really, I've only one change of under-pants. I could live nowhere else, of this I swear … I cannot imagine not being a Lancastrian. My children are trained in the ways of Lancashire and are wonderfully responsive to a rhino whip…[56]

And so it goes on, extolling the delights of 'Miresea-on-Crouch', that classic Lancashire seaside resort where,

> you can try on gloves in a shop or listen to a Dutch clairvoyant giving lectures on amputation … on the jetty there is a Polish flute band which plays laments about the days of the Black Death and the disused leper colony is ideal for kids wanting to play hide-and-seek.[57]

Dialect literature

A distinctive Lancashire dialect literature began in the mid-nineteenth century though its roots are earlier. John Collier ('Tim Bobbin') from a handloom-weaving community near Rochdale was the first to set down dialect speech in literature, with his 'Tummus un Meary' in 1746. Others followed but it was Edwin Waugh, again from Rochdale, who made the real breakthrough in the 1850s with his poem 'Come whoam to thi childer an' me'—largely thanks to middle-class sponsorship.

A popular tradition of Lancashire dialect literature developed during the second half of the century, with poets and prose writers including Waugh, Samuel Laycock, Ben Brierley and other lesser-known working men, mostly from handloom-weaving backgrounds. Towards the end of the century a small number of women were writing in dialect, such as Margaret Lahee. Dialect, both spoken and written, helped to underpin a strong regional identity.[58]

By the turn of the century it had achieved enormous popularity. Perhaps the high point of Lancashire dialect literature was the unveiling of the Dialect Writers' Memorial in Broadfield Park,

Rochdale in 1900. The Lancashire Authors' Association (see below) was formed in Rochdale not long after, in 1909.

Clarke's early writing, in papers such as his own *Labour Light* can hardly be said to be original. It was when he began using the Lancashire vernacular to put over a socialist message that he really came to life as a great writer, as we see in the novels, the early poetry and also many of the 'Tum Fowt' sketches. Clarke's invention of 'Teddy Ashton' as the archetypal Lancastrian was following a well-established literary convention. His fellow Boltonian, J.T. Staton (above) was one of several dialect writers in the 1860s and 1870s who created a standard character—in his case 'Bobby Shuttle'—who could be used as a commentator on issues of the day. The character was usually, superficially, slightly daft, but with plenty of common sense and homely wisdom. In later years George Formby became such a stage creation—the seemingly thick Lancashire lad who always managed to turn the tables on the 'toffs'. Clarke created a character with whom his working-class readership could identify—Bill Spriggs, but also his wife Bet. His supporting characters, Joe Lung, Patsy Filligan, Ben Roke and other denizens of 'The Dug an' Kennel' were used to poke fun at authority and affirm a strong sense of pride in being part of the Lancashire working class. 'Teddy Ashton' featured as a character in some of the sketches, occasionally acting as secretary to 'The Tum Fowt Debatin' Menociation'.

The initial 'Tum Fowt Sketches' were written as light entertainment, to soften the harder political material in Clarke's publications. However, Clarke began using the sketches to poke that 'sly fun and undermining sarcasm' against social ills of the time. By the early 1900s Clarke had published sketches such as 'Bill Spriggs at the Labour Church', 'Bill Spriggs as a Vegetarian' and even 'Bill Spriggs and the New Theology'. During a major strike in one of the Bolton weaving sheds in 1906 over the introduction of modern looms which would be managed by fewer weavers, he wrote a series of letters in dialect from 'Billy Pickinpeg' and also a sketch called 'Th'Patent Automatic Cemetery Looms' which helped win support for the strikers.[59]

Clarke's 'Teddy Ashton' claimed to have sold over a million copies of the *Tum Fowt Sketches*. Whatever, there is no doubt he built up a mass readership. Working-class readers of the local press eagerly lapped up 'homely' dialect sketches and poems, or heard them recited at tea parties and soirees, often organised by local co-operative societies. The attempt, and a highly successful one it was, by writers like Clarke to use dialect to get across a simple socialist message was very much a product of its time, and its popularity began to wane in the 1930s.

Edwin Waugh remained the most celebrated figure in Lancashire dialect writing. The centenary of Edwin Waugh's birth, in 1917, was celebrated in great style, despite the intrusion of war. The report in the LAA's *Record* described what must have been a remarkable occasion:

> Our glorious meeting at Waugh's Well, on Saturday June 23rd last, will long live in the memories of those privileged to take part in it. Despite the somewhat gloomy weather, the chilly winds, and the long steep ascent, an assemblage of several hundred persons, of both sexes and all ages, gathered to pay eloquent and heartfelt tribute to the dead poet who had so loved and immortalised the district. At 3.30 prompt, our members, augmented by a goodly contingent of the Bacup Natural History Society, left the Rawtenstall Free Library for the well, after undergoing the almost inevitable photographic ordeal. One section proceeded by tram to Waterfoot, and thence mounted the hills via Cowpe and Rough Lee, guided by Councillor Compston; and a second travelled on foot by way of Bury Road and Balladen Quarries...[60]

The two groups met near to Waugh's Well, from where they would have enjoyed commanding views across the Rossendale hills. Some of Waugh's poems were recited, no less than three scholarly papers were read, with a musical interlude which included Waugh's song 'The Sweetheart Gate'. The account notes that, "the proceedings terminated with the singing of the National Anthem ... subsequently many members returned via Waterfoot and were delighted by an inspection of the orchid house at Vice-President Ashworth's home at Ashlands".

The Lancashire Authors' Association and dialect

As we have seen, the Lancashire Authors' Association was formed in 1909, at the behest of Allen Clarke, to provide a forum for

Lancashire writers.[61] Its first secretary was Robert H. Brodie ('Billy Button') of Eagley, himself a talented writer.

The LAA was always anxious not to appear as a 'dialect' literary organisation. In an article for *The Radcliffe Times* (coinciding with a visit by the association) Samuel Hardman explained that the object of the association was "to promote and further the cause of Lancashire literature, and to provide for the wants and wishes of writers and lovers of Lancashire literature and history, and not, as widely supposed, for the sole purpose of encouraging and preserving the Lancashire dialect in its multiplicity of forms".[62]

The LAA never had a totally comfortable relationship with writing in dialect. Herbert Kirtlan, a prominent member of the association, caused controversy in 1959 when he gave a talk to the Edwin Waugh Dialect Society on 'Dialect under the Microscope'. The speech was reported in the *Rochdale Observer* as 'Speaker Gives Dialect Society a Severe Jolt'. The newspaper report said:

> Mr. Kirtlan questioned whether on the whole dialect literature was worth reading for its content. He said there was no point in writing in dialect unless the author was portraying a character speaking ... most dialect verse lacked imaginative figures which distinguished it from poetry. Dialect poetry had kept aside from the historical developments of English poetry and today's dialect writers were writing the same kind of stuff written by their fathers and forefathers. The reasons for dialect writing were aesthetic, historical and sentimental rather than literary.[63]

It is hard to disagree with Mr Kirtlan. By the 1960s, dialect writing had retreated to the realms of nostalgia and sentimentality—terrain on which it was always comfortable, but occasionally strayed from.

Several working-class writers who were members of the LAA used dialect to get over a radical message, often to the disapproval of other members. It was used in many local socialist papers from the 1890s, on both sides of the Pennines. The Lancashire-based *Cotton Factory Times* and its sister the *Yorkshire Factory Times* carried regular poems, short stories and even novels which made much use of dialect.

A later dialect writer who integrated a socialist message with a 'homely' dialect sketch was Hannah Mitchell, who wrote in *Labour's*

Northern Voice as 'Daisy Nook'.[64] She was working very much in the socialist dialect tradition of Allen Clarke, though writing in the 1920s. Many of her sketches express a strong working-class feminism, which is unsparing in its criticism of working-class male attitudes towards women.

* * *

Lancastrians: Major David Halstead 1860–1937

Halstead was a key figure in the Lancashire Authors' Association, serving as its chairman, then president, for many years. He held a senior position in the family bleaching business, in Haslingden, and had a distinguished military record. During the First World War he volunteered for active service and served 'with great distinction' in Egypt. However, he was invalided out and returned home. His politics were of the old-fashioned Tory paternalist kind and he worked well with other writers from different political backgrounds.

In 1917 he was elected Mayor of Haslingden and he was re-elected the following year. In 1922–3 he served as an MP. His writings included Annals of Haslingden, Sketches of Lancashire Dialect, History of the Fifth East Lancashire Regiment *and* Geology of Rossendale. *He was an avid collector of autographs, coins and books. His library included 5,000 books of 'Lancashire interest' and he had over 33,000 coins in his collection. He wrote occasional pieces in dialect, including the poem 'Billy Suet's Song' which featured on the LP* Deep Lancashire, *sung by Bernard Wrigley.*[65]

* * *

Dialect poetry and prose continued to be popular in the inter-war years, with most Lancashire newspapers publishing dialect sketches and poetry. Regional radio experimented with dialect readings; during the mid-1930s Jim Fleetwood, of Bolton, read some of the 'Teddy Ashton' sketches to appreciative listeners. The BBC introduced 'The Northern Muse' broadcast during the 1930s which featured dialect prose, poetry and song.[66]

* * *

Lancastrians: T. ('Tommy') Thompson 1880–1951

Thompson became one of the most popular Lancashire dialect writers of the mid-twentieth century. He was born into a poor working-class area of Bury and he "learnt what poverty and penury meant to people who have lived a hand-to-mouth existence dependant on the corner tick-shops and periodical visits to the pawnshop". At the age of 10 he started as a half-timer in a local mill but didn't last long—he hated "the noisy, steamy, smelly weaving shed and the prison-like atmosphere of the factory". He got a job as an apprentice bookbinder and for the next fifty years bookbinding was his main profession. As a young man he met several 'working-class intellectuals' including botanists, musicians and sportspeople.

At the age of 35, in 1915, he started writing for The Bury Times *and also contributed to the* Cotton Factory Times, Millgate Monthly *and* Manchester City News. *In 1923* The Manchester Guardian *accepted the first of his Lancashire Sketches—'Back Plum Street Memories' which continued for over a decade. He wrote two novels and many short stories, published in collections such as* Lancashire Mettle *(1933),* Lancashire Brew *(1937) and* Lancashire Fun *(1938). During the 1930s and 1940s he was in demand as a broadcaster, reciting many of his dialect sketches for the BBC's* North Countryman *programmes. He used the pseudonym of 'Owd Thatcher' for his radio series* Under the Barber's Pole.[67]

* * *

Working-class literature in Lancashire

The early 1900s saw a flowering of regional working-class literature, encouraged by the two *Factory Times* newspapers on either side of the Pennines, and Clarke's *Northern Weekly* which lasted until 1908. Many local socialist newspapers encouraged working-class writers, some—though by no means all—in dialect.

Allen Clarke encouraged a circle of writers which included Fred Plant of Stockport, Arthur Laycock of Blackpool, (son of the famous Samuel), the cartoonist, cotton worker and poet Sam Fitton of Shaw (see below), Ethel Carnie, the weaver, poet and novelist from Great Harwood, and Sarah Robinson, poet and short-story writer, from Padiham.

Ethel Carnie was a talented poet who had work published in both local newspapers like *The Blackburn Mail* and labour publications such as *Cotton Factory Times*. She became editor of *The Woman Worker*, an off shoot of *The Clarion*, moving to London at the behest of publisher Robert Blatchford in 1909. The move was not a success and she appears to have fallen out with Blatchford. By the following year she was back home in Great Harwood, working as a warper and beamer in a local mill. This did not put an end to her writing, and her first novel *Miss Nobody* was published in 1913. Her most overtly socialist novel, *This Slavery*, was published in 1925. Her novel *Helen of Four Gates* was made into a film in the 1930s and was shown at the 2011 Bradford Film Festival.

Miss Nobody was one of her most important novels, about the lives of working-class women in Lancashire at the turn of the century. The setting is Great Harwood, a weaving community situated between Blackburn and Burnley. It was one of the most hard-hit textile communities in Lancashire during the 1920s and 1930s, having an over-dependence on plain weaving which was prone to foreign competition.

In recent years several of Ethel's novels have been republished and most recently the poet and comedian Ruth Cockburn led a research project called *Miss Nobodies—Celebrating the Great Women of Great Harwood and Lancashire*.[68] The book is a collection of interviews, comments, poems, recipes and observations by the women of Great Harwood. A touring theatre show was created around the book by Spot-on Lancashire.[69]

Both Fred Plant and Arthur Laycock, the first socialist councillors to be elected for Stockport and Blackpool councils respectively, were talented novelists. Many of Plant's novels and short stories, several about life in Lancashire mills and mines, were only published in serial form in Allen Clarke's newspaper, *Teddy Ashton's Northern Weekly*. His novel *The Conductor's Sweetheart* is set during a strike on the local tramways, in which police mounted a series of baton charges against the tramway workers. W.E. Tirebuck, born in Liverpool in 1854, wrote several novels and short stories including *Miss Grace of All Souls*, set during the 1893 miners' lock-out in Lancashire.[70]

A Lancashire socialist aesthetic?

Walter Crane, head of the Manchester School of Art, epitomised the romantic style of socialist art developed in the 1890s and was strongly influenced by art nouveau. Women are bounteous goddesses, men are fustian-clad peasants, earthy, of the soil. They are invariably gazing towards the rising sun of socialism. Crane's romanticised imagery of the workers was fairly quickly superseded by the equally unrealistic Bolshevik images of heroic industrial workers toiling over anvils, hammers in hand. However, while Crane was very much part of the Manchester arts scene, it would be difficult to say that there was anythings pecifically 'regional' about his work—as with most socialist artists of the time, he saw his work as being universal, rather than local or regional.

In the early 1900s, Sam Fitton, a mill worker in Shaw, near Oldham, emerged not only as a talented dialect poet but a highly skilled cartoonist, illustrating many of Allen Clarke's sketches about mill life. Many of his cartoons had socialist, or at least pro-Labour, messages.[71]

Trade union banners, particularly those of local or regionally-based unions, might have had more regionalist messages but they generally fell into a very clear pattern, with idealised images of the craft or industry.[72] There are occasional exceptions, including the present-day Barrow-in-Furness RMT union which depicts the red rose of Lancashire alongside images of the railway.

Many local co-operative societies produced their own crockery, often supplied by local manufacturers. The images are usually those of store buildings or leading members of the society.[73]

A new Lancashire sensibility? An emerging regional consciousness

The 1950s saw a cautious emergence of a 'Northern' regional consciousness, reflected in the BBC's northern programmes broadcast from Manchester. This consciousness found a focus in arguments over the location of the National Theatre during 1953. The Conservative government, almost unthinkingly, proposed to locate it in London. However, Ellis Smith, MP for Stoke-on-Trent South argued differently: "The North has a culture of its own and it should find expression in a national theatre." He went on to say that he knew "the Northern accent was not popular in the South, indeed among people of all political parties. *Too many people forget where the Labour Movement started!*" (author's emphasis).[74]

Hannah Mitchell continued to write on Northern culture in the early 1950s. Her last piece in *Labour's Northern Voice* was a review of the Yorkshire Dialect Society's collection of dialect poetry, *A Northern Broadsheet*, in September 1956.

But it was the emergence of a new generation of writers, Northern-based and in some cases working class, which did most to stimulate an awareness of 'The North'. The late 1950s saw a string of successful novels, many made into films, with 'Northern' and 'working-class' themes. Dismissed by some conservative critics as 'kitchen sink drama', works such as *A Taste of Honey* by Salford's Shelagh Delaney, Walter Greenwood's *Love on the Dole*, Yorkshire's Stan Barstow's *A Kind of Loving*, John Braine's *Room at the Top* and Alan Sillitoe's *Saturday Night and Sunday Morning* (admittedly set in Nottingham) changed the way 'The North' was perceived—internally and externally.

Most of these were not overtly political novels of the sort encouraged by the inter-war Communist Party. To an extent they were 'anti-political' verging on nihilistic in the case of some, such as *Saturday Night and Sunday Morning*. But what they did do was to create a sense of pride in both region and class.

13

MUSICAL LANCASHIRE

Lancashire's musical tradition stretches from early sacred music including the 'Deighn Layrocks' (Larks of Dean) of the eighteenth century through to the Hallé Orchestra, Royal Liverpool Philharmonic, William Walton, Hans Richter, the Beatles, Buzzcocks and The Fall.

Lancashire, and Manchester in particular, became second only to London for its classical music and it was very much down to the efforts of a German refugee, Charles Hallé. The later influence of Thomas Beecham and his friend Neville Cardus, and the work of the Royal Northern College of Music and Chetham's College, sustained a strong musical culture which continues today.

Lancashire became famous for its popular music. George Formby and Gracie Fields became household names well beyond Lancashire in the twentieth century. It was also home to one of the country's greatest opera singers, the Leigh miner Tom Burke, who had unfulfilled ambitions to set up a 'Lancashire Opera Company'. Lancashire produced some important composers including William Walton (Oldham), Thomas Pitfield (Bolton), Peter Maxwell-Davies (Salford) and Harrison Birtwistle (Accrington). The Manchester-based Royal Northern College of Music and Chetham's College continue to produce great music and musicians.

* * *

Lancastrians: George Formby 1904–1961

There were two 'George Formby's—the most famous was George Hoy Booth, son of music hall entertainer George Formby (Senior), from whom he took his stage name. He was born in Wigan and never strayed far from his Lancashire roots, dying in Preston and being buried in Warrington. His first concert was given in Earlestown, but he became a world figure. He remained 'Lancashire' to his core.

He adopted much of his father's material and developed it under the influence of his wife Beryl. He became almost synonymous with Lancashire— one of his songs was 'The Emperor of Lancashire' and in a way, he was. People loved his homespun humour and catchy (often risqué) songs, accompanied by his trademark ukulele. He starred in numerous films, many having a 'Lancashire' theme and became the nation's most popular entertainer in the 1930s and 1940s. During the Second World War he worked for ENSA (Entertainments National Service Association) and travelled extensively entertaining service personnel.

He gave free concerts for charities and worthy causes and raised £10,000 for the Fleetwood Fund on behalf of the families of missing trawlermen. George kept his politics to himself but he stood up against encroaching racial segregation during a tour of South Africa in 1946, refusing to perform before racially segregated audiences. He caused a furore amongst the country's racist politicians by having the temerity to embrace a young black girl after a performance. Nationalist Party leader Prime Minister D.F. Malan telephoned the Formbys to complain about the incident. Beryl picked up the phone and told the Prime Minister, "why don't you piss off, you horrible little man!" He was a strong anti-Nazi and his film Let George Do It features him landing in the middle of a Nazi Rally and giving Hitler his come-uppance.

Formby was loved by millions; dozens of entertainers still make a living as 'George Formby' impersonators.

* * *

The second half of the twentieth century saw Lancashire at the forefront of a revolution in music, led by the Beatles but including Manchester and Salford bands. Later, Tony Wilson almost succeeded in making Manchester the cultural capital of Britain through his various projects including Factory Records and the Hacienda Club.[1] Wilson was a passionate 'Lancastrian' and made serious efforts to revive the flagging fortunes of the east Lancashire cotton towns, creating the 'Pennine Lancashire' brand.

The sacred musical tradition

Lancashire's classical musical heritage is much more than the Hallé Orchestra and the Royal Liverpool Philharmonic, or even its distinguished composers. Let Thomas Newbigging, the historian of Rossendale and son of Scots Owenites,[2] start us off. In 1891 he wrote:

> In no part of England has the musical art been more cultivated, or even at the present day is more cultivated, than in the two northern counties of Yorkshire and Lancashire. The interpretation of musical thought and expression, it is true, is now left more to the professional singer and performer, and people crowd to the concert hall to listen to the strains as rendered by the cultured exponent of musical language. In former days the practice of music was more of a subjective pursuit. The people themselves were to a greater extent than now the exponents of the art in which they delighted. Like the woven fabrics of the time, much of their music was home-made, and nearly all their power of interpreting the compositions of the great masters was of home growth and nurture...[3]

The main subject of Newbigging's article was James Leach, born in Wardle, near Rochdale, in 1762. His parents were spinners and weavers and he became a handloom weaver himself. His grandfather, William Howorth, was a stonemason in the local quarries and was proficient in several instruments, but Leach says that his favourite was 'the hautboy', an early form of oboe, and "he became familiarly known all over the neighbouring hills as 'Billy wi'th'Pipes'".[4]

He composed sacred music, publishing his first volume in 1789. He performed in national musical events and performed in the King's Band. Many of his compositions have biblical titles, such as 'Mount Pleasant', 'Bethel', 'Pisgah', and others. Some, such as 'Oldham', 'Bacup' and 'Blackburn' have obvious local references, reflecting the strong sense of community identity within the handloom-weaving community but perhaps also with an eye to local popularity and commercial advantage. He was able to become a professional musician, earning a modest income as a teacher, composer and instrumentalist. He and his family moved to Salford in 1795 but he died in an unusual road accident in February 1798 when his coach overturned. As Newbigging writes, he was "only thirty-six years of age, in the full plenitude of his powers and rising rapidly into fame".[5]

In 1924, the Reverend J.V. Wylie produced a substantial book devoted to composers of religious music in a relatively small area of north-east Lancashire, stretching from Accrington to Burnley. The foundation of this culture was, once again, these self-educated working men and women who had either been handloom weavers or were sons and daughters of weaving families.

Wylie writes about Thomas Healey, better known as 'Owd Tom Yealey', organist and choirmaster at Goodshaw Church, in Rossendale. He was known as 'the father of Burnley musicians' and there is a monument to 'Owd Tom' in Rose Grove Cemetery. His daughter, Rebecca, was soloist in Burnley Choral Society.[6]

He mentions the achievements of Molly Harwood of Hoddlesden, near Darwen. She was a handloom weaver in the 1780s and 'sang over her loom'. Her beautiful voice was recognised by a local philanthropist and she was admitted to the London College of Music in 1784. She sang as principal in the Handel Festival at Westminster Abbey.[7]

Perhaps the most remarkable musical phenomenon of early industrial Lancashire was the group of weaver-musicians known as 'The Deighn Layrocks' or 'Larks of Dean'. Dean is a small hamlet in Rossendale, north of the village of Weir.[8] Like many small settlements in the mid to late eighteenth century its people combined cotton spinning and weaving with hill farming. We are fortunate that Moses Heap, who lived in Dean for many years, wrote a detailed diary which gives us a record of 'the Larks' and their activities. Nearly a century later Samuel Compston, local councillor, JP and antiquarian, wrote a series of articles for the *Rossendale Free Press* providing more information about this musical phenomenon.[9] There are a number of aspects to the story of the 'the Larks' which stand out. Firstly, this was a real community of musicians, not one or two isolated figures. They practised and performed together, entertaining each other late into the night. Much of their music was religious.

* * *

Lancastrians: Moses Heap 1824–1913

Moses Heap was a mill worker from Crawshawbooth, Rossendale. He was born in the small settlement of Doals on 8 May 1824 and died at Southport on 24 April 1913. He started work in a local mill at the age of 8, for a shilling a week. He wrote My Life and Times *in 1906, a remarkable memoir of life in the Rossendale hills of the nineteenth century.*

Samuel Compston wrote about Heap in his series of articles for the Rossendale Free Press, *when Heap was still alive and 80 years old. He had recently donated his Manuscript Book to Rawtenstall Library which included works by several of the 'Larks of Dean' which included musicians from nearby Loveclough and Goodshaw. Heap did Lancashire musical history a great service by chronicling the lives of the hugely talented handloom weavers and which was put to good use by Compston and later Roger Elbourne in his* Music and Tradition in Early Nineteenth Century Lancashire.[10]

On Whit Sunday 1852, Heap walked 14 miles (and back) to Stonyhurst College to hear a performance of Mozart's Twelfth Mass. Compston wrote that Heap "brings before us reminiscences of our grandfathers' days, their love of song, their devotion to psalmody, their harmonious ability, and their Rossendale humour. Thus we who live in the twentieth century are enabled to take a glance back to the middle of the eighteenth century, and see the style of music sung, played, and delighted in from the year 1750 to 1860 by the famous company of folk called 't'Deighn Layrocks' or the Larks of Dean."[11]

In his memoir, Heap makes an interesting comparison between the 'Larks' and railway preservation! He said: "Verily the Lumb and Crawshawbooth valleys have something to be proud of in the musical achievements and status of the Layrocks of the present as well as those of the past. May the reputation never become tarnished, nor the musical faculty ever be used for other than uplifting and ennobling purposes. Let no one despise the simple life, rustic manners, or old-time music and work of 'the rude forefathers of the hamlet' who have long slept. Rather, as the rough earliest locomotives are carefully preserved at South Kensington and Darlington as the parents of our present powerful and finished engines, and only unpatriotic and conceived noodles can look upon the rough handiwork of George Stephenson and his men without reverent interest, so no true Lancashire or musical soul can scan the Layrock manuscripts, and consider the work of the men and women of that period without pride, as being amongst the efficient causes of the present greater musical scope and capability of Rossendale, and of the glorious counties of Lancashire and Yorkshire."

Heap was an avid musician himself and used to sing in choirs in the small village chapels dotted around the Rossendale area. For most of his life he worked in the local mills around Loveclough.

* * *

The great favourites of 'The Larks' were Handel and Haydn. They also composed their own pieces, such as 'Bocking Warp' and

'Shepherd'. Women were not excluded from the group and Susan Ashworth ('Susy o'James's') and Jane Ashworth ('Jinny o't'Clough') were prominent figures. Other women mentioned by Moses Heap and recounted by Compston included Betty Nuttall, Mary and Anne Whittles, and Mary Nuttall.[12] The Larks were at their peak in the years up to the Napoleonic Wars. Public transport was, of course, non-existent and the musicians walked considerable distances, often over bleak and wet moorland, to attend and perform at concerts. Moses Heap mentions Henry Whittles walking to Manchester and back to inspect a copy of the score of Handel's Samson.[13]

The Whitaker at Rawtenstall has Heap's manuscript book of 255 tunes, many of which were in use in Goodshaw, Lumb and the Dean Valley between 1750 and 1860. These were composed principally by the Deighn Layrocks. In everyday life the Layrocks were mainly weaver-farmers and quarry workers.

After the religious conversion of their leader John Nuttall around 1747, these 'moorland minstrels' not only sang the compositions of others, but produced psalm tunes and chants themselves, some of which are still sung in the Rossendale Valley today. Some of their more famous tunes include 'Spanking Roger', named after Roger Aytoun of Manchester. Another who made a significant contribution to the hymnody of Lancashire was James Leach, the violinist of Wardle who, according to the dialect writer John Trafford Clegg, delighted John Wesley by setting tunes to some of Charles Wesley's hymns.

The handloom-weaving communities around Darwen produced their own distinctive musical tradition. Shaw, in his *History and Traditions of Darwen and Its People*, refers to Edmund Harwood, father of Molly Harwood, who wrote a popular hymn called 'The Vital Spark'. James Hunt (1807–87), a weaver from Darwen, was the first person to introduce the chanting of psalms into Nonconformist chapels. The first such performance was in the small moorland chapel alongside Pickup Bank Cottage School, with the singing of the 34th Psalm 'I will bless the Lord of all time'.[14]

Samuel Crompton, more famed for his spinning mules than for his music, was the honorary choirmaster at the New Jerusalem Church in Bury Street, Little Bolton. He composed many hymn tunes.

* * *

Lancastrians: Tom Burke ('The Lancashire Caruso') 1890–1969

One of the most remarkable tenor singers that Lancashire produced was Thomas (Tom) Burke, from Leigh. He is commemorated, appropriately, by having the Leigh Wetherspoons pub named after him. While the drinkers of Leigh celebrate their talented predecessor, Burke himself is little known in the musical community, despite the very fine biography by John Vose.[15] Vose commented that Burke "has been omitted from the vast majority of musical reference books; is seldom mentioned in operatic literature; was not included in the selection for the HMV Great English Tenors *LP and failed to be represented in* Irish Tenors Through the Years *for which he could have qualified by parentage".*

Vose makes great claims for Burke, 'the Lancashire Caruso', stating that "Burke sang with the panache never achieved by an English man before or since. His voice possessed an urgent enthusiasm which was typically Italian … Most of all he was an exciting singer. What could we give for a man of Burke's vocal stature in England today. He would be a sensation."[16]

His father, James Vincent Burke, came from Athlone and arrived in Leigh in the 1880s. He got a job in one of Leigh's many collieries and married Mary Josephine Aspinall—also from an Irish background—in 1889. They lived on Mather Lane, a strongly Irish working-class part of town, close to St Joseph's Catholic church. Thomas Aspinall Burke was born on 2 March 1890. He recalls sitting on his father's knee while Dad sang him Gaelic lullabies.

There is an air of romance surrounding the story of Tom Burke's rise to stardom. At the age of 12 Tom left school to work 'half-time' in a local silk mill and went 'full-time' a year later. When he was 14 he got a job in one of the local mines at the weekly wage of 12/6d. He was employed as a 'lasher-on' at the colliery surface. He found the job tedious but relieved the boredom by singing, including many of his father's beloved Irish ballads. His adult colleagues enjoyed the lad's singing and dubbed him 'The Minstrel Boy', after one of the most well-loved Irish songs of the time, popularised by John McCormack.

He joined Leigh Borough Brass Band, playing the cornet. He also earned some extra cash by singing in local pubs. As John Vose recounts, "Publicans vied for his patronage and gave him free beer to keep him in their pub singing to the customers … Pub singing became his hobby, the presence of a piano an irresistible magnet to the young singer, and it was in this environment, singing to colliers and mill workers in some of the town's roughest hostelries, that he served his vocal apprenticeship."[17]

He left the pit at the age of 17 and appears to have done various jobs, with his pub singing complementing his wages, most of which would be handed over to his father and mother. However, it seems he returned to mining after his initial attempts to become a professional singer were thwarted. In 1909, at the age of 19, he walked the 30 miles to Blackpool to see his hero, Enrico Caruso, sing at the Winter Gardens. The experience was transformative and cemented his determination to become a fully professional singer. He finally managed the breakthrough, by chance, being discovered by a musical family when he was walking from the pit with his mates, singing at the top of his voice. [18]

He was offered a contract by London impresario Hugo Goerlitz. It was the vital first step in his operatic career which led him to sing the lead tenor role in Rigoletto, *at The Lyric Theatre, Milan. It was a resounding success and Tom Burke's operatic career went from strength to strength. By the mid-1920s he had become one of the world's great tenors, with a string of performances across Europe, England and the United States. He kept his links to his home town, Leigh, and in 1928 gave a performance in Leigh's Co-operative Hall. John Vose quotes from a 'national daily' who ran a piece headed 'Pit-Boy Sings to His Own People'. Burke walked on the stage to 'thunderous applause'.*

The report continued: "Prominent businessmen and colliers, freshly washed from the afternoon shift, clapped side by side; Lancashire housewives and mothers stamped their feet in excitement. They would have cheered him if he had told jokes or stood on his head. To speak to elderly people in Leigh is to fairly realise the pride the folk of this little town, noted more for grime than culture, felt for the local boy who conquered the world of music by sheer determination ... Then all was deadly still, the tenor's knuckles showing white as he clutched a handkerchief in his fist—suddenly a volley of chords from Percy Kahn at the piano, and the audience was swept away in the enchantment of Andrea Chénier; *then a succession of arias. Burke announced to great applause that he had been asked to sing* Turandot *in Rome, and as if to celebrate the honour with his friends, sang 'Nessun Dorma' from the opera. At the finale he received a long standing ovation—a fitting amen from his own people.* [19] *Tom Burke is today celebrated with a display in Leigh Museum; you can press a button to hear Tom at his finest. And just across the road is The Thomas Burke, a Wetherspoons pub. I think he'd have liked that.*

* * *

Bands and choirs

Lancashire is a region of wind bands (brass and silver) and choirs, a heritage its shares with its Yorkshire neighbour.[20] The east Lancashire town of Bacup, for example, is typical of the number of musical groups that could co-exist in a small area. From 1840 onwards the town had a brass band, a choral society, a hand-bell ringing group and an orchestral society. In addition Bacup was the headquarters of the Rossendale Branch of the Lancashire Association of Campanologists. It should be noted that influential historians have turned to Manchester and the surrounding region to define and understand notions of class in the 'classic' period of formation.

By the end of the nineteenth century, brass band contests had become major events attracting thousands of people. They were made possible because of the dense railway network of Lancashire and cheap rail fares. In 1888, the contest at Belle Vue, Manchester was served by fifty special trains from across the North, carrying both bands and spectators.

While very much a working-class tradition, the cost of instruments and uniforms would have been way beyond the reach of most people. The main impetus behind the emergence of the brass band movement was, as we've seen, military in origin, through the expanding number of 'volunteer' regiments formed in the mid-nineteenth century. Government financial support was available for these local volunteer regiments and some of the cash was channelled into brass and silver bands, to the consternation of some civil servants! However, some of the earliest brass bands were sponsored by employers. This was partly a reflection of Northern paternalism but also perhaps an early piece of marketing. Examples of employer-supported bands included Horwich L&Y Band, sponsored by the Lancashire and Yorkshire Railway Company. A rival Horwich RMI (Railway Mechanics' Institute) Brass Band was formed in 1912 following a dispute between the Chief Mechanical Engineer, George Hughes, and the band members. The row was over the band's poor record of success in competitions. The Band of the Farnworth Cotton Mills was sponsored by the town's main spinning company, Barnes's.[21]

Dobcross Band, in a village straddling the Lancashire–Yorkshire border (but firmly in Lancashire) began with support of the West

Yorkshire Rifle Volunteer Band, in 1875. Most of the members were weavers, many coming from handloom-weaving families but by then working in the large weaving sheds which grew up in the Saddleworth area.[22]

Many bands that were not formed by military volunteers were saved or revitalised by the military connection. The Bacup Band, after break-up and amalgamation, were reconstituted in 1859 as the band of the 4th Lancashire Rifle Volunteers. The Oldham Band, formed in 1865, became the Oldham Rifles in 1871. Besses o' th' Barn Band is one of the North's most well-known brass bands, formed in 1887. The members registered themselves as a limited company to help fund their activities.

Wingates Temperance Band was formed in 1873 and is still a highly regarded part of the band scene, as 'Wingates Band'. Many of its members worked in the coal mines around Westhoughton and Atherton. The Pretoria Colliery Disaster had a huge impact on the band, with no less than nine players or officials being killed in the explosion, which took the lives of 344 men and boys.[23] The centenary was marked in December 2010 with several major events including performances by the band of 'In Pitch Black' by composer Lucy Pankhurst, who also wrote 'Newton Heath Variations' in 2008 (see pages 314–5).

The Northern band tradition is still very much alive, exemplified by the annual Saddleworth Brass Band Contest. Following a two-year gap caused by Covid, the contest returned with renewed vigour in 2022. Over thirty bands performed through six villages, using a well-organised fleet of coaches to ferry bands around. For the 2022 event I caught the train to Greenfield and was thrilled to hear the first band set off to the strains of 'Slaidburn', the classic Lancashire marching tune composed by William Rimmer, conductor of Wingates Band (above) c.1910. The band contest takes place mostly in 'the historic West Riding of Yorkshire'. However, the Lancashire parts of Mossley, as well as the Lancashire moorland village of Lees, feature in the contest.

* * *

The early nineteenth century saw the growth of village- and town-based balls; they were quite rumbustious affairs. A press report of the Goosnargh ball in May 1845 observed that "Polkas, Mazurkas and Lancers found no favourites; country dances, jigs and reels were preferred and then the merry swains of Goosnargh tript it gaily."[24]

A fascinating aspect of Lancashire musical culture was the hugely popular 'string band' movement of the late 1890s. Seth Sagar of Read, near Padiham, recalled forming the Read String Band in 1895 with a couple of friends.[25] The phenomenon of 'social dances' started in Lancashire in the 1880s and became something of a craze. Musicians were recruited from more formal bands or local orchestras; members of the famous Larks of Dean formed a Quadrille Band in Rossendale, under the leadership of 'Robert o't' Carr' according to Samuel Compston.[26]

One ensemble in east Lancashire was known as 'The Black Pudding Band', led by brothers Dicky o'Dicks and Thomas o'Dicky's. David Middlehurst commented that "both played the curious instrument known as 'the Serpent' or 'black pudding', so named because of their extraordinary shape and jet black colour".[27]

Typical concert hosts would be local friendly societies, co-operative societies and sometimes trades unions. Blackburn and District branch of the Weavers', Winders' and Warpers' Association organised a well-attended concert and dance at Whittle-le-Woods in February 1912, with entertainment provided by Marsden's String Band.[28] Longridge Orchestral Band performed at the first Co-operative Ball organised in the town's Co-operative Hall in February 1887. The Furness Railway had its own 'Ferry Band' which performed on its lake steamer excursions up to the start of the First World War. The Whittingham Asylum String Band was formed at the hospital in 1873 and made good use of the institution's large ballroom.

Lancashire music in the twentieth century

Neville Cardus was a major figure in twentieth-century music. He was born and grew up in Rusholme, a working-class part of Manchester, and described himself as a 'staunch Lancastrian'[29] in an interview with Lancashire writer Joan Pomfret. He became both the music critic of *The Manchester Guardian* and its cricketing correspondent. Writing in 1929, Cardus used a sprinkling of dialect to make a universalist claim for music:

Perhaps it is impossible for the North of England really to live, move and have its being in music—that is, to project its attitude to life (and the getting and spending thereof) by means of an art so immaterial in its substance as music. A local psychology can give account of itself only through a local idiom; the Manchester School of Drama was very much a matter of idiomatic speech. In music, you cannot say "jannock" or "sithee" or shake a loose leg at Blackpool during the Wakes of Hindle. The language of music is international; musical Manchester certainly first became famous beyond the county's borders exactly in so far as it was truer to Germany ... than it was to Bury and Throstle's Nest ... great music was brought to the City [of Manchester] by the Germans...[30]

Cardus raises big issues about the nature of music and its descriptiveness. Several English composers have written magnificent pieces of music that have a strong sense of place, such as Delius's *North Country Sketches*, Elgar's *Severn Suite*, Bax's *Tintagel* and Holst's *Egdon Heath* (and we'll come to some specifically Lancashire pieces shortly). Cardus would probably ask, would you know it was the River Severn if Elgar hadn't given it that title, or recognise the Cornish coast in 'Tintagel' if Arnold Bax hadn't called it that? Almost certainly not, but it comes back to that strong sense of place and the ability of music to conjure up and reinforce a cultural patriotism that was regional in nature.

Cardus was making the point that classical music in Lancashire is forever in debt to one man—Charles Hallé—creator of the great orchestra which is synonymous with Manchester's musical life today as well as its history. Cardus tells us that Hallé arrived in Manchester from Paris, out of work and with little money, and was invited to conduct an orchestra that had been formed for the Manchester 'Art Treasures Exhibition' in 1857. Cardus says:

> The orchestra and chorus formed for the exhibition were not disbanded; they were kept together for the inauguration, in the following year, of the Hallé concerts. Until his death, some thirty-seven years later, Charles Hallé was the informing genius of 'musical Manchester'. His influence spread to all parts of the north of England ... He founded the Royal Manchester College of Music; better still he gave birth to that tradition of culture in music which, to this day, continues to attract to the City the best brains in the art.[31]

As well as Hallé, Manchester provided a welcoming home to musical figures such as Richter, Brodsky, Hecht, Speelman and many more. Cardus notes that "none of them is a name racy of Lancashire soil, but the county grew to know and honour them all".[32]

Manchester's cultural links with Germany are perhaps less well known than those of its cross-Pennine neighbour, Bradford, but they were important. The city possessed its Schiller Club and the Midland Hotel had a German restaurant.

Thomas Beecham, born in St Helens in 1879, was a good friend of Cardus who encouraged publication of *Beecham Stories*, comprising various stories and sayings of the great conductor. Cardus summed up his friend's personality as "witty, then waggish, supercilious, then genial, kindly, and sometimes cruel; an artist in affectation, yet somehow always himself. Lancashire in his bones, yet a man of the world."[33]

Beecham's family were prosperous industrialists who made a substantial fortune in the chemical industry, from the famous 'Beecham's Pills'. They encouraged his musical interests. A Lancashire upbringing rubbed off on him in many ways—his taste for Eccles cakes and Morecambe Bay potted shrimps became legendary.[34] He played a key role in reviving Manchester's fortunes as "the true musical capital of England"[35] along with Cardus during and after the First World War. Beecham was conductor of the Hallé during the First World War and resisted attempts to 'cancel' German music. However, it was a near-impossible task and Cardus tells that, "when the War came, crisis descended on musical Manchester. The Germans were driven underground, and the fate of the Hallé concerts hung in a terrible balance."[36] Beecham decided that the best line of defence was attack, and began a series of summer promenade concerts, which Cardus says "saw Manchester's music go to a full flower of culture" featuring composers such as Wagner, Mozart and Beethoven.[37]

The Hallé continued to be a central part of Lancashire musical life throughout the twentieth century. Writing in 1970, Michael Kennedy said that,

> unlike the Cotton trade, it has remained a premier feature of Lancashire life ... the orchestra's tradition is not a cliché, it is a living thing. There is a warmth, a personality about the Hallé that

immediately impresses visiting conductors. It has Lancashire humour and character...[38]

The Hallé has a magnificent new home at the Bridgewater Hall, close to its former home at the Free Trade Hall. It opened in 1996 and is one of Britain's outstanding concert halls, alongside Liverpool's St George's Hall. There are other great regional concert venues including Blackburn's King George's Hall, Bolton's Victoria Hall and the Winter Gardens in Blackpool.

The second half of the twentieth century saw Lancashire, and Liverpool in particular, give us the Beatles and many other outstanding bands and singers. The Beatles themselves, with so many of their songs, and singers like Cilla Black, had a very strong 'Liverpudlian' sensibility, though whether you could say there was anything specifically Lancastrian about it is doubtful. Gerry and the Pacemakers' hit song 'Ferry Across the Mersey' is a wonderful work of *local* patriotism.

Some years later, 30 miles away in north Manchester, Mark E. Smith and The Fall were writing and performing powerful, not to say aggressive, songs such as 'Lucifer Over Lancashire' and 'The North Will Rise Again'.

The folk song and dance revival

Lancashire was at the forefront of the Folk Song Revival of the 1960s and later, with singers such as Gary and Vera Aspey, Harry Boardman, the Oldham Tinkers, the Spinners, Houghton Weavers, Bernard Wrigley and many more.

Some of the singers helped revive old dialect songs and put the poems of Laycock and Waugh to music. There was always a risk of the 'Lancashire folk singer' falling into self-parody, with a *de rigueur* uniform of cloth cap, waistcoat and neckerchief, or clogs and shawls for the women. Peter Kay gave us a wonderful parody of a Lancashire folk group in *Phoenix Nights* when the hapless club secretary, Potter, decides to hold a 'Lancashire Neet' and the band turns out to be a bunch of racists.

Like its stablemate, dialect poetry, Lancashire folk song is an invented tradition and there is no sign of it disappearing. The revival of 'Lancashire Day' on 27 November has encouraged more 'Lancashire Nights' complete with traditional song and music, 'prato' pie' and all the accompaniments.

More recently, Jennifer Reid has built a strong reputation for her interpretation of old Lancashire songs which take us beyond the pastiche that has passed for some 'Lancashire folk' in the past. Sid Calderbank is an excellent reciter of the dialect classics, bringing a strong north Lancashire voice to his performances. The annual gathering of Lancashire folk musicians was traditionally the Fleetwood Folk Festival, held every summer but cancelled in 2022.

Lancashire is strongly associated with clog dancing; although, like morris dancing, it isn't exclusive to the county. Alex Fisher and Jennifer Reid have done much to revive interest in clog (or more properly, 'step') dancing and are regular performers at events across the North.[39] There was a growth of interest in step-dancing in parts of Lancashire in the late 1890s and early 1900s and the Robinson family, living in the area around Allithwaite and Costhwaite, did much to popularise the step-dancing tradition in the Lakeland area, mostly within 'Lancashire North of the Sands'.[40]

Less formal 'clog dancing' was popular in more urban parts of Lancashire in the late nineteenth and early twentieth centuries. Small industrial towns such as Horwich were proud of their local dancers and a report in the local newspaper proclaimed that "T.H. Fox, of Horwich, claims to be Champion Clog Dancer of the World. Horwich is first in the world for something..."[41] Fox was a pupil of the well-known step-dancer Dan Leno and defeated a challenger to the title of World Champion at a contest at the Grand, Bolton, on 3 September 1904.

An unlikely venue for a performance of clog dancing was provided by Accrington Police Court in September 1904 when Mary Hardacre was in the dock charged with drunkenness and "with doing damage in a cell". She was sentenced to six weeks' imprisonment at which point she performed a clog dance in the dock, before being carried out by the police.[42]

Johnny Haslett has documented the remarkable growth of morris dancing, a specific branch of clog dancing, in Lancashire between the late 1880s and late 1920s, in four volumes of material collected from the local press. The 'tradition' seems to have begun in the

Leyland area as part of a Rose Queen festival and spread to different parts of the county, mainly west Lancashire.[43]

The content of a talk by Johnny Haslett to members of the Morris Federation was reported thus:

> By the end of that month (May 1890) Leyland had about a score of Morris Dancers at their May Festival. The group continued through-out the 1890s with a couple of trainers and an additional group of juvenile dancers with a different trainer appearing in the mid-1890s ... Chorley was next up. The Rose Festival started in June 1890 with assistance from their Leyland friends and the engagement of Leyland Morris Dancers. By the following year Chorley had its own team of 29 dancers under the leadership of Mr. H. Gent. from Chorley, [the talk] moved on to Horwich in 1891 where the Rose Queen procession was denounced by the local corps of the Salvation Army as the 'work of the devil'. In July 1891 Chorley Morris Dancers appeared, but also mentioned is a juvenile Morris team at the Juvenile Rose Queen a month later. By the following year the Rose Queen Festival had its own home-grown team—the newspaper proclaimed that Horwich did not need to seek foreign aid to provide Morris Dancers.[44]

Although morris dancing has declined from its early twentieth-century popularity, Lancashire still has several active troupes includ-ing Rivington, Horwich, Rumworth and Tanhouse (Skelmersdale). Britannia Coconut Dancers of Bacup (see p. 31) continue to per-form every Easter Saturday around Bacup as well as being in demand across Rossendale and east Lancashire.

Rivington Morris is a women's troupe and describes itself in the following uncompromising terms:

> These demure cultured women hail from near Bolton in Lancashire. Their clogs have been heard as far afield as Sidmouth, Germany, France, Holmfirth, Wigan, Accrington and Blackrod Carnival. Hundreds have looked on in awe and marvelled at their stunning stepping, precision, music and reinforced foundation garments. On-lookers have been heard to say 'Rivington have that certain indefinable something that Northern teams have...' or 'Make room—these women take no prisoners'. Do not refer to these women as 'ladies', or you may encounter one of their infa-mous 'Clog Butties'.[45]

Bodies such as the Rivington Morris reflect a changing Lancashire which is proud of its cultural identity but modern in its championing of independent-minded women. Long may they continue to dance!

Lancashire composers

Lancashire has a strong tradition of locally born composers, including Harrison Birtwistle, Arthur Butterworth, Alan Rawsthorne, Peter Maxwell-Davies, Thomas Pitfield and others. Above all, William Walton stands out—though his 'Lancashire patriotism' was not particularly strong. He was described by music critic Michael Kennedy as "one of the three indisputable leaders of the first generation of twentieth century British composers, together with Michael Tippett (three years younger) and Benjamin Britten (eleven years younger)".[46] He was born in Oldham in 1902, son of Charles Walton, an office worker at Platt's and also a trained musician; he became organist at St John's, Werneth, and music teacher at Hulme School.[47]

He was interviewed by the *Oldham Chronicle* in 1926 and said:

> I expect I have been singularly fortunate for home influences have been the greatest possible aid in a career such as mine. My father, the late Mr. C.A. Walton, was a well-known local musician, and my mother, Mrs. Louisa Walton, who now lives at Werneth Hall Road, still teaches singing. In some households it is dangerous to dabble with art, and to sit down and write music often meets with a good deal of ragging and bullying. In fact, most people, I think, will agree that an artistic career is a very difficult one, but my parents never raised any objections and from both I have had every possible encouragement in my work.[48]

His musical talent was quickly recognised and he won a place at Christ Church Cathedral School at the age of 10. His father took him to Hallé concerts in Manchester and he attended performances of Sir Thomas Beecham's famous opera seasons in Manchester in 1916 and 1917. He went on to become one of the great composers, but to a degree was 'from Lancashire but not of it'. Music critic David Ward wrote that "he shed his accent and later explained that he was driven to begin composing by a desire to stay in the sophisticated south". "I must make myself interesting somehow or when my voice breaks, I'll be sent home to Oldham," he said as a young boy.[49] Oldham awarded their son (reluctant or otherwise) the freedom of the borough in 1961. In 2002 several events took place in Oldham and Manchester to mark his anniversary. Gary Cannon wrote:

> Approaching age eighty, Walton described Oldham as "home of cotton mills, brass bands and other things ... not my favourite part of the world". Walton's life story is a steady journey south, fleeing the dour and sooty Oldham for the halls and towers of Oxford, the glitz and glamour of London, and finally the sun and repose of the Italian island of Ischia. Yet, though Walton had left Oldham at age ten, its smokestacks and terraced houses, but especially its citizens' character, remained with him. Oldham had always been a home of hard-working individuals, and Roy Campbell observed this trait in Walton at Oxford. The typical Oldhamer is frugal and financially sensitive. Certainly through his Oxford period Walton demonstrated this trait, and after that as well. He also embraced a sense of independence that stemmed from Oldham, for even though Walton lived on the generosity of others for several years, his appeals for funding were appropriately humble and he was always grateful. When Walton's means became more comfortable, he then demonstrated generosity liberally, by helping his aging mother and his elder brother financially just as Thomas Strong, Siegfried Sassoon, Lord Berners, and the Sitwells had helped him. Many young composers commented on his generosity as well, even those like Humphrey Searle whose music shared little affinity with Walton's. Perhaps the most intrinsically Lancashire-esque quality that Walton retained in his character was his contrarianism. This is found not only in his personality, but also in his music...[50]

Music teacher John le Grove commented that "he became an international figure, and in some ways rather turned his back on Oldham, but I hear an authentic Lancashire voice in some of his music from *Façade* on, though that is difficult to define, of course".[51]

Peter Maxwell Davies, born in Salford 1934, and Harrison Birtwistle, born in the same year, were probably the most important composers working in Britain in the late twentieth and early twenty-first centuries. John le Grove commented:

Printed and Published by J. L. Butler, West House, Grange-over-Sands.

20: Mast heading of *Teddy Ashton's Northern Weekly*.

21: Allen Clarke and his wife Eliza, at The Daisy Colony, Carleton, near Blackpool, c. 1904.

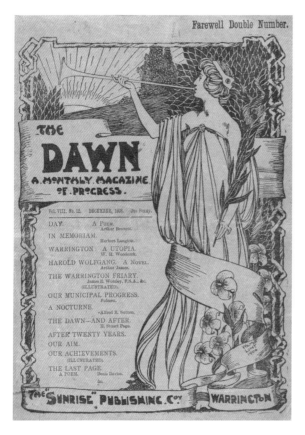

22: *The Dawn: A Monthly Magazine of Progress*, published in Warrington, 1908 (final issue).

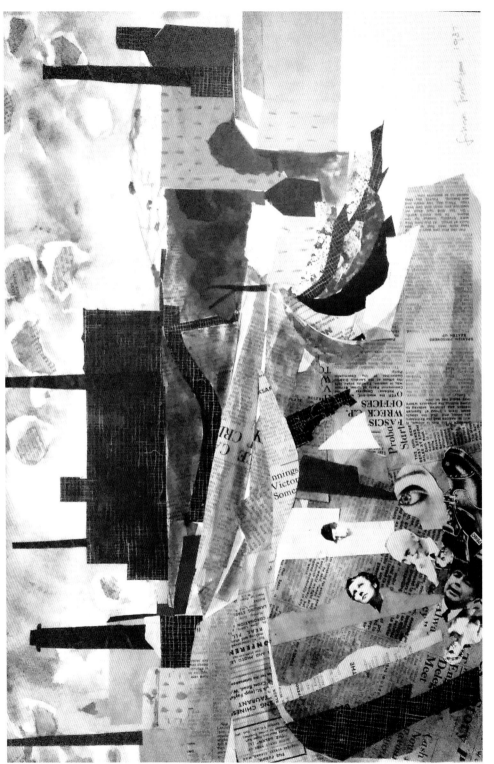

23: Lancashire art in the twentieth century: Julian Trevelyan's collage *Bolton* (1937).

24: Bolton Whitmanites' Garden Party, Rivington, 1894.

25: Thomas Newbigging: gas engineer, politician, poet and historian.

26: 'I am a Lancashire Woman!' Emmeline Pankhurst statue, St Anne's Square, Manchester.

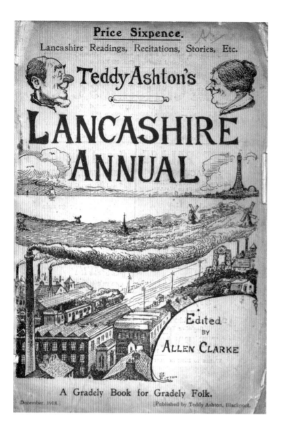

27: Cotton mills and windmills. Cover of *Teddy Ashton's Lancashire Annual*, 1918.

28: Cover of *Teddy Ashton's Lancashire Annual*, 1931, with 'gradely lass' Gracie Fields.

29: Haslingden Grane.

30: The Ulverston Canal: view of Canal Foot.

31: The steam yacht 'Gondola' on Coniston.

32: Young Asian girls play amid derelict housing, Bolton, 1969.

33: Lancashire Miners on Strike: an NUM march in Leigh, 1985, with the banner of Coppull and Chorley Miners' Wives.

34: Cultural Fusion! The Shree Muktajeevan Swamibapa Pipe Band of Bolton, performing in Leigh, 2022.

35: Mill girl at the seaside… and back at home.

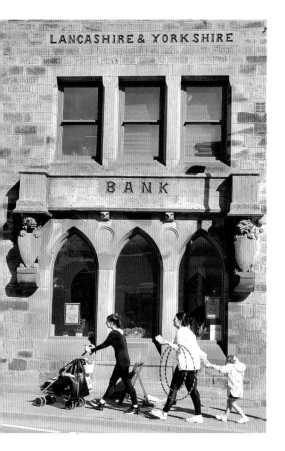

36: Local Banking: The former Lancashire and Yorkshire Bank, at Bacup.

37: Morecambe Bay.

Both were international figures. Whether either's music has a Lancashire sound is hard to say: Birtwistle is often craggy, obstinate—perhaps a northern 'grit'. 'Max' Davies liked to parody the popular music of his childhood, especially in the theatre pieces of the 1960s such as *Vesalii icones* and *Eight Songs for a Mad King*. He often incorporated fox trots or Victorian-style hymns played on a honky-tonk piano—things he heard while cowering in an air-raid shelter in Leigh. I knew Max a bit, and appreciated his utter lack of pomposity and propensity to deflate portentousness. Definitely Lancastrian in spirit right to the end.[52]

* * *

Lancastrians: Thomas Pitfield 1903–99

Thomas Pitfield was born in Bolton and spent his childhood and youth living at his parents' home on Bury New Road. His father was a builder and his mother was a dressmaker. They were a reasonably well-to-do family and owned some property. Thomas started school at the age of 5, attending Ridgeway's Endowed School and then the Bolton Municipal Secondary School. His mother sent him out rent-collecting on Saturday afternoons. Although he hated the job, exploring Bolton and surrounding villages developed his love of nature and encouraged him to write poetry—an activity of which his parents disapproved. It seems they disagreed with most of the things Thomas actually enjoyed, though his father did teach him carpentry skills and, perhaps grudgingly, bought him a piano.

He wanted to become an artist but instead was apprenticed to Hick Hargreaves of Bolton, one of the main engineering firms in town. In August 1917, at the age of 14, Thomas started in the millwrights shop at Hick Hargreaves, Crook Street. He spent seven years 'on the tools' and hated much of it. However, his artistic skills were able to develop through work in the drawing office. In his spare time he learned to play the piano, and earned extra cash by giving piano and cello lessons.

At the age of 21 he enrolled at the Royal Manchester College of Music as a part-time composition student. He had very little money and seems to have lived a hand-to-mouth existence. Part of that appealed to his increasingly ascetic character. He drank only water and became vegetarian.

In 1931 he won a scholarship to Bolton School of Art and developed his skill as a painter and etcher. His musical work blossomed and an increasing range of his work was performed in the great concert halls of Manchester and

Liverpool. Shortly before his father's death he turned up to hear a perfor-
mance of his son's work by the Hallé Choir in Manchester—"the only mem-
ber of my family who ever went to hear one of my works performed".

He married Alice Astbury, the daughter of a Bolton mill manager, at
Bank Street Unitarian Church. She was a fascinating character in her own
right, born in Russia in 1903, when her father was running a cotton mill
at Balashikha, 20 miles outside Moscow. She attended Bolton School (Girl's
Division) and was fluent in both Russian and English. Thomas and Alice
discovered a number of letters written by Tchaikovsky which she translated
into English.

Thomas and Alice left Bolton soon after they were married, first moving
to the Midlands before settling down to life in Bowdon, near Altrincham.
Although in a leafy Cheshire suburb, Thomas retained a strong sense of
his Bolton roots and the first volume of his autobiography is titled A
Cotton Town Boyhood. *He was elected president of Bolton Musical*
Artists Association.

His musical output was substantial, but he continued to write poetry and
illustrate his works. This included the carved-oak covers of his collection The
Poetry of Trees, *published in 1944. He also painted steam engines—*
Hick Hargreaves (as Benjamin Hick and Son Ltd) built some of the world's
first locomotives, which may have inspired his interest. He was a true
'renaissance man'. In 1960 he was made an Honorary Fellow of the Royal
Northern College of Music, where he rose to become Professor of Composition.

He produced several concertos as well as choral pieces and songs. He was
strongly influenced by the English folk-song revival and his music has echoes
of Ralph Vaughan Williams whose 150th anniversary was celebrated in
2022. He was a popular and committed teacher and often wrote music for
local societies and schools. He had strong ethical beliefs, remaining a pacifist
for all of his adult life.

Pitfield identified strongly as a Lancastrian. He contributed poems in
Lancashire dialect to The Journal of the Lancashire Dialect Society *and*
included a selection in his autobiography.[53]

He died on 16 November 1999. His obituary in The Independent
summed up a varied life: "Jack of many trades—artist, engraver, poet,
teacher, calligrapher, bookbinder, furniture designer, builder, ornitholo-
gist—and master of most of them, too. Thomas Pitfield will none the less be
remembered chiefly as a composer of unemphatic, beautifully crafted music."

* * *

Another unjustly neglected figure is Gordon Crosse, born in Bury in 1937; he died in 2021. He also became a national figure, with performances at the Proms, Aldeburgh Festival, and other major musical events.[54]

Hugh Wood (1932–2021) was a significant Lancashire composer, born in Parbold, between Wigan and Southport. John le Grove met him and remembered "his fairly acerbic, yet good humoured delivery of various musical points during a rehearsal. His musical language was quite modernist—a follower of the Second Viennese School of Schoenberg and Webern (who were not Lancastrians!)."[55]

Arthur Butterworth (1923–2014) was perhaps the most 'Lancastrian' of composers, though his later years were spent near Skipton, Yorkshire. Paul Conway, in his obituary, described him as a "composer, conductor and trumpeter with a passion for all things northern".[56] Butterworth was closely associated with the brass band movement and became music director of the National Youth Brass Band between 1975 and 1981. He wrote several pieces for brass bands, including *Odin*, a symphony commissioned by the Black Dyke Mills Band in 1986. *Odin* typifies the composer's passion for all aspects of the North, including art, literature, landscape and culture, which also lies behind his most performed works such as the tone poem *The Path Across the Moors* (1958) and *A Dales Suite* (1965). His *First Symphony* was premiered by the Hallé under Sir John Barbirolli at the Cheltenham Festival in 1957. Butterworth's second symphony was titled *A Moorland Symphony* and commissioned for the Saddleworth Festival in 1967. It is perhaps one of the most consciously 'Northern' pieces of music ever written. The libretto comprises poems by the Saddleworth poet Ammon Wrigley. Though not in his characteristic dialect, each poem reflects the moors that Butterworth and Wrigley both loved so well. The symphony was dedicated to his two great inspirations, Sibelius and Nielsen. Butterworth and Pitfield were both closely involved with the Manchester—and later Royal Northern—College of Music (see below).

Chris Gibbs is a composer from 'Lancashire North of the Sands' and became a friend of Butterworth. He taught piano and composition in Grange-over-Sands, and also held weekly classes in improvisation (classical, jazz and contemporary) with young instrumentalists at Cartmel Music Centre, near Grange. His compositions include a large-scale *Violin Concerto* and several shorter pieces for orchestra, and a piece for brass quintet—*Over Sands*. His one-act music drama *Across an Unknown Sea* received its first performance at the Sedbergh Festival in summer 2004. His *Forest of Bowland Suite* is perhaps his best-known work, again reflecting his strong sense of place. He is a member of 'The Lakeland Composers'—a group of active composers, dedicated to writing and performing new works. They are based in the North-West and organise regular performances of their own and others' music.[57]

Music education in Lancashire

Manchester's pre-eminent position in British music owes much to the contribution of its music colleges, particularly the Royal Northern College of Music (RNCM) and Chetham's School of Music.

Although Chetham's origins go back much earlier than the RNCM—it first admitted pupils in 1656—it did not emerge as one of the country's premier music schools until much later. The RNCM was formed in 1973 through the merger of the Royal Manchester College of Music and Northern School of Music. The Royal Manchester College opened in 1893, the brainchild of Sir Charles Hallé who became its principal. It was initially based in a former club building on the corner of Ducie Grove and Ducie Street. The building was adapted for use as a college by the architects Salomons and Steinthal, and contained a 400-seat concert hall as well as classrooms, a library and offices.[58] What we today know and love as the Royal Northern College of Music owes its existence to the support of several public bodies—above all Lancashire County Council, who were the principal funders, as well as Cheshire County Council and Manchester City Council. Most of its first students were drawn from Lancashire and Cheshire, with an outer periphery of Derbyshire, Yorkshire and Lincolnshire.[59]

The origins of the Northern School of Music go back to 1920. It was established by Hilda Collens, a talented piano teacher. The school became known as The Matthay School of Music, Manchester Branch. It was originally private but 'went public' in 1943 and was re-named The Northern School of Music. In 1954 the principal of the RMCM, Frederic Cox, raised the possibility of amalgamating with the Northern School of Music. It wasn't until 1972 when 'The Royal Northern College of Music' was established.

The RNCM has always had a strong commitment to working in the community, with an extensive programme of schools work. Perhaps its most unusual concert took place at Manchester's Newton Heath train maintenance depot in 2008. The RNCM Brass Band, together with Wardle Youth Band, performed a series of railway-themed pieces before an invited audience of railway workers and community representatives. Music included excerpts from Arthur Butterworth's *Trains in the Distance*. The concert concluded with the premiere of *Newton Heath Variations* by RNCM student Lucy Pankhurst, which featured sounds of a railway workshop and culminated in the entry of a steam locomotive into the auditorium.[60]

Chetham's became a music school during the 1950s building on Manchester's strong musical tradition. In 1969 the school decided to change the boys' grammar school into a fully co-educational specialist music school, with boarding accommodation extending its reach to students far beyond Manchester. Students lived and studied in the former Palatine Hotel and the former college buildings. Fifty years later, Chetham's enjoys an enviable reputation as one of the world's most celebrated and internationally renowned schools of music. The opening of the Stoller Hall in 2017 provided a new performance venue forging links between professional and student musicians.

14

LANCASHIRE AT PRAYER

Religious faith across Lancashire is remarkably varied, now more so than ever with Islam vying with Christianity, in a friendly way, as the largest active faith in terms of attendance for worship. Historically, Lancashire was at the heart of Catholicism in Britain and the 'recusants' fought running battles with the post-Reformation state for freedom to practise their religious beliefs.

However, the idea that Lancashire was a particularly devout place is a myth. John Walton observed of the years before the middle of the nineteenth century that, "the influence of organised religion on the population at large had never been strong; and its difficulties were compounded by population growth and redistribution from the late eighteenth century onwards."[1] In terms of religious attendance across faith divides, only five counties had lower levels of church attendance than Lancashire in 1851; in the case of the Church of England, Lancashire was the fourth lowest. The growth of Roman Catholicism in Lancashire helped to push the numbers up.

None of this is to suggest that religion wasn't important: it was a major factor in politics and local identity. E.P. Thompson wrote powerfully about 'the transforming power of the Cross' in *The Making of the English Working Class*, and nineteenth-century Lancashire saw the growth of several militant sects, often led by charismatic individuals such as Joanna Southcott, Joseph Rayner Stephens and John Wroe.[2]

Lancashire Catholicism

For centuries, before and after the Reformation, Catholicism was a strong force in Lancashire, particularly in the west of the county

north of Liverpool, and the Fylde. Most of the long-established—
and powerful—Lancashire families subscribed to 'the old faith' and
this cost some of them dearly in the English Civil War. Tensions
reached a high point in the late sixteenth century following the
Pope's excommunication of Elizabeth I. Thomas Hoghton (of
Hoghton Tower) had already gone into exile in 1569 and supported
the establishment of the English college at Douai, founded by
another Lancastrian, William Allen of Rossall. Public worship
became increasingly dangerous and some of the Catholic gentry
attended Anglican services to avoid persecution. Legend has it that
Richard Shireburne of Stonyhurst attended the 'upstarts'
(Protestant) church but put wax in his ears to avoid listening![3]
Despite the difficulties, most of them survived being on the losing
side of the Civil War, though somewhat bruised through the loss of
land and privilege. They still kept quite a bit.

It was the much-maligned Irish who revived Roman Catholicism
across Lancashire. The first Relief Act, passed in 1778, enabled Roman
Catholics in Britain to acquire land and property. In 1791 another bill
was passed that enabled them to practise their religion without fear of
civil penalties. Daniel O'Connell led a powerful mass campaign for
Catholic Emancipation in Ireland and his election in 1828 forced the
hands of the Duke of Wellington and Sir Robert Peel to promote the
Emancipation Act of 1829 in Parliament. This act admitted Irish and
English Roman Catholics to Parliament and to all but a handful of
public offices. The Universities Tests Act of 1871 opened the universities to Roman Catholics, making 'Catholic Emancipation' in the
United Kingdom virtually complete. However, while Britain's
Catholics had won legal rights, intolerance was still the norm.

By 1767 Lancashire had about two-fifths of all Catholics in
England. These were a mix of the traditional Lancashire Catholics
with their numbers swelled by Irish immigration. Wigan had the
largest concentration, with 26.5% of its population being Catholic.
Liverpool had the greatest number of Catholics, with 1,641 accounting for 5% of the population.[4] By 1850 the Irish-born population of
Wigan had grown to 4,502, with the proportion of the town's
population having remained much the same at 5.8%. Warrington's
Irish-born population was 10% of the town's 36,000 inhabitants.[5]

Lancashire's Catholic communities originally came under the
Chester Diocese. This was split into two with the creation of the

Liverpool Diocese which in turn lost most of east Lancashire with a further re-organisation which created a new Salford Diocese. The dominant figure in Lancashire Catholicism for many years was Bishop Goss who gloried in his faith but also his 'Englishness' and Lancashire identity, frequently reminding his flock that, "I am English, I am a real John Bull, indeed I am a Lancashire man!" He told an audience in Preston that "we have been born on the soil and have all the feelings of Englishmen. And we are proud of the government under which we live."[6]

* * *

Bolton was a fairly typical example of a growing industrial town, which had a very strong Protestant tradition. The first Catholic place of worship was St Peter and Paul's, established in 1794 with Father Joseph Shepherd as the priest. He was born of local parents—his father was one of only six registered Catholics in the mid-eighteenth century. He was educated at St Alban's English College in Valladolid and was ordained in 1791, arriving back in Bolton the following year. Catholics had met to worship, in semi legality, in a small room in the town centre, for several years. However, a licence was granted on 21 January 1795.

Father Shepherd was a tough character, travelling on horseback to Bury and Rochdale to conduct services as well as developing his congregation in Bolton. By the end of 1796 he had bought land to erect a purpose-made chapel. At the time Bolton was a staunchly Protestant town and religious hatred was rife. Construction of the chapel was the subject of frequent attacks, leading to the few parishioners taking turns each night to guard the building work. The chapel opened in 1798.

Few members of the original congregation were Irish, though that was to change very rapidly. Bolton's economy was booming as the cotton industry expanded and people flooded in to seek work. Many came from surrounding villages but there was a growing Irish migration in the early 1800s. Extreme poverty was a fact of life in Ireland and in 1831 fund-raising sermons were held at the Bolton chapel to help relieve starvation in Ireland. Bolton itself was far from being 'a land of milk and honey'. Living conditions were appalling with many of the immigrants crammed into damp, insanitary buildings where disease was rife.

The commanding figure within Bolton Catholicism at the time was Canon Edmund Carter, parish priest between 1847 and 1875. He was respected and feared, thinking nothing of going round Bolton pubs at night to quell fights and excessive drinking—often using his cane and bare fists to restore order. Other Catholic churches were built to meet the needs of the predominantly Irish incomers, including St Gregory's in Farnworth, a growing town in its own right with 800 Catholics resident by 1851.

Many of 'Cotton Lancashire's' Catholic communities started the tradition of 'Trinity Sunday' walks as early as the 1840s. These grew into huge displays by the 1880s, overseen by senior members of the clergy. Many continued to the 1960s. I remember my mother complaining at the cost of having to pay for the uniform each year, to be worn just once, only provided by Bolton's main Catholic tailors, McCartney's.

Anglicanism

Anglicanism in Lancashire deserves a book of its own (like so many subjects in this book). There is a lazy idea that the Church of England was completely aligned with Toryism in Lancashire but there were exceptions to the rule. If we look at Anglicanism overall, the picture in Lancashire is incredibly diverse. Most of Lancashire formed part of the Chester Diocese up to 1847 when the Diocese of Manchester was created. North and east Lancashire formed a new Blackburn Diocese which was founded in 1926 by the then Bishop of Manchester, William Temple, who was concerned to emphasise Christian pastoral support for the expanding cotton towns. This was underlined by transforming the fine Blackburn parish church into Lancashire's Anglican cathedral.[7]

* * *

Lancastrians: The Reverend John Wilcockson 1871–1969

John Wilcockson was born in Manchester in 1871. He came to Farnworth in 1915 as Vicar of St Thomas's Church, Dixon Green and remained vicar until he moved to the south of England in 1943.

He started a 'sanitary crusade' in 1916, opening a campaign against dirt, disease and bad housing. He became involved in politics because of his belief that it was a parson's job to look after the welfare of his flock in all its aspects, not just spiritually. It was his dynamic personality and political career that made him a household name in Farnworth and District for almost 30 years.[8]

He was first nominated as a Labour candidate in 1919 and soon demonstrated he was a man of action as well as words. Housing and health were his main concerns and he chaired both committees. It was due to his initiative that Farnworth became the first local authority in the country to clear slums under the 1930 Housing Act and embark on new housing developments.

When he was appointed chairman of the Urban District Council in 1930 he refused to wear the chain of office stating that, "had he wanted decorations he would have joined the Freemasons or Oddfellows and would therefore have had plenty of decorations".

He was president of Farnworth and Kearsley Co-operative Society in the early 1930s and chairman of the Bolton Board of Guardians. He was also chairman of the Fire Brigade Committee and chairman of the local ARP Committee in the late 1930s. He wrote a regular column for the Farnworth Weekly Journal called 'The Voice of Labour'.

He was unanimously elected as 'Charter Mayor' in 1939 and became the first Church of England clergyman in the country to be mayor of a borough. He was the mayor in the year that Farnworth was granted borough status.

He left Farnworth in 1943 citing the war 'and all its consequences' as his reason for leaving, as well as the fact that he felt he could achieve no more. He retired to Worthing and died in 1969 aged 97. He is buried in Farnworth Cemetery. A block of flats called Wilcockson House in Farnworth is the only memorial to a remarkable cleric and politician.

* * *

Nonconformity: fifty shades of grey?

Nonconformity covers a multitude of organisations, some being in effect 'sects', colourfully portrayed by E.P. Thompson:

> Puritanism—Dissent—Nonconformity: the decline collapses into surrender. *Dissent* still carries the sound of resistance to Apollyon and the Whore of Babylon, *Nonconformity* is self-effacing and apologetic: it asks to be left alone.[9]

Thompson, it could be argued, was being a tad unjust to the Nonconformist tradition which took in a plethora of groupings, ranging from the staid, but perhaps not apologetic, Wesleyan Methodists to the 'despiritualized fury' of Joanna Southcott and her followers.[10]

Methodism was by far the largest of the Nonconformist faiths; at various times it split into numerous groupings including the 'Primitive Methodists' who were strong in south Lancashire. Important outliers of Nonconformity were the Unitarians and Society of Friends (Quakers) who were numerically small but very influential (see pages 327–9). The Baptists and Congregationalists were also an important force in Lancashire, but their respective strength varied enormously. As with the Catholic faith, it is easy to generalise even on a regional level.

* * *

A closer look at one particular chapel, in Rawtenstall, might shed light on Nonconformity in Rossendale and east Lancashire.

Kay Street Baptist Church, Rawtenstall, opened its doors in 1872. Its history notes that:

> The decade of the sixties may justly be considered the darkest and gloomiest of industrial Lancashire of all the nineteenth century ... small wonder then, would it be that the working people of the towns of Lancashire, still stupefied by the shock which the Civil War in America had given them, should be reluctant to make any new venture in social or religious life. Yet it was in the period immediately following those days of trial and suffering that the Churches, and especially the Sunday schools, experienced a time of unwanted blessing and activity.[11]

Or perhaps it was precisely because of the desperate times of the 1860s that religion was seen to offer a palliative? There had already been a Baptist service held at nearby Goodshaw, a much smaller village, led by John Jefferson. He was born in Sunderland in 1823 and moved to Goodshaw, in Rossendale, in 1852, on a stipend of £60 per annum. His ten years at Goodshaw were "years of hard struggle" both personally (both he and his wife suffered from poor health) and with the onset of the Cotton Famine. The congregation diminished and he was ready for a fresh start. After a temporary move to Southport, where he seems to have fallen out with the local Baptists, he settled in Rawtenstall and began preaching at a local school: "This time I consulted nobody nor asked anybody's aid, but took Holly Mount School *on my own responsibility* and on March 3rd 1872 began to preach once a day."[12] The arrangement with the school proved short-lived and the growing congregation began meeting at the Co-operative Hall, underlining the close links between the Baptists and the co-operative movement. An entirely new building opened in 1872.

Jefferson was the driving force behind the Baptists of Rossendale and wrote regularly for *The Rossendale Baptist* magazine. He was described as having "a richly-dowered mind, bespeaking years of painful study and culture and was a man of wide and varied scholar-ship".[13] Jefferson died in 1900 "after some six weeks of severe illness and suffering." His place was taken by Charles Williams, noted for being "ever the fearless defender of the weak, champion of the oppressed, with the tenderness of a woman for those who had erred and strayed by the way".[14]

Who were the members of the Kay Street Baptist Church? It mostly comprised working men and women. The first members included eleven women, three more than the men shown in the por-trait gallery of the history. Although the history does not give the occupations of its members, the addresses given suggest the 'respect-able' working class and lower middle class formed the active core. Despite the mixed membership, there was a clear division of labour:

> After a hard day's work (not one of eight hours) you might have seen Betty Lonsdale, Nancy Eccles, Ruth, Mary Jane, Elizabeth and Ellen Greenwood and Elizabeth Haworth scrubbing, sweeping or dusting, while outside if spring or summer, Tom Brown, Robert Worswick or Major Lord gazing on a wealth of colour in the flower beds to the front of the chapel such as was not to be rivalled in the whole district.[15]

It sounds like the men had the better half of the bargain.

The church was determined to promote itself as widely as pos-sible and they took an advertisement with the Bacup Carriage Company on their omnibus operating between Bacup and Haslingden, a remarkable early example of marketing! It was aware of its global social responsibilities and in 1906 "raised her voice against the diabolical cruelties that were being inflicted on the Congolese, by the inhuman officials of the Belgian King, Leopold. The resolution was sent to L.V. Harcourt, at that time the member for Rossendale."[16]

Lancashire spirits and socialists

There was a close but highly complex relationship between religion and socialism, stretching back to Owenism in the 1820s. Many of the radical handloom weavers were 'free thinkers' who espoused varying degrees of atheism, pantheism or agnosticism. It has been argued that the 'ethical socialism' of the Independent Labour Party (ILP) which developed in the North during the 1890s owed much to Methodism.[17] This has been challenged to an extent. Certainly some leading figures in the ILP such as Philip Snowden, were brought up in the Methodist faith but the new socialism of the 1890s marked a turn away from not only Liberalism, but also its stablemate, nonconformist religion.

The links between the early socialist movement and spiritualism have been well documented by Logie Barrow.[18] Both movements enjoyed strong support in the industrial North, with links going back to Owenism, Chartism and secularism in the 1860s. Montague Blatchford, brother of Robert, adjudicated the choirs of the North-East Lancashire Lyceums. *The Bolton and District ILP Pioneer* had contributions from at least three spiritualists within its seven issues.

Barrow points out the close links between the Labour Church movement and spiritualism in east Lancashire, with several members of Blackburn Labour Church being involved with the local spiritualist church. James Swindlehurst of Bolton was involved in the Chartist movement in his youth and wrote an account of old Owenite and Chartist handloom weavers whom he chatted with in a Bolton park. *Summer Evenings with Old Weavers* is a fascinating account of a way of life that was rapidly becoming extinct but whose political echoes still reverberated in the North. He was a 'moral socialist' who believed that 'individual effort is required before man can work out his own salvation'. He was victimised for his radical beliefs and his family suffered eviction, with his wife giving birth in the street.[19]

Even the Marxist Social Democratic Federation (SDF) had a body of spiritualists amongst its ranks, though it was stronger within the ILP. J.T. Ward, an ILP councillor in Blackburn for 12 years, was a spiritualist 'healer' and director of the spiritualist magazine *The Two Worlds*, which Allen Clarke wrote for, and Rochdale ILP'er Peter Lee edited. Clarke wrote a popular account of his own experiences following the death of his first wife and two of his children.[20] He also wrote a novel based on his real-life experiences which was published as 'The Spirit Mother' and serialised in the spiritualist paper for the North of England, *The Two Worlds*.

Many of the socialist propagandists adopted the trappings of religion, with speakers like Snowden using a rousing 'come to Jesus' style of oratory. One of his most famous speeches was 'The Christ That Is To Be'.

The 'Labour Church' movement, founded by John Trevor in Manchester in 1891, was not so much a theological movement as an attempt to wean working-class men and women away from the embrace of Methodism and Anglicanism and provide a non-sectarian and non-denominational meeting point for local socialists who had an allegiance, however broadly defined, to Christianity. It was particularly strong in south-east Lancashire and the West Riding before the First World War.

The 'Socialist Sunday Schools' had a similar format to the traditional religious Sunday schools with a programme of songs, stories and discussions which were largely secular and socialist in character. 'The Socialist Ten Commandments' are a good example of early socialism's use of the form of popular religion to put over a socialist message.

Islam and Hinduism

A Bolton friend remembers walking past one of the town's first Hindu temples, some years ago. Work was still underway to convert the former Anglican church into a temple for the town's growing Hindu community. She peeked in and noticed some elaborately-decorated roses around the walls. An Indian gentleman, 'obviously in charge', came up to welcome her and asked if he could help. She pointed to the rose motifs, asking if they were some sort of ancient Hindu iconography. "Nay lass," he replied, "it's th'red rose o'Lancashire!" Perhaps Hindusim and Islam have integrated into Lancashire's spiritual tradition more than we imagine.

The Abdullah Quilliam Mosque in Liverpool was the first Islamic place of worship in Lancashire; in fact the first in Britain. It was founded in 1889 by a Victorian convert to Islam, Abdullah Quilliam. It fell into disrepair in the 1990s but a group of Muslims took over the building in 1999 and set up the Abdullah Quilliam Society. It re-opened in 2014.

The British Muslim Heritage Centre is located in Whalley Range, Manchester, in a former religious college. Originally it had trained ministers for the Congregational Church, providing further education for Nonconformists at a time when they were excluded from the Universities of Oxford and Cambridge. The college later established links with Owens College which became the Victoria University of Manchester, today's Manchester University. The building was acquired in 1985 by the GMB trade union, and used as their national training and conference centre until 2005.

It was only in the late 1950s that Lancashire began to experience large-scale migration from South Asia, with a consequent increase in both Muslim and Hindu congregations. Today, Blackburn with Darwen has the third highest Muslim population of England and Wales with 27% of the borough's population, and nearby Pendle at 17.4%.[21] The first places of worship were in people's homes; only later in the 1960s, when the communities were more settled (and prosperous) did mosques or temples begin to take shape. In Blackburn, the Jaame Masjid mosque opened in 1962, in two converted terraced houses in Audley Range. The Jamia Mosque Sultania was the first official mosque in Brierfield. The small two-room mosque was registered on 6 April 1976 and remained the focal point for Muslims in Brierfield for several decades until a new mosque opened in 2013. In Oldham the first mosque was established in 1967 in a terraced house on Church Hill Street off Waterloo Street. It moved to larger premises at 87 Greengate Street in 1971. A new, purpose-built mosque opened in 1997 and holds up to 2,000 people. Often, redundant Anglican churches were bought or rented, before purpose-built mosques like Oldham's were constructed.[22]

Lancashire had a smattering of Hindus in the earlier years of the twentieth century, mainly professional people often 'just passing through'. L'Hoondi Raj Thangdi, an important figure in the Indian

National Congress, lived in Lancashire during the 1930s and had links to the Bolton Whitmanites. Today, the Hindus in Lancashire are fewer than the Muslim population but still numerous. Towns such as Preston and Bolton have large Hindu populations, based mainly on migration from Gujarat in the 1960s. In Preston, about eighty families arrived from Gujarat in the 1960s and initially met in one of their homes on Glover Street. Hindu festivals were celebrated by hiring venues such as the town hall, schools and leisure centres. By the 1970s Lancashire's Hindu community had expanded, with newcomers arriving from Kenya and Uganda.

In Preston, the community comprised some 400 families by the end of the decade. Eventually funds were raised to purchase a former school which had been vacated when a new primary school was built nearby. In Bolton, the Shree Kutch Satsang Swaminarayan Temple was built in 1973 and was the first orthodox purpose-built Hindu temple to be constructed in the UK. Today, the Bolton Hindu Forum, formed in 2000, is active in a very wide range of community activities and has its own radio station, BHF Radio, founded by the late Manu Mistry.

Quakers and Unitarians

Numerically, the Quakers and Unitarians were a small part of Lancashire's religious make-up. Yet their size hides the considerable influence they exerted. Members of both faiths were active in industry, politics and culture. Lancashire has a strong claim to be where it all began.

* * *

Lancastrians: Katharine Bruce Glasier 1867–1950

Katharine Bruce Glasier was a highly influential figure in Lancashire socialism throughout the first half of the twentieth century. Like many other socialists of her time, including Carpenter, she was an admirer of the writing of Rabindranath Tagore, the Bengali poet and philosopher. She edited the ILP's paper, Labour Leader, *from 1916 to 1921. Katharine's drift into a highly spiritual form of socialism, which included becoming a Quaker, accelerated following the death of husband Bruce in 1920 after a prolonged illness and the tragic death of her son Glen in 1928. She was a frequent visitor to the home of Whitman 'guru' J.W. Wallace at Anderton. After Bruce's death she had a nervous breakdown and spent several weeks at Anderton with Wallace and his house-keeper Minnie Whiteside. By the end of April she began a steady recovery. They went for walks round Rivington and the moors. On 22 April she recorded having 'a wonderful time' with Minnie and Glen. During this period at Wallace's she seems to have undergone a form of spiritual renewal akin to Wallace's 'illumination' in 1885. On 25 April she wrote: "At last I understand—I know I am deathless." On 10 November she records: "Walk to Lake [i.e. Rivington]—I have cosmic consciousness of my own."*[23]

The tribute to her son, The Glen Book, *first serialised in Labour's* Northern Voice, *is at the same time a strong celebration of Whitman and his philosophy, with numerous excerpts from* Leaves of Grass. *She quotes extensively from Whitman about a coming new age, "rounding forward to another springtime of the Spirit of the Whole ... an age of reason and faith with far more wonderful works than man has yet seen is drawing near".*[24]

* * *

In 1652 George Fox had his vision of 'a great people to be gathered', leading to the formation of the Society of Friends, or Quakers. He conducted a pilgrimage taking him over Pendle Hill and into 'Lancashire North of the Sands'. He arrived in Ulverston and met Margaret Fell of Swarthmoor Hall, whom he subsequently married. Several small, secluded Quaker meeting houses sprang up across Lancashire, including at Cartmel, Freckleton, Crawshawbooth and larger centres such as Lancaster and Bolton. The Friends Meeting Houses in Manchester and Liverpool became major centres of Northern culture, used for a multiplicity of progressive causes. It would be fair to say that 'Lancashire North of the Sands' is the home of the Quaker movement and Swarthmoor Hall is its historic centre.

If Methodism's contribution to Socialism has been exaggerated, the role of the Quakers in socialism has, if anything, been under-rated. Many of the Quakers who went to prison rather than fight in the First World War were also members of the ILP.[25]

Unitarianism was a popular faith amongst the Liberal middle class of Lancashire and provides a relatively easy 'fit' with the Quakers;

it goes back to a similar age when alternative faiths were barely legal. The 1662 Act of Uniformity required all clergymen to use the Prayer Book of the Church of England and nonconformists were not allowed to worship in their own chapel or in their homes, until the Toleration Act was passed in 1689. They managed to circumvent the law, but it was not easy. Full toleration of Unitarian worship was not granted in this country until 1813 and there was gradual transition, in some congregations, from Presbyterianism to Unitarianism, with various splits and divisions taking place during the eighteenth and early nineteenth centuries.

One of the most delightful Unitarian places of worship is Rivington Chapel, closely connected to Lancashire's Walt Whitman 'fellowship' and the last resting place of several members of the group, including the Unitarian minister himself, Samuel Thompson who often entertained the Whitmanites in the period between 1890 and 1918. Its history is remarkable. Following the passing of the 1662 Act of Uniformity the local vicar, Samuel Newton, refused to take the oath and was expelled from the Church in what became known as 'The Great Ejection', together with about 2,000 other clergymen. He remained in the area and pursued what was in effect an 'underground' existence. He led worship for Nonconformists (or Dissenters) outdoors, possibly at Noon Hill on the slopes of Winter Hill. In 1672, he was granted a licence as a Presbyterian teacher and was allowed to hold meetings, probably at a farm on the edge of Rivington. The present chapel at Rivington was built in 1703 and is a lovely spot, with a tea room next door in the former chapel hall.

Walmsley Unitarian Church is situated on the moors above Egerton. The congregation was founded before 1672, and the chapel built in 1713. During the period of illegality they used to assemble in a wild and lonely spot named Yearnsdale Holmes. A watchman was appointed to warn of the approach of any hostile party!

In 1961 Captain John Crompton of Rivington Hall, chairman of the Trustees of Rivington Chapel, and Reverend Eric Shirvell Price, Minister of Bank Street Unitarian Chapel, Bolton, suggested a national pilgrimage as a way of marking the 300th anniversary of the Great Ejection of 1662. About 360 people made the first pilgrimage in the following year and it has continued, at three-yearly intervals, since. The last was held in 2022.

15

LANCASHIRE

POLITICS AND GOVERNANCE

Myths and realities

The 2019 General Election ushered in a Conservative government with a greatly-increased majority which included several gains in the North, Lancashire in particular. Constituencies such as Leigh, Heywood and Middleton, Burnley, Bury South, Bolton North East and several others that had been seen as 'safe' Labour seats changed hands. The idea emerged of a 'red wall' of Labour-held constituencies in the North that had 'fallen' to a Tory upsurge. Yet it's possible to exaggerate the change. Some of these constituencies, such as Bury South, Bolton North East and Burnley had been 'swing seats' which had alternated between Labour and Conservative—or in the case of Burnley, Liberal Democrat. True, Heywood and Middleton and Leigh were longer-standing Labour strongholds, but the 2019 election highlighted something distinctive about Lancashire politics: working-class conservatism is nothing new, and goes back to the days of what was termed 'clog Toryism' in the late nineteenth century. It should also be said that some aspects of Labour politics were a long way from the 'revolutionary socialism' of figures such as Liverpool-born Victor Grayson who won a by-election in the West Riding's Colne Valley in 1907 on an uncompromisingly radical socialist programme. Equally, the myth (like all myths there's an element of truth in it) of inter-war Nelson as 'Little Moscow' shouldn't hide the fact that many working people of east Lancashire were voting Tory throughout the same period.

* * *

Lancastrians: Sarah Alice Nall 1880–1952

Sarah Nall was a popular figure in Lancashire Conservative politics as well as dialect circles. She was born in Castleton and started working 'half-time' in a local mill at the age of 10, after being "literally kicked out of school at the age of four for being a dunce". The family moved to the Blackpool area and the young Sarah won essay prizes from the Blackpool Co-operative Society.

She became active in local politics, as a Conservative. At the age of 22 she was co-opted onto Bispham Parish Council as secretary of the Ladies' Committee and became a Sunday school teacher. She worked as a baker and confectioner and set up her own business, in Middleton. She was a member of the Primrose League for over forty years and was secretary of the Assheton Habitation in Middleton. She was secretary of the Women's Divisional Conservative Association for many years and was vice-chairman of the local Conservative Association for a period. She was an 'enthusiastic member' of the Lancashire and Cheshire Antiquarian Society and a member of the Lancashire Authors' Association, and a frequent contributor to its events and publications.[1]

* * *

Is there something distinctive about Lancashire politics that sets it apart from other parts of Britain? I think so. The politics of Lancashire Toryism had a very distinctive flavour in many of the cotton towns, and Liberalism put down strong and distinctive roots in Rossendale and the north-east Lancashire weaving districts. I've argued, in *Socialism with a Northern Accent*, that a distinct form of socialist politics emerged in the 1890s that was particularly strong in 'Cotton Lancashire' and the West Riding textile districts.[2] It leant more towards Christianity than Marxism and was often character-ised as 'ethical socialism'. The Independent Labour Party (ILP) formed an institutional home for this kind of politics; it was under-pinned by a political culture that included walking and cycling clubs, social clubs, socialist Sunday schools and choirs.

A more mainstream Labour culture took shape in Lancashire dur-ing the 1920s and 1930s, a blend of traditional Liberalism and mod-erate socialism, personified in its early years by former cotton weaver David Shackleton, MP for Clitheroe from 1902. His obituary by Tom Shaw in *The Manchester Guardian* said he was "intensely Lancashire in his pre-war outlook; and looked upon government action as interference and as reprehensible".[3] He wasn't of 'the left' but probably personified the views of many working men and women who made the transition from Liberalism to Labour in the inter-war years.[4]

But let's start from the beginning and consider how Lancashire politics evolved into blue, red and yellow.

* * *

Historically, political affiliation in England has usually been largely down to a combination of class and religious identity. The Lancashire of the seventeenth century was dominated by a small number of families, many of whom adhered to 'the old faith', Catholicism, which was particularly strong in west and north Lancashire. It fed naturally into support for King Charles I in the Civil War, and Toryism.[5]

However, a quite different religious and political tradition took shape in parts of south-east Lancashire, particularly in Manchester, as well as Bolton, which became known as 'Geneva of the North' on account of its Protestantism.

Lancashire can claim the mantle of being home to the great seventeenth-century radical Gerrard Winstanley, born near Wigan in 1609. He moved south and set up as a cloth merchant in the London area. He made a name for himself in the English revolution as one of the main figures in the 'Digger' movement, in 1649 establishing a community of radicals in Walton-on-Thames. His book *The Law of Freedom in a Platform*, published in 1652, outlines his vision of a communist society. Winstanley is an important figure in political history but perhaps more importantly he continues to inspire Break word at modern-if possible-day radicalism. The annual Diggers' Festival in Wigan began as a modest event in 2002 organised by a few local radicals and has grown into a major festival, taking place in September.

* * *

A new kind of politics was taking shape in Lancashire in the latter years of the eighteenth century. The influence of the French

Revolution was considerable in some parts of Lancashire, particularly in the handloom-weaving communities. The ideals of 'liberty, equality and fraternity', introduced to an English readership by writers such as Tom Paine, inspired many radical handloom weavers; *The Rights of Man* featured on many weavers' bookshelves.

Events in Ireland also had an impact on Lancashire. Many Irish people had already settled in parts of Lancashire and brought the democratic ideals of Wolfe Tone and Robert Emmet with them. The United Irishmen rose against English rule in 1798 and were defeated, with many killed; some fled abroad including to England. In parts of Lancashire and the North, a sister organisation, 'The United Englishmen', provided support for their Irish comrades and harboured their own revolutionary dreams.

E.P. Thompson, in *The Making of the English Working Class*, charts the development of this radical political culture.[6] Men such as Samuel Bamford and Richard Pilling embodied the radicalism and intellectual culture of the handloom-weaving communities which flourished across the Pennines in the late eighteenth and early nineteenth centuries. It was a culture that was not only highly literate, but as we have seen in previous chapters, included musicians, artists and scientists.[7]

* * *

Lancastrians: Samuel Bamford 1788–1872

Bamford was born in the handloom-weaving community of Middleton in 1788. His father was a weaver and admirer of Tom Paine. Bamford himself became a weaver in his early twenties and followed the family tradition of devouring the works of Paine—The Age of Reason, Common Sense *and* The Rights of Man. *In 1816 he formed a reform club in Middleton. His activities came to the attention of the authorities who arrested him for treason in March 1817. He was acquitted on the grounds of insufficient evidence.*

The high point of Bamford's political career came two years later. He led a large number of people from Middleton to attend the meeting at St Peter's Fields, Manchester, which has gone down in history as 'The Peterloo Massacre'.

After the massacre several men, including Bamford, were arrested and charged with "assembling with unlawful banners at an unlawful meeting for the purpose of inciting discontent". Bamford was sentenced to one year's imprisonment.

After his release he ceased to be active in the campaign for parliamentary reform. He returned to handloom weaving but the trade was in headlong decline due to competition from the new power looms. He attempted to supplement his income by selling poetry and local sketches such as his Walks in South Lancashire, *published in 1844. Bamford wrote in both standard English and dialect, a form which was yet to be popularised by writers such as Edwin Waugh and Samuel Laycock in the 1850s and 1860s.[8] He was a strong advocate of Lancashire culture and was recorded in* The Ashton-under-Lyne Reporter, *in 1868, talking to friends about the importance of preserving "all that was good and pure in the Lancashire dialect".[9] He published* The Dialect of South Lancashire *in 1854.*

Bamford was a tetchy character, easily given to offence. He refused to take part in the Chartist movement and even enrolled as a special constable, to the disgust of his radical friends. His books Early Days *and* Passages in the Life of a Radical *provide an invaluable source for working-class life in Lancashire in the early nineteenth century.*

* * *

For some years before Peterloo, Lancashire women had their own reform organisations. Samuel Bamford tells of women attending radical meetings and voting alongside men: "female political unions were formed, with the chairwoman, committees, and other officials".[10]

* * *

At the extreme end of working-class protest were the 'Luddite' disturbances in Lancashire and Yorkshire during 1812. These outbreaks, a reflection of the extreme poverty facing the weavers by this time, were ruthlessly suppressed with many of the leaders executed. Two events—the burning of a mill at Westhoughton and the assassination of an unpopular mill owner in Huddersfield—led to the execution of several people, including a boy aged 12 from Westhoughton. He was hung at Lancaster.[11]

The executions left an enduring sense of injustice which fuelled support for the Chartist Movement years later and even radicalism

in the 1860s. J.T. Staton, the radical Bolton dialect writer, recalled
the Westhoughton executions in an election sketch published in his
Bowtun Loominary in 1853,[12] attacking the Tories:

> Remember now Westhoughton mill
> How many there you stooped to kill
> Think of that infant voice so shrill
> That at Lancaster you hung

Luddism was more than just a crude reaction to rapid industrialisation. It was a revolt against the loss of that community and culture
so well described by Samuel Bamford. There are parallels with the
reaction of mining communities in the 1980s to the loss of not just
mining jobs but to the destruction of entire communities and their
way of life.

Lancashire Toryism

What of Conservatism in Lancashire, in the period up to the Reform
Act of 1832? In the West Riding of Yorkshire there was a 'radical
Toryism' personified by Richard Oastler and Michael Sadler.
Oastler described himself as a 'Church and King' Tory; with his
friend and near-neighbour Michael Sadler, he campaigned against
the new Poor Law of 1834 and in support of factory reform. Was
there a Lancashire equivalent? To a qualified extent, there was.
Joseph Rayner Stephens (see biography below) was one of the most
colourful figures of early nineteenth-century Lancashire radicalism,
but he always described himself as a Tory.

* * *

Lancastrians: Joseph Rayner Stephens 1805–79

*Stephens was born in Edinburgh but the family moved to Lancashire and he
entered Manchester Grammar School in 1819. He became a Methodist
preacher, and was appointed in 1826 to a mission station at Stockholm. He
was soon able to preach in Swedish, and acquired a taste for Scandinavian
literature. He was ordained as a Wesleyan minister in 1829, and was
located at Cheltenham in 1830.*

His Wesleyan career ended in 1834, when he resigned after being suspended for attending disestablishment meetings in Ashton-under-Lyne. He joined the 'factory movement' to improve conditions of factory workers. Francis Place said of Stephens that he "professed himself a Tory, but acted the part of a democrat". The opposition of leading Liberals to the Ten Hours Bill confirmed him as a 'Tory Radical'; later, he threw himself into the agitation for the People's Charter which swept Lancashire from the late 1830s for over a decade.

He was a powerful orator; he could be heard by gatherings of 20,000 people in the open air. He became known as 'the tribune of the poor'. On 27 December 1838 he was arrested at Ashton-under-Lyne on the charge of 'attending an unlawful meeting at Hyde'. He was tried at Chester in August the 1839 and was imprisoned in Chester jail.

He settled in Ashton-under-Lyne in 1840 and preached to large crowds. He liked producing newspapers including Stephens's Monthly Magazine *(1840), the* Ashton Chronicle *(1848–9), and the* Champion *(1850–1). He effectively formed his own sect, known as 'The Stephensites', "more of a political order than a religious institution, notwithstanding the fact they met on stated occasions for worship and instruction".[13]*

He took part in various local campaigns, retaining his power and popularity as a speaker well after Chartism had subsided. He became a member of the Stalybridge school board.

He died in Stalybridge on 18 February 1879 and was buried in the churchyard of St John's, Dukinfield. On 19 May 1888 a granite memorial to Stephens was unveiled in Stamford Park, Stalybridge.[14]

* * *

Blackburn has been the subject of particular attention for its 'Clog Toryism', thanks in large part to the work of Patrick Joyce. Long before he completed *Work, Society and Politics*, historians had commented on the town's 'popular Toryism'. The Liberal journalist and chronicler of Blackburn, W.A. Abram, in his *Blackburn Characters of a Past Generation*, devoted a chapter to 'Tom' Mullineaux, 'butcher and councilman'. He highlights divisions and dissension within the seemingly monolithic Tory political apparatus in the town. He was born in Blackburn in 1810 and built up a modest business as a butcher. He burst onto the political scene relatively late in life, in his mid-50s when he was elected to the council. He seems to have made it his mission to cause as much trouble as he could. Abram describes his politics thus:

> Politically, Thomas Mullineaux was a staunch Tory of the good old "Church and King" school. Mr. William Henry Hornby, senior, at one time the Conservative leader in Blackburn, was his personal friend, and in his business he counted amongst his customers some of the most wealthy families in the town. It was a strange event that one, always regarded as a Tory of the Tories ... should have become a persistent caviller at the proceedings of the party in power in municipal affairs, which was his own party, and a thorn in the side of the responsible leaders of it, during nearly the whole term of his service in the Town Council.[15]

During Mullineaux's frequent interventions in council debates he was rebuked with equal force by the sitting mayor, 'Jack' Smith, who Abram says "retorted as roughly and as rudely as he knew how to".[16] Smith himself was a remarkable character: "a big stone hewn from the quarry, but unsquared and undressed", Abram described him.[17] Although he began his political career as a 'radical' he fell out with the local Liberals and stood as a Conservative, though Abram was of the view that "he might best be described as an 'opportunist'". He served two years as mayor and made an impact. Abram said that "the town has never, before or since, had for mayor a man so utterly a stranger to all the graces of refined society and the rules of politeness, or to the dignity of mien people look for in the first citizen ... of a great town".[18]

Smith spoke, whether in the council chamber or in the tap-room of one of his many favoured pubs, with a strong Blackburn dialect which Abram reproduces in his character sketch. Smith was, however, able to confront rival political mobs during the years of his mayoralty with courage and firmness, threatening to have them all shot 'like rapputs' as Abram described. Smith had particular priorities, for which the people of Blackburn should thank him. He was a strong advocate for sewage and waste disposal and took an avid scientific interest in sewage, keeping samples at home in jars.

Mullineaux and Smith were 'characters' that formed Blackburn Toryism, though the figure of William Hornby dominated the town's politics; his statue still stands in Blackburn's town square. Although from a wealthy, upper-class family, he was able to relate to the town's popular culture and could speak 'broad Lancashire' when the occasion required. He was known to generations of Blackburnians as 'Th'Owd Gam Cock'.

Peterloo and its legacy in Lancashire politics

On Sunday 16 August 1819, some 60,000 working men and women, many with their children, gathered from all parts of Lancashire and the West Riding to hear Henry 'Orator' Hunt and other radicals of the day, to demand universal suffrage. They were peaceful and in carnival mood; many contemporary accounts describe the marchers decked out in their 'Sunday best'. Yet within a few minutes carnival turned to carnage as the local yeomanry were let loose on the crowd, hitting out blindly with their sabres as they tried to get to the stage where Hunt was speaking. At least seventeen people died and hundreds were seriously wounded.

The impact of 'Peterloo' echoed throughout nineteenth-century Lancashire, and beyond. Immediately, it stimulated demands for radical reform; during the Chartist period of the late 1830s and 1840s, 'Remember Peterloo' was a rallying cry against the establishment. Radical Liberals, in the 1870s and 1880s, recalled the massacre in their speeches and later, socialists in the North of England would refer to the massacre as an indication of the depths to which the ruling class would sink in its attempt to thwart the 'will of the people'.

Radical movements multiplied in the North during the 1820s and coalesced into the Chartist Movement, with its six demands focused around universal male suffrage. It took in peaceful reform, strike action and, on occasions, insurrection. The Chartist-influenced 'General Strike' of 1842 was undoubtedly strongest in the textile districts of Lancashire and was accompanied by some sporadic violence.[19] One of the great events of the Chartist period was the monster demonstration on Blackstone Edge on 2 August 1846, which brought together thousands of working men and women from both sides of the Pennines to hear the great orator Ernest Jones. Jones wrote:

But waved the wind on Blackstone Height
A standard of the broad sunlight
And sung that morn with trumpet might
A sounding song of liberty![20]

The event is still commemorated each May. Allen Clarke wrote a seven-part feature on the life of Ernest Jones in his *Northern Weekly* newspaper during 1900.[21]

After Chartism: the radical liberal tradition

Chartism petered out after the great, but ultimately ineffective, demonstrations of 1846 and in London in 1848. Many Northern towns had their venerated 'old Chartists' who lived to see the franchise extended to all men in 1884. They remained active in local political activities as well as trades unions, though the heady days of mass meetings on Blackstone Edge had long since passed. Allen Clarke, in his novel *The Knobstick* describes 'an old Chartist'—Joe Carklan—based on an historical figure known locally as 'Radical Grimshaw', well known in Bolton political circles through to the 1880s. In the novel, the old Chartist is looking back to the 1840s, before the storm clouds of the 1887 Engineers' Strike broke: "In them days men were full o'reform, and meant to alter every bad arrangement and right every wrong; but their enthusiasm deed away as soon as their ballies were full".[22]

In Rochdale, the leader of the local Chartist movement, Tom Livsey, went on to become a key figure in the Liberal Party, embodying the transition from Chartism to Liberalism which took place in the 1850s and 1860s. Livsey's first political speech, on 8 November 1837, was in the Chartist Rooms in Rochdale at a meeting commemorating Peterloo and the birthday of Henry Hunt. Livsey was involved in the battles of the Chartist period including the 1842 General Strike. He made the transition to political respectability with consummate ease, becoming a Liberal alderman on Rochdale Corporation, as well as an active co-operator. He was a strong, but unsuccessful, candidate for the mayoralty a year before he died in 1864.

Liberalism absorbed much of the energies of Chartism in the North. For several decades working-class politicians like Livsey played important roles in local Liberal politics in many Northern towns. Thomas Newbigging (see below) was one of Lancashire's most radical Liberals in the 1870s and 1880s, coming from an Owenite and Chartist background.

Liberalism and co-operation were easy bedfellows, often with Methodism sharing the company, particularly in the north-east of Lancashire. Both Lancashire and Yorkshire produced a Liberal political culture which retained strong radical elements, harking back to Chartism and Peterloo. It chimed well with the culture of working-class independence and 'respectability' which became particularly strong as the North's pre-eminence as the industrial powerhouse of the world became established.

Its success was based on a social compromise. Many key figures in Liberalism were major employers in the Northern towns and their interests were not always the same as their working-class, trade-unionised, fellow Liberals. The cross-class coalition which characterised Liberalism in many parts of the North began to show signs of stress by the 1880s as socialism gained popularity.

* * *

Lancastrians: Thomas Newbigging 1833–1914

Thomas Newbigging was the personification of the Northern radical Liberal tradition. He provides yet another link from Owenism through Liberalism towards Socialism. He was of Scots Presbyterian origins, born in Glasgow in 1833. His parents were brought up in New Lanark, Robert Owen's socialist community to the south of Glasgow, where they met and married. They settled in Glasgow in the early 1830s, with his father appointed manager of a large cotton mill. After some years in Galloway the family moved to Rossendale in 1844. At the age of 23 he was appointed manager of the Rossendale Union Gas Company, based in Bacup. He became one of Britain's leading gas engineers, spending five years in Brazil, where he was awarded the Brazilian 'Order of the Knighthood' by the Emperor. He wrote the standard text for the gas industry—The Gas Manager's Handbook—*published in 1881. He was elected president of the Institution of Gas Engineers for 1884–5.*[23]

However, it was his extensive non-professional interests which mark him out as exceptional. He wrote The History of the Forest of Rossendale, *a work which has yet to be surpassed for its detailed historical account of the area. He was a talented poet, strongly influenced by Burns. His* Poems and Songs *combine traces of Lancashire and Scots vernacular. Like many middle-class intellectuals of his day, he was fascinated by dialect and wrote a* Glossary of Rochdale-cum-Rossendale Words and Phrases, *with Henry Cunliffe. He was a member of the Manchester Literary Club and many other literary circles and was a good friend of the famous Lancashire dialect poet, Edwin Waugh.*[24]

His parental background inevitably instilled a strong social awareness in him from an early age. He was adopted as the Liberal 'Home Rule' candidate for Rossendale in the 1886 General Election. He was a passionate believer in Irish freedom, seeing 'Home Rule' as a stepping stone to complete national independence. He was a strong supporter and ally of fellow Rossendalian Michael Davitt (see page 376). At a speech in the Co-operative Hall in Rawtenstall, Newbigging spoke of the leader of the Irish Land League as having "imbibed many of his ideas of freedom in breathing the air of the Rossendale Hills". At a speech in Eccles he again returned to the Irish Question, observing that "the history of Ireland and its connection with England, both before and since the Act of Union ... is indeed such as to make even a heart of stone bleed".[25]

In response to accusations that Davitt and other Irish radicals were 'demagogues and agitators' he cited the English radical tradition: "We owe every shred of our English liberty to men who were called demagogues and agitators, and viler names than these ... the truth is we need more agitators". He attacked Tory attempts to 'play the Orange card' accusing Randolph Churchill of "opening wide the door of race and religious bigotry". He was passionate about religious equality, land reform, free education for all and strong local government. He was an early advocate of devolution for Scotland, Wales and England, as well as Ireland, objecting to "the unwieldy growth of London" sapping talent from the rest of the country.[26]

Newbigging was a great advocate of political decentralisation. His speech at Failsworth during the 1886 election campaign highlighted the dangerously centralised government in Britain, where "there is a magnetic force of attraction towards the governmental centre of the country. Talent, genius, the possessors of great wealth, the victims of poverty—all converge towards the central core of the nation's life; and when, as in the case of London, the growth becomes stupendous almost beyond conception, there is grave reason for apprehension."[27]

* * *

Political clubs

Political club culture grew rapidly from the 1880s and many fine buildings remain, often turned over to other uses, that were once Conservative or Liberal 'working men's clubs'. Labour clubs came later and were mostly less opulent. The Bolton Socialist Club, founded in 1895 survives—since 1905 housed at 16 Wood Street, Bolton, the birthplace of Lord Leverhulme. Nelson's Unity Hall, opened in 1907, has recently been refurbished and features displays of the early socialist movement in east Lancashire. Sadly, the grand Conservative Club in Accrington has been demolished.

Internationalism: the Cotton Famine, slavery and the Bulgarian atrocities

Perhaps the most legendary example of selfless support for an international cause was the Lancashire cotton workers' support for the anti-slavery cause during the American Civil War. A majority of the Lancashire cotton workers remained solidly in support of the North and emancipation of the slaves, despite the North blockading the southern ports and effectively destroying their livelihoods.[28]

A mass rally in support of the North took place at Manchester's Free Trade Hall on New Year's Eve 1862, the day before Lincoln's abolition decree came into effect. It was organised by local co-operators including J.C. Edwards. An historic resolution was moved by Edwards:

> That this meeting, recognising the common brotherhood of mankind and the sacred and inalienable right of every human being to personal freedom and equal protection, records its detestation at negro slavery in America, and of the attempts of the rebellious Southern slaveholders to organise on the great American continent a nation having slavery as its base.[29]

A letter of solidarity from the working people of Manchester was sent to Lincoln, saying: "The erasure of that foul blot on civilisation and Christianity—chattel slavery—during your presidency, will cause the name of Abraham Lincoln to be honoured and revered by posterity."

On 19 January 1863, Lincoln replied by sending an address to the working people of Manchester. He recognised their suffering as "an instance of sublime Christian heroism", and added: "It is indeed an energetic and re-inspiring assurance of the inherent truth and the ultimate and universal triumph of justice, humanity and freedom."

This was followed in February by the first food relief ship from New York to Liverpool. The *George Griswold* carried boxes of bacon and bread, bags of rice and corn and 15,000 barrels of flour and was greeted on the docks by a crowd of 4,000. It was the first of several.

In towns like Bolton and Rochdale most of the mills closed during the Cotton Famine and tens of thousands of previously well-paid cotton workers were made destitute. William Billington, a working-class writer from Blackburn, used dialect to express the feelings of many workers yearning for the war to end:

> Some factory maisters tokes for t'Seawth
> Wi' a smooth an' oily tongue,
> But iv they'd sense they'd shut their meawth,
> Or sing another song;
> Let liberty not slavery
> Be fostered an' extended –
> Four million slaves mun yet be free,
> An' then t'war will be ended.[30]

Some historians have claimed that Lancashire workers' support for anti-slavery was a myth, and have quoted some of the Labour Movement press to justify their view. Perhaps the most careful assessment of the arguments was done by Royden Harrison in *Before the Socialists*.[31]

In Staton's *Lankishire Loominary* he frequently dealt with 'Th'Spouters on th' Merriky Question' and maintained his non-commitment whilst attacking some of the tricks being used by both sides to gain support.

* * *

Many socialists and radical Liberals made common cause on international issues in the 1880s and 1890s, including protests against the 'Bulgarian atrocities'. The dialect writer J.T. Taylor, born into a handloom-weaving family in Oldham in 1861, became a co-operator and active Liberal and Unitarian. He celebrated the opposition of

Oldham workers to the Turkish government, at a time when the British Tories were supporting the despotic regime:

Aw'm gradely fain that Owdham folk
Are on their feet again
Contendin' for humanity,
An' liberty of men.
Aw'm glad to yer them lift their voice
To swell the leawd protest
Against these horrid, cruel crimes
That shook each human breast.[32]

Harrison refers to a mass meeting of cotton weavers in Blackburn in 1861, when local workers' leader Mortimer Grimshaw tried to get the workers to support a mediated settlement in America. The secretary of the Weavers' Association intervened and demanded a vote on his suggestion. It went against Grimshaw with over 4,000 hands raised against and a mere dozen in favour. In Stalybridge, a town particularly hard hit by the Cotton Famine, unemployed cotton workers passed a vote 'by an immense majority' stating that, "In the opinion of this meeting, the distress prevailing in the manufacturing districts is mainly owing to the rebellion of the Southern States against the American constitution."[33]

A sculpture by Jacob Epstein—*Slave Hold*—is a monument to the cotton workers' support for emancipation and is on display in Bolton Museum.

A Lancashire socialist culture

During the 1890s a distinctive socialist culture developed in the North—particularly in the industrial heartlands of Lancashire and the West Riding. It encompassed the Independent Labour Party (ILP) and the Social Democratic Federation (SDF),[34] local socialist groups, Clarion choirs, cycling and rambling clubs and relatively short-lived organisations like the Labour Church. The ILP was very different in shape and substance to the SDF, though the two co-operated at a local level in many Lancashire towns. Its socialism was primarily ethical rather than economic.

That culture was well described by Hannah Mitchell (see pages 349–50) in her autobiography in which she described a politics which, attracted a type of socialist who was not satisfied with the stark materialism of the Marxist school, desiring warmth and colour in human lives: not just bread, but bread and roses, too. Perhaps we were not quite sound on economics as our Marxian friends took care to remind us, but we realised the injustice and ugliness of the present system. We had enough imagination to visualise the greater possibility for beauty and culture in a more justly ordered state. If our conception of Socialism owed more to Morris than to Marx, we were none the less sincere, and many found their belief strengthened by the help and inspiration of the weekly meetings held in these Northern towns.[35]

Blatchford and *The Clarion*

Robert Blatchford probably did much more than either the Webbs, or even William Morris and Keir Hardie, to popularise socialism— particularly in the North of England. He achieved this through his newspaper *The Clarion*, as well as his best-selling book *Merrie England*, addressed to "John Smith of Oldham, a hard-headed workman, fond of facts".[36] The book won tens of thousands of converts to the socialist cause. However, Blatchford's politics were a kind of left-wing populism that could veer into support for nationalism and empire. He was acutely aware of the different landscape between the North and the South. In 1895 he said:

> If you asked a London socialist for the origin of the new movement he would refer you to Karl Marx and other German Socialists. But so far as our Northern people are concerned I am convinced that beyond the mere outline of State Socialism Karl Marx and his countrymen have had but little influence. No; the new movement here, the new religion which is Socialism, is the result of the labours of Darwin, Carlyle, Ruskin, Dickens, Thoreau and Walt Whitman.[37]

The ILP became the largest socialist party in the North, though in some towns the SDF retained its predominance, notably in Burnley and Salford. Co-operation between the two parties at local level was common, and in some places there were joint ILP/SDF parliamentary candidates, such as Allen Clarke in Rochdale in 1900. In Bolton, the two parties joined forces and formed the Bolton Socialist Party, which still exists.[38]

An interesting byway in the history of socialism was the Labour Church, set up by John Trevor in Manchester in 1891 and largely (though not exclusively) based in Lancashire and Yorkshire. It provided a cross-party meeting and discussion forum for socialists and radical Liberals. Contrary to some views, it did not have a 'theology' as such, but was loosely based on an amalgam of Christianity and Socialism.[39] Its 'manifesto', laid out by Trevor in 1891, said: "the Labour Movement is a Religious movement. We wipe out all distinctions between Secular and Sacred; we place Religion in the broad current of human progress…"[40]

The Labour Church was a national organisation but the majority of its branches were in the textile districts of Lancashire and the West Riding of Yorkshire. The Bolton branch included members of the local 'Whitmanite' group including its 'master' J.W. Wallace as well as Fred Wild. Allen Clarke was a frequent speaker, while Alice Collinge, poet and feminist, was the organist.[41]

The ILP had sunk some deep roots in Northern towns and cities by the outbreak of the First World War. However, many of the unions remained distrustful of the party, and of 'socialism'. Indeed, writers such as Allen Clarke saw one of the biggest obstacles to socialism being the conservatively inclined cotton unions. Clarke was most critical of the narrow trade unionism practised by the skilled textile workers, who combined very powerful organisation for themselves but were often deaf to the plight of underpaid workers. He wrote in *The Labour Prophet* that, "the factory folk of Lancashire are in the main antagonistic or apathetic to the Socialist movement", suggesting that the reasons were strong trade unionism combined with high wages for the skilled workers.[42]

* * *

Lancastrians: David Shackleton 1863–1938

David Shackleton was born at Cloughfold near Rawtenstall in 1863 and by the age of 9 was working in a weaving shed at Haslingden, running three looms by the age of 12, which was highly unusual. He walked to evening classes in Accrington after his daily work, and later obtained work there. At the age of 20 he married Sarah Broadbent, whose family were ardent trade unionists. He joined the Accrington Weavers' Association and was sacked for his union activities. He was out of work for seventeen weeks.

He became secretary of the Ramsbottom Weavers' Association and then Darwen Weavers' Association. In 1894 he was elected to Darwen Town Council. He lived in Victoria Street and later London Terrace. In 1902 he was elected Member of Parliament for the Clitheroe Division, becoming one of only four Labour MPs. In 1905 he became chairman of the National Labour Party.

He was a champion of women's suffrage and the trade union movement. He served on the Committee of the Board of Education, the Committee on Old Age Pensions and the committee dealing with steaming in weaving sheds.

He left Parliament in 1910 when he was invited by Winston Churchill to become Labour Advisor to the Home Office. In 1916 he became permanent secretary to the newly created Ministry of Labour. He never lost his affection for Darwen and his London residence was named 'Sunnyhurst', after his favourite beauty spot, Sunnyhurst Woods, Darwen. His wife, Sarah, was said to have retained a strong Lancashire accent unlike her husband in their later years.

Shackleton was a staunch teetotaller and non-smoker. He retired in 1925 and went to live in Beach Road, St Anne's. He died there in 1938 at the age of 74. However, he returned to his beloved Darwen at last. He was buried in Darwen Cemetery. Officers of the Lancashire Constabulary acted as pall-bearers.[43]

* * *

The period between the late 1890s and the First World War was a time of transition in working-class politics, as the Liberal Party fought a rearguard battle to hang on to the Northern working-class vote. A highly significant by-election took place in 1902 when Sir Kay Ughtred-Shuttleworth, Liberal MP for Clitheroe, resigned his seat after being ennobled. David Shackleton was selected by the newly formed Labour Representation Committee (LRC) to fight the seat as the 'Labour' candidate, but on a platform that was essentially Liberal in all but name. Remarkably, he was elected unopposed and remained MP for the constituency, which included the rapidly growing textile towns of Nelson, Colne and Brierfield, as well as Clitheroe itself.

* * *

Lancastrians: Hannah Mitchell 1871–1956

She was born in rural North Derbyshire, into a poor farming family. Forget the idealised images of rural poverty: it was hard and often violent, with Hannah becoming increasingly alienated from her mother. She managed just two weeks of schooling before leaving home to find work in Glossop, the nearest town of any size. She then moved to what must have seemed like the thriving metropolis of Bolton. She became involved in the embryonic socialist movement in the early 1890s and read Blatchford's Clarion *newspaper. One of her earliest influences was Katharine St John Conway (neé Glasier), another recent recruit to 'the cause' but from a very different class background. She heard the articulate middle-class clergyman's daughter speak at a packed meeting in Bolton about the new 'gospel of socialism'. She was fascinated by Katharine and her political passion and went away "with an inspiration which later sent me out to the street corners with the same message".*

Hannah Mitchell went on to become an accomplished speaker and activist for the fledgling Independent Labour Party. She got involved in the women's suffrage movement which was particularly active in the Lancashire mill towns and campaigned across the North of England. Her socialism was of the ethical, humanistic kind which became so popular across the North where the ILP was strongest.

She was actively involved in the women's suffrage movement and had a short stay in Strangeways prison after being arrested for disrupting a Liberal Party meeting in Manchester. To her annoyance, she was released after one night when her husband paid her fine; not out of sympathy for 'the Cause' but so that Mrs Mitchell could be at home to make his dinner! She was a lifelong opponent of war and maintained a principled opposition to the First World War, whilst doing much to support and help local boys who were called up, regarding them as victims rather than 'heroes'.

Hannah was a very practical activist. She became involved in local politics in Ashton-under-Lyne where she was elected to the local 'Board of Guardians' responsible for poor relief. A further move, to Manchester, led to her adoption as a council candidate in the face of some opposition from her male comrades. It took many years for her to be accepted by the Labour Party as a suitable candidate for the local elections. Though she was elected to the Ashton Board of Guardians in 1906 it was to take another seventeen years before she became a councillor in Manchester. Her local ILP branch nominated her in 1921, only for the nomination to be rejected by the city party; and when she was nominated by the ILP in 1923 she was turned down in favour of a disreputable local businessman. Shortly afterwards he became bankrupt, and it was only then, in her words, that "my opponents in the Labour Party swallowed their scruples and accepted me".

She was elected for the working-class ward of Newton Heath in 1924 and became one of Manchester's most effective local politicians. She was an imaginative and innovative local councillor, loved by her constituents and respected by politicians of all stripes. She suggested radical but achievable initiatives, such as 'electors' councils' in each ward, who would advise their elected members on important local issues, and a public wash house which transformed the lives of many working-class women. She was a community activist, arguing for cafes in parks so that tired mothers could have a cup of tea whilst taking the kids out for a walk; and she worked tirelessly on the Public Assistance (formerly Poor Law) Committee. But most of all she loved her time on the Libraries Committee. Another of her innovations was the 'travelling library' which toured areas without a branch facility, an idea she picked up from a visit to the United States.

She said, "The Labour Party itself was only lukewarm on such matters as equal pay, while on the employment of married women most of them were definitely reactionary." Sometimes, she continued, "they went all Marxian and stressed the bad economics of two incomes going into one home, while men with a capital "M" were unemployed".

During the 1920s she became a regular correspondent for the ILP paper Labour's Northern Voice. *She wrote dialect sketches as 'Daisy Nook', poking fun at petty injustice and arguing the case for socialism in a light, accessible style that was quintessentially 'Northern'.*[44]

* * *

The structure of the Labour Party, largely a result of the astute political brains of Ramsay Macdonald and Keir Hardie, provided a comfortable home for both Liberal-inclined trades unionists and the socialist activists of the ILP—which immediately affiliated to the new party. And once again it was the North which dominated the new organisation. The Labour leadership agreed a pact with the Liberals which ensured many candidates would get a free run against the Conservatives in the 1906 General Election. The LRC ran fifty candidates, of whom three-fifths were in constituencies in the North of England. A total of thirty were elected whilst the Liberals won a staggering 400 seats. The Labour success brought a strong influx of working-class men into Parliament. A total of twenty-three of the new MPs were active trade unionists and eighteen described themselves as 'socialists'.

An historic compromise

Most political histories tend to focus on the national scene and parliamentary elections, often ignoring the huge importance of local government politics. It was at the local level that socialists, particularly in the ILP, began to make a real difference in the early 1900s, though their real achievements became more obvious in the inter-war years: housing, sanitation, public transport, public health, education.

Local politics in the 1890s was often riddled with petty corruption and favouritism. Many Lancashire towns had only limited forms of local government, such as a school board and local boards of guardians who administered poor relief. Towards the end of the century the pace of incorporation—by which towns formed their own councils, or 'corporations'—accelerated and provided electoral opportunities for the rapidly growing socialist movement.

The Independent Labour Party began making headway in local elections and opportunities opened up to improve local government accountability, with an emphasis on extending municipal ownership to major utilities such as gas and water, and taking over ownership of tramways. 'Fair wages' for council work was another major plank in the reform manifesto. It was not particularly exciting stuff, but the work of often quite small councils such as Nelson and Farnworth transformed local communities.[45] It was practical socialism in action.

Nelson Council became the first Lancashire local authority to be Labour-controlled, from 1905. The influence of the Weavers' Union was particularly strong in this part of north-east Lancashire and the union threw its weight behind the ILP campaign to capture the council. It remained a progressive Labour-controlled council throughout the inter-war years. St Helens Council became Labour controlled shortly after Nelson, whilst Barrow's Poor Law Guardians had a Labour majority from 1904. On the other hand, Oldham only elected a single Labour councillor as late as 1910 and he remained a lone voice until 1914, reflecting the strength of both the Conservative and Liberal working-class traditions in the town. Manchester City Council had fifteen Labour councillors by 1901, mostly ILP members. Liverpool was more difficult territory, having only two Labour councillors before 1911. In the aftermath of the violent 1911 Transport Strike several more Labour men were elected.

Lancashire to the fore: the fight for women's suffrage

Lancashire produced many outstanding working-class women leaders who played an important part in the suffrage campaigns of the early twentieth century. Selina Cooper of Nelson, Annie Kenney of Oldham, Teresa Billington of Manchester and Sarah Reddish of Bolton were not untypical. The work of historians such as Jill Norris and Jill Liddington have finally put paid to the myth that the suffrage battle was exclusively conducted by middle- and upper-class women. Nowhere was the campaign stronger amongst working women than in Lancashire and Yorkshire. Some male socialists supported them, most notably Keir Hardie. Allen Clarke, in his *Northern Weekly*, ran pro-suffrage articles by men like John Tamlyn as well as writing editorials himself, including the provocative 'Are Women More Fit to Vote Than Men?'[46]

The comic character Bet Spriggs, of the *Tum Fowt* dialect sketches, was recruited to the cause, placing the blame for unemployment and low pay squarely on male politicians:

> That comes o' men havin' a vote an aw t'power an' electin' th'Government. Why, they'n noan sense to put up an umbrella when it rains; they hannot gumption to look even after theirsels, let alone their wives an' kids.[47]

Many of the women who were prominent in the ILP were also active in the National Union of Women's Suffrage Societies—Selina Cooper, Hannah Mitchell, Ellen Wilkinson and dozens of others.[48] Despite Keir Hardie's support, other leading ILP men were vehemently opposed to the women's suffrage campaign which they tried to dismiss as a 'middle-class' campaign. Yet the formation of the Lancashire Women Textile Workers' Representation Committee gave the lie to that view. During 1906 a delegation to London met Prime Minister Campbell-Bannerman and walked down the Thames Embankment with banners proclaiming that 'Women Produce the Wealth of Lancashire' and '306,000 Women in the Cotton Trade Want Votes'.[49]

Blatchford established *The Woman Worker* which lasted a few years before the First World War, ending in 1910. For a brief period Ethel Carnie, the Lancashire mill worker, edited the paper and contributed poems and short stories about the lives of working-class women in the North.[50]

Coalitions for municipal reform

Both the SDF and the ILP contested local elections. Initially these were for the school boards and local boards. James Shufflebotham, the Bolton SDF organiser, was elected onto the local school board and served on it for many years. Quite often radical Liberals cooperated with socialists in the cause of municipal reform.

Allen Clarke was strongly influenced by Solomon Partington (see pages 210–12). the radical Bolton journalist who played a key role in the 1896 Winter Hill Mass Trespass. Partington was a Liberal but became increasingly sympathetic to the ILP cause. The two friends were closely involved in producing the monthly *Municipal Reformer* which was printed and published in Bolton. The inspiration came initially from the socialist Rev. H. Bodell-Smith, another friend of Clarke's living in Blackpool.[51] In 1898 Bodell-Smith established a Municipal Reform Society and the newspaper was established shortly after, with Bodell-Smith as editor and Clarke a contributor. It developed a national circulation and carried features on a wide range of local political issues. Several local 'municipal reform associations' were established, including one in Bolton. However, the paper was not a great commercial success and after four years was handed over to the northern branch of the Land Nationalisation Society. The impetus for municipal reform developed a new momentum in 1904 when a major national conference in Manchester attracted several hundred delegates and established the Local Government Reform League, with Bodell-Smith as secretary.

Bolton's Municipal Reform Society appears to have flourished in the mid-1900s following Partington's election. It advertised a series of lectures during 1905 on 'Citizenship and Town Council Work' with speakers including Sarah Reddish on 'Women and Citizenship' and Solomon Partington on 'Rights of Way'. Sarah Reddish was elected onto the local board in 1907, the town's first female councillor and well before women won the right to vote in parliamentary elections.

Socialists and the radical wing of the Liberal Party continued to co-operate. The newly formed Labour Party (established in 1900 as the 'Labour Representation Committee' but becoming 'The Labour Party' in 1906) agreed an electoral pact with the Liberals in 1906 which allowed Labour to win an unprecedented number of seats. On issues like municipal reform, Home Rule for Ireland, pensions, 'fair wages' and even state ownership they shared much in common.

* * *

Lancastrians: Samuel Compston 1842–1934

Compston was one of the outstanding figures in Lancashire Liberalism and local government but also an important figure in the literary and historical world. He was born in Radcliffe and educated at Giggleswick School; most of his adult life was spent in Rossendale, living in Crawshawbooth, near Rawtenstall. He campaigned for Rawtenstall to become an incorporated borough and was one of the first members to be elected when it was established in 1891. He served on the council for 43 years and was created a 'Freeman' of the borough in 1919. He promoted the establishment of Rawtenstall's public library, museum and art gallery and chaired the relevant council committee.

He was active in the temperance movement and lectured for the British Temperance Society. He joined the Lancashire Authors' Association in 1919 and became its honorary vice-president. He wrote extensively on local history and culture, often for the Rossendale Free Press. *His publications included* Quakerism in Rossendale, The Old Musical Deyne Layrocks, Alcohol and the Nervous System *and* The History of Ewood Dale. *He was particularly active on public-rights-of-way issues, his obituary in the Lancashire Authors' Association* Record *noting that, "as a public representative he helped to preserve for the people the use of several moorland paths threatened with closure, including that to Waugh's Well".*[52]

He also did much, with fellow-Liberal Thomas Newbigging, to perpetuate the memory of the 'Deighn Layrocks'.[53]

As his obituary in the LAA's Record *recalled, "his sturdy figure, and kindly bearded face, were familiar to most of us, as also was his voice; for from time to time he had addressed us on Lancashire subjects, notably on Edwin Waugh at the Waugh centenary celebrations held in June, 1917, and on Rossendale and Rossendale folk at our gathering June 1930".*

* * *

After the First World War, the two traditions diverged. Labour succeeded in winning large swathes of the industrial working class for its cause, reflected in electoral successes nationally in 1924 and in 1929, but equally importantly in local government, with many Northern towns and cities electing Labour administrations. Ideologically, Labour became increasingly centralist and statist in its outlook, though the 'co-operative' tradition of local democracy and participation was never entirely extinguished.

The ILP cut itself off from the mainstream, with disastrous results, in 1932. It disaffiliated from the Labour Party and drifted closer towards the Communist Party. The Labour Party of Herbert Morrison was in the ascendant and the Liberal Party entered a coalition with the Conservatives in 1931 hoping to destroy the Labour Party. Any scope for an alliance with the Liberals was killed for generations.

Further divisions within the ILP led, in 1934, to the formation of a short-lived 'Independent Socialist Party' based mainly in Lancashire and led by veteran Chorley socialist and former Labour MP and councillor, Elijah Sandham.[54]

The Communist Party and 'Little Moscow'

The Communist Party (CP) in Lancashire, from its formation in 1921, was small but locally significant. It was particularly strong in Nelson, which became known as 'Little Moscow'.[55] Despite the Moscow-imposed principles of 'democratic centralism' the party was very much of the community; the Nelson party banner showed a Lancashire woman weaver at her loom.[56] The party played an important role in the unemployed movement of the 1930s, but was also involved in the 'More Looms' strikes, against increased work-loads for weavers, in 1932. It was particularly active during the Spanish Civil War; many of its members, including Lancastrians such as Sid Booth and George Brown, went to fight in Spain.[57]

The party was active in many Lancashire towns as part of the 'Aid Spain' movement and was often the leading force locally in mobilis-ing against the growing fascist threat. Mosley and the British Union of Fascists were very active in some of the Lancashire cotton towns and the CP, often with support from ILP members, were involved in violent clashes with the blackshirts.

* * *

The war and after

During the Second World War a 'Women's Parliament' was formed for Lancashire. It met in Manchester and was mainly composed of delegates from the Labour and Communist parties and trades union organisations.

The 1945 General Election saw Labour take power, winning hundreds of seats across the country including many where it had hardly campaigned. The dominant ideology of post-war Labour was centralist and state-oriented. However, there were minority voices which questioned the model of state ownership chosen by Labour. T.E. Nixon of the National Union of Railwaymen in Lancashire produced a pamphlet arguing for 'workers' control of the railways', noting that "it is a remarkable fact that the foster-parent of modern democracy—The Labour Party—should have made no attempt to reconcile progressive democratic tendencies with its policy of the socialisation of industry".[58]

Francis Andrews, a leading figure in the Union of Post Office Workers and a Lancashire ILP activist, argued that nationalisation without workers' control had little to do with socialism.[59]

At a conference in Manchester in January 1949, a North-West League for Workers' Control was formed, to complement a similar body established earlier in London. Price Jones, a Lancashire NUM activist from Gin Pit, near Leigh, proposed an elaborate scheme of workers' control for the mines, with pit, area, regional and national decision-making bodies.[60]

These voices gained little hearing within the Labour government. The state-owned industries gave token recognition to employee participation but the reality was very top-down and management-led. The Attlee government did lots of good things *for* working-class people, but they were expected to be grateful, and passive, recipients of Labour's largesse.

* * *

Lancastrians: Bessie Braddock 1899–1970

Bessie Margaret Braddock was born on 24 September 1899 in Liverpool. She was a lifelong activist in the Labour Party and Liverpool's first female MP. She was an ardent socialist and campaigner with special interests in maternity, child welfare and youth crime.

She was elected onto Liverpool City Council in 1930 and in the words of Labour historian Sam Davies, "she put on an almost one-woman show there for a decade".[61] During the 1930s she was very much on the left of the party, often at odds with the party leadership. She chaired the city's Maternity and Child Welfare sub-committee and was instrumental in opening a maternity and childcare centre in Everton in 1936, the first in the country. She organised a major national conference in Liverpool in the same year, working with many women's organisations. The conference called for birth-control clinics to be established by all health authorities and improved pre- and post-natal care.

She was elected Member of Parliament for Liverpool Exchange at the 1945 election and represented the seat for 24 years. She was a member of the Labour Party National Executive Committee and served as vice-chairman of the Labour Party in 1968.

She is commemorated by a statue in Lime Street station, and by a blue plaque erected at her home in Zigzag Road.

* * *

Within the Labour Party, the 1950s and early 1960s saw a new flowering of local activity which has been little documented. There was a plethora of Labour Party local newspapers, perhaps foremost being the Lancashire-based *Labour's Northern Voice*, which spawned many more local editions, initially in the Northern towns and cities but later extending southwards. The papers were highly conscious of Labour traditions and frequently ran articles celebrating ILP heroes and heroines of the early years.

The red wall dismantled?

The idea of a 'red wall' in Lancashire, or any part of the North, needs treating with a lot of care. While some towns have been quite solidly Labour since the 1920s, most have fluctuated. The traditional working-class Toryism has never gone away, though the Lancashire Liberal tradition seems fatally wounded. After a disastrous performance in 2019, Labour may well bounce back. What we are seeing is a loosening of traditional political affiliations. The cities—Manchester and Liverpool—have remained Labour but the same cannot be said for the large former industrial towns, still less the more rural areas. Yet Labour in Lancashire has a strong heritage, including the co-operative movement, which makes it distinctive and potentially popular. Whether an increasingly metropolitan-centred Labour Party will recognise this remains to be seen. Perhaps it is time for a new 'historic compromise' between Labour and the Liberal Democrats, building on common ground including voting reform, better public services and regional devolution.

16

LANCASTRIANS ABROAD

Lancashire has experienced large-scale emigration for 200 years. The 'push' factor, what forced people to leave, was overwhelmingly economic—particularly the desperate poverty of the first half of the nineteenth century, up to and after the Cotton Famine of the 1860s. There was, in a smaller number of cases, the enforced 'push' of being sent to Australia as convicts. Some of the leaders of radical working-class organisations in the 1820s, such as Richard Pilling, suffered this fate. Most, on release, stayed in Australia and built new lives there. The 'pull' factor was the promise of a better life. In some cases people simply emigrated and hoped (usually correctly) that 'something would turn up'. Very often though, skilled Lancashire workers were recruited to help set up textile mills in the United States, Russia and elsewhere. Communities of exiled Lancastrians sprang up around the world, particularly in America, Canada, Australia, Russia—and also in London.

During the 1960s a substantial number of societies for 'exiled Lancastrians' existed in both Britain and abroad. A report in the Lancashire Authors' Association's *Record* in 1965 commented on the prevalence of Lancastrian societies where,

> news of the mother country is devoured—newspapers and magazines of the towns back home … are avidly read and exchanged, and at meetings of Lancashire history, life, character and humour come to the fore—songs are played and sung, Lancashire prose and verse recited, slides are shown, tape-recordings played back and conviviality abounds, maybe over a potato pie or a Lancashire hot-pot.[1]

The writer identified some twenty-eight Lancastrian societies within England, mostly in the south. In addition he notes the existence of societies in Los Angeles, Mashonaland (owing loyalty to Yorkshire as well as Lancashire), Montreal, Nyasaland and Vancouver. This was almost certainly only the tip of a large iceberg; there would have been many more.

Some Lancastrians pursued eminent careers in unlikely places, often spending substantial amounts of time abroad, or even 'settling'. *The East Lancashire Review* applauded the achievement of Mr J.R. Pilling in winning a substantial railway building contract, commenting that,

> it is ... agreeable as well as interesting to find that Mr. J.R. Pilling, of Bacup, has obtained a concession from the Sultan of Turkey to construct a railway from Damascus to the Bay of Acre, opening out the country to the shores of the Mediterranean, with branch lines to the most important stations on the route. The projected main line will be 115 miles long. A good deal of the money will no doubt be raised in Lancashire.[2]

Sadly, the railway was never built.

Exiled in London

The 'Association of Lancastrians in London' was formed in 1892 by twenty-eight Lancastrians living or working in the capital. It describes its work as "seeking to promote friendship and good cheer among Lancastrians living in and around London". It met in February 1892 for the first Annual Dinner, with Samuel Pope QC 'in the chair'. Pope was leader of the Parliamentary Bar, much respected by fellow barristers and by members of both Houses. When not needed in London he was working on the Northern circuit or in Bolton, where he was Recorder. He was born in Manchester in 1826, eldest son of a Manchester merchant with interests in London. He was educated privately and later attended the relatively new London University. He seemed set to follow his grandfather, father and uncle into trade or manufacture though he also had a literary bent and delighted in recitations and song.

Lord Stanley (Earl of Derby) addressed the annual dinner of the association in 1932 and commented on Lancashire dialect being "not so prevalent as formerly ... There was a danger of losing the prerogative of all Lancashire people of telling a Lancashire story in the Lancashire dialect, as there were so few people who were practised in this highly specialised form of art."[3]

The London association appears to have taken His Lordship's plea to heart. The following year they requested the help of dialect exponent Riley Stansfield in writing their dinner menu card in dialect! It included a toast:

> An' he that scorns ale to his victual, is welcome to let alone. There's some can be wise with a little, an' some that are foolish wi' noan; an' some are so quare i'their natur, that nowt wi' their stomachs agree; but he that would leifer drink wayter, shall never be stinted by me.[4]

The association remains active, with over 500 members.

* * *

The great migration: America

The nineteenth century saw a large-scale migration from Lancashire to the United States, mostly from the textile districts. Some Lancastrians were recruited directly by the growing US cotton industry, others found work in textiles or in other trades.

The story of Bolton's counterpane weavers and the significant number who emigrated has been told by historians Erin Beeston and Laurel Horton. This was a highly specialised part of the handloom-weaving industry and was even localised within Bolton itself, at the small hamlet of Tonge Fold (later immortalised as *Tum Fowt* by dialect writers James Staton and Allen Clarke). The counterpane weavers enjoyed relatively high status and respectable pay among Lancashire's weavers during the late eighteenth century, but these advantages gradually eroded during the early 1800s. As Beeston and Horton commented, "The industry experienced periodic economic fluctuations, and many weavers emigrated to the United States. In 1825, a factory in Dover, New Hampshire, recruited English weavers to operate newly installed power looms. Ironically, these may have included workers displaced by the introduction of power looms in their home country."[5]

Some craftsmen and loom-tuners emigrated to the United States. In 1817, John Sutcliffe, from Bolton, informed 'the Weavers and

Manufacturers' of Lexington, Kentucky, that he had commenced the business of making weavers' reeds, in 'brass, steel and cane', having twenty-five years' experience in the business.[6] The evidence from Erin Beeston's research suggests that some immigrant counterpane weavers continued to ply their specialised trade in their new communities. New York's Metropolitan Museum owns two counterpanes combining central images of eagles and stars, surrounded with typical, repeated Bolton motifs. These may have been the work of emigrant weavers from Bolton or, possibly, made in Bolton specifically for the American market.[7]

Not much has been written about the impact of Lancashire emigration to America, yet it was significant. Rather than dispersed into a thousand or more places across the continent, some distinct Lancashire communities emerged in the developing cotton towns of the north-east: Fall River, Lowell (Massachusetts), Paterson (New Jersey) and other towns.

Many Oldham people settled at Paterson, New Jersey, in the early 1860s, escaping from the Cotton Famine. Bateson makes a fascinating reference to how this 'little bit of Oldham in the New World' evolved, referring to,

> a prosperous colony of Oldhamers who remained tenaciously loyal to the customs of their native town. In the year 1869 they formed an Oldham Society and planned to celebrate Oldham Wakes by conducting yearly excursions. They selected Echo Lake as their pleasure resort and here boat races, sack races and foot races were held annually ... Paterson was still celebrating Oldham Wakes as late as August 1887.[8]

By the 1860s a number of Oldham people had settled in Manayunk, Philadelphia. Many had emigrated during the Cotton Famine and found work in the carpet weaving factories of James Dobson who had left Oldham in the early 1850s "under the stress of poverty".[9] He became one of the most prominent industrialists in the area alongside fellow Oldhamers Ammon and John W. Platt, grandsons of the well-known Oldham figure Bill o' Jack's. They and Dobson organised a public meeting in the Mechanics' Hall at Manayunk in 1863 to help raise funds to alleviate the 'distress' then rife in Oldham. It was agreed to send one hundred barrels of flour to the Oldham Central Relief Fund.[10]

The Russian connection

A fascinating aspect of Rochdale and Bolton's role as major centres of textile engineering was their strong links with pre-revolutionary Russia. During the second half of the nineteenth century, Bolton engineering firms helped to equip Russia's emerging cotton industry. It wasn't just machinery that Lancashire exported—it was also people.

Russia in the nineteenth century was an autocratic state ruled by the Romanov dynasty. In the eighteenth century both Peter and Catherine the Great had used the state as a means of promoting industrial development, with textiles as a key lever. However, much textile production remained small-scale with spinning and weaving mostly done by hand, using serf labour. Alexander II (1818–81) attempted to bring in reforms and industrialisation, following his accession to the emperor's throne in 1855, after Russia's defeat by Britain and her allies in the Crimean War. He was keen to industrialise parts of his vast empire and state support for a Russian textile industry was seen as a means to force an industrial revolution. To a certain extent, his strategy worked and despite the political upheavals of the nineteenth and early twentieth century, Russia's textile industry grew to become the fourth biggest in the world—after Britain, the United States and Germany. And it was largely down to the expertise it used from Lancashire.

Russia developed what became known as 'technology transfer' using British engineering to equip and run the growing number of cotton mills in Russia. The key figure in making this happen was Ludwig Knoop who acted as an intermediary between the Russian authorities and Lancashire-based textile engineering companies. These included Oldham-based Platt Brothers and Howard and Bullough of Accrington. Bolton-based firms Hick Hargreaves, John Musgrave and Sons and Dobson and Barlow all developed strong links with Russia's cotton industry.

This involved much more than shipping out steam engines and boilers to power the mills. Expertise was in short supply and firms such as Platt's, Hick's and Musgrave's sent out skilled engineers for extended periods of time—with some actually becoming adopted Russians. Ivanovo, about 100 miles north-east of Moscow, became

known as 'the Manchester of Russia' and developed as a major cotton manufacturing centre. A 'Rochdale Street' remains in one of the
former textile districts around Moscow.

Some Lancashire cotton manufacturers invested in the Balkans.
The Shaw and Crompton-based firm of Crompton and Milne
established a weaving mill in Belgrade in the late 1890s, and
shortly after set up a larger mill in Bucharest. The firm was anxious to put down roots in the region and contributed to several
charitable causes including the Armenian Famine Fund, 'The
Persecuted Jews', the Belgrade Orphanage and other flood appeals
in Romania and Serbia. The firm's activities in the Balkans were
affected by the First World War and revolution in Russia. The
German army confiscated looms in Bucharest and shipped them to
Bulgaria. However, trade revived after the end of hostilities and
the firm rebuilt its markets in the Balkans, with an office in Sofia
established in 1930. The historian of Crompton commented that
"in all these countries the 'CROMPTON' mark could be found in
every town or village shop". In addition, a strong market was
developed in Lithuania "until relations were interrupted by the
German seizure of Memel in 1939".[11]

One of the oldest cotton manufacturing companies in Lancashire
was Kenyons, of Bury, with a history stretching back to the 1660s.
James Kenyon was keen to break into the Russian market and in
1872, at the age of 26, made the journey to Russia to see what the
opportunities were. He had already built up a close relationship
with de Knoop and Company which was importing Lancashire-
made textile machinery but struggled to find sufficient experienced
managers to run the factories. It was Lancashire that filled the gap,
or tried to. By then, there was a large community of Lancashire men
working in the Russian mills as engineers and managers and several
had shares in the factories:

> [Kenyon] made it his business to get in touch with as many as pos-
> sible of these British managers, some of whom proved to be owners
> or part-owners of spinning and weaving mills, calico printing works,
> paper-making mills and sugar refineries. He visited the firm of
> Braithwaite, one of his best customers, before leaving for home and
> decided there and then to return the following year.[12]

It was the first of several visits to eastern Europe. The relationship with de Knoop and Company developed to the extent that the sister of the UK representative of de Knoop married James Kenyon!

* * *

Whilst in many cases individual engineers went out to Russia, often for extended stays, scores of Lancashire families also migrated to the growing textile centres around Moscow. They set up their own social clubs in places like Ivanovo. Much of their history is lost but some family records have survived.

Robert Crompton was born in Bolton in the 1840s and became an apprentice in one of the Bolton mills. He rose to the ranks of overseer and qualified as an engineer. In the 1850s he was asked by his firm to travel to Kiev to help establish a mill that had installed machinery that he was familiar with. It was clearly seen as an extended job and he made the difficult journey to Russia with his young wife Ann. His great grand daughter Dorothy says that "he worked at the mill, creating a strong friendship with the mill owner and was respected by the workers".[13]

The Cromptons had four children, all born in Ukraine, then part of the Russian Empire. Two died young and were buried in Odessa. The third, Mary Alice Crompton, was brought up in Kiev and could only speak Russian until the age of 5, when the family returned to Bolton in the 1870s. There were concerns for the family's safety owing to growing political and industrial unrest in the country. The return to Bolton was short-lived. Not long after, the mill owner in Russia asked Crompton to come back to help him at the mill. However, he quickly succumbed to illness and died soon after his return. He is buried with his two children in Odessa.

Another fascinating link is through the family of Bolton suffragette Sarah Jane Carwin who was born in Bolton in 1863. Her father, John, was an engineer and in 1866 the entire family sailed to St Petersburg, though it isn't clear where John and his family settled. However, his wife Jerusha died shortly after their arrival and John re-married a Russian. They were wed in 'the chapel of the British factory' at St Petersburg and returned to Bolton in 1874.

The reference to 'the chapel of the British factory' also raises some Lancashire connections, through the architect Richard Knill

Freeman. He was commissioned to design the only Anglican church in Moscow, which was built specifically for British expatriates in the city, in 1884. Knill Freeman knew John Musgrave, the owner of the engineering firm which supplied many Russian mills with machinery. It is possible that Musgrave helped Knill Freeman win the contract to build the church which was located near to some of Moscow's largest mills.

The Lancashire migrants were well paid for their skills. Articles of agreement, signed in 1899 between Bolton firm John Musgrave and Sons and Moscow-based De Jersey & Co. for the engineering services of William Fisher, give his wages as £6 a week, as well as £15 for travel costs to and from Russia.

An engineer called Smith worked for Hick Hargreaves and went out to work in the Russian mills in the 1870s. He married there in 1876 and had three children who were born and raised there, only coming to England when revolution was looming. One of the boys won an apprenticeship at Hicks and returned to Russia after marrying a Bolton woman who went with him.

* * *

Lancastrians: Thomas Moran 1837–1936

Thomas was born in Tonge Fold, part of the strong handloom-weaving community that was still flourishing. However, the fortunes of the handloom weavers changed very quickly in the early 1840s and the family emigrated to America when he was 7 years old. The family settled in Philadelphia and the young Thomas trained as an artist. He became a highly regarded landscape painter, specialising in the Yellowstone region which he first visited with F.Y. Hayden, director of the US Geological Survey. Moran was credited with having a major influence in the creation of the Yellowstone National Park with his striking images of the canyons. He was strongly influenced by the work of J.M.W. Turner and returned to England in 1862 to study the artist's work at the National Gallery. He came back twenty years later and visited Bolton for an exhibition at Bromley's Art Gallery. The exhibition included work by his wife, Mary Nimmo Moran, who was a highly regarded print-maker.

He was passionate about the Rocky Mountains and the Yellowstone area in particular, adopting a signature 'T-Y-M, Thomas "Yellowstone" Moran'.

An early work was his enormous painting of a far-western natural wonder, The Grand Canyon of the Yellowstone, *which the US government purchased in 1872 for $10,000.*

Moran was elected to the membership of the National Academy of Design in 1884 and The Three Tetons (1895) *was displayed in the Oval Office during Barack Obama's term as president. The Thomas Moran House in East Hampton, New York is a National Historic Landmark. He is possibly the only Lancashire artist to have a mountain named after him—Mount Moran in the Grand Teton National Park. His work is kept at the Gilcrease Museum in Tulsa, Oklahoma; Cooper-Hewitt, the National Design Museum; the Amon Carter Museum of American Art; R.W. Norton Art Gallery; and the Berkshire Museum in Pittsfield, Massachusetts.*

* * *

Lancashire cotton men can take the credit for introducing football to Russia. The first competitive and regular football games in Russia started in the textile town of Orekhovo-Zuevo, about 50 miles east of Moscow. The area saw a huge boom in textile production in the 1840s, with the Morozov family being the dominant employer. The firm invited engineers and managers from Lancashire to maintain the machinery and they brought football with them. At first, they played among themselves, or against teams of British engineers from the Hopper Factory in Moscow.

Chorley-born Harry Charnock was managing director at the Nikolskoye Textile Factory near Orekhovo-Zuevo. In the 1880s he began to organise regular matches, involving Russian players as well as Englishmen; he became the vice-president of the Moscow Football League. Whilst in Russia he met and married Anna Hedwig Schelinsky and had two sons.[14]

A Christmas postcard has survived written from a Bolton family to a 'Mr. and Mrs. Ashcroft' living in Orekhovo-Zuevo in the early 1900s. Other family recollections include those of Tim Baines whose great-grandfather went out to Russia with his wife to work in the mills but returned just before the revolution of 1917. The connections between the Russian textile industry and Lancashire came to an abrupt end after the revolution, though by then the industry was well established. There are records of an

'Olga Snape' who was born in Russia but who came to Bolton at the time of the revolution, almost certainly having family connections in the town.

* * *

Lancastrians: John Taylor 1884–1947

John Taylor, son of a loco driver at Accrington, left Liverpool in 1904 as a 21-year-old lad on board RMS Umbria *bound for New York. He had an adventurous time in America, riding the freight cars in search of his fortune. His great-nephew, Andrew Rosthorn, describes him jumping a freight train and reaching a yard near Albuquerque on the roof of a box car. It was a bitterly cold night; his fingers had frozen to a steel heating pipe on the vehicle: "He was very fortunate when he called out for help. Someone in the freight yard found time to warm the steel pipe with live steam and release the frozen fingers before the train started rolling. Maybe they were intrigued by his Lancashire accent or maybe they were impressed by his engine driving ancestry, but someone in that freight yard offered John a job as a locomotive fireman."[15]*

His employer was the Atchison, Topeka and Santa Fe Railroad, which promoted itself as 'The Nation's Number One Railroad', linking Chicago with the south-western states. His mate the driver, or 'engineer' in US railroad parlance, often let John drive the loco and he did many turns on supply trains into San Francisco after the great earthquake of April 1906, which left 3,000 dead and 300,000 homeless.

He served fifteen years as a loco fireman, including a stint on the Santa Fe in California. In April 1918 he saw an advertisement for skilled railway employees for the Canadian Railway troops who were building and operating railway lines behind the Western Front in northern France. He was recruited into the Canadian Overseas Expeditionary Force as 'Sapper 2204799' of the Railway Construction Corps and arrived in France in October 1918. He worked on the temporary narrow-gauge lines which fed troops and ammunition to the front and managed to survive the war unscathed. He briefly returned to east Lancashire and had an entertaining conversation with his father 'Owd John' who questioned his son's ability to get a ticket to nearby Padiham. He returned to Canada in March 1919 and was discharged a month later. John did not return to the railroads but got a job in aeronautical engineering.

* * *

South Africa

A substantial 'colony' of Lancastrians settled in South Africa. Arthur Laycock, son of the famous dialect writer Samuel Laycock of Stalybridge, spent many years in South Africa during the 1930s, in the Durban area. He wrote a feature on 'Lancashire in South Africa' for *The Durban Daily Tribune* which also announced a forthcoming radio broadcast by the writer, commenting that:

> Lancashire has good cause to be proud of the many writers who have set down stories of Lancashire life in dialect verse. Samuel Laycock is one of the best-known of the Lancashire poets and his son, Mr. Arthur Laycock, will come to the Cape Town microphone tonight to talk about some Lancashire dialect poets.[16]

Australia

About one hundred Chartists were transported to Australia for various alleged crimes. However, the numbers of political radicals transported earlier, in the period between 1800 and 1840 is probably much greater. Richard Boothman, a Lancashire weaver, was convicted of killing a policeman in a riot at Colne on 10 August 1840. Boothman maintained his innocence, but after his original sentence of death was commuted to transportation for life, he sailed for Tasmania on the *Barossa*, arriving in Hobart on 13 January 1842. After two years at Impression Bay, Boothman went to work in the north of the island. He continued to deny responsibility for the crime and to ask relatives to petition for his return in letters home, but he was to die in Launceston, Tasmania, in 1877.[17]

James Stott, from Oldham, was tried with a number of others at Liverpool Crown Court in December 1848 for 'sedition' and 'compassing or devising to levy war against the Queen'. Unlike his other comrades on trial, Stott was also charged with 'Chartism'. He was sentenced to transportation for life. He sailed for Australia on the

Adelaide, arriving at Hobart on 29 November 1849. Others included James Constantine of Manchester and Thomas Kenworthy of Ashton-under-Lyne. The nine Chartist convicts transported on the *Adelaide* were immediately granted 'tickets of leave' allowing them to seek paid work subject to certain police checks on their activities on their arrival, and were pardoned seven years later in December 1856.[18]

Canada

In the early 1900s, a Blackburn couple moved to Valleyfield in Canada. Grandson Ken Dolphin told how his relatives and many others took a piece of Blackburn with them across the Atlantic:

The Montreal Cottons Company is responsible for many English families putting down roots in Valleyfield, about 35 miles south west of Montreal. Imagine working in a cotton mill in Lancashire at the turn of the last century: grimy, sooty with smoke emanating from the coal-fired boilers. My grandmother would tell us about working alongside her mother when she was three years old. She would help change the spindles and carry the full baskets of twine back and forth so that her mother could work faster and make a few more pennies. When my grandparents decided to move to Valleyfield, they had seen a publication put out by the mill called: *Valleyfield, Canada, The cotton factory town of Canada*. This booklet was filled with pictures of the town around 1905. It depicts a town that is centred around the mill. A town where wages are good and the cost of living low. A town surrounded by lakes and rivers teeming with fish. A town already populated by English-speaking people from the same area as them. The mills in Valleyfield are well built, kept scrupulously clean, well lighted, and well ventilated. The surroundings are charming, being beautified by trimly kept lawns and flower beds. The mills are lighted by electric lamp, enabling the air to be kept pure and wholesome at all times. No live steam is used in the weave rooms. The mill recruited people from Blackburn because the looms that they operated here were manufactured in Blackburn by Henry Livesey Ltd. This small neighbourhood had its own churches, of many denominations, a new school with free education, a sports and leisure club and a co-operative society (general store) organised by employees who have been members of a similar society in England, selling boots and shoes, groceries, and all manner of useful commodities. In fact, it was a small enclave of Lancashire life transplanted here.[19]

* * *

The phenomenon of 'Lancashire societies' abroad underlines the depth of people's attachment to their home county. Even those who emigrated willingly often retained that sense of longing, what the Welsh call 'hiraeth', for home. Perhaps the 'Lancashire Sensibility' remains stronger overseas than it does at home.

17

NEW LANCASTRIANS

Lancashire has been a focus of migration for centuries. Some of the earliest 'new Lancastrians' were Flemish weavers fleeing persecution in the fourteenth century. A significant number of Catholic priests sought refuge in Lancashire during and after the French Revolution, from 1793. The trickle of Irish immigration in the later eighteenth century became a flood by the 1840s, particularly during the 'famine' years of the 1840s, though large numbers of young men and women left Ireland during the inter-war years to get work in Lancashire.

Liverpool became one of the most cosmopolitan cities of Europe and was host to a large Chinese community from the nineteenth century. Jewish immigration tended to focus on Manchester, though thousands escaping persecution in eastern Europe landed at Hull and travelled across the Pennines by train to Liverpool to embark for the crossing to America. The massive population movements during and immediately after the Second World War had an inevitable impact on Britain, with Lancashire receiving large numbers of Polish migrants in particular but also families from the Baltic states. The Hungarian exodus following the ill-fated uprising of 1956 saw several Hungarian communities formed across the Lancashire industrial towns, bolstered by more recent immigration.

The British Nationality Act 1948 gave citizens of the British colonies the right to settle in the UK. It applied to everyone who was at that time a British subject, born in a British colony. The Act, with encouragement from British government recruitment campaigns in Caribbean countries, led to a wave of immigration. Nearly half a million people moved from the Caribbean to Britain, becoming known as the 'Windrush Generation'. Many found work in Lancashire.

Large-scale Asian immigration started in the early 1960s while the cotton industry was still a major employer and finding it increasingly difficult to recruit. Asian communities developed in the 'cotton belt' stretching east from Bolton and Preston to east Lancashire, Oldham and Rochdale. New waves of immigration were a feature of the 1980s through to the present, with successive wars and persecution forcing people to escape their mother countries for a better life. Towns such as Oldham, Rochdale, Blackburn, Burnley and Bolton each have their own distinct communities of Syrians, Afghans, Iraqis, Iranians, Albanians and, most recently, 'new' Ukrainians swelling the ranks of the post-war Lancashire Ukrainian communities.

It hasn't always been easy for newcomers. As far back as the 1860s there were anti-Irish riots in Ashton-under-Lyne. In Liverpool, in 1919, a Black man was killed in a racially-inspired riot. More recently, far-right groups have created disturbances in many Lancashire towns and cities, notably in Oldham in 2001, which led to a formal government inquiry. Yet without diminishing the terrible experiences of racism which many 'new Lancastrians' have endured, others tell a story of generosity and friendship when they came to England. It's a mixed experience.

The Irish

For well over a century Ireland provided the main bulk of migrants into Lancashire. The trickle of Irish immigration increased to hundreds of thousands in the 1840s; during the years of 'The Great Famine' about half a million arrived through the port of Liverpool alone. The population of Ireland dropped by two million, through death and emigration. The arrival of hundreds of near-starving Irish families in Bolton in the early 1840s could not have come at a worse time. The prosperity of the previous decades was just a memory as a severe depression—'The Hungry Forties'—dramatically affected the cotton industry.

In 1841, 10,000 people in Bolton alone were receiving 'parish relief'. Many eked out a precarious living in the dying trade of handloom weaving. Typhus claimed hundreds of lives and the burgeoning Irish population was particularly hard hit, due to the living conditions they had to endure. The parish priest, Father Dowdall, contracted the disease himself while organising relief work among his parishioners and died in November 1847. 'Fever sheds' were erected on Fletcher Street, close to the chapel, with a large pit dug as a communal grave. The dead were simply thrown into the large pit which was covered with a few planks. A couple of years later, in 1849, a cholera epidemic hit the town and once again an 'open grave' was dug out into which the dead were cast, after a perfunctory religious service. The master of the workhouse was forced to complain about the smell of the rotting corpses.

The Irish immigrants were blamed, wrongly, for bringing disease with them. There were frequent instances of anti-Irish violence, leading to occasional deaths. Yet many of the Lancashire towns were already rife with typhus and cholera; the Irish were worst affected because of their living conditions. The first Irish immigrants were fleeing dire poverty and starvation. They settled in Bolton, Wigan, Rochdale, Oldham and other developing industrial towns and created their own institutions—cultural, religious, educational and political. By the middle of the twentieth century they were very much integrated into community life, but kept their distinctive cultural identity.

Ireland has been a touchstone of both international solidarity and anti-imperialism in the North of England for 200 years and more. The influence of Irish republicanism was strong in the North of England in the early 1800s; although Wolfe Tone's United Irishmen were brutally suppressed following a series of uprisings in 1798, their politics of secularism, universal suffrage and national independence echoed throughout the nineteenth century and linked into the Chartist movement. Many Lancashire towns and cities with large Irish communities made common cause, at different periods, with Irish radicalism.[1] By the mid-1860s, the younger members of the Irish community in towns like Haslingden were increasingly drawn to the Fenian movement and established secret local groups which were dedicated to achieving Irish freedom by any means necessary. Davitt (see below) became the leader of the Rossendale 'centre' and was soon appointed organiser for Scotland and the North of England, and became involved in arms smuggling activities.

* * *

The large-scale Irish immigration of the first half of the nineteenth century had a major impact on religious life. The vast majority of the Irish immigrants were Roman Catholic and they swelled the ranks of Lancashire's existing Catholic population. It was not always a happy combination, with some of the long-established Catholics resenting the Irish incursion.[2]

Allen Clarke was part of the large Irish community whose numbers had been swelled by emigration during the Potato Famine of the 1840s. His father rose to the ranks of 'minder', one of the skilled and highly unionized cotton spinners. His grandfather was a supporter of the United Irishmen and Robert Emmet, and his son and grandson inherited some of that Irish revolutionary zeal. The young Clarke was taken by his father to see 'The Fenian Arch' where three Irishmen, Allen, Larkin and O'Brien, attempted to free two of their Fenian comrades from the van escorting them to prison. A policeman was shot—probably accidentally—but the assailants were condemned to death and became 'The Manchester Martyrs'.

Clarke commented: "I should think my father sympathised with the Fenians—though perhaps not with their methods—as the natural outcome of an oppressed race. I know he used to denounce the tyrannisation of England over Ireland."[3]

* * *

Lancastrians: Michael Davitt—Irishman and Lancastrian 1846–1906

The story of Michael Davitt, honoured as national hero in Ireland but virtually forgotten in Britain, personifies the course of Irish radicalism in the North of England in the second half of the nineteenth century. Davitt's family were evicted from their cottage in Straide, Co. Mayo, during the Irish Famine in 1850. They landed in Liverpool and settled in Haslingden, a small cotton weaving community in Rossendale. They lived in the town's 'little Ireland' and the family became part of the rapidly growing Lancashire Irish community. Davitt went to work in a local mill at the age of 9 but lost his arm in one of the frequent accidents which befell children working in a dangerous industrial environment. This may have been a blessing in disguise, since he was taken under the wing of the local postmaster and Englishman called Cockroft, and got the basis of an education.[4]

The ability to access guns proved invaluable when anti-Catholic mobs attacked local churches. In 1868, Davitt led the defence of St Mary's church in Haslingden; he and a small group of fellow Fenians fired above the heads of the approaching mob which quickly dispersed. Davitt was eventually apprehended and sentenced to a heavy term of imprisonment, serving much of his time in Dartmoor.

When he came out of jail he turned from the politics of Fenianism to popular mass struggle on a huge scale. One of the most burning issues in rural Ireland was landlordism and the inhuman treatment of the peasantry. The Irish Land Wars of the late 1870s and early 1880s culminated in a remarkable victory for Davitt and the Irish Land League, after facing mass evictions and savage repression by a police force which sided totally with the landlords. Davitt developed the policy of 'passive resistance' which later directly inspired Gandhi. It proved successful, with legislation passed during the 1880s which gave a large degree of security to Ireland's rural workers.

Davitt was hugely popular in the North of England, idolised by the Irish community but widely respected amongst liberals and socialists alike.

During the 1886 'Home Rule' General Election, Thomas Newbigging described him as 'The Lord Nelson of the Irish Party'. Addressing a packed meeting in Davitt's home town of Haslingden, he said: "You know Michael Davitt. He was reared in your midst, in this very town he grew from youth to manhood. I think he must have imbibed many of his ideas of freedom in breathing the air of the Rossendale hills ... He is a man of unblemished character, and his nobility of soul is ungrudgingly recognised both by friends and opponents."[5]

The experience of prison had taken a disastrous toll on his health and he died at the age of 60, in 1906. If forgotten by mainstream British politics, he is remembered by the Lancashire Irish community. In his home town of Haslingden a memorial has been erected which reads: "This memorial has been erected to perpetuate the memory of Michael Davitt with the town of Haslingden. It marks the site of the home of Michael Davitt, Irish patriot, who resided in Haslingden from 1853 to 1867. He became a great world figure in the cause of freedom and raised his voice and pen on behalf of the oppressed, irrespective of race or creed, that serfdom be transformed to citizenship and that man be given the opportunity to display his God given talents for the betterment of mankind. Born 1846, died 1906. Erected by the Irish Democratic League Club, Haslingden (Davitt Branch)."[6]

Much of Davitt's campaigning took place outside of Ireland. He travelled extensively across the United States as well as Britain. There is a plaque on the side of the Portree Hotel, Skye, commemorating his visit to the island during the crofters' struggle for land rights in 1887. There are two plaques, one in Gaelic, the other English. Davitt spoke with a strong Lancashire accent and was fluent in Irish (the family language) as well as English. I wonder if he addressed the thousands of assembled Sgiathanach (Skye folk) in Irish or Scots Gaelic, English or Lanky?

* * *

Many Irishmen worked as labourers, or 'navvies' in the building trade. In Allen Clarke's novel *The Knobstick*, set in 'Spindleton' in the mid-1880s, the tramping hero's first experience of kindness is from a group of Irish building workers whom he meets as he approaches the town. They offer him and his young child some food and a few pence of their hard-earned cash to help him find lodgings. It's a small act of kindness that means a lot.

Girls and women found employment in services or, as the century wore on, the textile industry and shop work. Gradually, a small middle class emerged, formed of first- or second-generation Irish. Teachers, doctors and small traders put their mark on the Lancashire cotton towns. A growing number of priests in the local churches came from Ireland. One of Bolton's best-loved doctors in the late nineteenth century was Dr James Dorrian who came from County Down. He had a surgery in a poor Irish community off Deane Road. Allen Clarke, who knew him as a child, says he was 'beloved by the poor'. A statue, funded by public subscription, commemorates him in Bolton's Queens Park.

At the same time, a new sense of Irish national identity was taking hold which led to war and independence in 1921. Bolton held its first Irish cultural festival 1909, in the King's Hall. The seventh took place just days before the Dublin Easter Rising in 1916. St Joseph's, Halliwell, was active in promoting Irish culture, particularly dance.

Irish immigrants had mixed views about the rise of nationalism. Many Irishmen had fought under the Union Jack in the First World War but wanted to see, at the very least, home rule for Ireland— what today we'd call 'devolution'.

One of the leading figures in radical Irish nationalism was James Connolly, born in Edinburgh and who spent much of his time doing 'propaganda work' in the North of England, before the 1916 Easter Rising in Dublin. Connolly made numerous visits to Salford in the early 1900s, being warmly welcomed by the large number of Irishmen working in local collieries. Joe Deighan, writing over fifty years later, commented:

> At street corner meetings and in lecture rooms, day in and day out, he endlessly explained to both British and Irish workers that the bosses that kept the miners underground hewing coal so long that they seldom saw God's daylight, were the same imperialists who kept Ireland in subjection.[7]

Connolly set up branches of the Irish Republican Socialist Party in some Lancashire towns, including Pendleton, with its large Irish working-class community. Connolly emphasised that the new branch should not compete with either the local ILP or SDF branches, who supported the cause of an independent Ireland.[8]

The Irish Democrat newspaper, for many years edited by Marxist, poet and professional chemist C. Desmond Greaves, was aimed specifically at Irish people in Britain. It was avidly read by Irishmen working on the building sites of Manchester and I well remember their weekly visits to the Communist Party offices in Longsight to collect copies of *The Democrat* for distribution on the sites.[9]

Jewish Manchester

Jews arrived in significant numbers into Lancashire during the later years of the nineteenth century and were dotted across its towns and cities. However, by far the greatest concentration was in Manchester, and north Manchester in particular. The present-day Jewish History Museum is a magnificent testimony to a very rich, and geographically focused, community of 'new Lancastrians'. Their history has been well documented by Bill Williams, who was instrumental in setting up the museum in the 1980s.

The earliest references to a Jewish presence in Lancashire was in 1740, when Jewish hawkers travelled around the county as pawnbrokers, opticians, dentists and 'quack doctors'. A group of Jewish peddlers settled in Liverpool in the mid-eighteenth century, some of whom were immigrants from Bavaria. Some of them moved to Manchester a couple of decades later and set up as shop-keepers.[10] The community grew steadily and a kosher restaurant opened on Long Millgate in 1819, run by Sarah Levy. Manchester's rapid growth as a commercial centre for textiles encouraged Ashkenazi traders from Germany and Holland to settle in Manchester. Sephardi merchants arrived from the Mediterranean coastlands in the 1840s. By the 1860s they had established several warehouses in central Manchester.

In some cases it was a story of 'rags to riches'. Benjamin Hyam set up as a hawker of old clothes, but developed a pioneering business in Manchester to establish what Bill Williams considers to be "probably the world's first shop to make and sell ready-made suits".[11]

The 1850s saw an increasing number of migrants from eastern Europe arriving in Manchester from the east coast ports, notably Hull. Some were en route to Liverpool and America, but many stayed. By 1875 there was a densely packed community of around 3,000 Jewish workers living in appalling housing around Red Bank. There were tensions between the settled, anglicised Jewish community of Manchester and the poorer incomers, seen as 'bringing down the quality of life' for those Jewish families that had settled in the Cheetham Hill area.[12]

The Jewish community expanded from the north Manchester suburbs to the south side of the city. A large synagogue opened in Fallowfield in 1873. In the twentieth century Manchester's Jewish working-class community was prominent in the trade union movement and also in the small, but influential, Communist Party. Many young Jewish men and women became involved in anti-fascist activity and supported the Republican side in the Spanish Civil War.[13] A new wave of Jewish refugees, fleeing from the Nazis, arrived in Manchester in the mid to late 1930s. Bill Williams estimates that by 1938 around 500 German refugees had arrived, mostly from professional occupations. The Manchester Ladies Lodge of B'nai Brith created a Hospitality Committee to give social and financial support to young refugee women arriving as domestic servants.[14]

The Jewish communities scattered across England had, by the late nineteenth century, established a network of friendly societies, mostly catering for working-class men. The Provincial Independent

Tontine Society was formed amongst a group of Jewish garment workers in Cheetham Hill in 1922. It was based on a particular firm which was mostly Jewish—Neville and Harris Blond. It provided assistance to members 'in need', issued annuities, and also donated to Jewish charities, including the 'Jewish Fresh Air Home' in Delamere and the Jewish Hospital in Manchester.[15]

* * *

In the late nineteenth century there was some 'local migration' of Jewish people from Manchester, and to a lesser extent London, to smaller Lancashire towns. The growth of the Jewish community in Blackburn commenced in the 1880s; by 1893 Blackburn had its own synagogue. Some of the trades in which Jewish people worked were tailoring, cabinetry, and shop owners. Doubtless, a number also worked in Blackburn's cotton mills as weavers and possibly engineers and office staff. The Jewish population peaked before the First World War, with about 250 Jewish families resident. This had declined to just twelve by 1980. Why the decline? Perhaps people left Blackburn because of worsening employment opportunities in the 1930s coupled with the decline of the cotton weaving industry.

The first synagogue opened in 1893 and closed in about 1976. In 1899 it held a special service in aid of the Blackburn and East Lancashire Infirmary. The report of this event notes that a 'fair sum' was collected and that the service was attended by a number of Christians including the mayor of Blackburn and other municipal authorities. At a service in 1901, attended by a number of dignitaries including the mayor of Blackburn and a large number of Christians, the Rabbi's sermon commented upon the harmony between Christians and Jews in England.

The Lancashire seaside town of St Anne's was a popular place for the more affluent Manchester-based middle classes to move to. Several Jewish families settled there and by 1909 there were around fifty Jewish families in the area. Many of the Jewish businessmen continued to work in Manchester, taking the famous 'club train' each morning into Manchester, often to visit the Cotton Exchange or do other business. The daily travel pattern featured in Allen Clarke's *Lancashire Annual* for 1924, with a selection of 'Club Train

Yarns'. He introduces this rather special 'luxury' train as, "the train that takes to Manchester and brings back to Blackpool the business men who toil in the smoke so that their spouses may revel by the sea".[16] He quotes one Blackpool-based traveller who seems to have resented the Jewish businessmen of St Anne's and Blackpool monopolising the best seats: "I've nought agen' 'em, for my motto is to live an' let live ... but it's funny to see the crowd of 'em making for the train every morning and coming out of the station every evening. They manage to monopolise most of the seats!" Descending into overt anti-semitism, he says that some people are asking, "now that the war has been over for so long, when is the railway going to hand over the Club Train to the British?" Clarke adds that "at Kirkham the porters shout 'Change here for Lytham an' Palestine'", presumably meaning St Anne's.

A St Anne's Hebrew Congregation existed by the 1920s. It began as a Sephardi congregation established by a number of Jewish textile merchants. In the 1930s more Manchester families moved to St Anne's and changed the community to Ashkenazi. Since 1946, the Jewish population in St Anne's has varied between 350 and 520 in 1965, and in 2004 there were about 300. Blackpool was considered the primary Jewish Orthodox community in the area, but with the decline of Blackpool's Jewish community, in 2012 it was decided to close its synagogue and merge with St Anne's.[17]

Liverpool: 'Blackness in many different shades'

Liverpool is one of the oldest continuous Black communities in Europe. Black people have been in Liverpool as sailors, soldiers and slaves for over 300 years, long before the Windrush Generation (see below) and post-war migration from the Caribbean.

Ray Quarless, 69, can trace his family back to the 1800s. The community activist told the *Liverpool Echo*: "My great grandfather is Jamaican, my great grandmother is English, my grandfather is Bajan, and my grandmother is a Liverpool-born Black woman. And on my mother's side, my grandparents are first generation Irish."[18]

Liverpool was home to one of the first permanent Chinese settlements in the UK as well as one of the first Black communities. Sailors from around the world were stopping and settling there, having families and children, with more doing the same in the generations after. Ray Quarless said: "The significant thing about Liverpool's Black community is that its Blackness comes in many different shades. Unlike Birmingham, Manchester, Leeds, Bristol, and London, we don't have this direct umbilical cord for Jamaica, which they all do. But Liverpool, its connections are Africa, the Caribbean, the Far East, the Near East, the Americas. That's what Liverpool is."[19]

Ray's own family history parallels the history of Black people in Liverpool. His grandfather came from Barbados in the 1890s, staying in a boarding house on Pitt Street near the docks. Ray's family lived in a seafaring community. He said, "I grew up with Chinese, Irish, Welsh, Scottish, African, Caribbean, both East and West Africa, Nigerians, Liberians, Malay, Singapore, Italian, German. Where I grew up was sort of a microcosm of what Liverpool 1 used to be."[20]

After the First World War around 5,000 Black people lived in Liverpool. As servicemen returned home looking for jobs, tensions grew. Riots broke out in 1919 and a mob attacked a Black seafarers' boarding house. Twenty-four-year-old Charles Wooton was chased to Queens Dock and murdered. No arrests were made.[21]

Destruction from bombing of the docks during the Second World War pushed Liverpool's Black community out to Granby in Liverpool 8, now known as their historic home. Lucille Harvey, 35, was elected to represent Princes Park, the ward covering this area, on Liverpool City Council in May 2022. She describes herself on Twitter as 'Melanin challenged Barbadian-Irish-Glaswegian Scouse'. She explained: "My mum is half-Barbadian, half Irish-Glaswegian, and then my dad is Scouse. Growing up in Toxteth, this was perfectly normal."

Chantelle Lunt, the 34-year-old founder of Merseyside Black Lives Matter, was born in Toxteth but grew up in a majority white area in Halewood. "There's a massive identity crisis to go from wanting to fit in and be more white, to wanting to fit in and be more Black. It was just, it was horrible."

In speaking to family about her past, Chantelle discovered her grandad was a mixed race man from Barbados, similar to the family history of many people in Liverpool, like Ray and Lucille. "My identity is basically a reflection of how I've grown up. So in terms of my Black identity, to be comfortable in my Black identity is not to shy away from conversations about who I am."

The Windrush generation

The *Empire Windrush* docked at Tilbury on 22 June 1948, carrying 802 Caribbean migrants. Some stayed in the London area but several moved north where there was a labour shortage after the war. Most of the men who settled in Manchester and the surrounding area found work in construction, at the Salford docks and in the new factories around Trafford Park. Many women got jobs as nurses in the new NHS. A community history project records:

> Far from being the magical country many Commonwealth citizens had heard about in stories and their education, Britain often seemed a grey and hostile place. Poverty was common, especially in the cities, and racism was prevalent. Accommodation was hard to come by for many settlers, who were turned away from available lettings on account of their skin colour.[22]

There were only 350 Caribbean settlers in Manchester during the early 1950s but numbers soon grew to 2,502 in 1961 and 6,263 in 1981. Many found homes in Moss Side and Hulme. Although the Black community still faced issues like poverty, racism, and police harassment, there was a keen sense of community spirit. White children mixed with Black children, families looked out for each other, and neighbours traded goods and essentials. From the early 1960s, clubs like the Reno, the Nile and the Bengwema opened up and became popular venues.

* * *

Lancastrians: Alvin Guy 1928–85

Alvin Guy set sail for Britain aboard the Empire Windrush *on 24 May 1948 from Kingston, Jamaica. On 22 June he arrived safely and made his way to Manchester, where he managed to rent a room in a house on Park Street. Alvin, then 28, found his first job on a construction site, helping to build council houses in a city that was still recovering from wartime damage. However, Alvin was a skilled engineer by trade and eventually settled in Oldham where he worked, at Entwistle Engineering. Just like many other Windrush settlers, Alvin and his family faced racism. Alvin's daughter,*

Kathryn Holland, said: "My dad experienced racism as we did as children. I remember experiencing it from about the age of six.

"We would try to play with the white children in our area but their parents would call them back inside." She added: "Dad was the only Jamaican on our street where I lived for 16 years but it improved when I got to about 10-years-old. He helped anyone who needed a home, a job, money, or a friend. Everyone who knew him loved him and he was known for always having a smile on his face."

Kathryn also added that Alvin was a keen musician and that he and his wife, Margaret, who met in 1960, both played music in bars and clubs as a duet. Kathryn said: "Music was so important to dad. He told us his mum didn't want to go into music and he said he used to climb trees in his youth to play his trumpet in secrecy. His mum would beat him when he came down. Our headmaster at Hathershaw School in Oldham used to let them hire a room to rehearse in on a Wednesday or Thursday night once a fortnight. He loved listening to them and asked my dad if he could teach him so he did."

* * *

Migration from eastern Europe

Bolton has a well-established Ukrainian community which is working with its neighbours as well as Ukrainian groups across the country to help their brothers and sisters in the current war (2023), many of whom have either had to flee their country or are facing relentless bombardment.

Bolton's Ukrainian community took shape after the Second World War. Ukraine had endured immense suffering under Stalin's rule as boss of the Soviet Union. During the early 1930s the eastern part of Ukraine endured a calamitous famine which led to the deaths of between four and seven million people. Stalin sat back and allowed it to happen: it was a man-made catastrophe. What Ukrainians call 'The Holodomor'—death by starvation—is etched deeply in the hearts and minds of present generations of Ukrainians, in much the same way that the Irish Famine of the 1840s continues to be recalled with deep sorrow and anger by Irish people.

Bolton born and bred, Yaroslaw Tymchyshyn is chairman of the Bolton branch of the Association of Ukrainians in Great Britain. His father, along with thousands more Ukrainians, arrived in Britain after the Second World War hoping for a better life. Many settled in Bolton, where there was a labour shortage in the cotton industry and coal mines. Several of the men got jobs at Agecroft Colliery. Yaroslaw's father worked at Dobson and Barlow's engineering works before joining Bolton Corporation as a bus conductor in 1953. According to Yaroslaw, he got the job because he was good at maths!

"A branch of the Association of Ukrainians in Great Britain was formed in 1948—it was one of the first in the country," said Yaroslaw. "There had been an earlier influx of Ukrainians into Manchester, at the end of the nineteenth century, but it was only really in the 1940s that the flow became significant." Alongside the association, a youth group was also established.[23]

The association raised funds to get its own cultural centre where the community's heritage could be cherished and maintained. The association ran classes in Ukrainian for the children, as well as encouraging national music and dance. Ukrainian history and culture was taught, countering the idea that Ukraine had no national identity. The Saturday School, which focused on language teaching, reached ninety-three pupils, boys and girls. Some delightful photos have survived of children in traditional Ukrainian costume.

The vast majority of the Ukrainian community are Roman Catholics. In the early years, mass, delivered in the home language, was heard at St Patrick's Church on Great Moor Street. The first generation of Bolton Ukrainians felt strongly about ensuring their children would get the sort of education that many of them had been denied. Most of the boys went to Thornleigh College, while those who failed the 11-plus often went to Rome to train as priests. The majority of girls went to the convent school, Mount St Joseph's, with some attending the former St Cuthbert's in Bolton.

* * *

A trickle of Hungarian refugees came to England towards the end of the Second World War. However, many more were forced to flee Hungary following the bloody defeat of the 1956 insurrection against Russian domination.

Many found their way to Blackpool, a seemingly unlikely destination, but the town had a lot of vacant accommodation by late

October—the end of 'the season'—when the majority of refugees arrived. Two hundred Hungarian refugees were accommodated. The following year, in gratitude to the people of Blackpool, the Hungarians gave a spectacular performance of theatre, music and opera in the Winter Gardens which supported the mayor of Blackpool's charity fund.

A blue plaque was unveiled at the Winter Gardens in October 2021 to celebrate Blackpool's role in supporting the Hungarian refugees in 1956. At the unveiling, Dr Csaba Balogh, State Secretary of the Ministry of Foreign Affairs and Trade of Hungary, said: "We are here to express our deepest appreciation to you, the town of Blackpool and the United Kingdom."[24]

Further immigration from Hungary into Lancashire took place in the 1990s and 2000s. Towns such as Rochdale and Bolton have sizeable Hungarian communities with local shops selling traditional Hungarian food. The town of Chorley has a twinning arrangement with Székesfehérvár, which has included educational and artistic links over the years.

The first main group of Poles came to Bury in September 1946 on a detachment of the Polish Army Second Corps to guard the army barracks situated at Lowercroft. After demobilisation, some of the troops decided to stay–joined by the main influx of Poles into Bury during 1948. Many of the disabled ex-servicemen were placed in Remploy Hostel, Radcliffe, which was attached to a furniture manufacturing factory. Able-bodied ex-servicemen found private accommodation or some were able to purchase their own homes having obtained work in cotton mills, brickworks, quarries, tanneries or paper mills.

During 1948, the families of many ex-servicemen began to arrive in Bury from various camps and orphanages scattered over Africa, India and Europe, predominately young, ranging from 10–18 years of age. The history of Bury's Polish Centre says:

> Learning the English language and getting started in a new life, work or business was not easily achieved and it took time. In that period, all over the UK in nearly every city or town new Polish ex-servicemen's clubs, churches and social centres were founded to cater for the need of social contact, friendly chats over a coffee or drink, or a meal, keep national identity and exchange of information with

each other as well as to keep abreast of what was going on back in Poland where their families and friends lived.[25]

The initial influx of Poles was mostly male. Many wives and children had to stay behind in Poland, and for many it wasn't until some ten years later that they were allowed to join their husbands. In 1958, a number of wives and children began to arrive from Poland, after agreement was reached between the British and Polish governments to allow family re-unification. As the community developed, it was decided to establish a social centre to act as a focus for Bury's expanding Polish community; it opened in 1962 and has since expanded further.

> Second and third generation Poles can now appreciate their parents' and grandparents' tremendous effort, determination, hard work and input they made to have their own centre. The centre gels the Polish community together to maintain its proud history and identity, where they can meet socially and attend Services in their own Chapel.[26]

South Asian migration

The largest immigration into Lancashire after the Irish influx of the nineteenth century was from the South Asian region—India and Pakistan (and subsequently Bangladesh). Bolton's Asian community began to grow in the late 1950s, mostly by Asian men coming to work in the mills, in some cases hopping over the Pennines from Bradford, or from Preston. The majority of the first Asians got jobs in the mills but some found work in engineering or on the railways. The first influx of Asians, mostly men, experienced little discrimination. Before 1967, Bolton's Muslim community worshipped at two small, terraced houses. People clubbed together to buy the former Emmanuel Church which also offered advice and English language classes and served as a community centre. Bolton's Asian communities put down roots during the 1970s but racism increased as well, with the activities of the National Front.

Fatima Irani's story is not untypical, arriving in Liverpool from Karachi in October 1962 with her three children:

> My husband, the late Moosa Irani, had come before us and told us to bring as much as we could as there was not much available here,

warm clothes, pillows and blankets, as it was really cold in England. As we settled things got easier as we adapted to change and made lots of new friends. I was a seamstress so began sewing clothes for the Asian ladies from home, as Asian clothes were not readily available. Coming to England and starting a new life at first was a very hard struggle with culture, language and food, but we soon became accustomed to it and made many happy memories with all those around us to treasure.[27]

Unlike neighbouring Oldham, Bolton's Asian population in the 1970s was split evenly between Muslim and Hindu. From as early as the 1950s, Blackburn began experiencing steady migration from a significant number of mainly Muslim migrants from India and Pakistan. The large majority of this migration originated specifically from the Bharuch or Surat areas of Gujarat in India and the Mirpur region of Pakistan-administered Kashmir. Both are rural areas and, in some ways, share similarities with the general landscape of east Lancashire. Mohammed was born and bred in Blackburn:

Though set in deepest Lancashire, growing up in Blackburn felt like a mini-India or Pakistan at times, divorced from the rest of Britain by place, race and time. I lived amongst a mainly Muslim Gujarati community; all my local streets were inhabited by South Asian families. Even in the early 1980s there were three main mosques in our area alone, split along lines of ideology as well as national, sometimes regional, South Asian identities. All meat was halal and every grocer sold the curry essentials. The bygone era that teachers would reminisce over in school, where doors were left open and children would be free to safely walk in and out of homes, was still a lived reality in our area. As a result, by the time I was five I was fluent in English, Gujarati and Urdu, as well as my own mother-tongue, Kutchi. At school I would learn of the town's proud industrial heritage; a time when every home was a mini-factory. I would return home to live that reality too as my mother sewed cloth and my father and I would cut the threads, delivered and collected by wealthier immigrants with more business sense. We would go to school during the day, attend mosque to learn the Qur'an in the evening, and play the South Asian street game, *Galli-Danda* (a kind of cricket but with sticks) in between. My parents were wise to ensure my primary education was delivered at an all-white school on the other side of town, otherwise my only interaction with White England would have been at the hands of the National Front who would pass by occasionally to touch up their graffiti and steal our toys.

Integration and the far-right were the major challenges facing the working-class Muslim community in Blackburn, at least while I was growing up. Integration and the far-right, with, I must add, dashes of poverty. Naturally, my experiences of growing up are inextricably linked to the history of the area. A former mill town, Blackburn sits nestled between solid Lancastrian hills, visible demarcations defining natural limits. It became one of the world's first industrialised towns, off the back of its thriving textile manufacturing industry, a proud trailblazer and boom town of the industrial revolution. Since the mid-twentieth century however, it has suffered greatly, like many other Northern England post-industrial towns, with issues of deindustrialisation, unemployment, poor housing and poverty. There was another feature which would, inevitably, exert upon the town yet another dimension of transformation. From as early as the 1950s, Blackburn began experiencing steady migration from a significant number of mainly Muslim migrants from India and Pakistan. The large majority of this migration originated specifically from the Bharuch or Surat areas of Gujarat in India and the Mirpur region of Pakistan-administered Kashmir. Both are rural areas of the Subcontinent and, in some ways, share similarities with the general landscape of east Lancashire: Mirpur has hills of its own and Gujarat had a thriving textile industry, which Blackburn would have sought inspiration from during the period of the Raj...[28]

Cotton, curry and commerce

The first Asian businesses in Lancashire were overwhelmingly concentrated in catering. Oldham was typical of the larger cotton towns. The Heritage Lottery Fund supported a project called 'Cotton, Curry and Commerce'—a history of Asian businesses in Oldham, which included a book and a community research project spanning three generations. The project was the result of a partnership between the Oldham Asian Business Association and Oldham Local Studies and Archives. The Asian Business Association (ABA)

was founded in 1998 to provide advice and assistance to local entre-
preneurs starting and running their own businesses. The ABA provided access to training and qualifications, and from 2001 instituted
the annual business awards and dinners. With the take-up of mainstream services by the Asian business community, and a consequent
diminishing need for their specialist service, the Asian Business
Association decided to dissolve its activities in 2011. However, keen
to ensure the survival of its archives and its legacy to the history of
Oldham, the ABA decided to embark on the project that became
'Cotton, Curry and Commerce'.[29]

In 1961, Raja Mohammed Mushtaq Ahmed lived in a small village in the Punjab region of Pakistan. By the age of 22 he was
married and working as a skilled draughtsman. His mother decided
that he should advance his career in England and raised the money
to cover his airfare and other living costs. His wife and daughter
stayed at home. He arrived in England on 18 August 1961, carrying an eiderdown and wearing as many warm clothes as he could!
His first home was with family friends living in Whalley Range.
"Home town culture and etiquette demanded that he would be
taken in regardless of crowded house conditions. The three bed-
room house with outside toilet was home to 21 people..."[30] His
first job was in the card room at Durban Mill, Hollinwood—'the
dirtiest job in the world'—before getting a better paid job on a
building site. He tried to get better jobs in local mills and eventually had to stage a sit-down protest in the reception of Ashton
Brothers' Mill in Hyde to get an interview. He learnt his trade as
a ring spinner and moved on to Wellington Mills in Greenfield for
a higher salary and better conditions.

Unions and politics

Many Asians were unionised, though attitudes amongst union officials sometimes revealed underlying prejudice. In 1965 a strike
broke out at Courtaulds in Preston. Of the 3,000 employees around
a thousand were of Asian and Caribbean descent. An unofficial strike
broke out in May 1965 over changes to the production process
which disproportionately affected the factory's Asian and Caribbean
workers. The union—the Transport and General Workers' Union

(TGWU)—refused to recognise the strike and relations with its Asian members soured.[31] The strike had strong racial overtones and led to some strikers suggesting separate union organisations for people of colour. This did not happen, but the process of changing entrenched union attitudes to become genuinely representative of its membership was, in some cases, a long one.

As Asian people put down roots in the cotton towns, some became involved in local politics. Labour was the obvious choice though there were tensions within the party in some towns, with a reluctance to adopt Asian people as election candidates. In one area of Bolton, an Asian (Yusuf Patel) was adopted by the Conservatives as their local election candidate and only lost, in what was a strong Labour ward, by a few votes. This was a wake-up call to Labour and more Asian people were adopted to fight—and win—council wards.

* * *

Successive waves of migration have made Lancashire a very diverse region, and it's the better for it. There remain tensions but the contribution of Lancashire's different communities in the fields of business, commerce, sport and culture is vast—and can only grow.

18

A LANCASHIRE RENAISSANCE?

What might a green, thriving and democratic Lancashire look like? We need to develop a modern vision which builds on Lancashire's historic achievements and culture, outlined in the preceding chapters.

The next few years are likely to see big changes in the make-up of this 'United Kingdom'. Scotland may become independent; we may see a more autonomous Wales and a united Ireland. The English regions will be forced into having a hard look at their future. Where stands Lancashire?

The Yorkshire writer, Colin Speakman, asked of his county, "What will be the role of what could and should be a strong vibrant Region of England, within the British Isles and even in Europe (which inescapably we are part of) in the difficult and perilous years of the mid twenty first century?"[1]

I'd like to take up Colin's challenge for Lancashire. As fellow Lancastrians (Colin is a Salford lad by birth) we share a common outlook on the North today and how we might navigate the stormy times ahead. I agree with Colin's arguments that real devolution, not the third-rate arrangements we have now in the 'city regions', is needed. Change must come from the grass roots,

> from individuals and communities, and not be something imposed by politicians with their own limited agendas ... real change comes from building on that powerful sense of localism, a pride in a community's shared values, a process that moves outwards from neighbourhood to district, from district to region, from region to nation.[2]

A starting point should be the revival of a 'Lancashire sensibility' which relates to what Colin Speakman has termed, for Yorkshire, a 'cultural province'. It's a helpful concept, used in both geography and anthropology. It can be defined as a complex of activities that, to some extent, have a degree of homogeneity, those 'traits in common', which I have tried to encapsulate in these chapters across a wide sphere of activities. It is flexible enough to allow for ethnic and social diversity, being 'Lancashire by adoption'. Indeed its strength, as argued in 'New Lancastrians', is its very diversity rather than a rigid homogeneity based on race or ethnicity.

The concept can cross political or even state boundaries and overlap with other cultures. It isn't without its difficulties; my preference might have been for a Lancashire 'cultural region' rather than 'province' which has come to mean something slightly negative. It says much of our centralist English culture that 'provincial' implies backwardness and conservatism. Yet what I'm saying is so similar to Colin's ideas, using a different term isn't helpful; let's find something that can unite us, these counties of the white and red rose—shared cultural provinces.

The Lancashire cultural province should take in all of 'historic Lancashire' including Liverpool, most of Greater Manchester north of the Mersey and 'Lancashire North of the Sands'. The flexibility of the term allows an overlap with, for example, Saddleworth which is part of the Yorkshire 'cultural province'.

I'm not going to jettison 'regions'—they work well as political and economic concepts, alongside the 'cultural province'. I'll explain, bear with me; firstly, let's start at the grass roots.

A new localism

We've seen that Lancashire has several political traditions and has been at the forefront of many reform struggles, perhaps above all Chartism and later the women's suffrage movement. These campaigns grew from the bottom up, from the small villages and towns as well as cities. We need to renew Lancashire's democratic and radical instincts, based on the *local*. Strong and democratic governance must be built from the bottom up, based on effective local bodies.

Local government has been hollowed out, as smaller authorities were merged into larger units which have little or no relevance to most people. Medium-sized towns, such as Darwen, Heywood, Farnworth, Radcliffe and others, should have their own voice and powers, co-operating with their neighbouring communities on issues of mutual concern within a Lancashire 'co-operative commonwealth' as argued below.

It need not require huge upheaval in the first instance. Town and parish councils could be given greater powers and take on some responsibilities currently owned by the districts or unitary authorities. Town (or parish) councils could be established where they do not exist, if there is local support for them. These do not have to be confined to rural areas.

The lessons from some town councils across the UK, such as Frome, show that small councils can revive civic pride, create active communities and do a range of very practical projects—and pull in extra funding. Parish councils don't have to be sleepy, old-fashioned committees who meet for the sake of it and whose main mission is to keep the precept as low as possible. Maybe we should find a better name for them; even 'village council' would be an improvement. In Scotland and Wales they have 'community councils' which could be another option; but keep 'town councils'. A sense of township is important.

While short-term reform isn't that difficult, local government restructuring is inescapable in the longer term. The creation of very large unitary authorities (e.g. just two local authorities for what was Cumbria) and proposals to carve up what little remains of 'Lancashire' take power and accountability away from people and result in them feeling disempowered and forgotten. The metropolitan borough councils in the Liverpool City Region and Greater Manchester need a strong 'lower tier' of town and parish councils which can work positively with the 'mets' but take on more responsibilities and collaborate between each other on issues of common interest.

A new regionalism—'county clanship'

We've seen that the great Lancashire Liberal, Samuel Compston, spoke of the virtue of 'county clanship, in no narrow sense'. He was onto something and his wording was carefully chosen. Regional pride does not pre-suppose antipathy to other regions and nations, and it needs to include everyone *within* the region. But it requires a democratic voice, not just one person elected every few years as 'mayor', nor a 'combined authority' of local leaders whose prime loyalty is to their own authority or even the council ward which they were elected to represent. How could a new political region that is much more than the fragmented and under-resourced dog's dinner of districts, unitary authorities, metropolitan councils and combined authorities take shape?

Lancashire was shrunk by an undemocratic diktat in the 1970s, as outlined in Chapter 2. Nobody asked the people of Bolton, Rochdale, Oldham, Wigan and other towns if they wanted to be part of a 'Greater Manchester'. There is an elected mayor but without the democratic oversight of an elected council, which at least the original Greater Manchester Metropolitan Council had, before it was abolished by Mrs Thatcher in 1986. Something else we weren't asked about.

Regional democracy should be the next big jump for our political system—with regional assemblies, elected proportionately, taking real powers out of Westminster.

Why? It's about the ugly but useful term 'subsidiarity'—making decisions at the most appropriate level. There are many things which are currently done centrally that ought to be devolved to a regional level—big enough to be strategic, small enough to be accountable and connected into regional and local networks. It should include long-distance transport, strategic health, land-use planning, driving forward a broad sustainability agenda that can address the big challenge of climate change, which is with us now. The powers that the Welsh and Scottish governments now have are a good guide to what strong regional government in England should possess. Remember that telling fact, Scotland is about the same size as Yorkshire but Yorkshire has very few of the powers the Scots have. Wales is considerably smaller than either Yorkshire or this re-imagined Lancastria, but with infinitely greater powers.

Choices

Above the metropolitan authorities there should be a tier of elected regional government, replacing the unaccountable combined authorities and bringing a common framework across England. It could be a fairly painless process and we should have choices, as I suggest below. There are at least four options.

The first is to carry on as we are with the current mish-mash of 'city regions' and unitary authorities that are too big to be account-able and too small to be strategic. A second approach could be mov-ing towards the sort of regional government envisioned by Labour's John Prescott in the early 2000s, with a 'North-West' regional government. The third is to 'go Northern', creating a combined region of 15 million people from the Humber and Mersey to the Scottish border. A fourth approach could involve a new approach which I'd call 'cultural regionalism'.

Can I dispense with the first option quickly? It was never wanted; after fifty years it is still unpopular in many parts of 'historic Lancashire', particularly the Lancashire towns that were forced into 'Greater Manchester', but perhaps also places like St Helens, Widnes and above all Southport that became 'Merseyside' and more recently Liverpool City Region. Many people in Barrow-in-Furness, Ulverston and Grange-over-Sands retain their Lancashire identities and it doesn't seem to be only the older generation. Staying as we are isn't an option that suits anyone, apart from those with a vested interest in keeping the *status quo*.

The second option, of new regional government based on the 'standard planning regions', makes some economic and geographi-cal sense. In the case of Yorkshire it chimes with people's historic cultural identities as well. Unfortunately, it doesn't work so well for 'The North-West' stretching south from Carlisle and the Scottish borders to Cheshire, with Yorkshire on its eastern flank. Back in 1992 Granada Television, from its Salford base, produced a series called *Homo Northwestus: A Quest for the Species, North-West Man*. It was produced by Bill Jones with Liz Andrew and presented by Ray Gosling.[3] The series, and subsequent publication, had worthy objectives: "perhaps by accident we might speed the process of evo-lution: awaken a truly proud, self-conscious northern race, west of the Pennine backbone".[4]

It's true that the 'North-West' makes sense on a map, and we had a North-West planning region for decades, followed by the North-West Regional Development Agency under Labour, but with limited powers. Today there's the excellent BBC regional news programme, *North-West Tonight* with a great team of presenters who have a real feel for the region. But you will struggle to find many people who identify as 'North-Western'. 'Lancashire' most certainly yes, but 'North-Western'? No, not really. It is a geographical concept, not a cultural, political and economic region that has grown over centuries, in the way that Lancashire and Yorkshire have.

The third option is to think big, to think 'Northern': a land of 15 million people bringing the three regions—North-West, North-East, and Yorkshire and the Humber—into one super-region, the North. It chimes with some recent thinking. There have been several books written in recent years on 'the North', all of them promoting a sense of Northern history and culture. Dave Russell's *Looking North* is probably the most scholarly. Paul Morley's *The North* is classic Paul Morley, and none the worse for that, with his knockabout approach to history. Brian Groom's *Northerners* represents a highly readable overview of a thousand years and more of Northern history. Kate Fox's *Where There's Muck There's Bras* is both an entertaining and a stimulating account of the great achievements of Northern women.[5]

It's interesting that since the publication of John Walton's magnificent social history of Lancashire in 1987,[6] publishers have generally shied away from 'Lancashire' and focused on 'the North'. These days, Lancashire has become decidedly 'uncool' and quaint, compared with Manchester or 'The North'. It conjures up images of L.S. Lowry, men in flat caps, clog dancing, dialect poetry, mill chimneys and cobbled streets. 'The North' has fared better and doesn't inspire that out dated image we have of Lancashire.

But there is a fundamental problem. There is certainly a broad 'Northern' identity, which can sit comfortably with an English, or even a *British* national identity, and also lots of local identities based on village, town or city loyalties, as well as regional identities within the North. However, 'the North' as a whole is too big to work as a manageable cultural, political and economic entity, whereas 'Lancashire' (and Yorkshire) could. If we look at the German approach towards regional government, there is great diversity in population size and geography, but what they have in common is a shared identity, often going back a long way. A typical population size is around 3 million; though Bremen has less than 700,000 and Nordrhein-Westfalen has nearly 18 million.

At the very least we should be looking at co-operation between the three (or arguably four) regions within the North: Yorkshire; Durham and Northumberland ('Northumbria'); Lancashire and Cumbria; and possibly Cheshire. 'The North' as a whole has a population much bigger than many European nations, let alone regions; not only is it too big, it masks strong regional identities within it; it's a country. Maybe, in the long-term, 'the North' might go the same way as Scotland seems to be going and embrace independence.[7]

Part of me hopes not. 'England' is an old country, with many great attributes and achievements, alongside some that are less worth holding on to. Many proud Lancastrians would equally say they are 'English'—and there's nothing wrong with that. Yet a Northern federation of regions, sharing and collaborating, connected by much-improved transport links, is an attractive vision.

The fourth option, of 'cultural regionalism', makes geographical and economic as well as political and cultural sense to me. It should be given a chance. It need not be coterminous with 'historic Lancashire' and represent what I've dubbed today's cultural province of Lancashire. It could grow outwards from what is already there, based on the democratic wishes of the people who live here.

In political terms a start could be to extend 'Greater Manchester'— why not call it 'Lancastria'?—to include the existing administrative county of Lancashire, extending as far north as Lancaster and Silverdale, east to Burnley and Colne and west to include Warrington. If the Liverpool 'city region' wanted to join, it should be up to them, or they could stay as they are, a powerful region in their own right with a strong identity and distinctive politics. Yet a region combining Liverpool and Manchester would be a real 'powerhouse' that could compete with London and the wider world. Just like it once did.

Lancastria should reach out to the other Northern regions and find areas of common concern. Transport is an obvious one and the existing 'Transport for the North', dependent on handouts from central government, should be the joint property of the democratic Northern regions and start to address the historically poor transport links within the North. There is already collaboration between

Northern universities, and scope for doing much more; the same goes for business development and co-operation.

The suggested Lancastria need not be exactly the same shape as the historic Lancashire (the cultural province) we've explored in this book, but could include a lot of it, with potential for taking in more. The key issue is 'what would it do' and 'how would it be democratically accountable'?

A democratic Lancastria

The current mayoral combined authority for Greater Manchester has several achievements to its credit and has aspirations to do more under its dynamic mayor, Andy Burnham. Yet the fundamental problem of accountability remains. The mayor is elected every four years and s/he has no team of fellow elected representatives to feed into the decision-making process and call the mayor to account.

The nearest model we have in England to the 'combined authority' is London, where the powerful mayor is scrutinised by the Greater London Assembly, which is elected on a proportional basis. It could be more powerful but at least it's an improvement on what we have. The devolved governments of Scotland, Wales and Northern Ireland have what amounts to classic 'regional' government, with assemblies elected by proportional representation and an accountable executive overseeing a civil service. Scotland is almost exactly the same population size as Yorkshire at about five and a half million, but with much greater powers. The new 'Lancastria' would have over four million, not including Merseyside or 'North of the Sands'.

Should there be an elected mayor for a new Lancastria region? Or would it be a distraction from an effective regional democracy? If there was a Lancastrian regional government, elected by a proportional voting system, the elected body should appoint its leader, and leave mayors to be ceremonial figures at the local level.

A red rose co-operative commonwealth?

What would a Lancastrian regional government do? It must be about addressing inequality, jobs, transport, the environment, health, education and having a thriving and diverse cultural sector. Allen Clarke's vision in 1895, below, of locally based and socially owned units of production make sense in a modern digital age, co-operating as equals with partners across the globe. A co-operative commonwealth of Lancastria.

His idea of a co-operative commonwealth could certainly work at a Lancashire level; after all, it's where co-operation began. Allen Clarke, with Solomon Partington, Sarah Reddish and Samuel Compston looking over his shoulder, would have said, "What are you waiting for?"

And we can't afford to wait. The coronavirus pandemic has focused people's minds on the dysfunctional way we have lived our lives. An even bigger threat is climate change which requires re-thinking every aspect of how we live, travel, work and play. Now is the time to create Allen Clarke's vision of a Lancashire Co-operative Commonwealth that can, in the words of Clarke's heroine in *A Daughter of the Factory*, Rose Hilton—get agate with the job of "washing the smoky dust off the petals of the red rose".[8]

Permit me one final quote from that pre-eminent Lancastrian, Allen Clarke. In 1895 he wrote:

> I would like to see Lancashire a cluster of small villages and towns, each fixed solid on its own agricultural base, doing its own spinning and weaving; with its theatre, gymnasium, schools, libraries, baths and all things necessary for body and soul. Supposing the energy, time and talent that have been given to manufacture and manufacturing inventions had been given to agriculture and agricultural inventions, would not there have been as wonderful results in food production as there have been in cotton goods production?[9]

Utopian? Perhaps, but we need our utopian visions. There was an element of realism there too. He recognised that capitalism had unleashed enormously powerful productive forces, but not necessarily with the best results. Food production has become the most pressing issue in many parts of the world and there is every likelihood that it will become so in Britain. We need to get much better at feeding ourselves; step forward the incredible, edible Lancastria. Clarke's vision is a localist one that has a strong cultural underpinning.

Humanity has the resources and skills to create a better world, for everyone. The consequences of not trying are worsening climate change and all that follows from it. Clarke looked forward to a Lancashire that was a greener, more self-sufficient place—within a co-operative rather than a capitalist system. Now, as we emerge from the pandemic, is the right time to think differently about the world we live in.

Lancashire has yet to find a new role that can build on its past achievements, without just being a dull collection of retail parks, charity shops and sprawling suburbia, or indeed a heritage theme park.

Most of the surviving Lancashire mills, with the exception of Manchester's Ancoats, don't have the inspiring mix of creative industries, office space and living accommodation that has been achieved with some of the mills in Yorkshire. At Saltaire, Salt's Mill is perhaps the finest example, though rivalled by the Dean Clough Mills in Halifax. More should be done to protect our own mills and find good uses for them. Why should Yorkshire have all the fun?

Allen Clarke would have loved the idea of putting the mill buildings to better use—as places to live, but also as office and art space, recreational centres and performance areas. How about mill roof gardens? There would be no shortage of space, with room to grow fruit and veg.

We need to build inspirational buildings that can take their place alongside the grand architecture bequeathed us by past generations. We need a vision, at least as radical as that of T.H. Mawson, of what our towns and cities should look like in the next 20 years, not what developers think is 'good enough' for us and makes the quickest return for them.

Alongside a vibrant urban society, economy and culture, we need to make the best of our countryside, the 'green lungs' that make Lancashire so special. The events of 1896, when thousands of Lancashire people fought to protect their countryside from the encroachments of landlords, demonstrated that people's love of their countryside isn't new, nor an exclusively middle-class preserve.

Places like Rivington, Pendle and Holcombe can be thronged with cars and motorbikes at weekends. At the same time, many stations that gave walkers access to the countryside have closed. Stations that Clarke used and wrote about—Chatburn in the Ribble Valley,

Helmshore, Waterfoot, Turton and Edgworth have gone. They should come back. Scores of bus services that once gave access to surrounding villages have either disappeared or are so infrequent as to be unusable. Never mind HS2, let's rebuild a world-class local transport network. For a fraction of the cost of the high-speed white elephant, we could have a network of modern, zero-emission trams and buses serving town and country, feeding into a core rail network.

Why not copy the example of some of the national parks in the United States, which prohibit car access to the most sensitive areas? If you get there by car, leave it in a 'parking lot' and either walk, get on a local bus or hire a bike. It could work in some of our national parks and popular visitor locations such as Rivington. The exciting plans for a 'South Pennines' regional park should include sensitive measures to restrict visitors' car access and promote use of public transport, cycling and walking.

Building a new Lancashire …

Let's not be too backward-looking; it's become a Lancashire trait these days. We should spend more time trying to imagine what a *new* Lancashire could look like. We have to understand and celebrate our past, but be careful about romanticising it, with unrealistic—and undesirable—returns to a mythical golden age. The daily, lifelong reality for many Lancastrians up to (at least) the 1940s was poverty, child labour and an early death from ill health caused by pollution and appalling working conditions. As Sophia Gaston wrote:

> Peddlers of nostalgic narratives emphasise the threat from a dismantling of the status quo and portray social change as a zero-sum redistribution of power. They too often fail to see that for many, particularly women and minority groups, the elevation of the past denies the hard-won rights, representation and agency of the present … Modern Britain needs a balance between openness and security, modernity and tradition, evolution and conservation … It's time for politics to leave nostalgia in the past and listen to the British people, most of whom find no discord in cherishing our heritage while looking with curiosity and ambition to the future.[10]

Her point is well made, though a feature of much contemporary thinking neglects the opportunity to imagine what sort of future we want to create, with the result that we become slaves to whatever is foisted on us.[11]

Sarah Gaston was referring to Britain, but her points apply equally well on a more regional or local level. Allen Clarke, of whom we have seen quite a lot in this book, wrote of Blackpool, and Lancashire, shortly before his death in 1935, that "it's a vastly changed world altogether ... and despite those old fogics, of both sexes, who are always telling the young generation that there were no times like their times, I add challengingly that it is a better world, a cleaner world and a pleasanter world in almost every way..."[12]

Lancashire and its people have much to look forward to if they 'got agate'. We do not have to accept everything that is thrown at us in the interest of 'efficiency' and 'modernity'; combining a respect for heritage and tradition with imagining and creating a new region is long overdue. Lancashire is an old county and it will take longer than fifty years to eradicate centuries of Lancashire identity. Let's look forward to a new Lancastria. Chuck the flat cap away (or keep it for when it rains).

NOTES

INTRODUCTION

1. Duxbury, Stephen, *The Brief History of Lancashire*, Stroud, The History Press, 2011, and for a more in-depth account which has never been surpassed see Walton, John K., *Lancashire: A Social History 1558–1939*, Manchester University Press, 1987.
2. Axon, Ernest, *Bygone Lancashire*, Brooke and Chrystal, Manchester, 1892, p. 9.
3. *Royal Commission on Local Government (The Redcliffe-Maud Report)* was published in June 1969 and accepted by the then Labour Government. However, the incoming Conservative Government shelved the report and a revised version of the proposals was implemented in 1974 following the passing of the 1972 Local Government Act.
4. See Fox, Kate, *Where There's Muck There's Bras: Lost Stories of the Amazing Women of the North*, Harper North, Manchester, 2022.
5. Williams, Raymond, *The Long Revolution*, Penguin Books, Harmondsworth, 1961, pp. 64–88.
6. Axon, op. cit. 'Preface'.

1. THE SHAPE OF LANCASHIRE

1. 'Gradely' is a Lancashire term for all that is good, proper and right. There is an old joke about a southerner coming to Lancashire and hearing the word used—but being unable to find it in his dictionary. "That's because," he was told, "it's not a gradely dictionary!"
2. Haslam, James, 'Lancashire Life. The Dialects and other Social Features', *The Record*, June 1936.
3. Ibid.
4. Ibid.
5. The southernmost equivalent, near Hale on the Mersey Estuary, has no monument nor even a notice to mark the spot.
6. Barnes, F., *Barrow and District*, Barrow-in-Furness Corporation, 1968 (2nd ed.) p. 86.

7. Ibid. pp. 24–6, also *Furness Abbey and Piel Castle*, historical notes by Jason Wood, English Heritage, London, 1998.

8. See Marshall, J.D., *Furness and the Industrial Revolution*, Barrow-in-Furness Library and Museum Committee, Barrow, 1958, esp. pp. 205–9.

9. Barnes, op. cit., pp. 109–10.

10. The classic history is McGowan-Gradon, W., *The Furness Railway: Its Rise and Development 1846–1923*, Altrincham, 1946.

11. Quayle, Howard, *Furness Railway: A View from the Past*, Ian Allan, Shepperton, 2000, is a well-illustrated account.

12. See Mowat, Jack and Power, Albert, *Our Struggle for Socialism in Barrow: Fifty Years Anniversary, Labour Party*, Barrow-in-Furness, 1949.

13. See White, Andrew, *Crossing the Sands of Morecambe Bay—Beauty, Drama and Tragedy*, Scriptorium Publications, Hornby, 2020. Andrew gives a list of known drownings since 1576 including the tragic deaths of up to twenty-four Chinese cocklers in February 2004.

14. Guide Over Sands Trust website https://www.guideoversands.co.uk/guides/ and see also Sutton, Lindsay, *Sands of Time: following in the footsteps of Cedric Robinson on Morecambe Bay*, Great Northern Books, 2021.

15. Bairstow, Martin, *Railways in the Lake District*, Halifax, 1995; also Cumbrian Railways Association, *The Coniston Branch*.

16. Hilton, Tim, *John Ruskin: The Later Years*, Yale University Press, 2000, pp. 559–60.

17. See https://www.cartmelagriculturalsociety.org.uk/history/

18. See *Grange and Cartmel: A Practical Guide for Visitors*, Dalesman Books, Clapham, 1980. For a more detailed history of the area see Dickinson, J.C., *The Land of Cartmel: a History*, Titus Wilson, Kendal, 1980.

19. 'Mr. Peter Cross remembering Joe Brown, Cark Station Master', Latter, Pam (ed.) *Looking Back: recollections of life in Cark, Flookburgh and District*, Kendal, 2001.

20. Ayre, Rev. Canon L.R., *Guide to Ulverston and Places of Interest in the Lake Land District*, Jas. Atkinson, Ulverston, 1904, p. 5.

21. See Chapter 2.

22. Bairstow, Martin, *Railways in the Lake Counties*, Pudsey, 2019.

23. Hewitson, Anthony, *Northward* was re-published in facsimile form by Landy Publishing in 1993 and 2003.

24. Waugh, Edwin, *Home Life of the Lancashire Factory Folk During the Cotton Famine*, first published serially in the *Manchester Examiner and Times*, later in book form.

25. Parker, N., *The Preston and Longridge Railway*, Oakwood Library of Railway History No. 30, Lingfield: Oakwood Press, 1972. See Chapter 5 for the fascinating branch line to the Whittingham Mental Hospital.

26. See Kean, Hilda, 'Public History and the Past: Slavery Memorial in Lancaster' in *North West Labour History Journal*, no. 45, 2020–1.

27. See Chapter 7 for the internecine rivalry between the city's two main employers.

28. Bairstow, Martin, *The 'Little' North Western Railway*, Pudsey, 2008.

29. Clarke, Allen, *The Story of Blackpool*, Blackpool, 1923, pp. 6–7.

30. Walton, John K., *The Blackpool Landlady*, Manchester University Press, 1978.

31. Ibid.

32. Clarke, Allen, *Windmill Land*, J.M. Dent and Sons, London 1916. Two years later (1917/18) he published a sequel, *More Windmill Land*.

33. Clarke, *Windmill Land*, op. cit. p. 80.

34. https://www.southportflowershow.co.uk/about-us.html

35. 'The Childe of Hale' was John Middleton (1578–1623) who grew to the improbable height of 9' 3" and had to sleep with his feet outside the cottage window.

36. See Chapter 10.

37. See Chapter 12.

38. See Heys, Harold, *Darreners*, Darwen, 2022. See also Chapter 8.

39. See Clarke, Stephen, *Clitheroe in Its Railway Days*, J. Robinson, Clitheroe, 1900.

40. *The Record*, December 1962, p. 10.

41. See Chapter 2 on the twentieth-century vision for a new Accrington, *Industry and Prudence*, and Chapter 6 on the library.

42. The history of Burnley has been well told in Bennett, W., *The History of Burnley*, four vols, Burnley Corporation, 1951. See also *Burnley: A Town Amidst the Pennines*, Lancashire County Council, 1982.

43. See Hill, Jeffrey, *Nelson: Politics, Economy, Community*, Keele University Press, Edinburgh, 1997.

44. See Chapter 8.

45. For an entertaining romp around the history of the town see Wightman, Peter, *Bonnie Colne*, Hendon Publishing, Nelson, 1976.

46. See Butterworth, Tim, 'Todmorden and the County Boundary', *The Lancastrian*, Spring 2020.

47. See Chapter 2.

48. Some readers may object! But east Lancashire never had buildings of such towering size as those of Oldham and Bolton's spinning mills.

49. Clarke, Allen, 'The Clegg Hall Boggart' in *Teddy Ashton's Lancashire Annual*, Blackpool, 1921. The story of 'The Battle of Boggart Hole Clough' is told in Chapter 15; see also for further information on Ernest Jones and the Chartist movement.

50. See Jones, Adrian ('Jones The Planner') and Matthews, Chris, *Towns in Britain*, Five Leaves, Nottingham, 2014, pp. 275–83.

51. See Chapter 12.

52. Fitton edited the local satirical dialect paper *The Crompton Chanticleer*.

53. There is a *Royton Town Centre Trail* published by Oldham Council and Royton Local History Society.

54. See Chapter 6 for the library and Chapter 8 for Queen's Park and its opening.

55. Ibid.

56. I could be wrong on this; the clever folk at the Bury Black Pudding Co. are working on it.

57. See Chapter 2 for short biography of Sixsmith.

58. See Chapters 14 and 15.

59. See Chapter 3.

60. O'Connor, Denis, *Barrow Bridge, Bolton, Lancashire: a model industrial community of the nineteenth century*, Bolton, 1972.

61. See Chapter 8.

62. See Chapter 5 on miners' housing.

63. Anderson, Donald and France, A.A., *Wigan Coal and Iron*, Smith's Books, Wigan, 1994.

64. See George, David, 'The Playhouse at Prescot and the 1592–94 Plague' in Dutton, R., Findlay, A. and Wilson R. (eds) *Region, Religion and Patronage: Lancastrian Shakespeare*, Manchester University Press, 2003. See Chapter 12.

65. See Diggle, George E., *A History of Widnes*, Corporation of Widnes, 1961.

66. Hadfield, Dave, *Up and Over: A Trek Through Rugby League Land*, Mainstream Publishing, Edinburgh, 2005, p. 158.

67. See Lane, Tony, *Liverpool: City of the Sea*, Liverpool University Press, 1997; also Hikins, H. (ed.) *Building the Union: Studies on the Growth of the Workers' Movement, Merseyside, 1756–1967*, Toulouse Press, Liverpool, 1973.

68. See Chapters 12 and 13.

69. See Chapter 13.

70. Wray, Tom, *Manchester Victoria Railway Station*, Peter Taylor Publications, Manchester, 2005.

71. See King, Ray, *Detonation: Rebirth of a City*, Clear Publications, Warrington, 2006.

72. Hampson, Charles P., *Salford Through the Ages*, Salford, 1930, p. 201.

73. See Hayes, Geoffrey, *Collieries in the Manchester Coalfields*, De Archaeologische Pers, Eindhoven, n.d. c 1970, also Davies, Andrew, *Coalmining in Lancashire and Cheshire*, Amberley Publishing, Sutton, 2010.

74. Hampson op. cit. pp. 237–8.

75. It became Pilkington's Royal Lancastrian Pottery and Tiles Co. in 1913 when King George V visited Lancashire as a guest of the Earl of Derby.

2. SHAPING LANCASHIRE

1. Haslam, James, 'Lancashire Life—The Dialect and other Social Features', *The Record*, June 1936.
2. CPRE, *Buildings in Lancashire*, 1938.
3. Sixsmith, Charles, 'Edward As I Knew Him' in Beith G. (ed.) *Edward Carpenter—in Appreciation*, George Allen and Unwin, London, 1931.
4. I am grateful to Barry Clark for his information on Sixsmith's involvement with the DIA and Red Rose Guild.
5. There are always exceptions to the rule and Girouard, Marc, *The English Town*, Guild Publishing, 1990, is one. Also Champness, Alan, *Lancashire's Architectural Heritage*, Preston, 1988, devotes a chapter to 'The Architecture of the Industrial Revolution'.
6. See Williams, Mike, with Farnie, D.A., *Cotton Mills in Greater Manchester*, Lancaster, 1992.
7. See Holden, Roger N., *Stott and Sons: Architects of the Lancashire Cotton Mill*, Lancaster, 1998.
8. See Salveson, Paul, *With Walt Whitman in Bolton*, Bolton 2019, also the recently acquired collection of Bradshaw Gass and Hope in Bolton Museum and Archives. See also Chapter 3 for the Bolton Whitman group.
9. See Fowler, Alan, and Wyke, Terry, 'Buildings in the Landscape', in Filson, J. (ed.) *King Cotton: A Tribute to Douglas A. Farnie*, Chetham Society, Lancaster 2009.
10. Ibid. p. 313.
11. See Price, James, *Sharpe, Paley and Austin: a Lancaster Architectural Practice 1836–1942*, Centre for North-West Regional Studies, Lancaster, 1998. The Grange Hotel was designed by E.G. Paley.
12. Ibid. p. 66.
13. Wood was recently the subject of a documentary by Middleton filmmaker Anthony Dolan. *Edgar Wood: The Painted Veil* (2018) documents his life and later years in Italy.
14. Parry, Keith, *Trans-Pennine Heritage: Hills, People and Transport*, David and Charles, Newton Abbot, 1981, p. 139.
15. Karol, Eitan, *Charles Holden: Architect*, Shaun Tyas, Donnington, 2007, p. 51.
16. Ibid. p. 179.
17. 'If Whitman had been an Architect', *Architectural Review*, June 1905.
18. Karol, op. cit. p. 472.
19. Lewis, Brian, *'So Clean' Lord Leverhulme, soap and civilization*, Manchester University Press, Manchester, 2008, p. 138. See pages 169–70 for short biography of Lever.

20. See Chapter 3.
21. Jacobs, Jane, *The Death and Life of American Cities*, Vintage Books, New York, 1992, p. 17.
22. Lewis, Brian, *'So Clean' Lord Leverhulme, soap and civilization*, Manchester University Press, Manchester, 2008, p. 137. See also Chapter 3 for his links with the University of Liverpool.
23. Howard, Ebenezer, *Garden Cities of Tomorrow: a peaceful path to real reform*, Swan Sonnenschein, London, 1898.
24. 'Beautiful Oldham! Why Not?' *Oldham Chronicle*, 11 December 1901.
25. Higgs, Mary, *Beautiful Oldham 1904–5, Annual Report*, p. 3. A response from the Lancashire and Yorkshire Railway to plant on some spare railway land produced a positive response, though the London and North Western was less positive.
26. Ibid. p. 14.
27. *The Record*, June 1937, p. 12.
28. Lees, Marjory, 'Mary Higgs M.A., O.B.E.—An Appreciation', *The Record*, June 1937, pp. 11–12.
29. Ibid.
30. In Talbot, C.M., *The Amazing Mary Higgs*, OWC Publishing, Oldham, 2011, p. 186.
31. Ibid. p. 137.
32. 'One Hundred Years of Life in the Suburb', *Oldham Chronicle*, 29 June 2009.
33. Quoted in *The Record*, March 1932, p. 14.
34. *The Dawn*, December 1908, vol. VIII no. 12. This was the final issue.
35. Ibid. p. 153. The author was presumably referring to *The Football Record* and its status as a free newspaper.
36. The title may in turn have inspired Thomas Mawson's book *Bolton As It Is and As It Might Be*, published in 1916.
37. Ibid. p. 156.
38. Ibid. p. 156.
39. Woodcock, W.H., *The Dawn*, December 1908, op. cit. p. 138.
40. Ibid. pp. 146–7.
41. Thompson, Laurence, *The Enthusiasts: A Biography of John and Katharine Bruce Glasier*, Gollancz, London, 1971, p. 76.
42. Clarke, Allen, *Can We Get Back to the Land?*, Bolton, 1904.
43. *Teddy Ashton's Northern Weekly*, 21 May 1904.
44. Salveson, Paul, 'Getting Back to the Land: The Daisy Colony Experiment', in *Labour's Turning Point in the North West 1890–1914*, North West Labour History Society, Southport, 1984, p. 36.
45. Coates, Chris, *Utopia Britannica vol. 1 British Utopian Experiments 1325 to 1945*, Diggers and Dreamers, London, 2001, is a good survey and complements Gillian Darley's *Villages of Vision*.

46. Doyle, Peter, *Mitres and Missions in Lancashire: The Roman Catholic Diocese of Liverpool 1850–2020*, Bluecoat Press, Liverpool, 2005, p. 282.

47. Op. cit. p. 283.

48. Cocker, W.W., Foreword to *Industry and Prudence: A Plan for Accrington*, Accrington Borough Council, 1950, p. xii.

49. Ibid. p. 157.

50. Ibid. p. 158.

51. Sixsmith, Charles, Foreword to *An Advisory Plan*, South Lancashire and North Cheshire Advisory Planning Committee, Manchester, 1947, p. v.

52. Ibid. pp. vii–viii.

53. Ibid. p. 7.

54. Ibid. p. 80.

55. Bowker, B., *Lancashire Under the Hammer*, Leonard and Virginia Woolf at The Hogarth Press, London, 1928.

56. Parry, Keith, *Trans-Pennine Heritage*, David and Charles, Newton Abbot, 1981, p. 188.

57. Ibid. p. 188.

58. Cumbria itself has now been split, with two unitary authorities created in 2022 to form 'Cumberland' and 'Westmorland and Furness'. The changes come into effect in 2023.

59. The Department for the Environment confirmed this position on 3 September 1991. See Friends of Real Lancashire leaflet, 2022. They point out that "no legislation has ever altered the boundaries of the County Palatine."

60. Goodhart, David, *The Road to Somewhere: The Populist Revolt and the Future of Politics*, Hurst, London, 2017.

61. Ibid. p. 3.

62. 'Decentralism and the Politics of Place' first published in *Society and Space*, vol. 2, 1984 and re-printed in Williams, Raymond, *Resources of Hope*, Verso, 1989.

63. Ibid. p. 3.

64. Speakman, Colin, *Yorkshire: Ancient Nation, Future Province*, Gritstone Publishing, Hebden Bridge, 2021, p. 35.

3. A LANCASHIRE SENSIBILITY

1. Tomlinson, George, Foreword to *The Journal of the Lancashire Dialect Society*, no. 1, December 1951. Tomlinson came from Rishton and spent his early years as a half-timer in the local mills. He was MP for the Farnworth constituency between 1938 and 1952. See Blackburn, Fred, *George Tomlinson*, Heinemann, London, 1954.

2. Open-air speech at Waugh's Well, 23 June 1917, reported in *The Record*, August 1917, p. 3. See brief biography in Chapter 14.

3. Reported in *The Record*, September 1947, p. 15.

4. In *The Record*, February 1960, p. 19.

5. The original report was in *The Ashton-under-Lyne Reporter* of 7 March 1868 and was reproduced in *The Record* in June 1935.

6. *Rochdale Observer*, 15 March 1890. See 'Defending Dialect' in Salveson, Paul, PhD thesis, 'Region, Class Culture: Lancashire Dialect Literature 1746–1935', University of Salford, 1993.

7. Partington, Solomon, *Romance of the Dialect*, Middleton, 1920, p. vii. Fred Moorman was a professor at the University of Leeds and an active member of the Yorkshire Dialect Society. Partington also self-published *The Future of Old English Words* in 1917, dedicating the book to 'the memory of The Old Lancashire Lion' (Sam Bamford) and to his and the author's native town of Middleton.

8. *The Record*, December 1938, p. 7. Thompson's lecture was also published in *The Manchester Guardian*.

9. *The Record*, March 1940, p. 15.

10. Reported in *The Record*, June 1929.

11. Reported in *The Record*, March 1932, pp. 12–13.

12. Allen Clarke, 'In Defence of the Dialect', in *The Record*, June 1929.

13. Reported in *The Record*, September 1933, pp. 4–7.

14. 'In Defence of the Dialect', *The Record*, June 1929.

15. Report in *The Record*, September 1944, p. 15.

16. *The Record*, June 1961, pp. 3–4.

17. Ibid.

18. Report in *The Record*, September 1966, p. 6. See also Chapter 12 and Herbert Kirtlan's critique of dialect writing.

19. Gramsci, Antonio, 'The Formation of the Intellectuals' in *Selections from the Prison Notebooks*, eds. Hoare, Quentin and Nowell-Smith, Geoffrey, Lawrence and Wishart, London, 1971.

20. Angus-Butterworth, L.M., 'John Dalton and the Manchester Literary and Philosophical Society' *The Record*, December 1931.

21. Wilson, Arline, 'Early Learned Societies 1790–1850', in *A Cultural History of Liverpool*, Historic Society of Lancashire and Cheshire, paper read on 14 May 1998.

22. Ibid.

23. Ibid.

24. See Chapter 11.

25. Axon, William.E.A., *Echoes of Old Lancashire*, Andrews, London, 1899 p. 169.

26. Walter Butterworth, 'Some Lancashire Authors and Illustrators', *The Record*, March 1931.

27. Manchester Literary Club archives M524/11/1/275.

28. See Archer, John H.H., *Art and Architecture in Victorian Manchester*.

29. L.M. Angus-Butterworth, 'The Life and Writings of Dr. Wm. Ed. Armitage Axon, Ma.A., LL.D., F.R.S.L., *The Record*, June 1954, pp. 8–9.

30. Abram, William Alexander, *Blackburn Characters of a Past Generation*, Blackburn, 1894.

31. Houlding, Henry, *Poems: Rhymes and Dreams: Legends of Pendle Forest, and Other Poems*, Burnley, 1895.

32. For an outline history of the society see https://www.hslc.org.uk/about-us/history/

33. *The Record*, March. Membership had dropped to 187 by 1959.

34. Pearce, A.H., 'The Rise and Progress of the LAA', *The Record*, June 1930, pp. 8–11.

35. Ibid.

36. *The Record*, August 1918, p. 15, and *The Record*, September 1926, p. 15.

37. Swann, J.R., *Lancashire Authors*, St Ann's-on-the-Sea, 1924, p. 171.

38. In 'Diary of Members' Activities', *The Record*, February 1953, p. 15. The report noted that "she is still very much in demand in feminine circles, and gives great service in connection with various churches".

39. Report in *The Record*, December 1992, by LAA librarian Frank Sunderland. See also George W. White, 'The Lancashire Dialect Society 1951–1992' in *The Record*, November 1993.

40. *Radcliffe Diamond Jubilee Exhibition*, Radcliffe, T.H. Hayhurst, 1897.

41. *East Lancashire Review* was edited by Thomas H. Hayhurst and was printed and published at the Steam Printing and Publishing Works, Radcliffe.

42. *The Record*, May 1916, p. 8.

43. Ibid.

44. Obituary of J.H.H. Smith in *The Record*, September 1931.

45. *Fifty Years 1882–1932 The Darwen Literary Society*, Darwen Literary Society, 1933.

46. Ibid. p. 10.

47. See Chapter 15.

48. Ibid. p. 13.

49. See Salveson, Paul, *With Walt Whitman in Bolton: spirituality, sex and socialism in a Northern Mill Town*, Lancashire Loominary, Bolton, 2019. See Chapter 2.

50. Clarke, Allen, *Moorlands and Memories*, 3rd ed., Blackpool, 1924, pp. 62–3.

51. See Chapter 3 for short biography.

52. Dixon, Wentworth, *An Old Friend*—Address to Men's Class, Bank Street School, 7 February 1926.

53. Wild, Fred, *Sketch of Life of J.W. Wallace*, typescript in Bolton Central Library.

54. See Chapter 2 for short biography.
55. *The Guardian*, 19 June 2009.
56. Originally published in *The Accrington Observer and Times*, 23 June 1941, summarised in *The Record*, September 1941, pp. 4–5.
57. Newbigging, Thomas, 'Inaugural Address as President of the Gas Institute, delivered at the twenty-second Annual Meeting, held in the Memorial Hall, Manchester, June 9th 1885', in *Speeches and Addresses, Political, Social, Literary*, John Heywood, Manchester, 1887.
58. Brindley, W.H. (ed.) *The Soul of Manchester*, Manchester University Press, 1929.
59. Grindon, Leo, 'Horsefield's Predecessors and Companions' in *Country Rambles and Manchester Walks and Wild Flowers*, 2nd ed. Manchester, 1882 (first published *Manchester Weekly Times*, 10 July 10 1858), pp. 194–5.
60. Bamford, Samuel, *Walks in South Lancashire*, Blackley, 1844, pp. 13–14.
61. See Davies, Bob, *The Luddites of Westhoughton*, Communist Party History Group, Manchester, 1971.
62. Weaver, Michael, 'Michael's Story' in *Voices*, Manchester, c.1981.
63. Featured in Salveson, Paul, *The People's Monuments*, Workers Educational Association, Manchester, 1983.
64. Clarke Allen, *The Red Flag: A Tale of the People's Woe*, Twentieth Century Press, London, 1908.
65. Much as I like a nice 'prato' pie, with red cabbage and mushy peas, I have to confess.
66. See Chapter 11. Cockburn, Ruth (ed.) *Miss Nobodies: A Book Celebrating the Great Women of Great Harwood and Lancashire*, Spot on Lancashire, Blackburn, 2021.
67. 13 October 2019.
68. The policy has now reversed back in support of fracking, so perhaps the Nanas will be back in action.
69. Personal communication with author, 26 November 2022. Councillor McKeon sits on Horwich Town Council.
70. Mitchell, W.R. ('Bill'), 'This Lancashire', *Lancashire Pride*, Dalesman Publishing Co., Clapham, 1981, p. 5.

4. FEEDING LANCASHIRE

1. Fort, Matthew, *Paul Heathcote's Rhubarb and Black Pudding*, Fourth Estate, London, 1998, p. 13.
2. Ibid. p. 11.
3. Bridge, Tom, *The History of English Cookery*, Printwise Publications, Bury, 1992.
4. Houlihan, Marjory, *A Most Excellent Dish: Tales of the Lancashire Tripe Trade*, Neil Richardson, Bolton 1988, p. 5.

5. Ibid. p. 10.
6. Clarke, Allen, *Teddy Ashton's Northern Weekly*, 17 August 1901.
7. Clarke, Allen, 'The Prince and the "Prato" Cake', *Teddy Ashton's Lancashire Annual*, 1914, pp. 13–15.
8. See Walton, J.K., *Fish and Chips and the British Working Class, 1870–1940*, Leicester University Press, 1992.
9. https://ivu.org/history/england19a/salford.html
10. Abbott, C.C., *A Legacy of Health*, Leigh, 1934, p. 10.
11. Clarke, Allen, *The Eternal Question*, London, 1919, p. 224.
12. Clarke, Allen, *Effects of the Factory System*, London, 1899, p. 174.
13. Lancashire County Council website: https://www.lancashire.gov.uk/media/896995/sector-a-agriculture-forestry-and-fishing.pdf
14. See Chapters 1 and 2.
15. Pearce, John, *The Life and Teachings of Joseph Livesey comprising his Autobiography with an Introductory Review of his Labours as Reformer and Teacher*, Manchester and Preston, 1885, p. lxxiii.
16. See Chapter 15.

5. LIVING IN LANCASHIRE

1. Clarke, Allen, *Effects of the Factory System*, Grant Richards, London, 1899, p. 42.
2. Ibid. p. 53.
3. 'Biography of Richard Lawrence Hool', introduction to Hool, R.L., *Common Plants and Their Uses in Medicine*, Lancashire Branch of the National Association of Medical Herbalists, Southport, 1922, p. 1.
4. See Moffitt, Derek, 'Stanley Worthington, Medical Herbalist', in Salveson, P. and Gleeson, M. (eds) *Lancashire Scrapbook*, Bolton, 1986.
5. Hool, Richard Lawrence, *British Wild Herbs* and *Common Plants and Their Uses in Medicine*, W.H. Webb, Southport, 1924.
6. Note pasted into Abbott, C.C., *Hocus Pocus?*, Leigh, 1933, dated 'November 1958'. Also Salveson, Paul, 'Before the NHS, Bolton relied on its community doctors', in *Bolton News*, 27 February 2021.
7. Broderick, Jack, 'The Strange Story of the Whitworth Doctors', *Rossendale Free Press*, 15 August 1970.
8. Robertson, William, *Rochdale and the Vale of Whitworth*, Rochdale, 1897, p. 310.
9. Diaries of Dr John Johnston, Bolton Local Studies.
10. Clarke, Allen, *Moorlands and Memories*, Bolton, 1920, p. 279.
11. Johnston refers to it as "a society consisting mainly of the (so-called) upper class and of which our F.R.C. Hutton is President". *Diaries*, 28 October 1891.

12. Johnston, John, *Musa Medica*, Bolton, 1897.

13. 'Taylor Family of Whitworth', Manchester Medical Collection, University of Manchester Library ref. GB 133 MMC/2/Taylor.

14. http://www.whittinghamhospital.co.uk/history/

15. See Hindle, David, *Victorian Preston and the Whittingham Hospital Railway*, Amberley, Stroud, 2012.

16. Cornwell, R.B., *History of the Calderstones Railway, 1907–1953*, 2010.

17. See Timmins, J.G., *Handloom Weavers' Cottages in Central Lancashire*, Lancaster, 1977.

18. Walton, John K., *Lancashire: A Social History 1558–1939*, Manchester University Press, 1987, p. 123.

19. See Darnley, Gillian, *Villages of Vision*, Five Leaves Publications, Nottingham, 2007.

20. https://manchestervictorianarchitects.org.uk/buildings/colliery-village-howe-bridge-atherton. Fletcher, Burrows was one of the few private coal mining companies to introduce pit-head baths, prior to nationalisation in 1947 when it was an early priority of the National Coal Board.

21. https://www.wythenshaweafc.com/a/wythenshawe-garden-city-46533.html

22. Quoted in Manchester Women's History Group, 'Ideology in Bricks and Mortar: Women's Housing in Manchester Between the Wars', in *North West Labour History*, no. 12, 1987, pp. 30–1.

23. Ibid. pp. 36–7.

24. See Chapter 14 for short biography of Wilcockson, also Chapter 1 for more references.

25. 'Town Builders of Today' in *Borough of Farnworth Charter of Incorporation 1939*, Borough of Farnworth, 1939, p. 27.

26. Ibid. p. 24.

27. *Souvenir Handbook: Jubilee of the Incorporation of the Borough*, Borough of Nelson, 1946, pp. 53–4.

6. EDUCATING LANCASHIRE

1. John Walton and Patrick Joyce have both debunked the idea that the nineteenth-century working-class of Lancashire were avid church-goers.

2. Clarke, Allen, *Moorlands and Memories*, Bolton, 1920, p. 13.

3. National Union of Teachers, *Morecambe, Lancaster & District: Souvenir of the Conference of the National Union of Teachers, Easter 1909*, Oxford University Press, 1909.

4. French, William, 'Education in Lancaster' in National Union of Teachers, *Morecambe Lancaster and District: Souvenir of the Conference of the National Union of Teachers, Easter 1909*, Oxford 1909

5. *The Liverpool Post*, 26 October 2009. See also Sekers, David, *A Lady of Cotton: Hannah Greg, Mistress of Quarry Bank Mill*, The History Press, Leicester, 2013.

6. *Lancashire Education*, Lancashire County, Preston, 1970.

7. Roderick, G.W., and Stephens, M.D., 'The Origins and Development of Adult Education in Lancashire 1870–1970' in *Lancashire Education*, published by Lancashire County Council, 1970.

8. Hudson, J.W., *The History of Adult Education*, Longmans, 1851. See also Tylecote, Mabel, *The Mechanics' Institutes of Lancashire and Yorkshire Before 1851*, University Press, Manchester, 1957.

9. Cowan, I.R., 'Mechanics' Institutes and Science and Art Classes in Salford in the 19th Century', *The Vocational Aspect*, Autumn 1968, Volume XX No. 47.

10. See Chapter 7 on Lancaster and the Storeys.

11. Roderick and Smith op. cit. p. 45.

12. See Chapter 11 for more on the co-operative movement and its libraries.

13. See Bateson, Hartley, *A Centenary History of Oldham*, Oldham County Borough Council, 1949.

14. See Smith, Stephen Craig, 'Wigan's Mining and Mechanical School' in *PastForward* issue no. 87 April/July 2021.

15. Anderson, Donald, and France, A.A., *Wigan Coal and Iron*, Smith's Books, Wigan, 1994.

16. *Industrial Lancashire*, H. Bannerman and Sons, Manchester, 1897. The author was John Mortimer, Chief Cashier at the company whose head-quarters was at 33 York Street, Manchester.

17. *A Short History of the Bolton College of Art and Design 1876–1976*, Bolton, 1976. Pupil teachers were common in Lancashire during this period, combining a teaching role with pursuing an education.

18. Ibid. p. 154.

19. *James Hargreaves Morton 1881–1918*, Darwen Library, 1981.

20. Weiss, F.E., 'The University of Manchester' in Brindley, W.H. (ed.) *The Soul of Manchester*, Manchester University Press, 1929.

21. Brazendale, David, *Lancashire's Historic Halls*, Carnegie, Lancaster 1994, esp. Chapter on 'Towneley Hall and the Lancashire Renaissance'.

22. See Muir, T.E., *Stonyhurst*, St Omers Press, Cirencester, 2006.

23. Weiss, op. cit. p. 63.

24. Ibid. p. 66.

25. See Macqueen, Adam, *The King of Sunlight*, Corgi Books, London, 2005, for the story of the libel case and Lever's gift to the university. See Chapter 2 for Lever's wider interests in town planning and civic design.

26. See Holmes, Gerard, *The Idiot Teacher*, Faber, London, 1952.

27. Ibid. p. 21.
28. *Farnworth Observer*, 25 June 1937.
29. Holmes, op. cit. pp. 188–91
30. Local government was given powers to levy a charge on the rates to support free libraries as early as 1850.
31. Sparke, Archibald, *Bibliographia Boltoniensis: being a bibliography, with biographical details of Bolton authors, and the books written by them from 1550 to 1912*, University Press, Manchester, 1913.
32. *The Record*, March 1940, p. 2.
33. *The Record*, September 1927, pp. 4–5.
34. http://blackburnmuseum.org.uk/blog/the-harris-private-press-collections-by-dr-cynthia-johnston/
35. *The Record*, December 1937, pp. 5–6.
36. *The Record*, December 1947, p. 3.
37. *The Record*, December 1936, p. 7.
38. *St Anne's on the Sea Express*, 7 March 1906.
39. See https://www.cottontown.org/
40. Garratt, Morris, 'Local Studies in Heywood', *Manchester Region History Review*, 2004. See Chapter 11 for Heywood Industrial Co-operative Society and its library.
41. See Chapter 3.
42. *Rawtenstall Public Library, 1905–1956*, Rawtenstall Borough Council, 1956.
43. https://www.amazingwomenbyrail.org.uk/attraction/accrington-library/
44. https://heylibraries.co.uk/05398399/Accrington_Library and see Chapter 1.
45. https://www.theportico.org.uk/about
46. For an excellent historical overview see Brooks, Ann and Haworth, Bryan, 'The Portico Library' in *Manchester Region History Review*, 2001, vol. XV.
47. https://www.independentlibraries.co.uk/working-class-movement-library
48. Wilson, Arline, 'Early Learned Societies' in conference paper for *A Cultural History of Liverpool*, paper read to Historic Society of Lancashire and Cheshire, 14 May 1998.
49. https://www.independentlibraries.co.uk/the-athenaeum-liverpool
50. Ibid.
51. See Chapter 3.
52. *The Record*, September 1921.
53. *The Record*, November 1921.
54. See Chapter 3 for short biography of Edith Pearce.
55. *The Record*, September 1940.

7. LANCASTRIANS AT WORK

1. See Alan Fowler's helpful introduction to the debate in *Lancashire Cotton Operatives and Work 1900–1950*, Ashgate 2003, and Walton, John K., *A Social History of Lancashire*, Manchester, 1998.

2. The argument is developed by Mary Rose in 'The rise of the cotton industry in Lancashire to 1830', in Rose, Mary (ed.) *The Lancashire Cotton Industry: A History Since 1700*, Lancashire County Books, Preston, 1996.

3. See Walton, J.K. op. cit. pp. 61–8.

4. Conway, Rebecca, 'Making the Mill Girl Modern? Beauty, Industry, and the Popular Newspaper in 1930s' England', *Twentieth Century British History*, Volume 24, Issue 4, December 2013, pp. 518–41

5. https://www.bolton.ac.uk/blogs/centre-for-worktown-studies-blog-cotton-queens/

6. See Foley, Alice, *A Bolton Childhood*, 1973.

7. See Timmins, Geoff, *The Last Shift: The Decline of Handloom Weaving in Nineteenth-Century Lancashire*, Manchester University Press, 1993. There is a large body of literature about 'the last handloom-weaver' in each Lancashire town.

8. Heaton's Mill at Lostock, on the outskirts of Bolton, employed female mule spinners for many years, to the outrage of the spinners' trades union. See Fowler op. cit.

9. Field Mill at Ramsbottom was one of the last to use mules; it survived until at least the mid-1980s but was the exception.

10. See Ruth and Edmund Frow, *The Half-Time System in Education*, Manchester 1970, also Winstanley, Michael (ed.) *Working Children in Nineteenth-Century Lancashire*, Lancashire County Books, Preston, 1995.

11. 'Half-Time Scholars', in *Returns of Schools Inspected for Year Ended August 31ˢᵗ, 1892*. Re-printed in *Farnworth: a collection of photographs and documents over the past century*, Bolton Environmental Education Project, c.1982.

12. See short biography in Chapter 3.

13. Johnston, John, *The Wastage of Child Life*, The Fabian Socialist Series No. 7, A.C. Fifield, London, 1909, p. 65.

14. Clarke, Allen, *Effects of the Factory System*, J.M. Dent for Vineyard Press, London, 1913, p. 80.

15. See Chapter 2.

16. *The Lancashire Miner*, January 1986.

17. *A Brief History of Astley Green Colliery 1908–2022*, Lancashire Mining Museum, 2022.

18. See below for more on the Lancashire NUM and the 1984/5 strike.

19. See John, Angela V., *By the Sweat of Their Brow: Women Workers in Victorian Coal Mines*, Routledge and Kegan Paul, London, 1984.

20. Holden, Mrs P., 'True Story of a Lancashire Pit Brow Lass', *North West Labour History*, 1985/6, Bolton, 1986, p. 1.

21. Councillor Marie Rimmer, in the 'Preface' to Winstanley, Ian, *Mining Memories: an illustrated record of coal-mining in St Helens*, St Helens MBC, 1992.

22. See Botcherby, Pierre, 'Queens of the Coal Age: Lancashire Women Against Pit Closures and the Parkside Pit Camp', in *North West Labour History*, no. 44, 2019/20.

23. https://www.royalexchange.co.uk/whats-on-and-tickets/queens-of-the-coal-age

24. Lancaster City Council's website has an informative account of the controversy: https://www.lancaster.gov.uk/the-council-and-democracy/civic-and-ceremonial/lord-ashton-the-lino-king

25. Clarke, Allen, *The Knobstick: A Tale of Love and Labour*, John Heywood, Manchester, 1893.

26. Clarke, Allen, (as 'Teddy Ashton') 'Th'Patent Automatic Cemetery Looms: Bill Spriggs Sweeps th'Manager Eaut o'th'shed', *Teddy Ashton's Northern Weekly*, 20 May 1905.

27. Beeching, Richard, *The Re-shaping of British Railways*, HMSO, London, 1962.

28. Matthews, Nick, 'The Co-op, anti-slavery and the Lancashire cotton famine', *Morning Star*, https://morningstaronline.co.uk/article/f/co-op-anti-slavery-and-lancashire-cotton-famine

29. Waugh, Edwin, *Home Life of the Lancashire Factory Folk During the Cotton Famine*, John Heywood, Manchester, 1867.

30. Ibid. p. 16.

31. Ibid. p. 30.

32. See Chapter 16 for more on Lancashire support for anti-slavery.

33. Laycok, Samuel, *Warblin's Fro' An Owd Songster*, Oldham, 1893, p. 4.

34. Ramsbottom, Joseph, *Phases of Distress: Lancashire Rhymes*, Manchester, 1864, p. 24.

35. Billington, William, *Lancashire Songs with Other Poems and Sketches*, Blackburn, 1883, p. 25.

36. Beckett, C.J., *Darwen Industrial Co-operative Society Souvenir*, Darwen, 1910, p. 23.

37. Walters, Charles, *History of the Oldham Equitable Co-operative Society Limited, 1850–1900*, Oldham, 1900, p. 46.

38. 'Lays of the Cotton Famine' in *Ballads and Songs of Lancashire*, Harland, J. and Wilkinson, T.T., 2nd ed. London, 1875.

39. Clarke, Allen, 'The Cotton Panic', *Teddy Ashton's Northern Weekly*, 6 October 1900.

40. https://cottonfaminepoetry.exeter.ac.uk/about/

41. Harker, Phil, with foreword by Smith, Rose and Edwards, Bob, *Lancashire's Fight for Bread: Story of the Great Lancashire Hunger March*, published by the Lancashire Marchers' Council, Bolton, 1933.
42. See also the account in Ainsworth, Jim, *Accrington and District 1927–1934: The Cotton Crisis and the Means Test*, Hyndburn and Rossendale Trades Council, Accrington, 1997.
43. Liddington, Jill, *The Life and Times of a Respectable Rebel: Selina Cooper 1864–1946*, Viargo, London, 1984, p. 381.
44. Harker, op. cit.

8. LANCASTRIANS AT PLAY: RECREATION, HOLIDAYS AND THE COUNTRY

1. 'Will Yo' Come o' Sunday Mornin'?' Clarke, Allen, *Teddy Ashton's Journal*, 9 September 1896. Revived by Clare, Nat, September 1982.
2. *Farnworth Park Souvenir*, 1864, in Farnworth Public Library.
3. Ibid.
4. *Heywood Advertiser*, 4 August 1879.
5. Ibid.
6. https://www.heywoodhistory.com/2017/03/park.html
7. Latiimer, Claire, *Parks for the People: Manchester and its Parks 1846–1926*, Manchester City Art Galleries, 1987.
8. Ibid.
9. See Peters, Rod, MA thesis, *Boggart Hole Clough and the ILP, May to August 1896*, 2014.
10. Laycock, Samuel, *Collected Writings*, Clegg, Oldham, 1900, p. 24.
11. Ramsbottom, Joseph, *Phases of Distress: Lancashire Rhymes*, John Heywood, Manchester, 1864, p. 26.
12. Anderson, Jessie Annie, in 'Foreword' to *Poems by Father and Son*, Tillotson, Bolton, 1919.
13. Latimer, op. cit. p. 41.
14. Stansfield, Abraham, *Essays and Sketches*, Manchester Scholastic Trading Co., Manchester, 1897.
15. Ibid. p. 234.
16. Ibid. p. 236.
17. See Chapter 2.
18. See Willies, Margaret, *The Gardens of the British Working Class*, Yale University Press, London, 2014, pp. 262–3.
19. Accrington Naturalists' Society, *Accrington Naturalist and Antiquarian Society Souvenir 1855–1905*, Accrington, 1905, p. 24.
20. Ibid. p. 11.
21. Walton, John K., *The World's First Working-Class Seaside Resort? Blackpool*

Re-visited 1840–1974, Lancashire and Cheshire Antiquarian Society, n.d. c. 1975, p. 11.

22. Clarke, Allen, 'The Things I Have Seen and Loved', *Blackpool Gazette*, 16 December 1935.

23. Clarke, Allen, *The Knobstick: A Story of Love and Labour*, John Heywood, Manchester, 1893, p. 116.

24. See Chapter 7.

25. Personal communication with the author.

26. Personal communication with the author.

27. Clarke, Allen, *Lancashire Lasses and Lads*, Bolton, 1906, p. 102.

28. Clarke, Allen, *The Knobstick*, op. cit. p. 59.

29. Clarke, Allen, *Lancashire Lasses and Lads*, op. cit. p. 113.

30. Clarke, Allen, 'A Man's Sake' in *Teddy Ashton's Northern Weekly*, 20 May 1899.

31. See short biography in Chapter 7.

32. Foley, Alice, *A Bolton Childhood*, Workers' Educational Association, Manchester, p. 72.

33. Ibid.

34. Pye, Denis, *Fellowship Is Life*, Bolton, 1995.

35. Clarke, *Moorlands and Memories*, Bolton, 1920, p. 119. See also Salveson, Paul, *Will Yo' Come o' Sunday Mornin'? The 1896 Fight for Winter Hill*, Bolton, 1982 and 1996.

36. Ibid. p. 199.

37. McKiernan, Julie, 'The Man Who Made Leigh Beautiful' in *PastForward*, Wigan, 2016.

38. Ibid.

39. Reported in Partington, S., *Winter Hill Right of Way Dispute* (no. 4 'Truth' Pamphlet') Bolton, 1900.

40. Clarke, Allen, *Teddy Ashton's Northern Weekly*, 9 November 1904.

41. Salveson, Paul, *Will Yo' Come O' Sunday Mornin'? The Story of the 1896 Winter Hill trespass*, 2nd ed., Bolton, 1996.

42. See Clarke, Allen, Windmill Land, Blackpool, 1915.

9. SPORTING LANCASHIRE

1. Walton, John K., 'The Origins of Working Class Spectator Sport: Lancashire, England 1870–1914', *Historia y Communicación Sociale*, vol. 17, San Sebastian, 2012.

2. Fox-Smith, Cicely, *Lancashire Hunting Songs and other Moorland Lays*, Manchester, 1909. Wrigley, Ammon, *Songs of the Pennine Hills*, Stalybridge, 1938.

3. Fox-Smith, op. cit., recorded by Gary and Vera Aspey on *From the North*, Topic Records, 1975.

4. Russell, David, *Looking North: Northern England and the National Imagination*, Manchester University Press, 2004, p. 240.

5. Russell op. cit. p. 245.

6. Holt, Richard, 'Heroes of the North: Sport and the Shaping of Regional Identity' in Hill, Jeffrey, and Williams, Jack, (ed.) *Sport and Identity in the North of England*, Keele, 1996, p. 157.

7. Hadfield, Dave. *Up and Over: A Trek Through Rugby League Land*, Mainstream Publishing, Edinburgh, 2004, p. 133.

8. *Lancashire County Cricket Club, One Hundred Years of Cricket*, Old Trafford, 1964.

9. Ibid.

10. Cavanagh, Ron, *Cotton Town Cricket: The Centenary Story of Lancashire's Oldest Cricket league*, Bolton, 1988.

11. Williams, Jack, 'Church, Sport and Identities in the North 1900–1930', in Hill and Williams op. cit., pp. 123–4.

12. Ibid. p. 27.

13. Ibid. p. 39.

14. Constantine, Learie, *Cricket and I*, Philip Allan, London, 1933.

15. *Viv Richards, Learie Constantine & Wes Hall: West Indies cricketers who charmed Lancashire*, BBC Sport, 2 October 2017.

16. Ibid.

17. Ibid.

18. Ibid.

19. Walton, John K., *Lancashire: A Social History 1558–1939*, Manchester University Press, 1987, p. 297.

20. Williams, op. cit. p. 127.

21. https://www.theboltonnews.co.uk/news/12969704.bolton-womens-rounders-sport-enjoys-a-120-year-tradition-rooted-in-the-mills/

22. http://www.holcombehunt.com/history.htm

23. Heys, Harold, 'Millworkers' Grand National to Stay in Lune Valley', *in Lancashire Magazine*, March/April 2006, p. 79.

24. *Bury Times*, April 7th, 1921.

25. Walker, Arthur N., *The Holcombe Hunt*, Sherratt and Hughes, The St Ann's Press, Manchester, Bury, 1937, p. 127.

26. Vose, John D., *Corner to Corner … and over the crown*, The Strule Press, Omagh, 1969.

27. Ibid. p. 30.

10. LANCASTRIANS AT WAR

1. Clarke, Allen, *The Lass at The Man and Scythe*, Pendlebury, Bolton, 1891. Later re-published as *John O'God's Sending*, Pendlebury and Sons, Bolton, 1901.

2. The graves of some of the rebels are in Garstang's parish churchyard, in Churchtown.

3. Clarke, Allen, *Moorlands and Memories*, Bolton, 3rd ed. 1924, p. 203.

4. Larysa Bolton, 'Working-Class Heroes: Researching First World War Working Class Soldiers', in *North West Labour History*, no. 34, 2009–10.

5. See Preece, Geoff, 'The Museum of the Manchesters', *in Manchester Region History Review*, Spring/Summer 1988.

6. 'News black-out on devastating explosion', *Lancashire Post*, 28 September 2017.

7. https://heatonwithoxcliffepc.org.uk/the-white-lund-explosions-october-1–4th1917/

8. *The Record*, June 1944, p. 15.

9. *Lancashire Evening Post*, 14 April 1995, re-printed with additional commentary by Mike Hill, 14 April 2020.

10. Ibid.

11. See Little, Eddie, 'Manchester City Council and the Development of Air Raid Precautions 1935–1939', *Manchester Region History Review*, vol. II no. 1 Spring/Summer 1988.

12. Makepeace, Chris 'Manchester at War' in *Manchester: A Second Selection*, Sutton Publishing, 1998, p. 67.

13. Makepeace, Chris op. cit. pp. 72–4.

14. See Trescathric, Bryn, *Barrow's Home Front 1939–1945*, Barrow, 1998.

15. Townend, Michael S., 'Wartime in Burnley and Pendle', East Lancashire Newspapers Ltd, Burnley, 1989, p. 38.

16. Letter from Mrs G. Whaittaker of Nelson, quoted in Townend op. cit. p. 40. Bradford also sent a number of evacuees to Colne and Nelson.

17. Parry, Keith, *Trans-Pennine Heritage*, David and Charles, Newton Abbot, 1981, p. 163.

18. I am indebted to Andrew Rosthorn for the Accrington story. One wonders how common the 'grab an evacuee' was!

19. Liverpool Museums website and https://www.mylearning.org/stories/women-at-war-the-role-of-women-during-ww2/743

20. Ibid.

21. https://www.lancs.live/news/lancashire-news/true-story-behind-battle-bamber-16526991

22. International Brigade Committee, *Greater Manchester Men Who Fought in Spain*, Manchester, 1983.

23. See https://www.wcml.org.uk/blogs/Lynette-Cawthra/Mary-Slater—the-story-of-a-photo-and-a-plaque/

24. https://www.lancashiretelegraph.co.uk/news/10172473.campaign-recognise-east-lancashires-forgotten-brigade/

25. See Chapter 7.
26. https://www.basquechildren.org/-/docs/articles/childreninmanchester

11. CO-OPERATIVE LANCASHIRE

1. See Turnbull, Jean and Southern, Jayne, *More Than Just a Shop: The History of the Co-op in Lancashire*, Lancashire County Books, Preston, 1995.
2. Mercer, T.W., *Towards The Co-operative Commonwealth*, CWS, Manchester, 1936.
3. See Chapter 2.
4. See Chapter 12 on libraries and co-operative societies.
5. Webb, Catherine, *The Woman with the Basket: The History of the Women's Co-operative Guild 1883–1927*. Women's Co-operative guild, London, 1927.
6. Clarke, C. Allen, *The Knobstick*, John Heywood, Manchester, 1893. p. 121.
7. 'Summat Abeaut Co-operation', *Teddy Ashton's Lancashire Annual*, Blackpool, 1923, p. 23.
8. Peaples, F.W., *History of the Great and Little Bolton Co-operative Society Limited, 1859–1909*, Manchester Labour Press, 1909.
9. Taylor, J.T., *Stories and Poems*, ed. Easthope, J.W., Oldham, 1928.
10. Easthope, J.W., 'Memorir and Poem', in Taylor, J.T., *Stories and Poems*, ed. Easthope, J.W., Oldham, 1928.
11. Taylor, J.T., *The Jubilee History of Oldham Industrial Co-operative Society 1850–1900*, Oldham, 1900.
12. Lawton, David, *Village Co-operation: A Jubilee Sketch of Greenfield Co-operative Society Ltd 1856–1906*, Manchester, 1906. See also biographical note in Swann, op. cit. p. 146.
13. Quoted in Harrison, John E., *A False Dawn: Co-operation in Chorley 1830–1880*, Chorley, 2020, pp. 10–11.
14. Ibid. pp. 22–4.
15. https://leigh.life/dokuwiki/doku.php?id=leighlife:mary_thomason, see Chapter 11.
16. For short biography of Haslam see Chapter 3.
17. Haslam, James, *History of Fifty Years' Progress*, Accrington, 1910.
18. Ibid. p. 14.
19. Ibid. p. 15.
20. Ibid. p. 26.
21. See Peaples, F.W., *History of the Great and Little Bolton Co-operative Society*, Bolton, 1909, p. 584.
22. Poem by A.H. Clough, born Liverpool 1819 and quoted in W.H. Brown, n.22 below.

23. Brown, W. Henry, *A Century of Liverpool Co-operation*, Liverpool Co-operative Society, 1929, p. 19.

24. Ibid. p. 29.

25. Ibid. p. 59

26. Ibid. p. 68.

27. Ibid. p. 104.

28. *1850–1950: A Century's Progress*, Littleborough Co-operative Society of Industry, 1950. Historical notes by N.H. Gregory.

29. Ibid. p. 22.

12. LANCASTRIAN ART AND LITERATURE

1. Thompson, op. cit. p. 323; also, for the weavers' musical culture, Elbourne, Roger, *Music and Tradition in Early Industrial Lancashire 1780–1840*, Woodbridge, 1980.

2. Bamford, Samuel, *Walks in South Lancashire*, Blackley, 1844, pp. 13–14.

3. See Bond, Peter and Jane, *Tim Bobbin Lives! The Life and Times of a Lancashire Legend*, Rochdale, 1986.

4. Davies, Peter, *A Northern School: Lancashire Artists of the Twentieth Century*, Redcliffe Press, Bristol, 1989.

5. Harrison, Stanley, *Poor Men's Guardians: a survey of the struggles for a democratic newspaper press 1763–1973*, London, 1974, p. 10.

6. Ibid. p. 12.

7. Axon, W.E.A., *Echoes of Old Lancashire*, Andrews, London, 1899, p. 70.

8. Ibid. p. 71.

9. See 'History of British Newspapers', News Media Association: http://www.newsmediauk.org/history-of-british-newspapers

10. Angus-Butterworth, L.M., 'Lancashire Writers of the Past: James Taylor Staton', *The Record*, December 1971, pp. 6–7.

11. Howarth, J.M., 'Lancashire Authors of the Past: J.T. Staton, 1817–1875', *The Record*, 1973, pp. 7–8. See also Button, Billy (Brodie, R.H.) 'Th'Bowton Loominary and its Author', in Clarke (ed.) *Teddy Ashton's Lancashire Annual*, Blackpool, December 1923, pp. 66–7.

12. *The Intelligencer* in its 3 January 1850 edition announced that it circulated 'throughout High and Low Furness, Cartmel, Millom and the districts of Lakes and the principal towns of Lancashire, Cumberland and Westmorland', though perhaps a rather extravagant claim.

13. Harford, C.E., 'Literary Manchester', in Brindley, W.H., *The Soul of Manchester*, Manchester University Press, 1929, pp. 136–7.

14. Chris Aspin in his introduction to *A Cotton Town Chronicle*, Accrington, 1978.

15. J.W. Easthope in his introduction to *Stories and Poems* by J.T. Taylor, Oldham, 1928.

16. *The Record*, November 1927, pp. 11–12.

17. See Cass, Eddie, 'The Remarkable Rise and Long Decline of The Cotton Factory Times', *Media History*, vol. 4 no. 2, 1998.

18. Clarke, Allen (as Teddy Ashton) 'Owdham Minstrel's Love Song', *Cotton Factory Times*, 24 September 1927.

19. *The Record*, September 1938, p. 13.

20. Ibid.

21. Biographical details in J.R. Swann, *Lancashire Authors*, St Annes, 1924.

22. Introduction to *Bits of Local History*, Leah Smith ('Owd Linthrin Bant') Radcliffe Library, 1971.

23. Biographical notes in Swann (ed.) op. cit. p. 84.

24. See Chapter 11.

25. See obituary in *The Record*, March 1931.

26. See above, and Conway, Rebecca, 'Making the Mill Girl Modern? Beauty, Industry, and the Popular Newspaper in 1930s' England', in *Twentieth Century British History*, vol. 24 Issue 4, December 2013, pp. 518–41.

27. See Salveson, Paul, *Lancashire's Romantic Radical: the life and writings of Allen Clarke / Teddy Ashton*, Bolton (2nd ed.) 2021. *Teddy Ashton's Northern Weekly* went through several name changes, starting as *Teddy Ashton's Journal*. Towards the end of its life it changed to *Fellowship*, then *Teddy Ashton's Weekly*.

28. Davies, Peter, *A Northern School: Lancashire Artists of the Twentieth Century*, Redcliffe Press, Bristol, 1989; Davies, Peter, *A Northern School Revisited*, ClarkArt Limited, Hale, 2015; Regan, Martin, *The Northern School: A Reappraisal*, Hale, 2016.

29. Regan, op. cit. p. 5.

30. Davies, *A Northern School* op. cit. p. 128.

31. Thomson, Susan W., *Manchester's Victorian Art Scene and Its Unrecognised Artists*, Manchester Art Press, Warrington, 2017, pp. 172–3.

32. Brierley, Ben, *Ab'o'th'Yate Sketches* vol. 3 (collected edition), Oldham, 1896.

33. Regan op. cit. p. 45.

34. *Lancashire South of the Sands 2: The Industrial Landscape*, Towneley Hall Art Gallery, 1987.

35. Ibid. p. 102.

36. Ibid. p. 107.

37. See Greenhalgh, Shaun, *A Forger's Tale: Confessions of the Bolton Forger*, Allen and Unwin, London, 2015.

38. Ibid. pp. 66–7.

39. Coombs, Trevor, *Rising from Reality: Art in Oldham from 1820 to 1890*, Oldham Art Gallery, 1990, p. 3.

40. Partington, Solomon, *Jubilee of the Middleton and Tonge Industrial Society and History of the Co-operative Movement: An Illustrated Souvenir for Members*, Middleton, 1900.

41. Holmes, James, *Manuscript Notes on Weaving for Second and Third Year*, Burnley, 1912.

42. See Schoeser, Mary, 'Shewey and Full of Work: Design', in Rose, Mary B. (ed.) *The Lancashire Cotton Industry: A History Since 1700*, Lancashire County Books, Preston, 1996.

43. See Chapter 2.

44. My thanks to Barry Clark for information on the DIA and Red Rose Guild.

45. Whittle, Stephen, 'Introduction' to *Creative Tension: British Art 1900–1950*, Paul Holberton Publishing, London, 2005, p. 6.

46. Ibid. pp. 110–11.

47. https://www.pilkingtons-lancastrian.co.uk/

48. https://www.erictucker.co.uk/about

49. https://www.clark-art.co.uk/company-profile

50. See Dutton, R., Findlay A., Wilson, R., *Region, Religion and Patronage: Lancastrian Shakespeare*, Manchester University Press, 2003.

51. https://shakespearenorthplayhouse.co.uk/about-us/

52. Angus-Butterworth, L.M., 'The Plays of Stanley Houghton, *The Record*, June 1936.

53. Clarke, Allen/Ashton, Teddy, 'The Most Humorous Literature in the World', *Teddy Ashton's Lancashire Annual*, Blackpool, 1917, pp. 26–7.

54. Owd Shuttle, *Tacklers' Yarns*, Manchester n.d. but probably c.1900. Also Mather, Geoffrey, *Tacklers' Tales: A Humorous Look at Lancashire and as Election of Lancashire Humour*, Palatine Books, Preston, 1993.

55. Fowler, Alan and Wyke, Terry, *Mirth in the Mill: The Gradely World of Sam Fitton*, Oldham Leisure Services, 1995.

56. Dawson, Les, *Les Dawson's Lancashire*, Elm Tree Books, London, 1983, p. 116.

57. Ibid. p. 117.

58. See Salveson, Paul, *Region, Class, Culture: Lancashire Dialect Literature 1746–1935*, Salford: PhD thesis, University of Salford, 1993.

59. Ashton, Teddy/Clarke, Allen in *Teddy Ashton's Northern Weekly*, 20 May 1905.

60. *The Record*, August 1917, pp. 1–2.

61. See Chapters 3 and 6.

62. Quoted in *The Record*, March 1932. See also Chapter 3 on 'Lancashire Sensibility' and the role of dialect.

63. *Rochdale Observer*, 21 November 1959, reported in *The Record*, June 1960, p. 5.

64. See Chapter 14 for short biography.

65. Tribute by 'Rambler Rose' (Edith Pearce) *The Record*, March 1944, pp. 13–14.

66. Report in *The Record*, September 1938 of the 17 July 1938 broadcast, featuring songs by W.F. Hampson and poetry by Ammon Wrigley.

67. Angus-Butterworth, L.M., 'Tommy Thompson', *The Record*, September 1970, pp. 9–10.

68. Cockburn, Ruth E., *Miss Nobodies*, Spot-on Lancashire and Ruth E. Cockburn, 2021.

69. Ibid. 'Foreword'.

70. See von Rosenberg, Ingrid, 'French Naturalism and the English Socialist Novel: Margaret Harkness and W.E. Tirebuck', in Klaus, Gustav (ed.) *The Rise of Socialist Fiction 1880–1914*, 1987.

71. See his *Gradely Lancashire*, 1929; also Fowler, Alan and Wyke, Terry, *Mirth in the Mill: The Gradely World of Sam Fitton*, 1995.

72. The number of specialist banner makers was also very restricted and the firms (e.g. London-based Tutill) tended to serve a UK-wide market, with well-established motifs. See Gorman, John, *Banner Bright: An Illustrated History of Trade Union Banners*, Scorpion Publishing, Buckhurst Hill, 1986.

73. A good general survey, including images of co-operative ceramics, is Birchall, Johnston, *Co-op: The People's Business*, Manchester University Press, 1994.

74. *Labour's Northern Voice*, July 1953.

13. MUSICAL LANCASHIRE

1. See Morley, Paul, *From Manchester with Love: The Life and Opinions of Tony Wilson*, London, 2021.

2. See Chapter 15.

3. Newbigging, Thomas, 'James Leach, the Lancashire Composer' in Newbigging, Thomas, *Lancashire Characters and Places*, Manchester, 1891, pp. 56–7.

4. Ibid. p. 60.

5. Ibid. p. 63.

6. Wylie, J.V., *Old Hymn Tunes: Local Composers and Their Story*, Accrington, 1924.

7. Ibid. p. 25.

8. Elbourne, Roger, *Music and Tradition in Early Industrial Lancashire 1780–1840*, Woodbridge, 1980.

9. See biographical note on Compston in Chapter 11. The newspaper articles ran in the *Rossendale Free Press* over several weeks, during November

and December 1904. Thomas Newbigging wrote an essay on 'The Larks of Dean' which was published in several publications.

10. Elbourne, op. cit.
11. Ibid. p. 115.
12. Ibid. p. 130.
13. Ibid. p. 124. For Compton biography, see Chapter 15.
14. Shaw, J.G., *History and Traditions of Darwen and Its People*, Darwen, 1889, p. 35.
15. Vose, J.D., *The Lancashire Caruso: Tom Burke, the Miner who became an Opera Star*, Blackpool, 1982.
16. Ibid. p. 11.
17. Ibid. p. 22.
18. Ibid. p. 30.
19. Ibid. pp 125–6.
20. Newsome, Roy, *The 19th-century brass band in Northern England: musical and social factors in the development of a major amateur musical medium*, PhD thesis, University of Salford, 1999.
21. Walker, Matthew, *The History of Farnworth and Walkden Brass Band*, Bolton, 2007.
22. See Livings, Henry, *That the Medals and the Baton Be Put on View: The Story of a Village Band 1875–1975*, David and Charles, Newton Abbot, 1975.
23. 'Nova Adjutor', *Wingates Band and the Pretoria Pit Disaster*, Wingates Band, 2010.
24. Quoted in Middlehurst, David, *The Lancashire String Band: Social Dance Musicians in the County 1880–1930*, Lancaster, 2015, p. 1.
25. 'Seth Sagars Memoirs', *Labour's Turning Point in the North West, 1880–1914*, North West Labour History Society, 1984.
26. *Rossendale Free Press*, 12 November, 1904.
27. Middlehurst, op. cit. p. 7, quoting from *Accrington Observer and Times* for 1903.
28. Ibid. p. 7.
29. Pomfret, Joan, 'Further Interviews with Lancashire Celebrities' in *The Record*, June 1955, p. 7.
30. Cardus, Neville, 'Music in Manchester' in Brindley, W.H., *The Soul of Manchester*, Manchester University Press, 1929, pp. 176–7.
31. Ibid. p. 178.
32. Ibid. p. 178.
33. Atkins, A., and Newman, A., *Beecham Stories: Anecdotes, Sayings and Impressions of Sir Thomas Beecham*, Robson Books, London, p. 13.
34. Beecham, Sir Thomas, *A Mingled Chime*, Hutchinson, London, 1944.
35. Ibid. p. 122.
36. Ibid. p. 180.

37. Ibid. p. 182.

38. Kennedy, Michael, *Portrait of Manchester*, Robert Hale, London, 1970, p. 99.

39. See Fisher, Alexandra, *Clog Dance: Revival, Performance and Authenticity: An Ethnographic Study*. MA Dissertation, University of Surrey, 2000. Alex makes the point that 'clog dancing' is a form of step-dancing performed in clogs. See also Meterhall, C. and Smith, A., *An Introduction to Clog Dancing in the North-East*, Newcastle, 1981.

40. Flett, J.F. and T.M., *Traditional Step-Dancing in Lakeland*, English Folk Dance and Song Society, 1979.

41. *Horwich Chronicle*, 5 November 1904.

42. *Preston Herald*, 14 September 1904,

43. Haslett, J., *Morris Dancers and Rose Queens*, 4 volumes.

44. Report of online talk by Johnny Haslett to the Morris Federation, 15 May 2021.

45. Description in 'About' section of Morris Federation website www.morrisfed.org.uk

46. Kennedy, Michael, quoted from 'Walton: A Celebration', 2002, on William Walton Trust website https://waltontrust.org/en/biography

47. Law, Brian R., *Oldham, Brave Oldham*, Oldham Council, 1999, p. 229.

48. *Oldham Chronicle*, 1 May 1926.

49. Ward, David, 'Oldham's Tribute for Composer and Most Reluctant Son', *The Guardian*, 15 July 2002.

50. Cannon, Gary D., *From Oldham to Oxford: The Formative Years of Sir William Walton*. Dissertation submitted in partial fulfilment of the requirements for the degree of Doctor of Musical Arts, University of Washington, 2014.

51. Personal communication with the author, 20 July 2022.

52. Ibid.

53. Pitfield, Thomas, *A Cotton Town Childhood*, Altrincham, 1993. His dialect poetry was published in *The Journal of the Lancashire Dialect Society*, September 1989, pp. 17–18.

54. Peter Dickinson, 'Gordon Crosse: the composer remembered', *The Gramophone*, February 2022.

55. Ibid. See also Obituary by Black, Leo, *The Guardian*, 26 August 2021.

56. Conway, Paul, 'Obituary: Arthur Butterworth', *The Guardian*, December 5th, 2014.

57. See http://www.lakelandcomposers.org.uk/index.htm

58. *Music Enriches Us All: The Royal Northern College of Music, the First Twenty-One Years*, Carcanet Press, Manchester, 1994.

59. Kennedy, Michael, *The Royal Manchester College of Music*, Manchester University Press, 1971, p. 10.

60. Northern Rail produced a DVD of the event: *Northern Brass: A Musical Celebration of Railways in the Community*, 2008.

14. LANCASHIRE AT PRAYER

1. Walton, John K., *A Social History of Lancashire*, University of Manchester Press, 1987, p. 184.
2. Thompson, E.P. *The Making of the English Working Class*, Pelican, London, 1963.
3. Referred to in Champness, John, *Lancashire*, Shire Publications, Princes Risborough, 1989, p. 4.
4. Doyle, Peter, *Mitres and Missions in Lancashire: The Roman Catholic Diocese of Liverpool 1850–2000*, The Bluecoat Press, Liverpool, 2003.
5. Ibid. p. 39. It would be wrong to assume that all Irish migrants would be Catholic. Peter Doyle (op. cit.) estimates that at least 80% of Irish migrants were Catholic, still a considerable number.
6. Ibid. p. 45.
7. See https://www.blackburn.anglican.org/our-history
8. See https://www.boltonsmayors.org.uk/wilcockson-j.html
9. Thompson, op. cit. p. 385.
10. Ibid. pp. 420–5.
11. *History of the Baptist Church, Kay Street, Rawtenstall*, Rawtenstall, 1922, p. 5.
12. Ibid. p. 6.
13. Ibid. p. 14.
14. Ibid. p. 16.
15. Ibid. pp. 23–4.
16. Ibid. p. 58.
17. For Merseyside see above; Smith, Leonard, 'Religion and the ILP' in James, Jowitt and Laybourn (eds) *Centennial History* (above).
18. Barrow, Logie, *Independent Spirits: Spiritualism and English Plebeians 1850–1910*, 1986.
19. Swinglehurst, James, *Summer Evenings with Old Weavers*, n.d. but c.1890. There is a short biography in Barrow op. cit. p. 123.
20. Clarke, Allen, *The Eternal Question*, 1901.
21. Office for National Statistics, *Data and Analysis for Census 2011*, London 2011.
22. https://www.asianimage.co.uk/news/16314236.first-mosques-north-west/
23. Bruce Glasier, Katharine, Diary, University of Liverpool Library, 10 November 1920.
24. Bruce Glasier, Katharine, *The Glen Book*, 1947.

25. See Pearce, Cyril, *Comrades in Conscience*, Huddersfield, 2001.

15. LANCASHIRE: POLITICS AND GOVERNANCE

1. *The Record*, June 1944, p. 12.
2. Salveson, Paul, *Socialism with a Northern Accent*, Lawrence and Wishart, London, 2012.
3. *Manchester Guardian*, 2 August 1938.
4. See below and *The Lancashire Giant: David Shackleton, Labour Leader and Civil Servant*, Martin, Ross M., Liverpool University Press, 2000.
5. See Chapter 14, also Blundell, Dom, *Old Catholic Lancashire*, vols 1 and 2, Burns Oates and Washbourne, London, 1925. Also Hilton, J.A., *Catholic Lancashire*, Phillimore, London, 1994.
6. Thompson, Edward P., *The Making of the English Working Class*, London, 1963.
7. See Chapters 12 and 13.
8. Vicinus, Martha, *The Industrial Muse*, 1974; and Salveson, Paul, *Region, Class, Culture: Lancashire Dialect Literature 1746–1935*, PhD thesis, Salford, 1993.
9. *Ashton-under-Lyne Reporter*, 7 March 1868, reported in *The Record*, June 1835. The report in *The Record* describes the meeting taking place at "Mostyn, where he now resides", but this is an error and should be 'Moston'. His last known address was at 109 Hall Street, Harpurhey, part of Moston.
10. Bamford, Samuel, *Passages in the Life of a Radical*, vol. 2, T. Fisher Unwin, London, 1903 ed., p. 141.
11. Thompson, E.P. (op. cit.) has much on the Luddites. For local studies see Davies, Bob, *The Luddites of Westhoughton*, Bolton, 1972.
12. *Bowtun Loominary*, 29 January 1853.
13. *The Record*, 16 November, p. 4.
14. Edwards, Michael, S., *Purge This Realm: The Life of Joseph Rayner Stephens*, Epworth Press, 1994.
15. Abram, William Alexander, *Blackburn Characters of a Past Generation*, Blackburn, 1894, p. 160.
16. Abram, op. cit. p. 162.
17. Ibid. p. 174.
18. Ibid. p. 182.
19. See Jenkins, Mike, *The General Strike of 1842*, Lawrence and Wishart, London, 1980.
20. https://radicalmanchester.wordpress.com/2009/12/04/ernest-jones-and-the-1846.
21. *Teddy Ashton's Northern Weekly*, 28 April–9 June 1900.

22. Clarke, Allen, *The Knobstick*, John Heywood, Manchester, 1893, p. 173. 'Chartist Grimshaw' features in Clarke's serialised novel *The Cotton Panic*, 5 January 1901. *Teddy Ashton's Northern Weekly*, 5 June 1901.

23. 'Lancashire and Scotland: Mr. Thomas Newbigging', Bowles, A.G., *The Record*, October 1972, pp. 6–7.

24. See Vicinus, Martha, *Edwin Waugh: The Ambiguities of Self-help*, 1984.

25. Newbigging, Thomas, *Speeches and Addresses*, p. 71.

26. Ibid., p. 71.

27. Ibid. pp. 222–3.

28. The extent of that support has been challenged; in some towns there was a degree of support for the South, as well as a more general 'plague on both your houses' attitude. Allen Clarke's novel *Black Slaves and White* was published in *Teddy Ashton's Northern Weekly* in 1897 and is a useful literary source.

29. Matthews, Nick, op. cit.

30. Billington, William, 'Aw Wod This War Wur Ended', *Lancashire Songs with Other Poems and Sketches*, 1883 p. 27

31. Harrison, Royden, *Before the Socialists: Studies in Labour and Politics 1861–1881*, Routledge and Kegan Paul, London, 1965.

32. Taylor, J.T., *Stories and Poems*, Oldham, 1928.

33. Harrison, op. cit. p. 66.

34. The ILP was founded in Bradford in 1892; the SDF pre-dated it, having been created in 1881 as 'The Democratic Federation' before becoming 'The Social Democratic Federation' in 1884. It was particularly strong in London and some of the Lancashire towns.

35. Mitchell, Hannah, *The Hard Way Up*, Faber, London, 1969, p. 116.

36. Blatchford, Robert, *Merrie England*, first serialised in *The Clarion*, Manchester, 1892–3. Published in book form by Clarion Press, London, 1895, then in numerous editions.

37. Blatchford, Robert, 'The New Party in the North' in Reid, Andrew, (ed.) *The New Party*, London, 1895, p. 14.

38. See Pye, Denis, *Bolton Socialist Party and Club*, National Clarion Publishing, revised edition, 2022.

39. Hargreaves, David, 'In Manchester I learned the Purpose: John Trevor and the Labour Church', *North West Labour History*, no. 40, 2015–16.

40. Trevor, John (ed.) *The Labour Prophet*, 1894.

41. Salveson, Paul, *With Walt Whitman in Bolton: Spirituality, Sex and Socialism in a Northern Mill Town*, Bolton, 2019.

42. Clarke, Allen, 'The Cotton Operatives and Socialism', *The Labour Prophet*, March 1897. The *Prophet* was the newspaper of the Labour Church movement, edited by John Trevor.

43. Martin, Ross M., op. cit. and https://www.cottontown.org/Politics/Blackburn.

44. See Chapter 3.
45. See *Borough of Farnworth, Charter of Incorporation, 1939*, for a typical example of local municipal pride.
46. In *Fellowship* (formerly *Teddy Ashton's Northern Weekly*) 8 October 1907.
47. Ibid.
48. See Liddington, Jill, *The Life and Times of a Respectable Rebel: Selina Cooper 1864–1946*, Virago, London, 1984.
49. Ibid. p. 170.
50. Her *Songs of a Factory Girl* was later published in book form, 1911. See also Chapter 12.
51. See Chapter 3 for Bodell-Smith's early life in Darwen and involvement in Darwen Literary Society.
52. *The Record*, March 1934, p. 18.
53. See Chapter 3 for more on Compston.
54. See obituary in *The Times*, 9 May 1944.
55. Macintyre, Stuart, *Little Moscows: Communism and Working-Class Militancy in the Inter-War Years*, Croom Helm, London, 1980.
56. Referred to in 'Seth Sagar's Memoirs', pt. 2, *North West Labour History*, 2009/10, p. 40.
57. See Chapter 10.
58. Nixon, T.E., *Workers' Control of the Railways*, n.d., c.1946.
59. *Labour's Northern Voice*, August 1947.
60. *Labour's Northern Voice*, 'Miners' Special', Spring 1953.
61. Davies, Sam, *Liverpool Labour: Social and Political Influences on the Development of the Labour Party in Liverpool, 1900–1939*, Keele University Press, 1996, p. 179.

16. LANCASTRIANS ABROAD

1. Mercer, S., *The Record*, June 1965, pp. 20–1.
2. 'Notes, Sentiments and Queries', *East Lancashire Review*, June 1890.
3. *The Record*, March 1932, p. 18.
4. Stansfield, Riley, 'In Appreciation of the Dialect' in *The Record*, September 1933.
5. Beeston, Erin and Horton, Laurel, 'Bolton's Cotton Counterpanes: Hand-Weaving in the Industrial Age', co-authored with Erin Beeston, in *Quilt Studies 14*, ed. Hazel Mills, Halifax: British Quilt Study Group, May 2013.
6. Ibid.
7. Ibid.
8. Bateson, Hartley, *A Centenary History of Oldham*, Oldham County Borough Council, 1949, p. 148.
9. Ibid. p. 147.

10. Ibid. p. 148.
11. Hargreaves, J.E., *A History of the Families of Crompton and Milne and of A & A Crompton & Co.*, Crompton Urban District Council, 1967, pp. 103–6.
12. Muir, Augustus, *The Kenyon Tradition: The History of James Kenyon and Son Ltd., 1664–1964*, Heffer and Sons, Cambridge, 1964, p. 55.
13. Correspondence with the author.
14. Salveson, Paul, 'To Russia with Love', *Bolton News*, 13 February 2021.
15. Rosthorn, Andrew, *The Typical, Topical; Tropical, Tramp*, Tockholes, 2020.
16. Quoted in *The Record*, December 1938, p. 11.
17. https://www.chartistancestors.co.uk/chartists-transported-australia/
18. Ibid.
19. Livesey, Roger, 'Blackburn Cotton Families who settled in Canada' in *Lancashire Telegraph*, 20 August 2018.

17. NEW LANCASTRIANS

1. See Thompson, E.P., *The Making of the English Working Class*, Pelican, London, 1968 ed., esp. pp. 183–8. See Chapter 14.
2. See Hilton, J.A., *Catholic Lancashire: From Reformation to Renewal 1559–1991*, Phillimore, Chichester, 1996. See also Chapter 14.
3. Clarke, Allen, 'Amongst the Agitators', *Teddy Ashton's Northern Weekly*, 3 June 1905.
4. See Moody, T.W., *Davitt and Irish Revolution*, 1984; also John Dunleavy's local study *Davitt's Haslingden*, 2006 and 'Michael Davitt's Lancashire Apprenticeship' in *Irish Studies in Britain*, Autumn/Winter, 1981.
5. Newbigging, Thomas, *Speeches and Addresses*, John Heywood, Manchester, 1887, p. 24.
6. See Salveson, Paul, *The People's Monuments: A Guide to Sites and Memorials*, Manchester, 1987, for a section on the Davitt memorials in Haslingden.
7. Deighan, Joe, *The Irish Democrat*, June 1954.
8. See Eddie Little, 'James Connolly in Salford' in *North West Labour History*, no. 40, 201506.
9. Desmond Greaves wrote the classic biography of Connolly, *The Life and Times of James Connolly*, Lawrence and Wishart, London, 1961. He lived for most of his later life in Birkenhead and travelled extensively around the UK and Ireland extolling the need for Irish unity. He collapsed and died on Preston station on 23 August 1985, on his way to speak to a meeting in Scotland. See https://archive.irishdemocrat.co.uk/greaves/greaves-brief-biog/
10. Williams, Bill, *Jewish Manchester: An Illustrated History*, Breedon Books Publishing, Derby, 2008.

11. Ibid. p. 17.

12. Ibid. p. 34.

13. See Chapter 14.

14. Ibid. pp. 143–4.

15. Liedtke, Rainer, 'Self-Help in Manchester Jewry', *Manchester Region History Review*, 1992.

16. 'Club Train Yarns', *Teddy Ashton's Lancashire Annual*, Blackpool, 1924 pp. 106–7.

17. https://shulbythesea.co.uk/

18. 'Being Black in Britain's Oldest Black Community', *Liverpool Echo*, 17 July 2021.

19. Ibid.

20. Ibid.

21. https://www.liverpoolmuseums.org.uk/liverpool-black-community-trail

22. Article by Peskett, Ted, in https://talkingaboutmygeneration.co.uk/memories-and-the-history-of-manchesters-Windrush-generation/

23. Salveson, Paul, 'Bolton's Ukrainian Community', *Bolton News* 17 March, 2022.

24. https://www.lancashiretelegraph.co.uk/news/19680253.blue-plaque-unveiled-commemorating-hungarian-people-fled-lancashire-1956/

25. http://www.polishclubbury.co.uk/history/

26. Ibid.

27. Jewell, Barry (ed.) *We Were There: The Recreational, Social and Sporting Lives of Bolton's First Asian Migrants*, vol. 1, Bolton Asian Migration, 2016, p. 69.

28. https://www.criticalmuslim.io/blackburn/

29. http://cottoncurryandcommerce.co.uk/

30. Stackey, Ed., (ed.) *Cotton, Curry and Commerce: The History of Asian Businesses in Oldham*, Oldham Council, 2013, p. 28.

31. See Hepworth, Jack, 'Britain's first migrant strike: labour militancy and radical politics at Courtaulds', Preston, 1965, in *North West History Journal*, 2019.

18. A LANCASHIRE RENAISSANCE?

1. Speakman, Colin, *Yorkshire: Ancient Nation, Future Province*, Gritstone Publishing, Hebden Bridge, 2021, p. 10.

2. Ibid. p. 11.

3. Jones, Bill, with Gosling, Ray, *Homo Northwestus*, Granada Television, 1992.

4. Ibid. pp. 2–3.

5. Russell, Dave, *Looking North: Northern England and the National Imagination*, Manchester University Press, 2004; Wainwright, Martin, *True North*, Guardian Books, London, 2009; Groom, Brian, *Northerners: A History*, Harper North, Manchester, 2022; Fox, Kate, *Where There's Muck There's Bras*, Harper North, Manchester, 2022. An important recent addition is Alex Niven's *The North Will Rise Again*, Bloomsbury Continuum, 2023.

6. Walton, John K., *Lancashire: A Social History 1558–1939*, Manchester University Press, 1987.

7. See the arguments of Niven, Alex, op. cit.

8. Clarke, Allen, *A Daughter of the Factory*, serialised in *Teddy Ashton's Northern* Weekly, 21 May–29 October, 1898. 'Agate' is a Lancashire millworkers' term for 'get started'.

9. Clarke, Allen, *Effects of the Factory System*, Grant Richards, London, 1899, p. 174. Published serially in *The Clarion*, 1895–6.

10. Gaston, Sarah, 'UK politics must leave nostalgia behind', *Financial Times*, 6 June 2022.

11. In particular, see Mulgan, Geoff, *Another World Is Possible: How to Re-ignite Social and Political Imagination*, Hurst, London, 2022.

12. Clarke, Allen, 'The Things I have Seen and Loved', *The Blackpool Gazette*, 14 December 1935.

BIBLIOGRAPHY

Books

Abbott, C.C., *A Legacy of Health*, Leigh, 1934.

Abram, William Alexander, *Blackburn Characters of a Past Generation*, Blackburn, 1894.

Adjutor, Nova, *Wingates Band and the Pretoria Pit Disaster*, Wingates Band, 2010.

Ainsworth, Jim, *Accrington and District 1927–1934: The Cotton Crisis and the Means Test*, Hyndburn and Rossendale Trades Council, Accrington, 1997.

Anderson, Donald and France, A.A., *Wigan Coal and Iron*, Smith's Books, Wigan, 1994.

Archer, John H.G., *Art and Architecture in Victorian Manchester*, Manchester University Press, 1985.

Aspin, C., *Lancashire—The First Industrial Society*, Helmshore Local History Society, 1969.

Atkins, A., and Newman A., *Beecham Stories: Anecdotes, Sayings and Impressions of Sir Thomas Beecham*, Robson Books, London.

Axon, Ernest, *Bygone Lancashire*, Manchester, 1892.

Axon, W.E.A., *Echoes of Old Lancashire*, Andrews, London, 1899.

Bairstow, Martin, *Railways in the Lake District*, Halifax, 1995.

Bamford, Samuel, *Passages in the Life of a Radical*, vol. 2, T. Fisher Unwin, London, 1903.

————, Samuel, *Walks in South Lancashire*, Blackley, 1844.

Baren, Maurice, *How It All Began in Lancashire*, Dalesman, Skipton, 1999.

Barnes, F., *Barrow and District*, Barrow-in-Furness Corporation, 1968 (2nd ed.).

Barrow, Logie, *Independent Spirits: Spiritualism and English Plebeians 1850–1910*, 1986.

Bates, Denise, Pit Lasses: Women and Children in Coalmining c.1800–1914, Wharncliffe Books, Barnsley, 2012.

BIBLIOGRAPHY

Bateson, Hartley, *A Centenary History of Oldham*, Oldham County Borough Council, 1949.

Beckett, C.J., *Darwen Industrial Co-operative Society Souvenir*, Darwen, 1910.

Beecham, Sir Thomas, *A Mingled Chime*, Hutchinson, London, 1944.

Bennett, W., *The History of Burnley*, four vols, Burnley Corporation, 1951.

Billington, William, *Lancashire Songs with Other Poems and Sketches*, Blackburn, 1883.

Blatchford, Robert, *Merrie England*, Clarion Press, London, 1894.

Blundell, Dom, *Old Catholic Lancashire*, vols 1 and 2, Burns Oates and Washbourne, London, 1925.

Bond, Peter and Jane, *Tim Bobbin Lives! The Life and Times of a Lancashire Legend*, Rochdale, 1986.

Borough of Farnworth, *Charter of Incorporation*, 1939.

Bowker, B., *Lancashire Under the Hammer*, Leonard and Virginia Woolf at The Hogarth Press, London, 1928.

Brazendale, David, *Lancashire's Historic Halls*, Carnegie, Preston, 1994.

Bridge, Tom, *The History of English Cookery*, Printwise Publications, Bury, 1992.

Brierley, Ben, *Ab o'th'Yate Sketches*, vol. 3 (collected edition), Oldham, 1896.

Brindley, W.H. (ed.) *The Soul of Manchester*, Manchester University Press, 1929.

Brown, W. Henry, *A Century of Liverpool Co-operation*, Liverpool Co-operative Society, 1929.

Bullen, Andrew and Fowler, Alan, *The Cardroom Workers' Union*, Amalgamated Textile Workers' Union, Manchester, 1986.

Cavanagh, Ron, *Cotton Town Cricket: The Centenary Story of Lancashire's Oldest Cricket League*, Bolton, 1988.

Champness, John, *Lancashire*, Shire Publications, Princes Risborough, 1989.

Champness, John, *Lancashire's Architectural Heritage*, Preston, 1988.

Chapman, Sydney J., *The Lancashire Cotton Industry*, Manchester University Press, 1904.

Clarke, Allen, *Can We Get Back to the Land?* Bolton, 1904.

———, *Effects of the Factory System*, Grant Richards, London, 1899.

———, *Lancashire Lasses and Lads*, Bolton, 1906.

————, *Moorlands and Memories*, Tillotson, Bolton, 1920.

————, *The Eternal Question*, J.M. Dent, London, 1901.

————, *The Knobstick: A Tale of Love and Labour*, John Heywood, Manchester, 1893.

————, *The Lass at The Man and Scythe*, Pendlebury, Bolton, 1891. Later re-published as *John O'God's Sending*, Pendlebury and Sons, Bolton, 1901.

————, *The Red Flag: A Tale of the People's Woe*, Twentieth Century Press, London, 1908.

————, *The Story of Blackpool*, Blackpool, 1923.

————, *Windmill Land*, J.M. Dent, London, 1916.

Clarke, P.F., *Lancashire and the New Liberalism*, Cambridge University Press, 1971.

Clarke, Stephen, *Clitheroe in Its Railway Days*, J. Robinson, Clitheroe, 1900.

Coates, Chris, *Utopia Britannica vol. 1 British Utopian Experiments 1325 to 1945*, Diggers and Dreamers, 2001.

Cockburn, Ruth E., *Miss Nobodies*, Spot-on Lancashire and Ruth E. Cockburn, 2021.

Collins, Herbert C., *Lancashire Plain and Seaboard*, J.M. Dent, London, 1953.

————, *The Roof of Lancashire*, J.M. Dent, London, 1950.

Constantine, Learie, *Cricket and I*, Philip Allan, London, 1933.

Coombs, Trevor, *Rising from Reality: Art in Oldham from 1820 to 1890*, Oldham Art Gallery, 1990.

CPRE, *Buildings in Lancashire*, Preston, 1938.

Crosby, Alan, A History of Lancashire, Phillimore, Chichester, 1998.

————, *Dictionary of Lancashire Dialect, Tradition and Folklore*, Smith Settle, Otley, 2000.

Crowley, Michael, *Comrades Come Rally! Manchester Communists in the 1930s and 1940s*, Bookmarks, London, 2022.

Darnley, Gillian, *Villages of Vision*, Five Leaves Publications, Nottingham, 2007.

Davies, Bob, *The Luddites of Westhoughton*, Communist Party History Group, Manchester, 1971.

Davies, Peter, *A Northern School: Lancashire Artists of the Twentieth Century*, Redcliffe Press, Bristol, 1989.

————, *A Northern School Revisited*, ClarkArt Limited, Hale, 2015.

Dawson, Les, *Les Dawson's Lancashire*, Elm Tree Books, London, 1983.

Dickinson, J.C., *The Land of Cartmel*, Titus Wilson, Kendal, 1980.

Diggle, George E., *A History of Widnes*, Corporation of Widnes, 1961.

Doyle, Peter, *Mitres and Missions in Lancashire: The Roman Catholic Diocese of Liverpool 1850–2000*, The Bluecoat Press, Liverpool, 2003.

Dunleavy, John, *Davitt's Haslingden*, Haslingden, 2006.

Dutton, R., Findlay, A. and Wilson R. (eds) *Region, Religion and Patronage: Lancastrian Shakespeare*, Manchester University Press, 2003.

Duxbury, Stephen, *The Brief History of Lancashire*, The History Press, Stroud, 2011.

Edwards, Michael S., *Purge This Realm: The Life of Joseph Rayner Stephens*, Epworth Press, 1994.

Elbourne, Roger, *Music and Tradition in Early Industrial Lancashire 1780–1840*, D.S. Brewer, Woodbridge, 1980.

Foley, Alice, *A Bolton Childhood*, WEA, Manchester 1973.

Fort, Matthew, *Paul Heathcote's Rhubarb and Black Pudding*, Fourth Estate, London, 1998.

Fowler, Alan and Wyke, Terry, *Mirth in the Mill: The Gradely World of Sam Fitton*, Oldham Leisure Services, 1995.

Fowler, Alan, *Lancashire Cotton Operatives and Work 1900–1950*, Ashgate, 2003.

Fox, Kate, *Where There's Muck There's Bras: Lost Stories of the Amazing Women of the North*, Harper North, Manchester, 2022.

Fox-Smith, Cicely, *Lancashire Hunting Songs and Other Moorland Lays*, Manchester, 1909.

Frow, Ruth and Edmund, *The Half-Time System in Education*, E.J. Morton, Didsbury, 1970.

Girouard, Marc, *The English Town*, Guild Publishing, 1990.

Gooderson, P.J., *A History of Lancashire*, Batsford, London, 1980.

Goodhart, David, *The Road to Somewhere: The Populist Revolt and the Future of Politics*, Hurst, London, 2017.

Gramsci, Antonio, *Selections from the Prison Notebooks*, ed. Hoare, Quentin and Nowell-Smith, Geoffrey, Lawrence and Wishart, London, 1971.

Greenhalgh, Shaun, *A Forger's Tale: Confessions of the Bolton Forger*, Allen and Unwin, London, 2015.

Greenwood, Walter, *Lancashire*, Robert Hale, London, 1951.

Gregory, N.H., *1850–1950: A Century's Progress*, Littleborough Co-operative Society of Industry, 1950.

Grindon, Leo, *Country Rambles and Manchester Walks and Wild Flowers*, (2nd ed.) Manchester, 1882.

————, *Lancashire: brief historical and descriptive notes*, Seeley, London, 1892.

Groom, Brian, *Northerners: A History*, Harper North, Manchester, 2022.

Hadfield, Dave, *Up and Over: A Trek Through Rugby League Land*, Mainstream Publishing, Edinburgh, 2004.

Hampson, Charles P., *Salford Through the Ages*, Salford, 1930.

Hardwick, Charles, *Traditions, Superstitions and Folk-lore of Lancashire*, Simpkin, Marshall and Co., London, 1872.

Hargreaves, J.E., *A History of the Families of Crompton and Milne and of A & A Crompton & Co.*, Crompton Urban District Council, 1967.

Harland, J. and Wilkinson, T.T., *Ballads and Songs of Lancashire* (2nd ed.) London, 1875.

————, *Lancashire Legends, Traditions, Pageants, Sports, etc.*, Routledge and Sons, London, 1875.

Harrison, John E., *A False Dawn: Co-operation in Chorley 1830–1880*, Chorley, 2020.

Harrison, Royden, *Before the Socialists: Studies in Labour and Politics 1861–1881*, Routledge and Kegan Paul, London, 1965.

Harrison, Stanley, *Poor Men's Guardians: A Survey of the Struggles for a Democratic Newspaper Press 1763–1973*, London, 1974.

Haslam, James, *History of Fifty Years' Progress*, Accrington, 1910.

Hayes, Geoffrey, *Collieries in the Manchester Coalfields*, De Archaeologische Pers, Eindhoven, n.d., c.1970.

Hewitson, Anthony, *Northward*, Landy Publishing, 1993 and 2003.

Hewlett, E.G.W., *Lancashire*, Oxford University Press, 1913.

Heys, Harold, *Darreners*, Darwen, 2022.

Hikins, H. (ed.) *Building the Union: Studies on the Growth of the Workers' Movement, Merseyside, 1756–1967*, Toulouse Press, Liverpool, 1973.

Hill, Jeffrey, *Nelson: Politics, Economy, Community*, Keele University Press, Edinburgh, 1997.

Hill, Jeffrey and Williams, Jack, (ed.) *Sport and Identity in the North of England*, Keele, 1996.

HIll, Samuel, *Old Lancashire Songs and Their Singers*, Stalybridge, 1898.

Hilton, J.A., *Catholic Lancashire*, Phillimore, London, 1994.

Hilton, Tim, *John Ruskin: The Later Years*, Yale University Press, 2000.

Hindle, David, *Victorian Preston and The Whittingham Hospital Railway*, Amberley, Stroud, 2012.

History of the Baptist Church, Kay Street, Rawtenstall, Rawtenstall, 1922.

Holden, Roger N., *Stott and Sons: Architects of the Lancashire Cotton Mill*, Lancaster, 1998.

Hollingworth, Brian, *Songs of the People: Lancashire Dialect Poetry in the Industrial Revolution*, Manchester University Press, 1977.

Holmes, Gerard, *The Idiot Teacher*, Faber, London, 1952.

Hool, R.L., *Common Plants and Their Uses in Medicine*, Lancashire Branch of the National Association of Medical Herbalists, Southport, 1922.

Houlding Henry, *Poems: Rhymes and Dreams: Legends of Pendle Forest, and Other Poems*, Burnley, 1895.

Houlihan, Marjory, *A Most Excellent Dish: Tales of the Lancashire Tripe Trade*, Neil Richardson, Bolton, 1988.

Hollingworth, Brian, *Songs of the People: Lancashire Dialect Poetry in the Industrial Revolution*, Manchester University Press, 1977.

Howard, Ebenezer, *Garden Cities of Tomorrow: A Peaceful Path to Real Reform*, Swan Sonnenschein, London, 1898.

Hudson, J.W., *The History of Adult Education*, Longmans, 1851.

International Brigade Committee, *Greater Manchester Men Who Fought in Spain*, Manchester, 1983.

James, David, Jowitt, Tony and Laybourn, Keith. (eds) *The Centennial History of the Independent Labour Party*, Ryburn Academic Publishing, Halifax, 1992.

Jenkins, Mike, *The General Strike of 1842*, Lawrence and Wishart, London, 1980.

Jewell, Barry (ed.) *We Were There: The Recreational, Social and Sporting Lives of Bolton's First Asian Migrants*, vol. 1, Bolton Asian Migration, 2016.

Johnston, John, *Musa Medica*, Bolton, 1897.

————, *The Wastage of Child Life*, The Fabian Socialist Series No. 7, A.C. Fifield, London, 1909,

Jones, Bill, with Gosling, Ray, *Homo Northwestus*, Granada Television, 1992.

Joyce, Patrick, *Work, Society and Politics: The Culture of the Factory in Late Victorian England*, Harvester Press, Brighton, 1980.

Karol, Eitan, *Charles Holden: Architect*, Shaun Tyas, Donnington, 2007.

Kennedy, Michael, *Portrait of Manchester*, Robert Hale, London, 1970.

————, *The Royal Manchester College of Music*, Manchester University Press, 1971.

King, Ray, *Detonation: Rebirth of a City*, Clear Publications, Warrington, 2006.

Klaus, Gustav (ed.) *The Rise of Socialist Fiction 1880–1914*, 1987.

Lancashire South of the Sands: 2: The Industrial Landscape, Towneley Hall Art Gallery, 1987.

Lane, Tony, *Liverpool: City of the Sea*, Liverpool University Press, 1997.

Latimer, Claire, *Parks for the People*, Manchester, 1997.

Law, Brian R., *Oldham, Brave Oldham*, Oldham Council, 1999.

Lawton, David, *Village Co-operation: A Jubilee Sketch of Greenfield Co-operative Society Ltd. 1856–1906*, Manchester, 1906.

Laycock, Samuel, *Collected Writings*, Clegg, Oldham, 1900.

———, *Warblin's Fro' An Owd Songster*, Oldham, 1893.

Lewis, Brian, *'So Clean' Lord Leverhulme, Soap and Civilization*, Manchester University Press, Manchester, 2008.

Liddington, Jill, *The Life and Times of a Respectable Rebel: Selina Cooper 1864–1946*, Virago, London, 1984.

Liddington, Jill and Norris, Jill, *With One Hand Tied Behind Us: The Rise of the Women's Suffrage Movement*, London, Virago Press, 1978.

Livings, Henry, *That the Medals and the Baton Be Put on View: The Story of a Village Band 1875–1975*, David and Charles, Newton Abbot, 1975.

Lofthouse, Jessica, *Lancashire Landscape: Discoveries South of the Ribble*, Robert Hale, 1951.

———, *Lancashire's Fair Face: Discoveries, Ribble to Lune*, Robert Hale, 1952.

Longden, Christina, *His Own Man: A Victorian 'Hidden' Muslim. The Life and Times of Robert 'Reschid' Stanley*, Past Truisms CIC, Huddersfield, 2019.

Macintyre, Stuart, *Little Moscows: Communism and Working-Class Militancy in the Inter-War Years*, Croom Helm, London, 1980.

Macqueen, Adam, *The King of Sunlight*, Corgi Books, London, 2005.

Marshall, J.D., *Furness and the Industrial Revolution*, Barrow-in-Furness Library and Museum Committee, Barrow, 1958.

———, *Lancashire*, David and Charles, Newton Abbott, 1974.

———, *The History of Lancashire County Council*, Martin Robertson, London, 1977.

Marshall, John, *The Lancashire and Yorkshire Railways*, 3 vols, David and Charles, Newton Abbott, 1969.

Mason, Eric, *The Lancashire and Yorkshire Railway in the Twentieth Century*, Ian Allen, London, 1954.

Mather, Geoffrey, *Tacklers' Tales: A Humorous Look at Lancashire and a Selection of Lancashire Humour*, Palatine Books, Preston, 1993.

BIBLIOGRAPHY

McGowan-Gradon, W., *The Furness Railway: Its Rise and Development 1846–1923*, Altrincham, 1946.

Mercer, T.W., *Towards the Co-operative Commonwealth*, CWS, Manchester, 1936.

Middlehurst, David, *The Lancashire String Band: Social Dance Musicians in the County 1880–1930*, Lancaster, 2015.

Midwinter, E.C., *Social Administration in Lancashire 1830–1860*, Manchester University Press, 1969.

Mills, W. Haslam, *Sir Charles Macara: A Study of Modern Lancashire*, Sheratt and Hughes, Manchester, 1917.

Mitchell, Hannah, *The Hard Way Up*, Faber, London, 1969.

Mitchell, W.R., *Lancashire Mill Town Traditions*, Dalesman, Clapham, 1982.

———, *Life in the Lancashire Mill Towns*, Dalesman, Clapham, 1972.

Moody, T.W., *Davitt and Irish Revolution 1846–82*, Clarendon Press, Oxford, 1981.

Moorhouse, Sydney, *Holiday Lancashire*, Robert Hale, London, 1955.

Morley, Paul, *From Manchester with Love: The Life and Opinions of Tony Wilson*, London, Faber, 2021.

Mowat, Jack and Power, Albert, *Our Struggle for Socialism in Barrow: Fifty Years Anniversary*, Labour Party, Barrow-in-Furness, 1949.

Muir, Augustus, *The Kenyon Tradition: The History of James Kenyon and Son Ltd., 1664–1964*, Heffer and Sons, Cambridge, 1964.

Muir, T.E., *Stonyhurst*, St Omers Press, Cirencester, 2006.

Mulgan, Geoff, *Another World is Possible: How to Re-ignite Social and Political Imagination*, Hurst, London, 2022.

Newbigging, Thomas, *Lancashire Characters and Places*, Manchester, 1891.

———, *Speeches and Addresses*, John Heywood, Manchester, 1887.

Niven, Alex, *The North Will Rise Again*, Bloomsbury Continuum, 2023.

O'Connor, Denis, *Barrow Bridge, Bolton, Lancashire: A Model Industrial Community of the Nineteenth Century*, Bolton, 1972.

Parker, N., *The Preston and Longridge Railway*, Oakwood Library of Railway History No. 30, Lingfield: Oakwood Press, 1972.

Parry, Keith, *Trans-Pennine Heritage: Hills, People and Transport*, David and Charles, Newton Abbot, 1981.

Partington, Solomon, *Romance of the Dialect*, Middleton, 1920.

———, *The Future of Old English Words*, Middleton, 1917.

Peaples, F.W., *History of the Great and Little Bolton Co-operative Society Limited, 1859–1909*, Manchester Labour Press, 1909.

Pearce, Cyril, *Comrades in Conscience*, Huddersfield, 2001.

Pearce, John, *The Life and Teachings of Joseph Livesey Comprising His Autobiography with an Introductory Review of his Labours as Reformer and Teacher*, Manchester and Preston, 1885.

Pearson, Harry, Connie: *The Marvellous Life of Learie Constantine*, Abacus, London, 2017.

Pitfield, Thomas, *A Cotton Town Childhood*, Altrincham, 1993.

Price, James, *Sharpe, Paley and Austin: A Lancaster Architectural Practice 1836–1942*, Centre for North-West Regional Studies, Lancaster, 1998.

Pye, Denis, (with Neil Duffield) *Bolton Socialist Party and Club*, Bolton, 1995.

Pye, Denis, *Fellowship Is Life: The Story of the National Clarion Cycling Club*, National Clarion Publishing, 1995 and 2004; revised edition 2022.

Quayle, Howard, *Furness Railway: A View from the Past*, Ian Allan, Shepperton, 2000.

Ramsbottom, Joseph, *Phases of Distress: Lancashire Rhymes*, Manchester, 1864.

Reach, Angus Bethune, *Manchester and the Textile Districts (1849)*, ed. C. Aspin, Helmshore Local History Society, 1972.

Regan, Martin, *The Northern School: A Re-appraisal*, Gateway Gallery, Hale, 2019.

Reid, Andrew, (ed.) *The New Party*, London, 1895.

Robertson, William, *Rochdale and the Vale of Whitworth*, Rochdale, 1897.

Roby, John, *Traditions of Lancashire* (2 vols), Longman, London, 1829.

Rose, Mary (ed.) *The Lancashire Cotton Industry: A History Since 1700*, Lancashire County Books, Preston, 1996.

Rosthorn, Andrew, *The Typical, Topical; Tropical, Tramp*, Tockholes, 2020.

Royal Commission on Local Government (The Redcliffe-Maud Report), 1969.

Russell, Dave, *Looking North: Northern England and the National Imagination*, Manchester University Press, 2004.

Salveson, Paul, *Socialism with a Northern Accent*, Lawrence and Wishart, London, 2012.

———, *Lancashire's Romantic Radical: The Life and Writings of Allen Clarke/ Teddy Ashton*, Bolton (2nd ed.) 2021.

———, *The People's Monuments*, Workers Educational Association, Manchester, 1983.

————, *With Walt Whitman in Bolton: Spirituality, Sex and Socialism in a Northern Mill Town*, Bolton, 2019.

————, 'Getting Back to the Land: The Daisy Colony Experiment' in *Labour's Turning Point in the North West 1890–1914*, North West Labour History Society, Southport, 1984.

Saunders, Langford, *Lancashire Humour and Pathos*, Fred Johnson, Manchester, 1911.

Shaw, J.G., *History and Traditions of Darwen and Its People*, Darwen, 1889.

Singleton, Frank, *Lancashire and the Pennines*, Batsford, London, 1952.

Sixsmith, Charles, 'Foreword' to *An Advisory Plan*, South Lancashire and North Cheshire Advisory Planning Committee, Manchester, 1947.

Smith, Leah ('Owd Linthrin Bant'), *Bits of Local History*, Radcliffe Library, 1971.

Sparke, Archibald, *Bibliographia Boltoniensis: being a bibliography, with bio-graphical details of Bolton authors, and the books written by them from 1550 to 1912*, University Press, Manchester, 1913.

Speakman, Colin, *Yorkshire: Ancient Nation, Future Province*, Gritstone Publishing, Hebden Bridge, 2021.

Stacey, Ed., (ed.) *Cotton, Curry and Commerce: The History of Asian Businesses in Oldham*, Oldham Council, 2013.

Stansfield, Abraham, *Essays and Sketches*, Manchester Scholastic Trading Co., Manchester, 1897.

Sutton, Lindsay, *Sands of Time: Following in the Footsteps of Cedric Robinson on Morecambe Bay*, Great Northern Books, 2021.

Swann, J.R., *Lancashire Authors*, St Ann's-on-the-Sea, 1924.

Swinglehurst, James, *Summer Evenings with Old Weavers*, Bolton, 1890.

Talbot, C.M., *The Amazing Mary Higgs*, OWC Publishing, Oldham, 2011.

Taylor, J.T., *Stories and Poems*, ed. Easthope, J.W., Oldham, 1928.

————, *The Jubilee History of Oldham Industrial Co-operative Society 1850–1900*, Oldham, 1900.

Thomson, Susan W., *Manchester's Victorian Art Scene and Its Unrecognised Artists*, Manchester Art Press, Warrington, 2017.

Thomson, T., *Lancashire for Me—A Little Biography*, George Allen and Unwin, London, 1940.

————, *The Lancashire Omnibus*, George Allen and Unwin, London, 1951.

Thompson, E.P., *The Making of the English Working Class*, Pelican, London, 1963.

Timmins, J.G., *Handloom Weavers' Cottages in Central Lancashire*, Lancaster, 1977.

———, *The Last Shift: The Decline of Handloom Weaving in Nineteenth-Century Lancashire*, Manchester University Press, 1993.

Tippett, L.H.C., *A Portrait of the Lancashire Textile Industry*, Oxford University Press, London, 1969.

Tongue, Steve, *Lancashire Turf Wars: A Football History*, Pitch Publishing, Worthing, 2018.

Townend, Michael S., *Wartime in Burnley and Pendle*, East Lancashire Newspapers Ltd., Burnley, 1989.

Trescathric, Bryn, *Barrow's Home Front 1939–1945*, Barrow, 1998.

Tulloch, Alexander, *The Little Book of Lancashire*, The History Press, Stroud, 2013.

Turnbull, Jean and Southern, Jayne, *More Than Just a Shop: The History of the Co-op in Lancashire*, Lancashire County Books, Preston, 1995.

Tylecote, Mabel, *The Mechanics' Institutes of Lancashire and Yorkshire Before 1851*, University Press, Manchester, 1957.

Vicinus, Martha, *Edwin Waugh: The Ambiguities of Self-help*, Geore Kelsall, Littleborough, 1984.

———, *The Industrial Muse*, Croom Helm, London, 1974.

Vose, John D., *Corner to Corner (and Over the Crown)*, The Strule Press, Omagh, 1969.

———, *The Lancashire Caruso: Tom Burke, the Miner Who Became an Opera Star*, Blackpool, 1982.

Wainwright, Martin, *True North*, Guardian Books, London, 2009.

Walker, Arthur N., *The Holcombe Hunt*, Sherrratt and Hughes, St Ann's Press, Manchester, Bury, 1937.

Walker, Matthew, *The History of Farnworth and Walkden Brass Band*, Bolton, 2007.

Walters, Charles, *History of the Oldham Equitable Co-operative Society Limited, 1850–1900*, Oldham, 1900.

Walton, John K., *A Social History of Lancashire*, University of Manchester Press, 1987.

———, *Fish and Chips and the British Working Class, 1870–1940*, Leicester University Press, 1992.

———, *The Blackpool Landlady*, Manchester University Press, 1978.

Waterhouse, Robert, *The Other Fleet Street*, First Edition Limited, Altrincham, 2004.

Waugh, Edwin, Collected Works (11 vols), John Heywood, Manchester, 1881.

———, *Home Life of the Lancashire Factory Folk During the Cotton Famine*, John Heywood, Manchester, 1867.

Weaver, Michael, 'Michael's Story' in *Voices*, Manchester, c.1981.

White, Andrew, *Crossing the Sands of Morecambe Bay: Beauty, Drama and Tragedy*, Scriptorium Publications, Hornby, 2020.

Whittaker, G.H., *A Lancashire Garland of Dialect Prose and Verse*, Geo. Whittaker and Sons, Stalybridge, 1936.

Whittle, Stephen, *Creative Tension: British Art 1900–1950*, Paul Holberton Publishing, London, 2005.

Wightman, Peter, *Bonnie Colne*, Hendon Publishing, Nelson, 1976.

Williams, Bill, *Jewish Manchester: An Illustrated History*, Breedon Books Publishing, Derby, 2008.

Williams, Joanna M., *Manchester's Radical Mayor: Abel Heywood*, The History Press, Stroud, 2017.

Williams, Mike, with Farnie, D.A., *Cotton Mills in Greater Manchester*, Lancaster, 1992.

Williams, Raymond, *Resources of Hope*, Verso, London, 1989.

———, *The Long Revolution*, Pengin Books, Harmondsworth, 1961.

Willies, Margaret, *The Gardens of the British Working Class*, Yale University Press, London, 2014.

Winstanley, Michael (ed.) *Working Children in Nineteenth-Century Lancashire*, Lancashire County Books, Preston, 1995.

Wray, Tom, *Manchester Victoria Railway Station*, Peter Taylor Publications, 2005.

Wrigley, Ammon, *Songs of the Pennine Hills*, Stalybridge, 1938.

Wylie, J.V., *Old Hymn Tunes: Local Composers and Their Story*, Accrington, 1924.

Articles

Angus-Butterworth, L.M., 'The Plays of Stanley Houghton, *The Record*, June 1936.

———, 'Tommy Thompson', *The Record*, September 1970.

———, 'Lancashire Writers of the Past: James Taylor Staton', *The Record*, December 1971.

Beeston, Erin, 'Bolton's Cotton Counterpanes: Hand-Weaving in the Industrial Age', *Quilt Studies 14*, ed. Hazel Mills, Halifax: British Quilt Study Group, Halifax, May 2013.

Bolton, Larysa, 'Working-Class Heroes: Researching First World War Working-Class Soldiers' in *North West Labour History*, no. 34, 2009–10.

Button, Billy (Brodie, R.H.) 'Th'Bowton Loominary and its Author' in Clarke (ed.) *Teddy Ashton's Lancashire Annual*, Blackpool, December 1923, pp. 66–7.

Cass, Eddie, 'The Remarkable Rise and Long Decline of the Cotton Factory Times', *Media History*, vol. 4 no. 1.

Clarke, Allen/Ashton, Teddy, 'The Most Humorous Literature in the World', *Teddy Ashton's Lancashire Annual*, Blackpool, 1917, pp. 26–7.

Clarke, Allen, 'The Things I Have Seen and Loved', *Blackpool Gazette*, 16 December 1935.

Conway, Rebecca, 'Making the Mill Girl Modern? Beauty, Industry, and the Popular Newspaper in 1930s' England', *Twentieth-Century British History*, Volume 24, Issue 4, December 2013.

Dunleavy, John, 'Michael Davitt's Lancashire Apprenticeship' in *Irish Studies in Britain*, Autumn/Winter, 1981.

Howarth, J.M., 'Lancashire Authors of the Past: J.T. Staton, 1817–1875', *The Record*, 1973.

Liedtke, Rainer, 'Self-Help in Manchester Jewry', *Manchester Region History Review*, 1992.

Little, Eddie, 'Manchester City Council and the Development of Air Raid Precautions 1935–1939', *Manchester Region History Review*, vol. II no. 1 Spring/Summer 1988.

Preece, Geoff, 'The Museum of the Manchesters' in *Manchester Region History Review*, Spring/Summer 1988.

Walton, John K., *The World's First Working-Class Seaside Resort? Blackpool Re-visited 1840–1974*, Lancashire and Cheshire Antiquarian Society, n.d., c.1975, p. 11.

Theses

Cannon, Gary D., *From Oldham to Oxford: The Formative Years of Sir William Walton*. Dissertation submitted in partial fulfilment of the requirements for the degree of Doctor of Musical Arts, University of Washington, 2014.

Newsome, Roy, *The 19th-Century Brass Band in Northern England: Musical and Social Factors in the Development of a Major Amateur Musical Medium*, PhD thesis, University of Salford, 1999.

Salveson, Paul, *Region, Class, Culture: Lancashire Dialect Literature 1746–1935*, Salford: PhD thesis, University of Salford, 1993.

INDEX

INDEX